# Trekking Atlas

## OF THE WORLD

# Trekking Atlas
## OF THE WORLD

NEW HOLLAND

CONSULTANT EDITOR JACK JACKSON

First published in 2006 by New Holland Publishers

London • Cape Town • Sydney • Auckland

www.newhollandpublishers.com

| | | | |
|---|---|---|---|
| 86 Edgware Rd | 14 Aquatic Drive | 80 McKenzie St | 218 Lake Road |
| London, W2 2EA | Frenchs Forest, NSW 2086 | Cape Town, 8001 | Northcote, Auckland |
| United Kingdom | Australia | South Africa | New Zealand |

ISBN 1 84537 179 8

CONSULTANT EDITOR  Jack Jackson

PUBLISHING MANAGERS  Claudia dos Santos & Simon Pooley

COMMISSIONING EDITOR  Alfred LeMaitre

DESIGNER  Nathalie Scott

PRODUCTION EDITOR  Anna Tanneberger

ILLUSTRATOR  Steven Felmore

CARTOGRAPHER  John Loubser

PICTURE RESEARCHER  Karla Kik

PROOFREADER/INDEXER  Elizabeth Wilson

PRODUCTION  Myrna Collins

Reproduction by Resolution, Cape Town

Printed and bound in Singapore by Tien Wah Press (Pte) Ltd

1 3 5 7 9 10 8 6 4 2

PAGE ONE  *Yerupaja 6634m (21,765ft), locally called El Carnicero (The Butcher – due to the sharp ridge), is the highest
point in Peru's Cordillera Huayhuash and the third highest mountain in Peru.*

PAGE 2-3  *A trekker gets an early morning start above Tagourt village en route to the Tizi n'Fedghat (pass), Morocco.*

LEFT  *A trekker above Yak Kharka (Yak Pasture) north of Marpha on the descent from Damphus Pass into the Kali Gandaki.*

OVERLEAF  *A young woman hiking along the picturesque west coast of Scotland, UK.*

## General Introduction 10

Brief definitions of different kinds of treks (with pros and cons): backpacking, self-contained treks, DIY treks and commercial treks • Physical fitness • Personal safety • Passports and permits • Insurance • Vaccinations and prophylactics • Altitude and acclimatization • Interacting with local cultures and the environment • Equipment • Food and water

# CONTENTS

## THE TREKS

### EUROPE

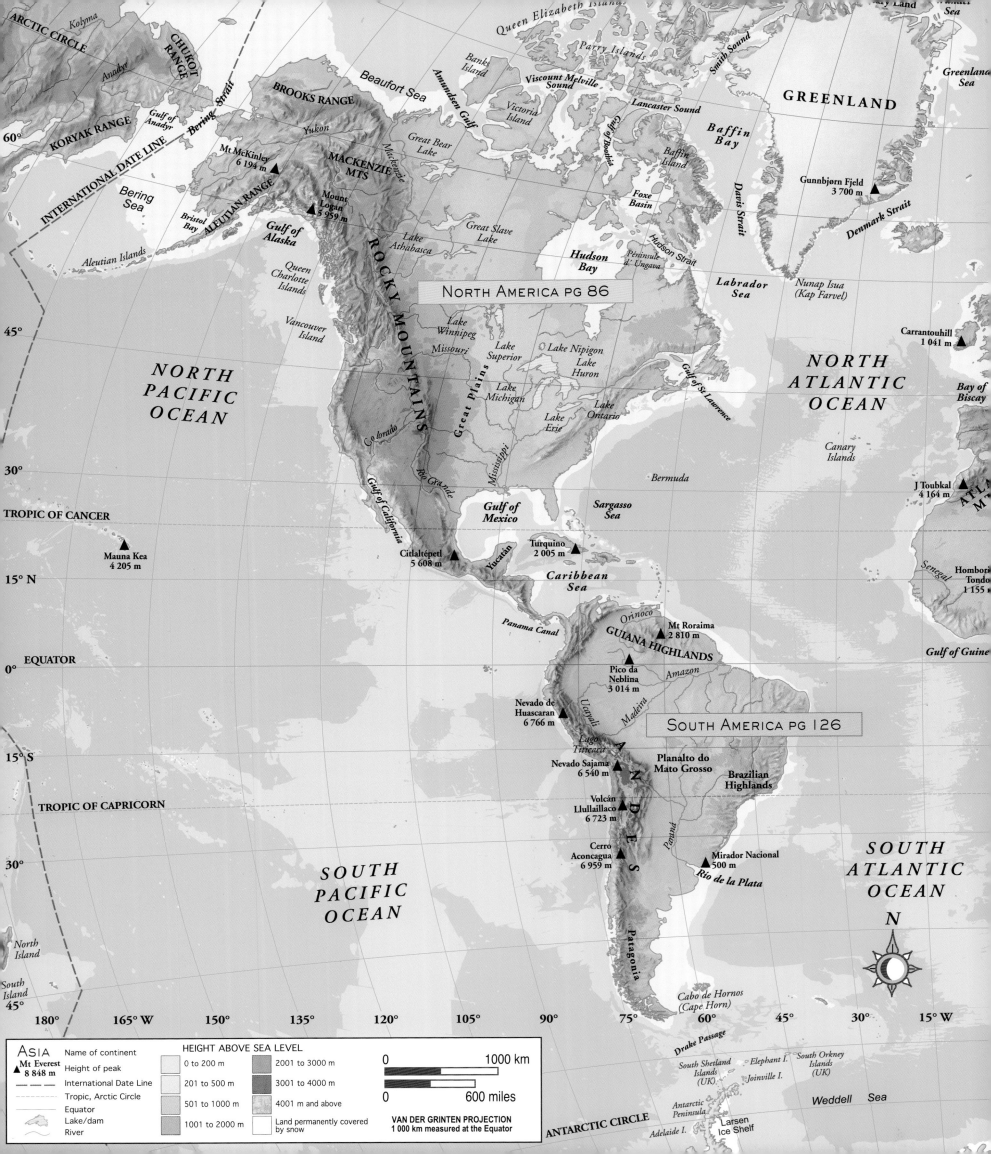

ARCTIC
OCEAN

ARCTIC CIRCLE

INTERNATIONAL DATE LINE

Barents
Sea

Kara
Sea

Laptev
Sea

East Siberian
Sea

CHUKOT RANGE

Tanana

Mt McKinley
6 194 m

60°

Nordkapp

Taymyr
Peninsula

Ozero
Taymyr

Chukot
Peninsula

Seward
Peninsula

Yukon

Lappland
Kola
Peninsula

Pechora

Taymyr
Peninsula

Korry

Anabar

Olenek

Indigirka

Kolyma

CHERSKOGO RANGE

VERKHOYANSK RANGE

Anadyr

Gulf of
Anadyr

KORYAK
RANGE

Brist
Ba

rwegian
Sea

Lake
Ladoga

Lake
Onega

Yamal Peninsula

Ob'

Yenisey

Siberia

Lena

Yana

Aleutian Islands

Bering
Sea

hopiggen
470 m

Baltic Sea

URAL MOUNTAINS

Ob'

STANOVOY RANGE

Sea of
Okhotsk

Kamchatka Peninsula

a

Volga

Ertis

Ozero
Baykal

DA HINGGAN LING

Amur

Sakhalin

EUROPE PG 22

CARPATHIANS

Don

Ural

ALTAI SHAN

Gobi Desert

45°

ALPS

Danube

CAUCASUS

Aral
Sea

Balqash
Köli

Youyi Feng
4 374 m

Manchuria

Hokkaido

APENNINES

Black Sea

El'brus
5 642 m

Caspian Sea

Syrdariya

Jengish
Chokusu
7 439 m

ASIA PG 150

Paektu-san
2 750 m

Sea
of
Japan

editerranean Sea

Qogir Feng (K2)
8 608 m

Qingzang
Gaoyuan
(Plateau
of Tibet)

Huang

Huang
Hai
(Yellow
Sea)

Korea Strait

Honshu

Fuji-san
3 776 m

PACIFIC
OCEAN

30°

Indus

HIMALAYAS

Jinsha Yangtze

Chang (Yangtze)

East
China
Sea

TROPIC OF CANCER

at
8 m

OGGAR

TIBESTI

Lake
Nasser

Thar
Desert

Ganges

Mt Everest
8 848 m

Hkakabo Razi
5 881 m

Luzon
Strait

Mariana Trench

Emi Koussi
3 415 m

Red Sea

Jabal Sawda
3 132 m

Arabian
Peninsula

Arabian
Sea

Bay
of
Bengal

Mekong

South
China
Sea

15° N

a h a r a

Lake Chad

Ras Dashen
4 619 m

Gulf of Aden

Andaman
Sea

Gulf of Thailand

Sulu
Sea

Mount Apo
2 954 m

AFRICA PG 212

Mt Cameroun
4 100 m

Great Rift Valley

ETHIOPIAN
HIGHLANDS

Lake
Turkana

Malay
Peninsula

Celebes
Sea

Congo

Mt Kenya
5 199 m

Sumatra

Borneo

Puncak Jaya
5 030 m

EQUATOR 0°

Congo
Basin

Lake
Victoria

Kilimanjaro
5 892 m

Java

Banda
Sea

Lake
Tanganyika

Lake
Nyasa

Maromokotro
2 875 m

Timor Sea

Arafura
Sea

Cape
York
Peninsula

Great Barrier Reef

Coral
Sea

15° S

Namib Desert

Tsodilo
Hills

Mulanje
3 002 m

Mozambique Channel

Timor Sea

Zambezi

Inyangani
2 592 m

North West
Cape

Great Sandy
Desert

Brandberg
2 592 m

1 401 m
Kgalagadi

Limpopo

INDIAN
OCEAN

GREAT DIVIDING RANGE

Orange

DRAKENSBERG

TROPIC OF CAPRICORN

Cape of
Good Hope

Cape
Agulhas

Great Victoria
Desert

Great
Australian Bight

Darling

Murray

30°

Cape
Leeuwin

Mount
Kosciusko
2 229 m

Bass Strait

Tasman
Sea

Mount
Cook
3 754 m

North
Island

AUSTRALIA & NEW ZEALAND PG 248

South
Island

45°

15° E

30°

45°

60°

75°

90°

105°

120°

135°

150°

165° E

180°

ANTARCTICA

ANTARCTIC CIRCLE

# INTRODUCTION

BY JACK JACKSON

Originally a *trek* was an Afrikaans word referring to migration by ox-wagon in South Africa, but nowadays it can cover any form of transport on land. The Collins English Dictionary quotes 'a long and often difficult journey' particularly one that occurs in stages. Adventure is more difficult to define, The Collins English Dictionary quotes 'a risky undertaking of unknown outcome' or 'an exciting or unexpected event or course of events', other dictionaries go further and define it as 'a hazardous activity'.

Trekking among non-mountaineers really began in the early 1960s when Lieutenant Colonel Jimmy Roberts opened a trekking operation in Nepal. A former Gurkha Officer, Military Attaché at the British Embassy in Kathmandu and logistics advisor to many mountaineering expeditions, Roberts fine-tuned the concept of using guides and porters who carried the gear, set up the camp, and did the cooking. This was similar to the expedition approach used by mountaineers to reach their objectives. It was particularly appropriate for Nepal since many of what are now known as trekking routes were already in use by the local people to get from village to village at that time – and the scenery was stunning.

Jimmy Roberts advertised in *Holiday* magazine in 1964 and the first commercially guided walking trek began on 25 February 1965. Three middle-aged American women – a paediatrician, a retired bacteriologist, and a school superintendent – set off on foot from Panchkhal, Nepal, bound for the Tengboche (Thyengboche) Monastery near Mount Everest. The women paid $450 each, walked for 35 days and 242km (150 miles), and were accompanied by three Sherpa guides, nine porters, and Roberts. Roberts, who had spent years of his life walking and exploring in the hills of Nepal, had managed to get permission from the king of Nepal to

walk through areas previously off-limits to foreigners. Roberts' trekking operation became Mountain Travel Nepal, one of the first adventure-travel companies, and the trekking industry was born.

## TREKKING TODAY

For this book we have concentrated on trekking on foot rather than by animal or vehicle. Adventure means different things to different people. Risk is self-imposed, so the individual decides what level of adventure or risk is acceptable. Trekkers with little experience of mountains will find The Inca Trail in Peru or hiking across Crete just as adventurous as trekking in high mountains; and those keen on religion will find designated religious pilgrimages fulfilling.

When establishing the criteria for treks in this book, with the exception of The Way of St James, we decided on the following:

1) It must be in a region that is not routinely traversed except by the local people.
2) It requires careful planning and/or expert guidance.
3) The region trekked through has very little modern infrastructure.
4) It passes through remarkable terrain.
5) It takes at least five days of active trekking from the point of departure to the end of the trek – not from arrival in the country or region.
6) It is at least 96km (60 miles) in length, although to some extent this depends on the difficulty of the terrain and how much ascent and descent is involved.
7) It is challenging in terms of fitness and/or psychological stamina.
8) It should not involve anything too

technical: no advanced specialist skills, such as ice climbing or rock climbing, are required.
9) The trek should involve an element of risk, or at least potential exposure to danger, the unknown or the unexpected.

In First World countries some treks may intentionally have to keep away from the local infrastructure, for instance by remaining on high ground. As far as physical fitness is concerned, one tends to overexert on the first day of the trek, ache like hell on day two, feel better on day three and then feel comfortably fit for the rest of the trek. On commercial treks, the first day is usually arranged so that if any participants demonstrate really poor physical fitness they can still be returned to the point of departure and, if necessary, repatriated. Psychologically, things are the reverse; some people are affected in weird ways by altitude, others do not sleep well at night and after a week of bad nights do inept things such as being constantly unpleasant to other group members or falling over and breaking bones. A common problem is that people who are on regular prescription medication forget to take it, with awkward and often disastrous consequences for themselves and the rest of the party.

The enjoyment of a trek often involves taking on a challenging journey: along a slippery mountain trail with a large drop into a river to one side; along a narrow ridge in a high wind; or wading rivers, all involving risk. Basic trekking can be enjoyed with the minimum of equipment so long as one can read a map and use a

**ABOVE** *Crossing the 5416m (17,769ft) Thorung La Pass between the valleys of Jomsom and Manang on the Annapurna Circuit, Nepal.*

compass. However, the introduction of hi tech equipment such as Global Positioning System (GPS) receivers, for navigation based on satellite fixes, and modern clothing has made a huge difference. In the 1960s many countries forbade the issue of accurate maps for civilian use. The best that I could find for trekking in Afghanistan and the Sahara Desert were British Military Survey Tactical Pilotage Charts, the aviation charts used by aircraft pilots – hardly a large enough scale for accurate route-finding on foot.

Communications were rudimentary: some military posts had field telephones, though few of these worked.

## COMMUNICATIONS TODAY

By the early 1970s, many remote settlements had satellite communication powered by diesel generators. Using one of these was like using a ship's radio: you spoke, waited a few seconds, heard an echo of your own voice and then received a reply. Nowadays, there are still a few places where communication remains a

problem, but for those who can afford them, there are portable satellite telephones and video transmission systems for remote use, even on the summit of Everest. More useful are Global Positioning System (GPS) receivers. Now that the degraded civilian signal has been discontinued, we can all receive the military-quality signal, provided there is no tree cover or mountain between receiver and satellite. However, electronics and batteries can fail so carry at least two GPS receivers and several sets of spare batteries.

## TECHNOLOGY

Large-scale maps are now available for most trekking areas and new technology has given us lightweight clothing. Rucksacks are better designed for carrying loads and trekking poles help to stabilize the body and reduce the stress on the knees and lower back when walking downhill. Boots, tents and cooking equipment are much lighter and food technologists have developed more palatable, lightweight dehydrated food. Modern medicines have reduced the chances of a bug turning your trek into a nightmare (some of the older remedies for diarrhoea are now illegal). New technology has done more than make existing treks easier: it has enabled us to take on longer and more adventurous routes; and, with improvements in transportation, to reach more remote regions.

Treks need not be a wilderness experience: there may be continuous habitation but with individual houses and settlements quite far apart. Trekkers may have to arrange air, vehicle or boat transport to the point where they commence their trek and a pick-up from the point where they intend to finish. Treks are not

climbing trips, although some scrambling may be involved or the wearing of crampons advisable, but no technical rock or ice-climbing should be required.

As well as narrow paths, local bridges can worry people. They can be no more than a few horizontal wooden planks with

prickly branches to keep the goats to the middle of the bridge or wooden planks suspended from ropes or cables, both with an occasional plank or two missing. In South America they can be made entirely of grass. A suspension bridge is very picturesque as it bends and snakes across a

ABOVE RIGHT *Trekkers crossing a river of glacier meltwater on narrow planks, above Rumboor, Kfiristan, northwest Pakistan.*
RIGHT *A footbridge made of local rope near Sher Qila (Lion's Fort) in the Punial Valley, northwest Pakistan. People crossing such bridges cause a sinusoidal motion, so it is best to go one at a time.*

gorge, but sways as you cross – not only from side to side, but also up and down in a sinusoidal motion. If someone else steps on the bridge while you are crossing, their rhythm creates waves of motion that interfere with yours. Keeping your footing on the move is a bit of a knack. It is easier to cross one person at a time.

## BACKPACKING TREKS

Also known as teahouse treks or lodge treks, in populated areas backpackers can rely on local accommodation for overnight facilities, so they do not have to carry tents, cooking equipment and food. In Nepal some hostelries now have solar-powered hot showers. Depending on the region, local meals can get very repetitive and, if there are many trekkers around, hostelries and teahouses can run out of food so some tasty, high-energy snacks should be carried. In some areas, trekkers are at risk of diseases spread by contaminated food, drink and poor hygiene, so they should be well versed in the various symptoms and carry the appropriate medications.

## SELF-CONTAINED TREKS

There are many remote regions where self-contained trekking is either necessary or especially enjoyable and there are others where it is unnecessary, but saves money. There is a limit to the amount of weight that anyone can carry comfortably day after day and still enjoy the trek, but one has to carry the basic necessities: tent, sleeping bag and mat, clothing, cooking equipment, fuel, food and items for water purification and personal hygiene. In general this means buying the lightest and

ABOVE *A high camp on Budzunge Bara with a panorama to the east, Nepal.*

most expensive equipment and food available. Living on freeze-dried or dehydrated food for more than two weeks at a time can drain your energy, especially at altitude where people tend to lose their appetite, so pack some tasty, high-carbohydrate foods as well.

In some areas, fuel and food-dumps can be set up in advance, but these caches can be raided by people or animals. Bear-proof or baboon-proof containers may be necessary, also for the animals' own protection (they start to associate humans with food and end up being shot as 'problem animals').

On this type of excursion, participants are less at risk of diseases spread by contaminated food, drink and poor hygiene, but in remote areas at least one member of the party should have some medical training and carry a good medical kit.

## DO-IT-YOURSELF TREKS

Given the time, it is possible to gather permits, porters or pack-animals, cooks, food and equipment and trek with all the comforts and facilities of a trek arranged through a local agency and a travel agent in your country of residence. The advantage of porters is that they can carry whatever you do not need during the day. As well as carrying larger, more comfortable tents they will also be able to carry stools or folding chairs, a more varied selection of food, extra sleeping bags for the colder nights at altitude and spare film and equipment for photographers. A properly organized trek will also have porters carrying kerosene or liquid petroleum gas for cooking so that local trees are not cut for

**ABOVE** *Porters taking a rest on the final slopes leading to the 5151m (16,900ft) Hispar La (pass) from the east, Pakistan*

firewood and some porters will be designated to dig latrines. This method of trekking is particularly enjoyable for a group of friends.

On the downside you may have to send out someone in advance to fully complete the arrangements; there may be a problem with language and keeping control of porters; you have no way of knowing the honesty of those that you hire; and they may well charge you more than the going rate. Porters hired in this way routinely strike for more pay as soon as you get far enough away from officialdom to be at their mercy. In some countries it may be law to organize treks through registered local trekking companies. However, if it is legal to organize your own trek, work with people recommended by friends. When organizing porters to do the cooking,

someone should watch over the cook's hygiene and at least one member of the party should carry a good medical kit.

## COMMERCIAL TREKS

Complete arrangements can be made through a local trekking agency and a travel agent in your country of residence .This will be the most expensive option, but it saves a lot of time and frustration; and ensures that you have all the necessary paperwork and the correct flight bookings. Even better, if the local agency handles large numbers of tourists, they will receive first choice on overbooked local flights. In many First World countries the travel agency through which the original bookings are done, is responsible in law if anything serious goes wrong. Participants will not have communication problems or

LEFT *Trekking beneath the 6634m (21,765ft) Yerupaja in Peru's Cordillera Huayhuash. This mountain is considered by many to be the most spectacular peak in South America.*

between the group and the porters, cooks and local people. The cooks will have been trained in hygiene. Money hassles are almost eliminated, the local leader is responsible for minor purchases along the way and can help individual members of the party with personal bargaining. Unlike normal tourism where it is normal for the guide to get at least 30% of the value on anything tourists purchase, trekking guides are generally more honest. Many commercial trekking companies offer reduced rates to medical doctors who are willing to act as official doctors on the trek.

Two major advantages of a commercial trek come about because of all the local agent's contacts along the route: communication and security. In an emergency, either back at home or on the trek, messages can be passed along the route in either direction. And in countries that are no longer 100 per cent safe, the party is large and the porters have an intimate knowledge of the area and the local people. This means that the party is less likely to attract trouble, in fact, in some countries the agency will have already paid off the local troublemakers to leave their trekkers alone.

In some countries it is a legal requirement that the trek be led by a local national. In some of the trekkers' countries of residence, for reasons of litigation, a

trouble getting permits. The porters and cooks will be tried, tested and of proven honesty; fuel for cooking will be carried so that local trees are not cut for firewood; and some porters will be organized to dig latrines. There will be a designated local leader who speaks the group's language and acts as a go-between and interpreter

person who has passed a short course and gained some form of mountain leadership certificate will be given precedence over someone with 30 years of Himalayan experience, but no certificate, as the agency's group-leader.

It is quite common for the porters to be very poorly paid and heavily reliant on gratuities from the group as acceptable remuneration for their work – so cost in a decent tip.

## PHYSICAL QUALIFICATIONS

Trekking, backpacking, bushwalking and tramping are physically demanding. Commercial trekking brochures are full of 'brochure-speak' that can fall anywhere between making relatively easy trips sound like major expeditions and making quite difficult ones sound easy. Most commercial treks are not that difficult or they would not attract enough clients for commercial success. Older people of the type that have completed many long walks over many years are usually very good at doggedly placing one foot in front of the other when they feel tired. Some treks are organized for photographers with plenty of time for stops where the sun is at the best angle for photography and therefore they can only cover short distances each day, such treks are also ideal for older people. The greatest deterrent is a history of knee or hip problems.

Those with diabetes have no problems if they carry the correct medicaments and sweet foods, consume them regularly and the (western) trek leader or doctor knows about their condition in case something

goes wrong. In 1971, I was leading a trek at altitude in Afghanistan when one woman collapsed in a coma. The trip had an official doctor, but she was junior to the many senior American and English doctors that formed the group. The patient was a very senior pathologist, yet she had not informed anyone that she was diabetic. This, plus the fact that no insulin or carbohydrate snacks were found in her bags, meant that all the doctors present discounted the possibility of diabetes as the cause of the coma for nearly two hours. Eventually, with her pulse getting very weak, the senior doctor made the decision that treating her for diabetes was all they could do and she came round. It is important that the western trek leader or the official trek doctor is kept informed about diseases that could cause emergencies. This information remains confidential, unless an emergency occurs.

## PERSONAL SAFETY

Several of the areas where groups have trekked safely in the past are now subject to civilian or religious strife. The current Marxist-Leninist-Maoist terrorists in Nepal, Peru's Maoist Shining Path guerrilla movement in the 1980s and 1990s, and banditry, kidnapping or robbery in ex-Russian States, Iran and Eastern Turkey are just a few examples. It is important to keep up to date with the advice given by your government's Foreign Office Travel Advice unit.

## PASSPORTS AND PERMITS

Your passport should be valid for six months longer than the expected length of

the trip and have six empty pages left to cover any bureaucracy. Some countries will also require proof that you have sufficient funds available and a return or onward air ticket. Some countries even require onward air tickets for overland travellers and others require a letter of introduction from your own government.

Photographers, writers, journalists and members of the armed forces often require special visas or special permission or even the attendance of a government minder or political liaison officer. Unless you are travelling officially as such, avoid mention of these professions in your passport. Carry spare passport photographs and several photocopies of all paperwork, separate from the originals. If officials want to take any paperwork away, only give them a photocopy, as they often misplace it.

## INSURANCE

Buy individual personal and medical insurance, preferably one that flies you home by Air Ambulance in a serious emergency. Many standard insurance companies do not fully cover 'adventure sports', including trekking. First World travel agents that organize Third World trekking will sell suitable insurance policies. Trekkers who organize their own trips can often buy suitable insurance policies from the governing body for mountaineering in their country of residence.

## VACCINATIONS AND PROPHYLACTICS

Make sure that you have all the required vaccinations and that they will remain

valid for the whole trip. If a trek passes through a country where dangerous diseases such as malaria are endemic, it is essential to take the correct advice, precautions and prophylactics. (It will depend on the area you're going to: your medical adviser can look it up on a chart). In recent years, people taking the antimalarial Mefloquine (Larium) have experienced psychological problems, with women affected more than men. However, some people also suffer side-effects when taking Chloroquine and Proguanil. Doxycycline is a good alternative short-term prophylaxis for women who are not on the contraceptive pill or pregnant and provided that you do not sunbathe.

People on prescription medication should carry enough for the whole trek and some extra to cover delays. It is wise to know the generic names for these medications in case you have to purchase more locally.

At the time of writing, no country officially requires cholera vaccination, but border officials in some countries may not always follow official government policies and may ask for proof of cholera vaccination. Tourists can get proof of vaccination (even if they did not actually receive the vaccine), or a letter from their doctor stating that the vaccine is medically contraindicated. All travellers should avoid being vaccinated at borders as the vaccines may be administered with contaminated equipment increasing the risk for acquiring AIDS or Hepatitis A or B. I had two people catch Hepatitis A in this way in Iran.

Two new cholera vaccines, Dukoral and Mutacol, were recently licensed for use in many countries, excluding America. Dukoral will help to protect travellers against enterotoxigenic Escherichia coli (ETEC), the most common cause of travellers' diarrhoea and in the UK is recommended for adventurous backpackers travelling to remote regions with limited access to medical care.

## ALTITUDE AND ACCLIMATIZATION

It is essential to acclimatize slowly to altitude. Serious mountain sickness usually occurs above 3650m (12,000ft) but can occur as low as 2150m (7000ft). The old adage of going high during the day but sleeping low at night still applies. Most people experience problems if they are transported high by road or air instead of walking up over several days. Successful acclimatization also depends on staying healthy during the weeks before the trek as well as on the trek itself. People suffering from altitude sickness should be brought down to a much lower altitude as soon as possible. If it is available, a Gamow Bag – a portable hyperbaric chamber that is pressurized with a foot-pump – and the administration of oxygen will help. There are prescription drugs such as Acetazolamide (Diamox) that can be used to relieve the symptoms of benign mountain sickness and by people who are only going to altitude for a very short time. However, these are no substitute for correct acclimatization.

Altitude manifests itself in several ways from Acute Mountain Sickness to psychological problems. In the late 1970s, while trekking from the Kalash Valleys near Chitral across to Buni Zom, Gilgit and Hunza in Northern Pakistan, I had a woman acting

ABOVE *Trekkers acclimatizing above Manang, a higly organized town where year-round tourism is possible in Nepal – Annapurna Circuit.*

strangely. She regularly complained that the metal tent pegs gave her bad vibes and that the young men in nearby tents kept casting spells on her. Two years later I had the same lady on a trip with higher ambient temperatures but very little altitude, she still had metal tent pegs and men in nearby tents, but never gave any problems.

At altitude people can lose their appetite, so having a good variety of food with different tastes can be good for morale.

## FOOD AND WATER

Food that is cooked properly from raw should be safe to eat. However, when certain cooked foods, such as rice and meat, are allowed to cool, some of the organisms that grow on them are not killed by reheating. This can happen in the higher-quality type of hotel that trekkers often use before and after a trek. Many hotels reheat precooked food or leave food standing around for many hours as a buffet where flies or cockroaches can contaminate it. People with special dietary needs must warn the trek organizers of this in advance.

When purchasing bottled water in the Third World, make sure that the seal is intact and do not contaminate the water by adding ice. The only way to be sure of purifying local water is to boil it vigorously for at least twenty minutes, longer at altitude. If you are above the snowline, you will save work and fuel by melting ice rather than snow. Chlorine tablets will not kill amoeba in the cyst form, this requires iodine, but some people are allergic to iodine. A small dropper bottle containing Tincture of Iodine, or tablets, can be used

**ABOVE** *A trek's cooks preparing food at the Berber village of Setti Fadma, Ourika Valley, Atlas Mountains, Morocco.*

to quickly purify the water supplied in cheap restaurants. Unless they are combined with chemical treatment, the filters sold in camping shops will not filter out tiny organisms such as viruses. They will also block up quickly if the water contains fine grit from glacier meltwater.

## RAMADAN

The Muslim fasting month of Ramadan should be avoided in Islamic countries. In 1977 I had a week to get from a trek that I had led in Ladakh in India to one starting at Gilgit in Pakistan. In the days of the British Raj I could have walked across from Srinagar in days, but with the problems between India and Pakistan my flights via Delhi and Lahore were held up and I arrived a day late. The group that I was to

lead had arrived the day before – the last day of Ramadan. During Ramadan, Muslims may not consume food or drink during the day, so, in my absence, when the group had a hotel lunch, the food, including rice and meat, would have been reheated from the day before. Within a few days, most of them were sick and they got worse throughout the trek. Most members of the group were doctors and they became more and more convinced that they had typhoid. However, on their return to the UK, tests proved the problem to be Giardiasis (Giardia lamblia), which could have been easily treated during the trek.

## ACCIDENTS

Statistically most accidents to tourists happen when travelling by vehicle. Good local

agencies will have safe drivers and reliable vehicles, but public bus drivers can be dangerous. Many use drugs to keep awake for the long hours necessary.

In 1974, while on what was then a remote trek among Hill Tribes on the Northern Thailand-Myanmar border, a woman tripped and broke her leg while dancing with the family in the yard of the dwelling where we were staying. The wound was open and we were four days' walk from the nearest river and then a further half-day from the nearest hospital so my main concern was not the break, but infection.

Transporting her back to safety was a major undertaking. We constructed a bamboo stretcher and gathered local porters to carry it, but it was not that simple. Many of the villages were at war with each other so I had to keep finding fresh porters as each group would only carry her as far as the next village. The villagers were also super-stitious about carrying an injured person through the village, and I had to buy a chicken and let them sacrifice it before we could continue. Although not a doctor, I do have some expedition-medical training so I risked giving her broad-spectrum antibiotics for the time it took to reach an American Mission hospital in Chiang Mai. Fortunately, we saved her leg and she was able to do another trip with me later.

## BEST-LAID PLANS...

Even the best-organized treks can have problems: earthquakes, avalanches, landslides and inclement weather can sweep away bridges or tracks, necessitating lengthy detours. Transport at either end of the trek can break down. Local strife, theft, altitude problems, illness, accidents and friction within the group are common.

In my experience, when local agency staff are used, theft is never down to the porters, since having and keeping the job is more important to them. It could be local people not connected with the group, but often it is within the group itself.

I started trekking in Norway's Jutenheimen Mountains in 1962. After covering the Austrian, French, Italian and Swiss Alps, I have trekked in the remoter parts of the Third World since 1967 and in that time have experienced seven coups d'état.

However, such problems are rare and usually do not impinge on one's enjoyment of the trip. There are many reasons to enjoy trekking, not least because it is a physical activity. Some people take pleasure from captivatingly spectacular natural scenery and where they exist, the exotic and diverse cultures of local ethnic groups living a subsistence lifestyle. Others prefer harsh environments and extreme terrain, while those on a pilgrimage have the satisfaction of making the journey for religious, respectful, nostalgic or sentimental reasons. Photographers prefer not having to dash to the next viewpoint, but to be able to stop and photograph often, allowing for different views and the nuances of the light.

Spectacular views embed themselves in one's memory. When well clear of light pollution in the wilds, the bright stars in a clear sky at night are amazing. In 1971, while bivouacking in the Sahara Desert, a shower of shooting stars appeared to be so close that we felt that they might hit us.

## REASONS TO GO

Finding oneself spectacularly close to wild animals can be rewarding. We came across bears near Skardu in Pakistan, lynx in Morocco, Desert Foxes in the Sahara, Bearded Vultures (Lammergeyers or Lammergeiers) in Afghanistan and Pakistan, Griffon Vultures, caracal, Hamadryas Baboons and Striped Hyenas in Yemen, ptarmigan in Iceland and wolves attacking sheep in Iran. Travelling with local porters, interacting with the local people and residing with them overnight can be very satisfying especially when the trek coincides with local festivals.

Apart from attending local festivals and visiting several tribal groups, my treks have

involved being guest of honour, starting a polo final and presenting the winner's cup in Gilgit and at a Fantasia in Morocco; having tea with the Mir of Hunza when it was still an autonomous state; dinner with the Mir of Punial in Pakistan; dinner with the Gurkha Chief of Staff in Ladakh; and dinner with a Maharaja in his palace in India; breaking Ramadan fasts with Afghan and Iranian chiefs and a Pakistani General; having coffee

with an Iranian princess; joining several marriage feasts in Yemen; and regularly being certified as alcoholics to legally obtain supplies of beer in Pakistan since it went dry.

Why lie on the beach for a holiday when you can have an adventure and see the world differently. If you take pleasure from walking then this book and the regions featured within it will provide inspiration for that next enterprise. Enjoy your trekking.

RIGHT *Nyinba woman with baby at Limithang village, Humla – the highest, most remote and most northerly region of Nepal lying on the border with Tibet.*

OPPOSITE *Looking to Ganglakarchung La (pass) at 5100m (16,732ft) from just before Narithang camp, Bhutan.*

# EUROPE

## By Jack Jackson

Although much of Europe is urban, there are too many national parks to list: large tracts of wilderness to be enjoyed; and bears, lynxes, wolves and other wild animals can still be found. Conditions vary from the hot, stark mountains of the Mediterranean islands to high alpine routes and almost unpopulated regions such as northern Scotland, some of Spain, eastern Europe, and Iceland – to as far north as you can go before it is best to use skis. Away from urban areas, the scenery can be varied. From gently-contoured hills to savage peaks of granite and limestone mountains,

ICELAND

REYKJAVÍK

Surtsey

Horn

Arctic Circle

ATLANTIC OCEAN

N

Belfas

IRELAND

DUBLIN

PEMBROKESHIRE COAST PATH

Celtic Sea

Land's End

Bretag

WAY OF ST JAMES

Bay of Biscay

Cantabrian Mtns

Bilbao

PORTUGAL

Porto

PICOS DE EUROPA

LISBOA (LISBON)

MADRID

S P A I N

La Mancha

Valencia

Sevilla

Córdoba

Murcia

Golfo de Cádiz

Málaga

Strait of Gibraltar

Costa del Sol

Tanger

Gibraltar (U.K.)

Ceuta (Sp.)

Melilla (Sp.)

RABAT

MOROCCO

Fès

Oujda

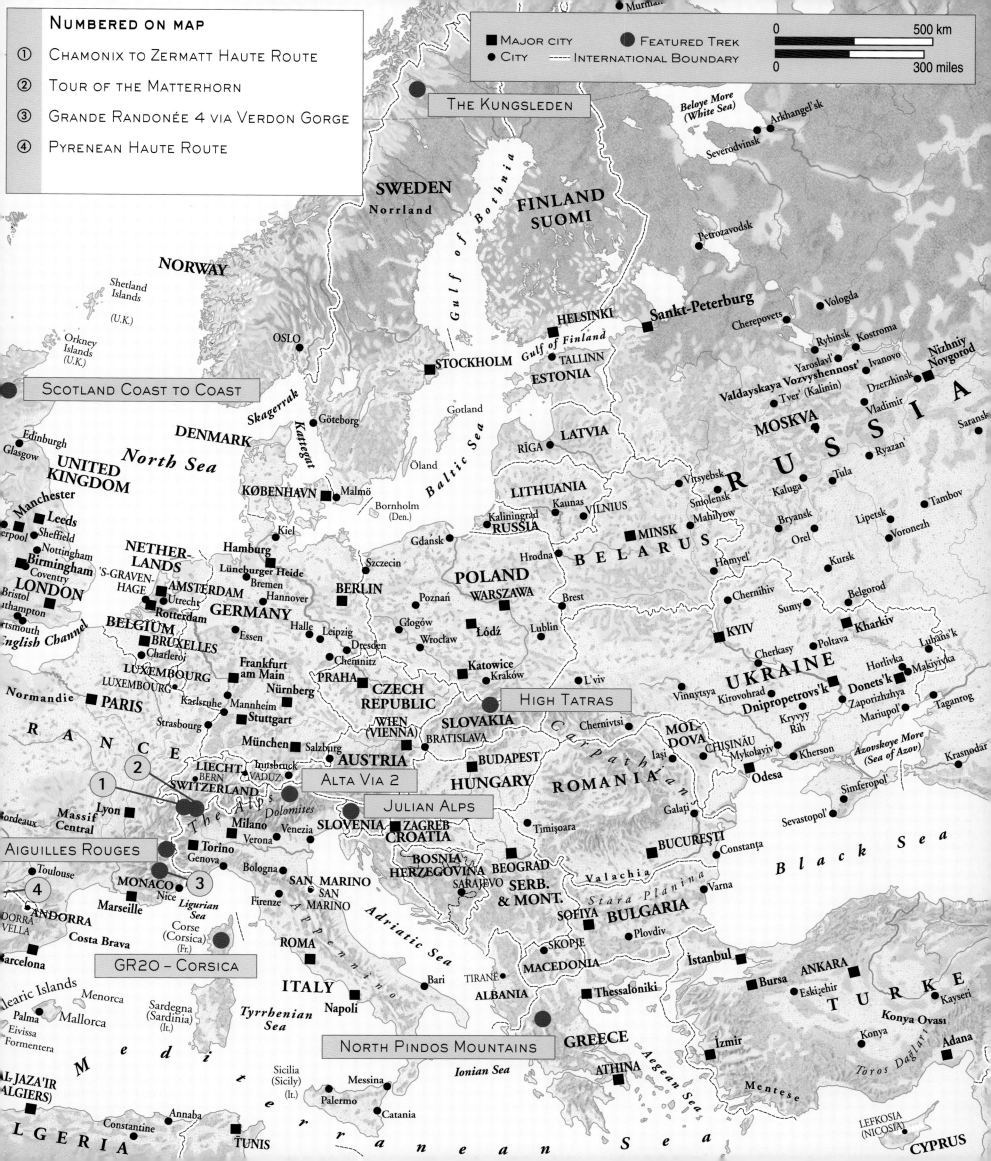

NUMBERED ON MAP

① CHAMONIX TO ZERMATT HAUTE ROUTE

② TOUR OF THE MATTERHORN

③ GRANDE RANDONÉE 4 VIA VERDON GORGE

④ PYRENEAN HAUTE ROUTE

■ MAJOR CITY    ● FEATURED TREK
● CITY    - - - INTERNATIONAL BOUNDARY

0    500 km
0    300 miles

THE KUNGSLEDEN

*Beloye More (White Sea)*

Murmansk
Arkhangel'sk
Severodvinsk

SWEDEN
*Norrland*

FINLAND
SUOMI

Petrozavodsk

NORWAY

Shetland Islands (U.K.)

Orkney Islands (U.K.)

HELSINKI
Sankt-Peterburg
Vologda

Cherepovets

SCOTLAND COAST TO COAST

OSLO

STOCKHOLM
TALLINN
ESTONIA

Rybinsk
Kostroma
Nizhniy Novgorod

Yaroslavl'
Ivanovo
Dzerzhinsk

*Gulf of Finland*

Valdayskaya Vozvyshennost'
Tver' (Kalinin)
Vladimir

Saransk

Edinburgh
Glasgow

DENMARK

*Skagerrak*

Göteborg

Gotland

*Baltic Sea*

RĪGA
LATVIA

MOSKVA
RUSSIA

Ryazan'

UNITED KINGDOM

*North Sea*

*Kattegat*

Öland

LITHUANIA

Vitsyebsk
Smolensk
Mahilyow

Vologda

Tula
Tambov

Manchester
Leeds
Sheffield
erpool
Nottingham

KØBENHAVN
Malmö

Bornholm (Den.)

Kaunas
VILNIUS

Kaluga

Bryansk
Orel

Lipetsk
Voronezh

Kaliningrad
RUSSIA

Kursk

Birmingham
Coventry

NETHER-LANDS

Kiel
Hamburg

Gdańsk

MINSK

Homyel'

Belgorod

Bristol
uthampton

'S-GRAVEN-HAGE
AMSTERDAM

Lüneburger Heide
Bremen
Hannover

Szczecin

BELARUS

LONDON

Utrecht

BERLIN

Poznań

WARSZAWA

Brest

Chernihiv

Sumy

rtsmouth

BELGIUM

Rotterdam

GERMANY

Halle
Leipzig

POLAND

Głogów
Wrocław

Lublin

KYIV

Poltava

Kharkiv

*English Channel*

BRUXELLES
Charleroi

Essen

Dresden
Chemnitz

Łódź

Katowice
Kraków

L'viv

Cherkasy

Luhans'k

LUXEMBOURG

Frankfurt am Main

PRAHA

HIGH TATRAS

Vinnytsya
Kirovohrad

Horlivka
Makiyivka

*Normandie*

LUXEMBOURG

Nürnberg

CZECH REPUBLIC

UKRAINE

Dnipropetrovs'k

Donets'k

PARIS

Karlsruhe
Mannheim

Stuttgart

WIEN (VIENNA)

SLOVAKIA
BRATISLAVA

Chernivtsi

MOL-DOVA

Kryvyy Rih

Zaporizhzhya

Taganrog

R    A    N    C    E

Strasbourg

München
Salzburg

AUSTRIA

BUDAPEST

Iași

CHIŞINĂU

Mykolayiv

Kherson

*Azovskoye More (Sea of Azov)*

Krasnodar

Lyon

LIECHT
BERN
VADUZ

Innsbruck

ALTA VIA 2

HUNGARY

ROMANIA

Odesa

Massif Central

SWITZERLAND

*The Alps*

JULIAN ALPS

*Carpathian*

Galaţi

BUCUREŞTI

Constanţa

*Black Sea*

AIGUILLES ROUGES

*Dolomites*
Milano
Verona

Venezia

SLOVENIA
ZAGREB
CROATIA

Timişoara

Toulouse

Torino
Genova

Bologna

SAN MARINO
SAN MARINO

BOSNIA HERZEGOVINA

BEOGRAD

*Valachia*

*Stara Planina*

Varna

ordeaux

MONACO
Nice

Firenze

SARAJEVO

SERB. & MONT.

GR20 – CORSICA

ANDORRA
DORRA VELLA

Costa Brava

*Ligurian Sea*

Corse (Corsica) (Fr.)

SOFIYA
BULGARIA

İstanbul

ANKARA

Marseille

ROMA

*Adriatic Sea*

SKOPJE

Plovdiv

Bursa

Eskişehir

TURKE

arcelona

leraic Islands

Menorca

Palma
Mallorca

Eivissa
Formentera

*Sardegna (Sardinia) (It.)*

*Tyrrhenian Sea*

NORTH PINDOS MOUNTAINS

*Appennino*

Napoli

Bari

TIRANË

MACEDONIA

ALBANIA

Thessaloniki

GREECE

ATHINA

İzmir

Konya Ovasi

Konya

Kayseri

Adana

*Toros Dağları*

L JAZA'IR ALGIERS)

LGERIA

Annaba
Constantine

*Mediterranean*

Sicilia (Sicily) (It.)

Messina
Palermo
Catania

TUNIS

*Ionian Sea*

*Aegean Sea*

*Mentese*

LEFKOSIA (NICOSIA)

CYPRUS

ITALY

**ABOVE** *The waymarked descent from Monodendri through the Vikos Gorge, which translates as Loud Voice, is much easier than the ascent.*

**PREVIOUS PAGE LEFT** *Taking in the view from above the Refuge d' Arremoulit, trekking poles are useful to steady trekkers on rockier or steeper slopes.*

**PREVIOUS PAGE RIGHT** *Glen Nevis viewed from the slopes of of the UK's highest peak, the 1343m (4406ft) Ben Nevis.*

alpine pastures, volcanic lava, glaciers, rivers and gorges, thick woodlands, and dramatic coastlines.

Many people think that Mont Blanc is the highest mountain in Europe, but it is not even in the top five. There are higher mountains in the Caucasus. Europe's highest peak is the 5642m (18,510ft) Mount Elbrus in the Russian Central Caucasus.

Long-distance, self-guided walking, and later backpacking, started in Europe, mainly as the routes of merchants and soldiers who were going about their business. There were also people undertaking religious pilgrimages. Whether you want gentle rambling, hiking or the more physically demanding trekking and backpacking, there is a network of long-distance routes that crisscross Europe from urban walks to pilgrimages and tough treks. Many of these routes follow a numbered system and are often signposted or have coloured waymarks (blazes). Most of them encompass beautiful scenery, but some are thematic.

Europe does not have trekking with porters and most walking/backpacking is self-guided, but there are plenty of commercial treks. Some organizations provide a van to carry food, drink, extra gear and even non-walking partners to pre-arranged meeting places. Very occasionally, a long-distance walker uses a donkey or mule as a pack animal.

France probably has the most extensive network of walking routes called randonnées, with 60,000km (37,200 miles) of long-distance routes and 80,000km (49,600 miles) of regional and shorter routes. Many of these follow ancient tracks used by merchants, soldiers and pilgrims and are divided into categories: Grandes Randonnées (GR) and Randonnées en Pays (PR). Grandes Randonnées (GR), or great walks, which are long-distance routes of more than 50km (31 miles), are waymarked or blazed with red and white markers on rocks, boulders and trees. Regional Randonnées, or Randonnées en Pays (PR), which are between 10 and 50km (6 and 31 miles), are waymarked with red and yellow markers. There are also local and urban routes. The Grandes Randonnées are given internationally recognized numerical identities and some spread across international borders. For example, the GR20 follows the mountainous spine of the island of Corsica. Other European countries have copied the system, but the colours of the waymarks and the signs used can vary.

There are also European Long Distance Paths (E-paths), designated by the European Ramblers' Association. E-paths are an international network of 11 ultra-long-distance walking routes over thousands of kilometres across Europe. They are usually superimposed on existing networks of routes, though some new routes have been developed to fill in gaps. E-paths mainly follow sections of existing routes so they are not waymarked in their own right, except at major junctions. Some E-paths are still being developed. Some people walk ultra-long-distance routes in one go, but it is more usual to do them in stages.

## VIA FERRATA

*Vie ferrate* (singular *via ferrata*), which means 'iron ways' in Italian, are unique to Europe. Originally set up in World War I to help alpine troops supply their outposts in the Dolomites, these are mountain routes over very steep ground. However, they are completely protected with fixed climbing aids – heavy-gauge steel wire, periodically fixed to the rock by thick metal bars with eyelets at the end, handrails, ladders, and bridges. Nowadays similar systems can be found in Sweden and France.

## INFRASTRUCTURE

Many regions have a lot of infrastructure, from the ability to call up helicopter or other rescue services by mobile telephone to mountain huts with or without permanent wardens or bivouacs, and the possibility of descending down into the valley for accommodation or to avoid a storm. For this reason, backpackers often deliberately make things more taxing by carrying the equipment for camping and staying high when they do not need to.

## BEST TIME TO GO

Generally the best time to trek in Europe is from May to the end of September, but the peak holiday month of August can experience lots of rain. Mosquitoes can be a problem in northern Europe including Iceland, and they seem to get worse in fine weather. When trekking on routes that are high, start early to avoid storms that often build up in the afternoon. At altitude storms can get very cold and windy, even in summer, and static electricity can be a problem on exposed ridges or faces. Static electricity can be a serious problem if you are carrying metal trekking poles, an ice axe or karabiners for protection. Having my hair stand on end during a descent in Austria was not a pleasant experience. At times of high pressure, winter days can be bright and sunny, though the hours of daylight are short and many people search out winter snow on lower mountains for the beauty of the scenery.

**ABOVE** *A path along the Chéserys Lakes leads to a series of easy ladders to reach the Refuge du Lac Blanc in the Aiguilles Rouges.*

# PEMBROKESHIRE COAST PATH

*By Tom Hutton*

Winding its way around 300km (186miles) of breathtaking coastline, the Pembrokeshire Coast Path provides an enthralling tour of the wild and rugged headlands that form the western tip of mainland Britain. The walking is challenging: the narrow path hugs the cliff tops – cutting lengthy diversions around every inlet, and dropping steeply down to sea level at regular intervals. Yet the rewards are tremendous, with abundant wildlife and sublime coastal scenery around almost every corner.

The official start is on the banks of the Afon Teifi in St Dogmael's – a small harbour-side village close to the town of Cardigan. It's an incongruous start, with the line of the path following minor roads along the banks of the river before climbing steeply out onto open ground, high above the broad mouth of the estuary. It's not until you reach Cemaes Head – the first of many proud capes you'll pass on the trail – that you really start to hear the calls of the gulls and taste the salt in the air.

The next section is broken up by Ceibwr Bay, a rugged, pebbly cove that makes an ideal spot for your first lunch, and then it's back up onto the cliff tops again to round Foel-goch and get your first views across the bay to Newport – an ideal stopping-off point at the end of day one.

If St Dogmael's to Newport made an obvious first day on the trail, Newport to Fishguard will provide an equally convenient second, with little in the way of civilization between the two. The opening leg, to Cwm-yr-Eglwys, is delightful: passing many secluded coves and climbing high above the surf in places. Then comes Dinas Island – a thrilling diversion that climbs to a lofty 142m (466ft) at its highest point.

Things become even more dramatic as you approach Fishguard: with rocky promontories breaking the coast into a succession of picturesque bays. This is a good place to spot Atlantic Grey Seals, which are usually seen bobbing up and

**ABOVE** *A gentle swell washes onto the golden sands of Swanlake Bay, a remote south Pembrokeshire beach, accessible only on foot.*

down in the water (called bottling) or, during their autumn breeding season, hauled up on the beaches, caring for their pups. Porpoises and Bottlenose Dolphins are also regularly seen from this stretch of coast.

West of the ferry port, the scenery continues to get wilder, reaching a climax on the rugged bluff of Strumble Head, where an ornate lighthouse warns passing ships of the treacherous waters that surround it. Towering cliffs and cairn-topped hills continue the wild and woolly theme to Aber Mawr and Trefin, which makes a convenient place to stop for the night. If you fancy a shorter day, however, you'll struggle to do better than the hostel at Pwll Deri – surely the most spectacularly positioned hostel in Wales!

## ATMOSPHERIC VILLAGE

Of all the villages passed on the trail, Porthgain has to be the most atmospheric. The tiny harbour, crowned with just a small cluster of buildings, looks like it comes straight from a film set; and the village pub, the Sloop Inn, is one of the best in the area. It's a steep pull back onto the cliff tops though – even more so if you've taken advantage of the wonderful facilities.

Once up, the next section slips easily beneath the feet; and unless you fancy whiling away a few hours on the lovely sands of Traeth Llyfn (a gorgeous but usually deserted beach) the next major landmark is the gothic-looking tower at Abereiddi, which has long been a favourite haunt of the author. A few metres beyond this, you'll pass a flooded quarry, known for obvious reasons, as the Blue Lagoon.

Abereiddi's eerie abandoned settlement – once quarry worker's cottages – is the last you'll see of civilization before St David's Head; and ahead now is a wonderful section of rugged coastline, made all the more impressive by the imposing crag-topped hills that tower above it. The finest of these, Carn Llidi, is one of the best places in Wales to watch the sunset.

The headland is remarkably beautiful, and worthy of the Patron Saint's name. Summer carpets the rough ground with the pinks and golds of heather and gorse, while winter bombards the rugged cliffs with

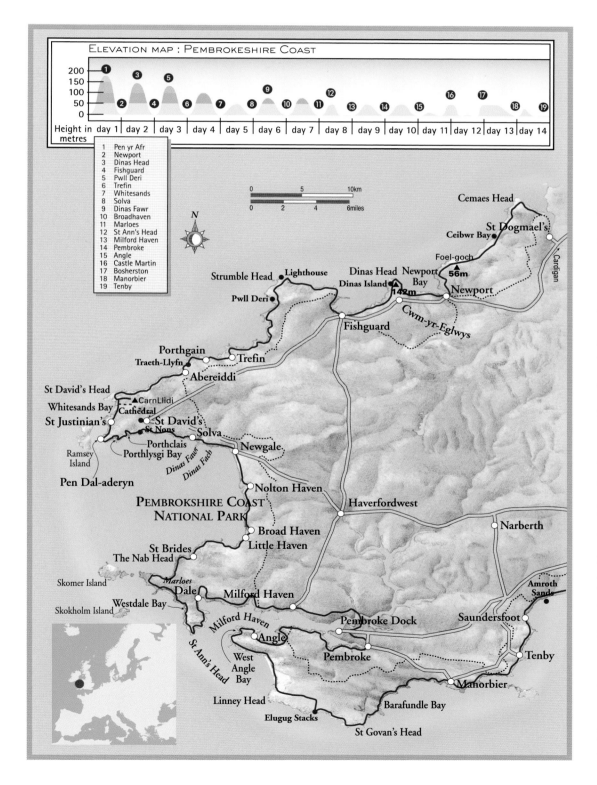

sizeable swells, sending clouds of spray high into the air. Whitesands Bay is just a short walk from here, but if you don't fancy the camp sites or the hostel above the beach, an easy 30-minute stroll will see you on the narrow streets of St David's – a city the size of a small village, and surely the spiritual capital of the Principality.

## ST DAVID'S CATHEDRAL

If you only see one attraction in Wales, then let it be St David's Cathedral – a stunning edifice that, in the 12th-century, was considered so holy that Pope Calixtus II suggested that two visits to St David's were the equivalent to one journey to Rome – an honour indeed.

From Whitesands, the path ducks behind the beach, hurdling a few small cliffs before dropping again to St Justinian's – which houses a sheltered lifeboat station and also acts as the boarding point for boat trips to the offshore islands. From here, the scenery develops a wilder flavour again and the path tracks along the edge of the gushing sound to Pen Dal-aderyn, where it enters St Bride's Bay.

Due south now, you'll see the Marloes Peninsula and the offshore island of Skomer – still some three to four day's walking away. West, beyond the lazy humps of Ramsey's grassy spine, you should be able to make out the jagged, whitened profile of Grassholm – a tiny sea stack, 13km (8 miles) offshore, that is home to some 33,000 breeding pairs of gannets.

The waters of St Bride's Bay are a little more tranquil than those further north, but the breathtaking scenery doesn't relent at all, with the sea turning almost turquoise as you cross behind Porthlysgi Bay and track inland around the narrow haven of Porthclais – a popular rock climbing venue.

## BIRTHPLACE OF ST DAVID

St Non's marks the actual birthplace of St David, modestly celebrated by a small shrine and a holy well, a few metres inland

ABOVE LEFT *Looking across Ramsey Sound from the lifeboat station at St Justinian's. The land on the horizon is the northernmost tip of Ramsey Island.*
LEFT *The view across Fishguard Bay from Pen y Fan, the high point of Dinas Island.*

of the coast path and close to the tumbledown ruins of a 13th-century chapel. Beyond this, you'll pass above the sheltered sands of Caerfai Bay – the nearest beach to the city. From here you climb above a rocky headland; drop to cross a river at Porth y Rhaw; hurdle a final lofty hillside before plummeting steeply down into the colourful harbour village of Solva.

If you think the sudden drop to the streets and the huge trek inland was cruel, wait for the climb back out: first onto a slender ridge called Gribin, and then back down to sea level again to ford a stream, before a final steep climb up onto Penrhyn.

It's easy going from here, though – especially if you can avoid the temptations of the inviting promontories of Dinas Fawr and Dinas Fach. Then it's a steep drop to Porthmynawyd and an equally steep climb back up for a final push to Cwm-bach. If the tide's low, you can short-circuit the next section, staying on the beach to Newgale; but if your timing is off, it's back up again to hurdle another steep gorse-covered hillside before dropping down to the huge, pebbly strand.

Newgale might not be the prettiest of Pembrokeshire's beaches, but it's certainly one of the wildest; particularly in winter when it's pounded by the full brunt of the Irish Sea swells. If the tide is low, you can enjoy the next section close to the tide-line; if it is high, keep to the road.

Nolton Haven breaks your stride, but at least it has a pub; then it is back up again, for an easy section that leads all the way down to Broadhaven – a traditionally-styled seaside resort and one of the less

**ABOVE** *Many different plant species decorate the cliff tops in spring and summer. This is English Stonecrop.*

picturesque villages on the path. Little Haven makes up for this, though, with a quaint harbour; and then it's west again, and slightly easier going, as you make your way along the cliff tops past St Bride's and onto the western tip of the peninsula.

## MILFORD HAVEN

The beaches on the southern side are some of the best on the trek – worth a visit if time allows – but from West Dale things become a little wilder again, as you climb steeply onto the tip of St Ann's Head. This lofty headland marks the entrance to Milford Haven – an expansive natural harbour. It also signifies the start of the 'inland' section of the walk; and the path follows the sheltered waterway inland past Dale and Sandy Haven and up the inlet to the more industrial landscapes of Milford Haven, Pembroke Dock and Pembroke. It is not the most scenic part of the walk, but at least there's no shortage of good places to eat and sleep.

West Angle Bay marks a welcome return to the coastal scenery – and if you'd forgotten just how beautiful this can be, the drop to Freshwater West will quickly jog your memory. The next section crosses a military zone and is often closed to the public, necessitating a lengthy road detour. Check before you start out. Assuming that it is open, the stretch between Elugug Stacks and St Govan's Head is one of the finest sections of the whole trek, with soft grass beneath your feet and barely any discernible rise or fall. The scenery is typically breathtaking and the tiny chapel at St Govan's is a must-see.

## BEACH, PUB AND CASTLE

From the dramatic limestone bluffs of St Govan's Head, you are probably only two days away from the finish – but what a fine two days they are. Stunning beaches, such as Barafundle and Swanlake, conspire to tempt you from the path; and the sunny village of Manorbier provides further distraction in the shape of a good pub and a fine castle. Even the bustling streets of Tenby and Saundersfoot feel welcoming at this late stage of the journey, and they also offer plenty of choice for a comfortable final night on the trail.

The broad sweep of Amroth Sands marks the end of your coastal odyssey, and although it's a lovely beach, punctuated at low tide by the stumps of ancient trees, it still feels like an anticlimax after the exhilaration of the last few days. Don't be surprised if you feel an overwhelming urge to turn around and walk straight back the way you came.

# SCOTLAND COAST TO COAST

*By Ronald Turnbull*

'Scotland small? Our multiform, our infinite Scotland small?' So asks one of Scotland's 20th-century poets, Hugh Macdiarmid. Compared with the rest of Europe, Scotland may not take up much of the map. And its mountains, all at about the 1000m (3300ft) mark, would count anywhere else as valley bottoms. What Scotland does have is empty country where you can walk for three days without crossing a road or passing an inhabited house. This emptiness is due, historically, to the despoliation after the 1745 rebellion of Bonnie Prince Charlie, followed by the Highland Clearances when the people were forcibly removed to make way for sheep. But add to this a universal right of access and wild camping, and the result is a country whose glens, loch sides and rocky ridges are just made for self-sufficient backpacking.

And as a country Scotland is not so much small as comfortably middle-sized. To walk right across it takes about two weeks. In that short time you'll see the sea lochs of the west and the rocky ridge of Ben Nevis. You'll cross remote Ben Alder, the heather hills of Central Scotland, and the granite plateau of the Cairngorms.

## CHOOSE YOUR ROUTE

Highland Scotland has no waymarked paths. It has no huts, though there are some simple unlocked shelters known as bothies. This is country where you choose your own route, and look after yourself. It's possible to make your way across, using the valleys, and finding yourself a village or hostel every night. But to see the very best of Scotland, you need to cross the mountain tops, and walk for three days at a time with a tent. The route suggested here is of that more demanding, more rewarding sort, with seven of the country's highest hills taken on the way, and some easy (always avoidable) scrambling on the rocky ridges.

The south-western corner of the Highlands has no hills above 914m (3000ft). This

**ABOVE** *In the west, mountains are steep and rather rocky. In the east, more rounded ones rise from forests of ancient pine. Glen Feshie leads in towards the Cairngorms*

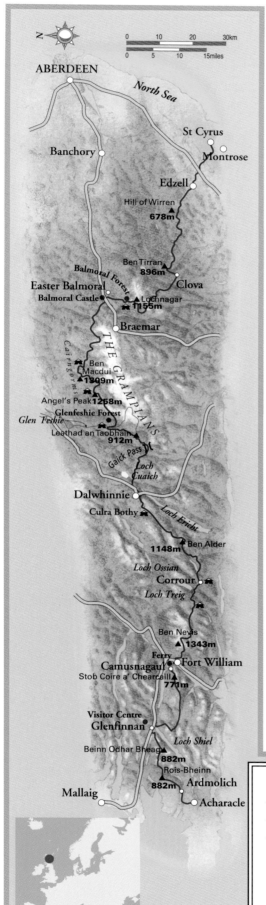

is the arbitrary altitude that Scottish hillwalkers pursue and, accordingly, this country west of Fort William is seldom visited. After a rough crossing to Ardmolich, the first two days take you along a high line of hills by Rois-Bheinn 882m (2894ft) and Beinn Odhar Bheag (also 882m) to Glenfinnan. High, shaggy slopes rise out of empty valleys, but the way along the top is among knolls of bare rock, on short, walkable grass. Sheltered beside a rock knoll somewhere on Druim Fiaclach is your first overnight stop. Wind rustles through the grass as you draw water from a chilly rock pool. Behind you, the Atlantic stretches into a sunset all spotted with islands.

Glenfinnan is where Prince Charles Stuart raised the standard of rebellion in 1745. This historical moment is important to walkers as it has resulted in a Visitor Centre with a useful café, as well as hotels and a hostel. A day's walking among the scattered Caledonian pines of the Cona Glen (valley) leads to Stob Coire a' Chearcaill 771m (2530ft) and a long gentle descent to Camusnagaul. A small passenger ferry carries schoolchildren, commuters, and the occasional long-distance walker across to Fort William.

## BIGGER, BUT EASIER, HILLS

Hills for these first three days have been relatively small and very quiet. The hills between the Great Glen and the A9 road are bigger, but at the same time easier. They are not so rough, and their ridges carry well-trodden paths. The trek now crosses the not-at-all quiet hill that is also Scotland's highest. But having taken the long, stony path 1343m (4406ft) up Ben Nevis, the way continues by a granite ridge that's less than a metre wide in places. The Carn Mor Dearg Arête is technically straightforward, a matter of clambering over granite boulders. However, it does have high, steep drops on both sides. Behind you, as you work your way along, the 3km (2-mile) wide crag of Ben Nevis's north face unfolds.

From the 1220m (4003ft) Carn Mor Dearg you could continue along the ridge of the Grey Corries to the bothy in Lairig Leacach – a splendid, but extremely strenuous, day. More reasonable is to descend the Allt Coire Giubhsachan into upper Glen Nevis. And in bad conditions, Ben Nevis can be avoided altogether by way of the beautiful Nevis Gorge.

Good paths lead eastward to Corrour. No public roads run to Corrour, whose buildings

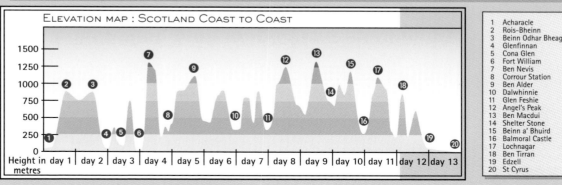

ELEVATION MAP : SCOTLAND COAST TO COAST

| | | | | | | | | | | | | | |
|---|---|---|---|---|---|---|---|---|---|---|---|---|---|
| 1 | Acharacle |
| 2 | Rois-Bheinn |
| 3 | Beinn Odhar Bheag |
| 4 | Glenfinnan |
| 5 | Cona Glen |
| 6 | Fort William |
| 7 | Ben Nevis |
| 8 | Corrour Station |
| 9 | Ben Alder |
| 10 | Dalwhinnie |
| 11 | Glen Feshie |
| 12 | Angel's Peak |
| 13 | Ben Macdui |
| 14 | Shelter Stone |
| 15 | Beinn a' Bhuird |
| 16 | Balmoral Castle |
| 17 | Lochnagar |
| 18 | Ben Tirran |
| 19 | Edzell |
| 20 | St Cyrus |

Height in metres: 1500, 1250, 1000, 750, 500, 250, 0

day 1  day 2  day 3  day 4  day 5  day 6  day 7  day 8  day 9  day 10  day 11  day 12  day 13

ABOVE *You don't have to go over the tops. The Steall waterfall, one of Scotland's largest, is on the low-level variant route taken to avoid Ben Nevis, the UK's highest hill.*

consist of a railway station, an independent hostel, and a youth hostel. More good paths run by Loch Ossian and the Bealach Dubh; but the high way is over hills of grass and heather, Carn Dearg and Sgor Gaibhre, to the 1148m (3766ft) Ben Alder. Moorland birds with melancholy piping calls fly across the stony plateau. Geologically, and in terms of atmosphere, it's a remnant of the land before the glaciers.

The plateau's northern corner is a sharp rocky arête called Long Leacas. Again, it's technically undemanding, but much less visited than Ben Nevis, and some of its delicately poised mossy blocks require care. It leads down to Culra Bothy, where an open door, a brightly burning fire, good company and a bottle of whisky may tempt you into a night on hard concrete rather than your comfortable tent in the

heather. The enjoyable way onwards is by the long grassy ridge of the 911m (2989ft) Fara. A tree gap leads down to a 20th-century castle alongside Loch Ericht, and so out to Dalwhinnie.

The A9 road runs along the line of a military one built to pacify the Highlands around the time of Prince Charlie's rebellion. Crossing it marks the dividing line between the Highlands and the Grampians: between sharp mountains of grass and rock, and rounded ones of heather. Dalwhinnie, close to the high point of the road, is a huddle of grey buildings between dark plantations and brown hills. It is not a pretty place. But those grey buildings include a shop, hotels and a café, and it's a welcome stop for walkers to wash themselves and their clothes, and dry out the contents of the rucksack.

Rounded and heathery could be quite unexciting. But for this first Grampian day, fast going along a track leads by Loch (lake) Cuaich and across a high moor into dramatic, steep-sided Gaick Pass. An invaluable small path along Allt Gharbh Ghaig (the rough stream of Gaick) leads onto the 912m (2991ft) Leathad an Taobhain. Once again, by staying on hills lower than the crucial 914m (3000ft)-mark, solitary walking is almost assured. A path by Allt Lorgaidh leads down into Glen Feshie.

## TREE COVER

Just 2000 years ago, all the lower ground of Scotland was under the spreading blue-grey foliage of the Scots pine, with deer grazing between the red-coloured trunks. In Glen Feshie a fragment of this lovely tree cover still remains, with Ruigh-aiteachain bothy standing close to the wide silver river.

While the Grampian range as a whole is less exciting, this does not apply to its high central area, the Cairngorms. Here the rounded slopes rise above the plant-line into bare tundra ground of boulders and gravel. And the plateau ends abruptly in 300m (1000ft) crags of pale granite, dropping to deep, glaciated valleys. The trek crosses the high, empty moorland of the Moine Mhor (Great Moss) to the 1258m (4127ft) Sgor an Lochain Uaine (Angel's Peak), a corner poised high above one of the great valleys. Its northeast ridge gives a scrambling descent; from Lochan Uaine, keep going down, staying 100m (100yd) left of the stream to reach the tiny Garbh Coire bothy.

Across the deep valley of the Lairig Ghru, a path to the right of Allt Clach nan Taillear leads onto the 1309m (4296ft) Ben Macdui, Scotland's second highest peak. Dwarf Azalea grows 2½–5cm (an inch or two) high among the boulders. A path leads down to Loch Etchachan, where you swing left to the head of Loch Avon. Here, below a tremendous crag of granite slabs, is the Shelter Stone: a fallen boulder with room below it for half a dozen people. The boulder hole is cramped and rather dirty, but its situation is magnificent at the head of a long lake, surrounded by high, craggy slopes.

## BALMORAL CASTLE

Head down Loch Avon to cross Beinn a' Chaorainn to the 1197m (3927ft) Beinn a' Bhuird. After walking 3km (2 miles) southwards along crag tops, the northeast ridge of A' Chioch gives an easy scramble down to Dubh Lochan. Paths and tracks lead east to the crossing of the 900m (2953ft) Culardoch and a heathery descent to Balmoral. Here is a large castle built by Queen Victoria (herself a keen trekker through the surrounding valleys). More importantly, here (at Easter Balmoral) is a small shop where Queen Elizabeth II occasionally purchases groceries. In 2005 the opening hours of this crucial shop were reduced to three hours daily; in this uncommercial country, researching food supplies is even more important than shelter.

Tracks lead south past Gelder Shiel bothy to Meall Coire na Saobhaidhe, which gives a dramatic approach to the last really large mountain, the 1155m (3789ft) Lochnagar. Curve round the White Mounth plateau on grassy paths to Broad Cairn, and descend an old cattle-drovers' path into Glen Clova. The

trek has now left the Cairngorm granite, and the more fertile schist crags are bright with birch trees. From Clova Inn, cross the 896m (2941ft) Ben Tirran and the 678m (2224ft) Hill of Wirren. A handy track runs down the last slope of the Highlands to Edzell. A band of lowland ground still separates you from the sea. Tracks and minor roads, to north of the River North Esk, lead between fields of Oilseed Rape, which has yellow flowers in season, and past villages where you can sample the different sorts of Scottish beer. Finally you reach the North Sea below the small sandstone cliffs of St Cyrus.

## DRAW YOUR OWN

Or else you don't! For there are at least a dozen ways to walk across the Highlands; and part of the pleasure of the exercise is in writing a line across the map, and then seeing if you can follow it, and thus finding out whether it was a good one. A way can be devised that passes from village to village, without ever needing a night out of doors –

ABOVE *Wild weather keeps the Cairngorm plateau bleak. But just below the rim, roseroot and globe flower grow in the hollows of Mullach Clach a' Bhlair*

though that way you won't get the very best of the empty country. A different sort of walk is when you look up at the mountains, from the glens and riversides. The trek just described has such valley routes alongside it almost all the way; and a classic route by Glen Clova, Braemar and Fort Augustus stays on good paths and tracks.

Walking eastwards, as described here, means you often have the rain and wind hitting you, less unpleasantly, from behind. On the other hand, walking westwards saves you the best of the country for the end. You can start (or end) at Stonehaven, Aberdeen, or even at Spey Bay. You can end (or start) at Shiel Bridge; or Torridon; or in the south at Oban. Then there's Inverie on Loch Nevis, only reached by a rail journey to Mallaig and a passenger ferry.

A magazine, published in Scotland, coordinates an annual event where 250 people walk coast-to-coast by many self-chosen routes in May. Taking part in this Great Outdoor Challenge makes it more sociable, since you meet each other in lonely bothies and hostels all the way across. The event organizers also appraise route plans for plausibility and such details as missing footbridges: a valuable service in particular for walkers from outside the UK.

Only by walking right across it will you discover the size of Scotland. From the sea inlets of the west, by way of the high rock-topped ridges or maybe Rannoch Moor; to the green pools and granite crags of the Cairngorms, the pine forests, and the heather – there's always one more glen, another line of distant hills. Some have walked from the Atlantic to the North Sea a score of times. Scotland small? Not at all!

# AIGUILLES ROUGES

## By Hilary Sharp

At 3096m (10,157ft) Mont Buet, delightfully nicknamed locally 'le Mont Blanc des dames' (the ladies' Mont Blanc), forms the highest point of the Aiguilles Rouges massif. Its wide, round summit towers above its neighbours, but it is so far into the mountain range that it is rarely seen from the valley, hiding its secrets from those who climb in the nearby ranges.

Mont Buet is a summit to aspire to, one to save for that perfect day when all the essentials come together – time of year and good weather, coupled with willing legs and lungs. The memory of its ascent will be one of those to reach for on dark dreary days in the office when the sunlit mountains seem a figment of your imagination.

To climb Mont Buet as the culmination of a multi-day trek discovering the Aiguilles Rouges, is the ideal. Its steep north ridge provides an exciting finale – just enough exposure to make the nerves tingle, but stopping short of provoking sheer terror.

The Tour of the Aiguilles Rouges is not an official long-distance trek. However, positioned as they are right opposite the Mont Blanc range the Aiguilles Rouges do beg to be discovered and the nature of this chain of peaks is such that several days are required to explore its many different facets. The massif runs from northeast to southwest and the north- and south-facing slopes are markedly different. The whole area is designated a nature reserve so development is regulated. Nevertheless the

south-facing slopes sport two major ski resorts and the consequent ease of access is much appreciated by day walkers who enjoy many trails across these hillsides, from where the views of Mont Blanc and its associated peaks are stunning.

Nip over to the north-facing slopes and it's a different story. No lifts here, just kilometres of wilderness, broken only by the occasional summer farm or mountain hut. This is the perfect counterbalance to the sunny playground on the other side and here the adventurous hiker can have a ball.

ABOVE *Walkers and Mont Blanc are reflected in the small lake near Lac Blanc during an early morning departure from the nearby refuge.*

The tour described takes in the best of the Aiguilles Rouges and is circular so could be started anywhere. It seems best to leave Mont Buet until last, so starting where you'll finish is a good idea. Le Buet is a tiny hamlet in the Vallorcine valley, separated from the Chamonix valley by the Col des Montets road pass. This pass has an effect way beyond its relatively modest height of 1,461m (4,793ft). Traditionally the Vallorcine valley was cut off from the rest of France for a good few months of the year by snow on this pass and that feeling of being at the back of beyond remains – not for nothing is Vallorcine known as *le bout du monde* (the end of the world) by the people of Chamonix. Vallorcine has an atmosphere completely different to that found in Chamonix. Its old-fashioned charm is expressed in its two tiny shops, the scruffy but friendly hotels and the mountain railway that links it to the outside world. Those searching for wild nightlife and trendy shops will hate it, but people looking for quiet and an escape from the rat race of city life will fall in love with this village.

Starting in Le Buet, at 1350m (4429ft), you walk up to the Col des Montets and then down a little way to pick up the delightful path that leads into spruce and larch forest, heading up to the slopes of Les Chéserys. Leaving the tree line, the trail butts up against cliffs popular with climbers and soon you reach a fine pinnacle – the Aiguillette d'Argentière. Take a break here to watch the climbers, and take in the views of the Mont Blanc massif.

## LADDERS

So far height has been gained by determined plodding up zigzags. Now you get to gain considerable altitude by having fun: a series of ladders and rung-equipped rock faces. In no time you reach the huge cairn at 2100m (6890ft) on Les Chéserys. Not far away, to the west, is the Lac Blanc hut, easily spotted as there will probably be an ant-line of hikers heading towards it. Its position, just a short walk from the Flégère cable car, makes it one of the most popular destinations for day walkers from Chamonix. The views from the hut are spectacular and they do a fine line in refreshments..

Take the well-marked path that leads along the shores of the Chéserys lakes (the brave will take a dip) and up a final section of trail, equipped with easy ladders and rungs, to the hut. The Refuge du Lac Blanc at 2352m (7,717ft) was rebuilt in 1991, after

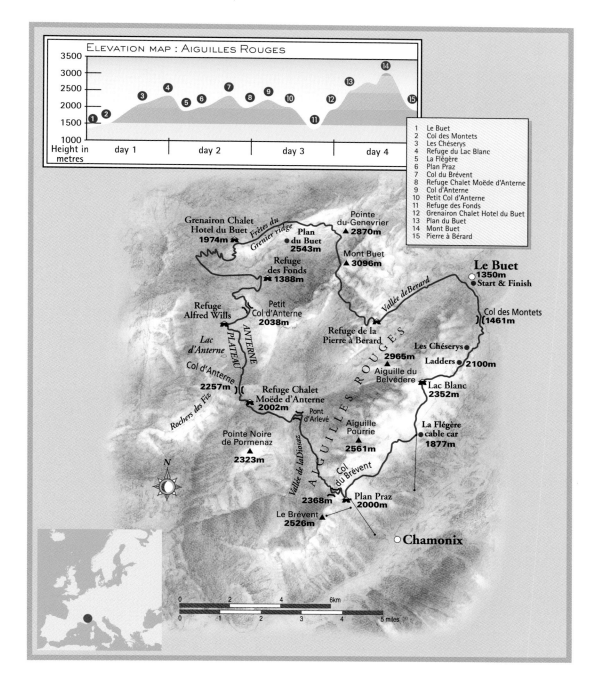

ELEVATION MAP : AIGUILLES ROUGES

1  Le Buet
2  Col des Montets
3  Les Chéserys
4  Refuge du Lac Blanc
5  La Flégère
6  Plan Praz
7  Col du Brévent
8  Refuge Chalet Moëde d'Anterne
9  Col d'Anterne
10 Petit Col d'Anterne
11 Refuge des Fonds
12 Grenairon Chalet Hotel du Buet
13 Plan du Buet
14 Mont Buet
15 Pierre à Bérard

the old hut was destroyed by avalanche. The new hut is very attractive, and is set in a much safer position.

In the evening calm returns and this is a great spot from which to watch the dying rays of the sun on the mountains. The dominant feature is the 4122m (13,524ft) Aiguille Verte, with the 3754m (12,316ft) Les Drus in the foreground. Keep your eyes open in the evening and you may see ibex roaming the nearby slopes at dusk.

In the early morning the path towards the La Flégère cable car at 1877m (6158ft) will be quiet and you can enjoy clear reflections in the mountain lakes, sharing the trail only with chamois, ibex and marmots whose piercing whistle will warn of your approach. From La Flégère quickly escape the horrors of lifts and bulldozed ski runs by the pleasant traverse which leads around the mountainside to the 2000m (6562ft) Plan Praz. This path undulates slightly, but is relatively flat and allows a full appreciation of the panorama ahead. The slopes are carpeted in Alpenrose shrubs, which bloom in July with pink flowers, while later in the season your progress will be hindered by the masses of billberries bordering the trail – partake to your heart's content!

Plan Praz is part of the Brévent ski area, and is also a major take-off zone for paragliders. Take the time to watch them as you enjoy refreshments here. This is the last real civilization you'll see for a while.

A well-marked path leads to the Col du Brévent at 2368m (7769ft) and this is the gateway to the wild, dark depths of the Diosaz Gorge, seen far below. Bid farewell to the cheery chaos of Chamonix and head off down the pleasant trail towards the Pont d'Arlevé. Ahead are the impressive limestone walls of the Rochers des Fiz; south and west is the Arve valley, stretching away hazily towards the Geneva plains; to the southeast are the ever-present snowy peaks of the Mont Blanc massif; and to the north is the large, rounded summit of Mont Buet. Your destination is visible on the other side of the valley, where the summer grazing (alpage) buildings of the Chalets de Moëde, can be seen, and the Refuge Chalet Moëde d'Anterne at 2002m (6568ft) is not far beyond (on some maps this hut is called the Refuge du Col d'Anterne). This is a superb spot for the night, with its privileged position opposite the massif. An extra day spent here allows time to explore the nearby summit of the Pointe Noire de Pormenaz and a swim in the Pormenaz lake for the brave.

## STABLE WEATHER

The next section of the trek requires good stable weather and equally stable legs. If there is any question about either then it is advisable to take the variant from here to ascend Mont Buet by its normal route (described below). From the hut take the obvious trail up to the Col d'Anterne at 2257m (7405ft). Now the views of Mont Blanc will be left behind as you venture into the remote Anterne plateau, formed by the huge rocky ramparts of the Rochers des Fiz. The blue waters of the Lac d'Anterne are deceptively attractive but usually arctic in temperature.

Beyond lies the Refuge Alfred Wills, named after a prolific British alpinist – a good spot for a coffee stop, but don't linger too long before heading off over the Petit Col d'Anterne 2038m (6686ft). The scenery changes quite dramatically as you leave the idyllic, pastoral meadows of the plateau and head down through steep forested slopes to the Refuge des Fonds 1388m (4554ft). Another refreshment stop presents itself before you start down the valley. Don't dwell too much on the map here, since you'll be frustrated at having to descend to go back up to the Grenairon

**ABOVE** *Marmots will be heard and hopefully seen throughout this trek. Their high-pitched alarm shriek will betray their presence even when you can't see them.*

Chalet Hotel du Buet. The way up to the refuge is steep and you don't emerge from the trees until just before the refuge at 1974m (6476ft). This is quite a climb at the end of the day, so it's important to pace this day carefully and not spend too much time sunbathing on the plateau!

## THE BIG DAY

The next day is the big one so start at dawn. Take the waymarked path, which leads up from the hut over polished limestone and onto the Frêtes du Grenier ridge. The way is intricate as it winds around rocky bastions, but in snow-free conditions with good visibility there is no technical difficulty here. Ahead is Mont Buet and the north ridge looks increasingly steep and improbable the nearer you get to it – look at the views instead! After the rocky Cathédrale, leave the ridge to traverse to the lake at the 2543m (8343ft) Plan du Buet. A rest is advisable here before tackling the shaly switchbacks that give access to the unnamed col 2808m (9213ft) between the Pointe du Genevrier and Mont Buet. Once here the views open up again, stretching away beyond Mont Buet to the Mont Blanc massif, while below lies the Vieux Emosson lake, home to dinosaur tracks from the Triassic era. This area feels quite remote. Wildlife abounds and if you're lucky you'll catch a glimpse of chamois or ibex on nearby slopes.

For the next part of the hike trekking poles should be strapped to your packs, cameras attached firmly and both hands kept free. The ridge is well-equipped with cables but is nevertheless quite impressive

**ABOVE** *The equipped north ridge of Mont Buet provides an exposed and memorable ascent. However, it is not difficult.*

and a certain amount of concentration is required. Once this section is overcome the final rounded summit ridge is a stroll, which enables you to arrive on the summit looking fresh and relaxed!

Unless the weather is bad it's unlikely you'll be alone here. Mont Buet is very popular, but everyone will have faced a walk at least as long as yours and a considerable number of folk do not reach the summit on their first try. This is a peak to be proud of, and it certainly rewards you for your effort. Views are 360° and you will

not know which way to face for lunch: Mont Blanc in all its splendour; the Aravis range capped by its highest peak the Pointe Percée, to the Rochers des Fiz and Anterne – savour it; you have earned this view.

However, reaching the top is only half of the game and the descent by the normal route is not to be underestimated – by the time you reach the oasis of the Refuge de la Pierre à Bérard at 1924m (6312ft), you will be impressed by all those people who come up by this route. A beer, or several, are called for at the hut before staggering down the beautiful Bérard valley. If you feel that exhaustion will prevent full appreciation of this part of the route, spend a last night at the hut and then take a leisurely amble out the next day, lingering by the river and reflecting on the last few days.

Just before emerging from the valley don't miss the view of the big waterfall from the small Café de la Cascade, which is known for its marvellous *tarte aux myrtilles*. For the best view of the waterfall follow the path behind the café and through the rocks to a superb viewpoint opposite and below the waterfall. While you're there take a look at Farinet's cave. Farinet lived in the 19th century, and was famous for making counterfeit money and giving it to the poor. Needless to say, the locals were happy to cover for him while he was hiding out in caves fabricating money.

The last section down to Le Buet takes you past some of the oldest dwellings in the Vallorcine valley, which are now being renovated as summer residences, and you arrive at the main road just next to the well-placed bar of the Hôtel du Buet.

# CHAMONIX–ZERMATT HAUTE ROUTE

## By Hilary Sharp

Walking from Chamonix to Zermatt through the high mountains is one of the most beautiful glacier walks in the Alps. This Haute Route was first done in 1861, by members of The Alpine Club (of Great Britain) with local guides. They called it the High Level Road. It was a different experience without the well-equipped huts and good, lightweight equipment we have today. This was a time of great exploration in the Alps, nearly 80 years after the first ascent of Mont Blanc in 1786, but still four years before the Matterhorn was summitted by Edward Whymper and his friends. Nowadays the Haute Route is often done on skis in the spring, but it is still popular as a walk in the summer, and justifiably so.

Chamonix is a major French alpine town situated in the shadow of Mont Blanc, the highest peak in western Europe at about 4807m (15,771ft). Mont Blanc has been re-measured several times recently, adding or losing a metre each time. Zermatt is the Swiss version, its mountain backdrop being the much-photographed 4477m (14,688ft) Matterhorn, unique for its soaring profile.

### HIGH PENNINE ALPS PEAKS

The Haute Route passes close to many of the high Pennine Alps peaks, with the opportunity to ascend some en route. The route follows glaciers throughout its length. However, over the years the recession of the glaciers has altered some

sections; and nowadays there is a danger of ice and rockfall, especially late in the season, so care should be taken in choice of route. Early starts are always recommended for glacier travel.

There are several variations to the route, but here I describe what seems to be the most popular way, both in terms of route and direction. There's no reason why you shouldn't go from Zermatt to Chamonix, but tradition and force of habit mean that this is done less often.

TOP *En route, via the Col Supérieur du Tour, to the Aiguille du Tour, which is an optional extra near the start of the Chamonix–Zermatt trek.*

Although known as Chamonix to Zermatt, the trek really starts at the head of the Chamonix valley at the village of Le Tour at 1450m (4756ft). Having taken the lifts to 2180m (7152ft), near the Col de Balme, the path to the Albert Premier Refuge 2702m (8865ft) takes a rising traverse around the hillside, and onto the glacial moraine leading to the hut. Perched just above the Glacier du Tour, this hut enjoys spectacular glacier and summit views, but it is one of the most popular in the Alps so expect it to be busy. If you plan to ascend the 3544m (11,627ft) Aiguille du Tour, a good beginner's peak, then it would be wise to stay the night at the hut, but if not, then I recommend you press on, unless you've made a late start.

ABOVE *On the crevassed glacier above Champex. The Haute Route follows glaciers throughout its length, making this one of the most beautiful glacier walks in the Alps.*

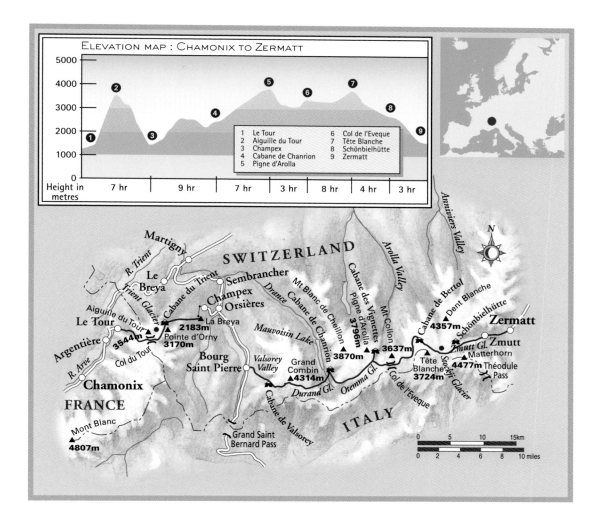

ELEVATION MAP : CHAMONIX TO ZERMATT

| | | |
|---|---|---|
| 1 | Le Tour | 6 Col de l'Eveque |
| 2 | Aiguille du Tour | 7 Tête Blanche |
| 3 | Champex | 8 Schönbielhütte |
| 4 | Cabane de Chanrion | 9 Zermatt |
| 5 | Pigne d'Arolla | |

## GLACIER TRAVEL

Just beyond the hut you'll set foot on a glacier for the first time on this trek. Your objective, the Col Supérieur du Tour at 3289m (10,791ft), is at the head of the glacier. This gives access to the Trient glacier, which forms a huge plateau where it would be easy to get lost in bad weather. The Cabane du Trient is at 3170m (10,400ft), under the Pointe d'Orny. From the Cabane du Trient you can enjoy superlative views of the east face of the Aiguille du Tour, and the Aiguilles Dorées.

During the next day's descent down the left bank of the Orny glacier, you can admire the spectacular profile of the rock spire of the Petits Clochers du Portalet, before continuing down the pleasant, well-worn path which eventually leads to the chairlift of La Breya. This

ABOVE *Ibex can be seen on the hillside near the glaciers. This one is posing against a backdrop of the Grand Combin.*

TOP *Arriving at the Valsorey Hut after a long climb from Bourg St Pierre. Like most huts on this trek, the Valsorey refuge occupies a wonderful position with good views.*

## AVOID IN BAD WEATHER

The next stage is serious and should not be attempted in bad weather. (Ask at the hut – and if conditions aren't right, retreat carefully from the Valsorey and take transport round to Mauvoisin lake.) Climb up northeast behind the hut and make a traverse rightwards to the Plateau du Couloir at 3664m (12,021ft). This can vary dramatically from easy snow early in the season to ice and scree later, at which time it can also be prone to rock fall. From the plateau, which is immediately under the Grand Combin, you head down onto the Glacier du Sonadon, quite flat at this point. The Col du Sonadon at 3504m (11,496ft) is directly ahead to the east, and is crossed easily to reach the Durand Glacier.

The climbing is over for a while, and you must descend the glacier, first on the left, then the right, to the valley above the Mauvoisin lake, coming out at the bridge at 2182m (7159ft). The glacier walking is all done for the day and you can relax and enjoy the views of the Grand Combin, La Ruinette and, down the valley, the Mauvoisin lake formed by what is allegedly the biggest dam of its kind in the world. The Cabane de Chanrion is just 280m (919ft) above.

## THE WEATHER DECIDES THE ROUTE

Two choices present themselves for the next day, and the decision depends largely on the weather. The first possibility, taking the Otemma glacier, involves no technical difficulties and stays relatively low, making

delivers you to the outskirts of Champex at 1466m (4810ft), a fine place to enjoy a break, before taking the bus or taxi to the village of Bourg Saint Pierre at 1632m (5353ft). The village offers a variety of accommodation, as well being interesting historically, since it is on the route to the Grand Saint Bernard Pass, a much-used route since Roman times and before. A good path leads out of town, starting relatively gently up the Valsorey valley, then steepening up, as it approaches the Valsorey hut, perched at 3030m (9941ft) under the southwestern slopes of the huge bulk of the Grand Combin 4314m (14,145ft).

it a good choice in less than perfect weather. The second, up the Brenay glacier, involves a section of steeper ground to pass a serac barrier and also allows for the ascent of the 3796m (12,454ft) Pigne d'Arolla. This is a fine peak to include on the way if you can, with no technical difficulties. The views are splendid, with Mont Blanc de Cheillon to the west and Mont Collon to the east. High peaks can be seen further away in all directions, and this is certainly one of the highlights of the trek.

Whichever route you choose, you end up at the Cabane des Vignettes 3160m (10,367ft), situated on a rocky promontory. A night spent at the Vignettes hut will be unforgettable, perched high above the Arolla valley, with the rocky summits of the Aiguille de la Tsa, the Dents de Bertol and the Bouquetins right opposite. People seem to find the situation of the toilet here quite memorable!

From the hut you need to reverse the Otemma route as far as the Col de Chermotane 3053m (10,016ft), and then continue up the Glacier du Mont Collon to the Col de l'Eveque at 3392m (11,130ft). Having passed the western side of Mont Collon you now pass under the eastern face, down the Haut Glacier d'Arolla until it is possible to leave it to pick up the path to the Plans de Bertol. Time for a rest here, before tackling the steep, but well-marked trail, and then the snow of the Bertol glacier to the Col de Bertol at 3279m (10,758ft). The hut is just above and to the north of the pass, high on the rocks, accessed by chains and ladders and surrounded by a sea of glaciers.

**ABOVE** *Martagon lilies are the one of the special alpine flowers to look out for in the early summer.*

## NEARING ZERMATT

For the next section you'll need the camera at the ready as you get to see the Matterhorn in all its magnificence. You also pass from French to German-speaking Switzerland. In good weather the traverse of the flat upper section of the Glacier du Mont Miné will cause no problems. It is taken in a generally southeast direction to gain the viewpoint of Tête Blanche at 3724m (12,218ft). The Matterhorn, the Dent d'Hérens and the Dent Blanche are suddenly really close, while further away are all the Zermatt peaks.

Finally, you must force yourself to continue down onto the Stockjigletcher, which is heavily crevassed, so you'll need to tear your gaze away from the visual delights of the peaks and watch out for holes and crevasses. From the rocky lump of the Stockji, a steep zigzag path descends to gain moraines leading to the Schönbiel glacier, which must be crossed to pick up the hut approach path, snaking up improbably through steep ground to reach the hut.

## VIEW OF THE MATTERHORN

Staying at the Schönbielhütte at 2694m (8839ft) is an experience you don't want to miss. A fit party could certainly continue on to Zermatt, and, if it's nightlife and shops you're yearning for, then go for it. However, this hut occupies such a marvellous position, with the north face of the Matterhorn right opposite the front door, that it's hard to imagine how anyone could want to miss it. The Matterhorn (Monte Cervino in Italian meaning the stag mountain) is such a unique summit that it's totally absorbing to study the different faces and ridges. Its neighbour, the Dent d'Hérens 4171m (13,684ft) is equally spectacular, and so this last night in the mountains will definitely be one to remember.

The next day there'll be plenty of time for a leisurely stroll down to the real world. A good trail goes above the left bank of the Zmutt glacier, eventually passing through the charming hamlet of Zmutt. It's worth stopping for refreshments here, and exploring the traditional houses. Zmutt is one of the oldest habitations of the area, and its importance dates back to Roman times, when it was the last staging post before the long climb up to the Théodule Pass, which was the route used to travel over to Italy.

Stroll down into Zermatt 1600m (5248ft) past ancient chalets and meadows bursting with brightly coloured gentians, orchids, geraniums, hawksbeards and rampions – a welcome contrast after days of snow and ice. Then celebrate!

# PROVENCE: GR4 VIA VERDON GORGE

*By Hilary Sharp*

The Côte d'Azur may not immediately spring to mind as a walking destination, but just inland from the glitzy palaces and casinos lies some of the most beautiful countryside in France. Rolling hillsides, interspersed with deep valleys and limestone cliffs, are home to charming villages. Fields of lavender and poppies stretch as far as the eye can see. The region's gastronomy, based on local products, is world-renowned.

Provence is at its most beautiful in the spring – warm, but not too hot, the hillsides painted in the pastel hues of aromatic flowers, the air redolent with the scent of thyme, so much a part of this region.

There is something magical about starting a hike from the coast and heading into the mountains. This trek follows part of the route known as the Grande Randonnée 4, which traverses France from Bordeaux to Monaco. This nine-day section passes through varied scenery, ranging from towering limestone cliffs to vast vistas of lavender fields to mountain passes to charming Provençal villages.

## GATEWAY TO THE MARITIME ALPS

Beginning in Grasse, the gateway to the Maritime Alps and known world-wide for its perfume industry, the route makes its way quickly into the mountains and remains at 600m (1969ft) and above throughout. The section through the Verdon Gorge provides a spectacular climax to the trek. This 800m (2625ft)-deep ravine is a much sought-after destination for rock climbers who cling to its sheer walls. It is also hugely popular with canoeists who descend its azure river, bouncing along over rapids and through deep tunnels. For walkers the hike along the base of the gorge provides an unforgettable experience, under the towering orange cliffs with the gushing river nearby. The trek continues for another day to the fascinating tourist village of Moustiers Sainte Marie, situated near to the large Sainte Croix Lake

ABOVE *The Ste Croix Lake seen from the plateau above. Any highpoint on this hike offers views such as this.*

and this is a pleasant place to end the trek and perhaps spend a few days resting or visiting surrounding areas by car.

The trek begins on the outskirts of Grasse 333m (1093ft). The world capital of the perfume industry, the town is surrounded by fields of flowers. The old town is a labyrinth of little streets and has hardly changed since the 18th century. This is a popular centre for walkers and many trails lead out of town into the foothills behind. The GR4 is well marked and heads in a long steady climb up to the Plateau de la Malle, over the Col du Clapier at 1260m (4134ft). It is important to take time on this early part of the trail rather than rushing along head down as the views stretch all the way to the Mediterranean coast, and the towns of Cannes and Antibes can be clearly seen. Their many hotels gleaming in the sun are in sharp contrast to the wild terrain on the trail.

## OLFACTORY FEAST

As you brush by the aromatic plants along the trail they release their perfumes and you will begin to understand the attraction of hiking in the Mediterranean regions: a visual and olfactory feast. The trail leads to the barren limestone Plateau de Caussols, which you cross to descend to the village of Cipières at 780m (2559ft). Gréolières, at 820m (2690ft), is reached by crossing the river Loup and then climbing up an ancient footpath, much worn by the timeless passage of feet. This typical picturesque village is situated at the foot of the Cime de Cheiron. Take the time to explore the winding streets and the old church, drinking in the atmosphere of Provence.

A steep climb leads out of town past the summit of Coutellade, a 1400m (4593ft) peak. The trail continues, wending its way through oak and beech woods, past high waterfalls and tiny, hidden hamlets to a well-marked detour to Aiglun, a charming village perched high on the hillside at 642m (2106ft) and surrounded by impressive, sheer, red and orange limestone cliffs. The local *gîte* is renowned for its food.

There are two types of *gîte* in France. It can be self-catering accommodation or, as in this case, a *gîte d'étape*: an inn offering dormitory accommodation, breakfast and dinner. Sometimes you need a sheet sleeping bag, since there are often just blankets for the beds.

Aiglun has a very deep ravine nearby, known as a *clue* in Provençal, and this has become one of the major sites for canyoning in the region. This *clue* is on the route as you leave Aiglun heading northwest to rejoin the GR4 trail.

Passing through pastures bordered by forests and ravines, the Esteron river is

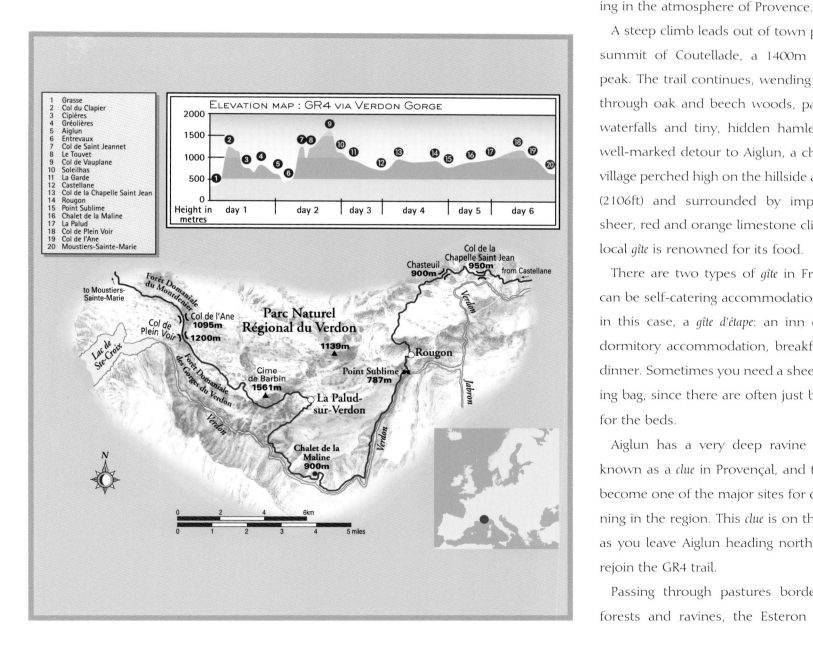

**ABOVE** *The water of the Verdon river has carved a huge gorge leaving towering limestone cliffs: a rock climber's dream and beautiful vistas for the hiker.*

crossed to reach the Castellet valley, which marks the regional border and you leave the Maritime Alps for the Haute Provence Alps. A final climb through woodland, and you emerge to beautiful views of Entrevaux, just below. This small town, situated at 480m (1575ft) on the River Var was, until 1860, strategically important as the frontier town between French Provence and the states of the King of Sardinia. It was fortified in the late 17th century and has a fine citadel perched high on a rocky outcrop. The interior of the town is the old part with tiny winding streets and ancient houses tightly squeezed one against the other. The cobbled streets and close-packed houses

give a real feeling of having stepped back in time and a day could be spent very happily here exploring the nooks and crannies and then relaxing by the riverside.

## FOSSILS AMONG THE ROCKS

It will certainly be with regret that you leave Entrevaux, heading west to climb through oak woods and beech groves up to the Col de Saint Jeannet at 1278m (4193ft), past the chapel of Jean du Désert, destination of an annual pilgrimage by an order of monks.

A descent through meadows takes you to the hamlets of Ubraye at 1000m (3281ft) and Le Touvet at 1250m (4101ft) before

tackling a long but gentle climb up a wild valley, with increasingly fine views across verdant plateaus until you arrive at the Col de Vauplane at 1650m (5413ft). Alpine flowers abound here in the spring and this is a beautiful highpoint, with fine views stretching away into the distant misty plains. Snow may remain early in the spring and in fact this is a small ski resort in winter. Coming down from this col the road is soon reached and a short detour to the left (southeast) leads to the tiny village of Soleilhas where there is accommodation for walkers.

From the turn-off for Soleilhas, the GR4 continues another few kilometres to the hamlet of La Garde at 927m (3041ft), passing the incredible Teillon cliffs on the way. This limestone buttress clearly shows the different layers in the limestone, twisted during the formation of the mountains to their vertical position. These strata were formerly layers of silt on the ocean floor and fossils abound among these rocks. A short, flat path along the valley takes you to Castellane 724m (2375ft), an interesting old town situated on the Verdon River, and known as the Gateway to the Gorges. This is a good place to linger after all that time in the wilds. There's plenty to explore here, from souvenir shops to a perfume farm to the famous chapel of Notre Dame du Roc, perched high above town. If you have the time, then follow the ancient worn trail up to this chapel, passing numerous oratories and Stations of the Cross. This ascent is undertaken as a pilgrimage annually. There is a short, circular walk marked in yellow paint up to and around the rock, which gives wonderful views of the red-tiled roofs of Castellane and the Verdon River that runs through the town.

The next part of the trek basically follows the Verdon River as it makes its way along the valley. The route stays well above the valley floor, taking a high line around the mountainside, giving tantalizing views of the turbulent, jade waters below. The trail joins an old Roman way which takes you over the Col de la Chapelle Saint Jean 950m (3117ft) to the charming village of Chasteuil 900m (2953ft) where there is a *gîte*. The Roman way continues up to another high plateau – far below are the huge cliffs marking the beginning of the Verdon Gorge. A good track leads down through Rougon, yet another fabulous village in a beautiful position, this time with wonderful views of the rocky depths of the Verdon Gorge. Below is Point Sublime 787m (2582ft), departure point for forays into the gorge and scene of one of the many big car parks for visitors. There is a good hotel here, known for its marvellous food – needless to say if you do not book in advance you may not get a room. The incredible Verdon Gorge now beckons and the huge, grey cliffs that form the entrance are dark and forbidding. The through route under the towering cliffs, named the Sentier Martel after the geologist who first explored the gorge, is a highlight of the trek but it can only be undertaken in good weather conditions. The walk takes about seven hours from one end to the other and there are no exit points en route. While the walking is basically straightforward, it can be very hot in the gorge and,

although you're following the valley, the path is undulating and surprisingly tiring. If in doubt you should either take the bus or a taxi to La Palud-sur-Verdon or take a series of paths that are shown on the map in a generally southwesterly direction to reach La Palud.

## TUNNELS

For the main route the trail first ventures into the gorge by means of two tunnels, constructed many years ago when a dam was planned. The first tunnel requires a torch since there are a couple of sections where it is pitch dark despite the windows hewn in the rock walls. After rain, puddles form that are difficult to avoid so prepare for wet feet. These tunnels are popular with visitors as a novel walk and a chance to see the gorge from the base.

Afterwards do not be tempted by any other tunnels; the path is clearly indicated. There are seven tunnels in total but the others are dangerous and not maintained. The route undulates, sometimes almost going down to river level, with several tempting beaches that you can visit, and then back to the higher slopes. There are many attractive places where you can sit and take in the ambience, but keep an eye on the time as the final part of the walk is an ascent and requires energy and daylight.

Where the river turns from heading south to west the path has to go over a rocky rampart and for this there is a short section of easy but quite vertiginous ladder to pass through the Brèche Imbert. In this direction you will ascend ladders, but on any sunny day in the holiday season there

will certainly be the potential for a bottleneck here. In fact there is an accepted one-way system but do not expect the French to take any notice of that!!

The finale for the day features a climb of 200m (656ft) up a treeless slope to the Chalet de la Maline 900m (2953ft)

From La Maline the GR4 route takes the road into the village of La Palud-sur-Verdon at 950m (3117ft). It may seem dull after all that spectacular wild walking, so it might be worth getting a taxi or a lift for this part. There are lots of cars on the road, so this probably will not pose a problem. Once in La Palud there are many distractions in the form of bars, bakeries, postcard shops and a few *gîtes*.

The GR4 continues ever onward, heading out of town by an increasingly impressive route along the hillside to the east of the Verdon River. The trail traverses around the Cime de Barbin and uses good forest tracks for most of the way. After some hours of walking views open up spectacularly and the huge Sainte Croix lake is seen far below. At this point you are walking right on top of very high cliffs and the Col de Plein Voir 1200m (3937ft) is certainly aptly named. Keep your eyes on the waymarks here as the trail can be indistinct as it wends down through bushes and among polished limestone to the Col de l'Ane 1095m (3593ft). The path makes its way through improbably steep hillside to descend to the Gorges road a couple of kilometres before Moustiers Sainte Marie. Walk into town, check out the ceramics (not to everyone's taste) and then visit the *pâtisseries* – definitely to everyone's taste!

# CORSICA: GR20

*By Hilary Sharp*

Corsica, *île de beauté* in French, known to the Greeks as *kalliste* – the most beautiful – lies just 160km (100 miles) south of the French coast and 80km (50 miles) west of the Italian coast. A French region or *département*, (*La Corse* in French), it is really a rocky massif in the sea. Although its highest peaks only reach 2700m (8858ft) they hold snow for much of the year and, despite the Mediterranean location and the beautiful sandy beaches, the mountains are renowned for sudden and violent changes of weather.

Regularly invaded throughout history, from the Greco Romans to the French intervention in the 18th century, Corsica now enjoys a more peaceful existence, although a small group of nationalists con-

tinue to demand autonomy from France. Napoleon was born there in 1769, the year that the French finally defeated Pascal Paoli and his independence fighters.

## STEP BACK IN TIME

Walking Corsica's mountains, you'll feel you've stepped back in time. Nowadays most people live on the coast. There are fewer than 10 people per square kilometre (fewer than 26 people per square mile) living in the mountains where life is hard and the farmers scrape a living from the land with sheep, goats and cows. The once infamous Corsican bandits and their vendettas are history, albeit quite recent, and there is a trend of emigration from the hill villages to the big towns or even to the mainland.

At around 180km (112 miles) in length and involving some 9700m (31,824ft) of ascent, the Corsican high-level long-distance walk is regarded as one of the toughest of the European Grande Randonnées (big walks). It's also considered one of the finest of its kind. Officially named the Grande Randonnée 20, this route begins in the northwest and makes its way along the mountainous spine of the island, staying high most of the time, to finally emerge near the attractive beaches on the southeast coast. The Parc Naturel Régional de la

**ABOVE** *Gaining altitude on day one, leaving behind the coastline of Calvi, while the mountains beckon.*

Corse was created in 1972 and protects the entire mountain chain. All the refuges found along this trek are owned by the PNR. Although this route is liberally supplied with huts, which are wardened to make sure you pay your dues, there is no reliable supply of food. Increasingly you will find basic foodstuff for sale in the huts and even cooked meals, but this service depends on the warden and cannot be relied on. Gas stoves and pots are provided, but at the height of the season you may have to queue to use these. Hut places are allocated on a first-come first-served basis, and you can arrive to find the hut is full. Carry some camping equipment, at least a bivvy bag and stove, if not a tent. Sleeping bags are necessary even in the huts, although the hut sleeping platforms do have mattresses.

The trek begins in the small village of Calenzana just north of Calvi, allegedly the birthplace of Christopher Columbus. Before setting off, visit the impressive Citadel at Calvi where, in 1794, the British Admiral Nelson lost an eye from 'an explosion of stones' while manning shore-based artillery during the British siege of the fort.

From the relatively low altitude of 275m (902ft) in Calenzana, the first day's walk takes you to the dizzying heights of 1570m (5150ft). You'll soon escape the oppressive summer heat, though, as you climb into the hills, and the views back to the north coast provide excuses to rest, while ahead are the tempting rocky peaks, rugged and mysterious. When you've finally toiled your way over two cols you'll arrive at the Crête de Fuca and the terrain eases up. Already you're in the mountains, far from the beaches, and a pleasant stroll leads around to the Ortu di u Piobbu refuge.

## A GENTLER DAY

The next day is gentler, although the walking is spectacular and varied: at times rocky, at times among juniper and scented alder bushes. The views are dominated by the summit of Monte Cintu, at 2706m (8878ft) Corsica's highest summit. The high rocky cols of Avartoli at 1898m (6227ft) and l'Inominata at 1912m (6273ft) lead to a steep descent and the Refuge de Carozzu (also known as the Refuge de Spasimatu) at 1260m (4133ft). It is surrounded by soaring cliffs, many of them equipped for rock climbing. This hut usually offers basic provisions, including the dark Corsican beer made from chestnuts, and rough red wine.

From the Carozzu hut a new, if rather wobbly, suspension bridge takes you to some innocuous-looking granite slabs. Climbing up these in dry conditions it is difficult to imagine the nightmare that can result when it rains and friction slabs become potential death traps. Above, the trail winds on endlessly through rocks and

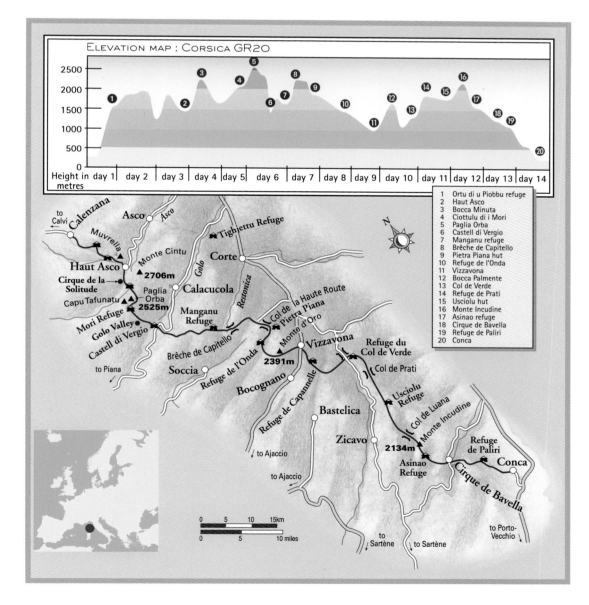

shrubs, past the Lac de la Muvrella at 1860m (6101ft) before surmounting the crest under the Muvrella summit. There you will be rewarded with a wonderful panorama, with Monte Cintu in the foreground, much closer now.

The descent is steep and a little tortuous, taking you to the tiny hamlet of Haut Asco at 1422m (4664ft). There are at least two refuges and a hotel. An extra day here would allow an ascent of Cintu, which has a marked and cairned path to its summit.

At Haut Asco you are poised to tackle the crux of this route, the Cirque de la Solitude. This imposing granite coomb is formed by rocky spires, and was first crossed by the bold Austrian adventurer Felix von Cube at the beginning of the 20th century. It took him several attempts to find the key to this section, whereas nowadays chains and cables make the passage relatively straightforward, if somewhat impressive. However, this is not a place to be caught in a storm or in snow (although this seems unlikely, in July 2000 several walkers were trapped in the cirque by snowfall and had to be rescued!).

Beyond the Bocca Minuta 2218m (7277ft) on the other side of the cirque is the Tighjettu refuge 1640m (5381ft), an alternative base for an ascent of Monte Cintu. Just below the hut is one of the delights of walking Corsica's high mountains – a *bergerie* (shepherd's dwelling) where local food can be bought. Regional specialities tend to involve goat or sheep – the cheese sandwiches are fabulous as are omelettes filled with brocciu cheese. These shepherds live by the age-old practice of transhumance –

**ABOVE** *Climbing the equipped via ferrata to get through the Cirque de la Solitude, the crux of the GR20 trek. While chains and cables make it straightforward, it is still impressive.*

they bring the animals up into the high pastures during summer, descending as the year goes on to spend winter down in the valleys. *Bergerie* meals will be among the best memories of the trek.

## TWO INTERESTING SUMMITS

The next refuge, Ciottulu di i Mori at 1991m (6532ft), is reached by a long valley climb. It is nestled under two interesting summits, both of which beg to be climbed if you can spare a day. The Paglia Orba at 2525m (8284ft) is ascended by an intricate gully and ledge system, while the Capu Tafunatu 2335m (7661ft) is climbed via its very characteristic hole – *tafunatu* in Corsican dialect – carved out of the granite by wind and rain. This feature is incredible,

especially after a storm when residual cloud billows through it. The hole itself can be reached by walkers following cairns so long as you have a good head for heights – a fall could be fatal.

The lovely pastoral Golo valley, with its rock pools where hikers can swim, leads to forests of distinctive Corsican long-needled pines to the hotel at Castell di Vergio 1404m (4605ft). The trail continues through the forest and along a delightful ridge walk to the Lac de Nino at 1743m (5717ft). Wild horses graze beside the still waters of the lake, which harbours bushes of fragile aquatic plants.

The Manganu refuge at 1601m (5253ft) is just beyond the Bergerie de Vaccaghia and attracts a lot of visitors, partly due to its relative ease of access from nearby roads, and because it's ideally situated for one of the gems of the Corsican mountains – the Restonica valley. This valley comes up from Corte and our route traverses the head of the valley via the stunning Brèche de Capitello, at 2225m (7300ft) the highest point on the trek. Arrive here early and you'll ascend in the shade, emerging into golden sunlight through the narrow rocky col. There follows a section of ridge walking that will delight any walker, however well-travelled. Views are immense, down to the Lac de Melo and the Lac de Capitello in the east, their inky depths glistening temptingly below, and the distant villages of Soccia and Orto in the west, misty in the morning light. The intricate trail finally leads to the Col de la Haute Route at 2206m (7238ft) where a whole new vista opens up, looking across southeast to Monte d'Oro.

This is pig territory, home to those famous semi-wild occupants of much of the Corsican interior. You'll hear loud snorting and grunting noises coming from the bushes. Rarely, you'll be mugged for your lunch, but it's far more common to have your valuable rations rifled from an unguarded tent or sac, consequently the huts in areas frequented by pigs have an enclosed camping ground.

From the Pietra Piana hut at 1842m (6042ft) there are two choices – either a valley walk past the Bergerie de Tolla, which is the way to go if you're hungry, or a shorter version along the ridge heading south. The Refuge de l'Onda at 1430m (4692ft) is the last stopping place before the valley of Vizzavona where civilization will be rediscovered. There are a couple of traditional, basic hotels, a restaurant and a railway providing an escape route to the coast for those who've had enough. Vizzavona at 990m (3247ft) marks the dividing point between the north and south sections of the trek (although distance and effort-wise it's a little over halfway). The southern part of the GR20 is markedly more gentle in scenery, with rolling grassy hills and wonderful views of the coast.

A steep forest path leads out of town, over the Bocca Palmente at 1640m (5381ft) and past the rather old Refuge de Capanelle at 1586m (5202ft). A continuing traverse through beech trees brings you out at the Col Verde at 1289m (4228ft), where there is also a refuge.

The next climb is most rewarding. After a long toil the Col de Prati is reached at 1840m (6037ft) and nearby is the Prati

**ABOVE** *Above of the clouds during the southern part of the trek. Cloud billows up from the valleys while the high mountain chain basks in sunshine.*

Refuge. The views are breathtaking – this is the first time you'll see the southeast coast, and you'll begin to realize just how far you've come. In clear weather you can see as far as the islands of Elba and Monte Cristo. A fantastic ridge provides a scenic walk to the Usciolu hut at 1750m (5740ft), which has panoramic views of the coastline. Later the scenery changes to beech woods, then a plateau where streams wind their way through lush green grass dotted with deep blue monkshood. The way ahead is obvious – a direct ascent to the only true summit actually on the GR20 route, the 2134m (7000ft) Monte Incudine.

A quick descent leads to the Asinao refuge 1536m (5038ft), from where it's only a short way to one of the most famous beauty spots on the island, the Cirque de Bavella. Arriving here early one morning,

we found a magical scene of granite spires swirled in bands of mist coming up from the valley. The path weaves in and out of the weird and wonderful sculpted rock formations, many of them honeycombed with *tafanatu*. The Col de Bavella at 1218m (3995ft) has accommodation and bus services, but it's worth staying at the next hut, the Refuge de Paliri at 1060m (3477ft), if only for the views of the Italian coastline, Monte Cristo and the neighbouring island of Sardinia. The last day is as good as all the others, with many impressive granite spires, orange in the morning rays. After reaching the narrow gap of the Bocca Uscioulu at 587m (1925ft) it's downhill all the way, the southeast coastline beckoning until you suddenly burst out of the footpath onto the road next to the fountain of Conca at 252m (827ft).

# Pyrenean Haute Route/Ordesa Canyon

*By Hilary Sharp*

The Pyrenees can be described as the mountain range that runs between the Atlantic and the Mediterranean, and forms the frontier between France and Spain. The peaks here are smaller than in the Alps, but no less impressive and there is a marked contrast between the Spanish and French sides of the massifs. The Pyrenees contain three National Parks, two of which feature here, the French Parc National des Pyrénées and the Spanish Parque Nacional de Ordesa y Monte Perdido.

Legend has it that, in ancient times, Hercules could not resist seducing Pyrène, the beautiful daughter of the King of Cerdagne, before leaving to accomplish a mission. In despair at her lover's departure, the princess took off in pursuit, only to be slaughtered by wild animals. On his return, devastated by grief, Hercules built a tomb around his beloved, piling up huge rocks which became the Pyrenees.

The Pyrenees were first really explored by the French geologist and botanist, Louis-François Ramond de Carbonnières, who began his exploration of this wild country in 1787. He climbed many peaks and passes and in 1802 was a driving force behind the first ascent (by two French guides, Laurens and Rondau, and a Spanish shepherd) of Monte Perdido, at 3355m (11,007ft) the third highest peak in the range. One of the indigenous flowers of the Pyrenees is named Ramondie des Pyrénées, in his honour.

Several long-distance treks cross the Pyrenees, notably the Haute Route Pyrénéenne (HRP), which takes a general line, with many variations, from the Atlantic to the Mediterranean; the French Grande Randonnée (GR) 10, which does the same but at a lower level; and the Spanish Gran Recorrido (GR) 11, which takes in some spectacular scenery on the south side of the massif, including the impressive Ordesa Canyon. The trek described here is a part of the HRP and GR11, sometimes coinciding with the

ABOVE *The Brèche de Roland is bathed in the golden light of sunrise in a dawn start from the Refuge des Sarradets.*

GR10, together forming a trek that is varied and interesting, discovering some of the most beautiful parts of this region.

## START AT THE LAKE

The trek starts at the Lac de Bious d'Artigues (1415m; 4641ft), a blue lake dominated by the Pic du Midi d'Ossau 2884m (9460ft), easily recognized by its double summit. The trail leads under the south face of the mountain and circles east around it, passing through meadows that are blue with wild irises in summer. Higher up, yellow spotted gentians replace the irises, up to the rocky boulder field above the Lac de Peygeret. The arduousness of

the final section of the climb is mitigated by the fine views and, on arrival at the Col de Peygeret at 2300m (7544ft), you're rewarded with the sight of the south face of the Pic du Midi d'Ossau. Ahead are the summits Palas and Balaitous which show the direction of the next day's walk and, just below, next to its glittering lake, is the Refuge de Pombie 2032m (6665ft). Bathing costumes will be put to good use here.

The early morning sun catches the top of the Pic du Midi d'Ossau, turning the face orange as you descend. Meadows are strewn with foxgloves and the blue thistle-like Pyrenean Eryngo. If you're lucky you'll see herds of isards, the Pyrenean chamois, running on the high slopes. Lower down, horses and donkeys graze peacefully, while the shepherds tend sheep.

The Arrious valley provides the main ascent on this day, with a steady climb out of the woods and into open country, littered with boulders, to the Col d'Arrious at 2259m (7410ft). There are two routes to the Arremoulit Refuge at 2305m (7560ft). If it's wet or stormy you must take the path that descends to the Lac d'Artouste at 1989m (6524ft) and then follow a clear and easy path back up to the refuge. In dry conditions, however, it's much more interesting, and less arduous, to take the Passage d'Orteig, which winds its way round the hillside, high above the lake, with a short section of cable hand-line where it would

ABOVE *Orange dawn light on the Pic du Midi d'Ossau, reflected in the lake near the Refuge de Pombie.*

### Elevation map : Pyrenean Haute Route and Ordesa Canyon

Height in metres — 4000, 3000, 2000, 1000, 0

day 1 | day 2 | day 3 | day 4 | day 5 | day 6 | day 7 | day 8 | day 9 | day 10

1 Lac de Bious d'Artigues
2 Pic du Midi d'Ossau
3 Refuge de Pombie
4 Refuge Arremoulit
5 Refugio de Respumoso
6 Grande Fache
7 Refuge Wallon
8 Col des Mulets
9 Vignemale
10 Petit Vignemale
11 Gavarnie
12 Refugio de Goriz
13 Le Taillon
14 Gavarnie

not be a good idea to fall. The excitement is fairly short-lived, though, and you soon reach the safety of relatively flat ground and the hut. It is situated among several azure lakes, which look tempting, but are glacially cold.

The Col d'Arremoulit at 2448m (8029ft) is reached by following cairns marking the path between the boulders. This brings you to the Spanish border and a panorama – the distant summit of Lurien behind and, ahead, the high peak of Balaitous, with its reflection in the lake below.

The path leads around the Arriel lakes and then takes a traverse eastwards, contouring the hillside, high above the Rio Aguas Limpais, to the dammed Respumoso lake. Flowers are abundant – houseleeks, gentians, rhaetian poppies, leopard's bane, thrift, wild chives and, of course, irises and there is an endless vista of distant mountains. Above the lake is the modern Refugio de Respumoso 2100m (6888ft), handy for cold drinks on a hot day, before tackling the hard, hot climb back to France. The path passes a beautiful lake – take a swim and you'll find the next part doesn't feel so difficult.

The return to France at the Col de la Fache at 2664m (8738ft) provides views of Vignemale, at 3298m (10,817ft) the highest of the French Pyrenean peaks. For those with excess energy, a jaunt up the 3005m (9856ft) Grande Fache from the col is highly recommended. Various routes are possible, more or less exposed, to a final easy scramble to the summit.

A long, steep descent will test tired legs. The Refuge Wallon, at 1864m (6114ft), is

**ABOVE** *The north face of Vignemale, an impressive rock wall, is seen to great advantage from the Refuge des Ourlettes de Gaube.*

visible long before you reach it. Then, suddenly, just when you've had enough, the rocks give way to grassy pasture and the hut in a fine open setting, with sun-worshippers by the pools in the river.

From Wallon the route crosses the river and makes its way into the Gave d'Arratille valley. A winding path rises near the river past stunted pine trees to the Lac d'Arratille at 2256m (7400ft), abundantly colonized by white flowers. The climb onwards to the Col d'Arratille at 2528m (8292ft) is arduous and once again you pass into Spain, but this time just for an hour or so, before hurrying back over the Col des Mulets at 2591m (8498ft) to discover Vignemale's north face and its glacier. The first ascent of this mountain was made by Henri Cazaux

and Bernard Guillembet in 1837, but it was the Irish-French Count Henry Russell who, having fallen in love with the summit, made the Vignemale famous: in 1899 he obtained a 99-year lease of the peak for the sum of one French franc a year. He excavated a few small caves in the rock around the summit where he could overnight with his friends. These are now often inhabited by impecunious climbers in summer.

The Refuge des Ourlettes de Gaube at 2151m (7055ft) is a rather basic refuge, redeemed by its fine position under the towering face of Vignemale and the welcome of the hut guardians. An excellently graded zigzagging path leads easily from the hut to the Hourquette d'Ossoue at 2734m (8968ft). However, early morning progress will be slow as your gaze is constantly drawn to the orange glow of the rising sun kissing the summit of Vignemale. From the Hourquette pass the Refuge de Baysellance at 2651m (8695ft) is just a short walk away. However, the summit of the 3032m (9945ft) Petit Vignemale, just to the south, calls for a quick ascent and excellent views of the Ossoue glacier leading to the summit of Vignemale itself.

From the refuge the path descends relentlessly and in the high season there'll be many people toiling upwards. After a couple of exposed sections, you reach the flat, boulder-strewn area before the Ossoue dam. It is a good lunch spot, with the opportunity to bathe sore feet in the icy waters of the river. The dam is at the roadhead, but Gavarnie is several kilometres away. Unless you enjoy road walking it's best to take the path that winds up above the road, through meadows of irises, gentians, houseleeks and orchids. This route is long, but views are very satisfying: looking back, Vignemale and Petit Vignemale dominate the horizon, while ahead is the striking pyramid of the summit of Pimené, situated just above Gavarnie. A final 20 minutes on tarmac leads into town, where the return to civilization is a little rude: the streets usually teem with people, and are littered with horse droppings, this being the preferred transport for reaching the famous and impressive Cirque de Gavarnie. Throughout this area you may spot huge Griffin vultures soaring overhead.

## DISCOVER ORDESA

The trek could finish here, but it would be a shame to miss Spain's Ordesa region, just across the Franco-Spanish frontier, home to some of the most spectacular scenery in the Pyrenees, notably the Ordesa canyon, a deep and impressive gorge, sculpted by glaciers, its walls formed of fascinating limestone strata.

To escape from Gavarnie, take the so-called Pilgrim's Route, named for those who embark on the long journey to the city of Santiago de Compostela. The trail leaves Gavarnie passing the old church where, in the past, pilgrims would spend the night praying before setting out to face the rigours of their journey. The path gains altitude gently through meadows, heading for the Port de Boucharo at 2270m (7446ft). There is a road, but the trail is much nicer. Note, though, that there is no shelter at the Cabane des Soldats, a locked-up building.

From the col our route heads into Spain down steep scree to reach the meadows. Ahead can be seen the huge cliffs and deep ravines of the Ordesa. Cedar forest welcomes you to the valley of Bujaruelo, while the Refuge St Nicholas de Bujaruelo at 1332m (4369ft) and the pools in the river may distract you from your journey.

Take the GR11 trail along the true left bank of the Garganta de Bujaruelo, and walk through forest to emerge on the road a few kilometres from Torla. This final stretch is rather tortuous, but can be avoided by following a trail on the far side of the Rio Ara. Either way, Torla is such a charming village that all pain will quickly be forgotten once installed in one of the *tapas* bars that line its narrow winding streets.

A regular bus service will take you to the entrance of the Ordesa Canyon from where you can pick up the high level Faja de Pelay trail, which takes the southern side of the Ordesa Canyon. The red walls of the canyon tower all around, while below is the fast-flowing Rio Arazas, continuing to carve out the gorge. At the head of the valley the path joins the main drag

**ABOVE** *The blue iris, found throughout the Pyrenees, flowers in July.*

coming up the valley at the Cascada de Cola de Caballa (horse's tail waterfall). The GR11 trail then continues up to the much-frequented Refugio de Goriz at 2170m (7117ft), situated at the head of the Ordesa Canyon. This is a good base for an ascent of Monte Perdido if conditions are suitable. It is called the lost mountain (*monte perdido*) because from the French side it is blocked from view by the frontier peaks. However, it has clearly been found and provides a popular ascent both by its glacier and, later in the season, by a non-glaciated route.

It is best to spend the night at Goriz, even if the peak is not your objective, otherwise the day is very long. The trail continues across featureless hillsides until it reaches the rocky notch of the Brèche de Roland at 2807m (9207ft). It was named after the hero Roland, nephew of Charlemagne, who is said to have cut this cleft in the ridge while trying to break his sword rather than have it fall into enemy hands.

The brèche is the gateway back into France. Gaze out to the distant mountains and hazy plains of Spain. Those with energy and time to spare can ascend the nearby summit of the 3144m (10 312ft) Le Taillon, before descending a snowy slope to the Refuge des Sarradets (also known as Refuge de la Brèche de Roland) just below at 2587m (9207ft). It is worth spending the night here even though it is one of the busiest huts in Europe, if only to watch the sun setting on the walls of the Cirque, before taking one of the trails back to Gavarnie. Be sure to take a look at the Cirque and Europe's highest waterfall before heading into town.

# PICOS DE EUROPA

## By Ronald Turnbull

The Picos de Europa range lies in the middle of the Cordillera Cantabrica on the north Atlantic coast of Spain. As the turkey vulture flies, it measures only 30km (20 miles); but those without wings will find it much larger than that, as they climb constantly up and down over fissured rockfields, or divert around a limestone crag. Deep, wooded gaps – the Duje river valley and the Cares gorge – slice the range into three massifs: East, Central and West. Very long, steep gullies (called *canales*) descend from the heights to river level. Above rise limestone towers and pinnacles, the most famous of which, El Naranjo de Bulnes, is a naked blade of rock about 500m (1600ft) high.

The steep gullies mean you need to be fit, keep the weight of your pack to a minimum, and make use of the huts and villages rather than try to be self-sufficient. Even the waymarked hut-to-hut routes are likely to have you clinging to a rock face or following tiny marker cairns across a wilderness of holes and boulders. Paths confidently lead along little ledges; become so narrow as to need a fixed cable for security; then deposit you on a field of forget-me-nots in the middle of a crag.

### MINERAL KINGDOM

High above the gorges, in between the rock peaks, the terrain is particularly interesting. Because of its porous nature, limestone doesn't hold water. So these hills don't have lakes; instead there are huge, dry hollows known as *jous*, whose shadows hold the gritty residue of old snow. This is a mineral kingdom, mainly, but an occasional mimosa or gentian sprouts from a crack, a mountain rebecco (the Spanish chamois species) hops across a distant skyline, while a turkey vulture wheels, patiently waiting for something to die. In misty weather the Picos are uniquely

ABOVE *The optional first day of walking is strenuous but scenic. Seen from the start of the descent to Tielve, the distant peaks of the Central Massif carry June snow.*

challenging. The path, where it crosses bare rock, simply vanishes; when reading the map's contour lines it is impossible to distinguish between knolls and hollows; and what appears to be level ground turns out to be a maze of little crags. Meanwhile, the limestone slashes your boots, wears away your fingertips and renders your legs very, very tired.

Trekkers choose the Picos because they haven't been developed and groomed for tourism. So be prepared for the closing of shops during siesta, which lasts the entire afternoon. Very few hut wardens and villagers speak English. The huts are well-placed and friendly, but the path system is rougher than elsewhere in Europe. Many waymarks have weathered to faded yellow paint, while 'fixed' cables are not necessarily fixed all that firmly. As treks go, the Picos de Europa is not among the tame ones!

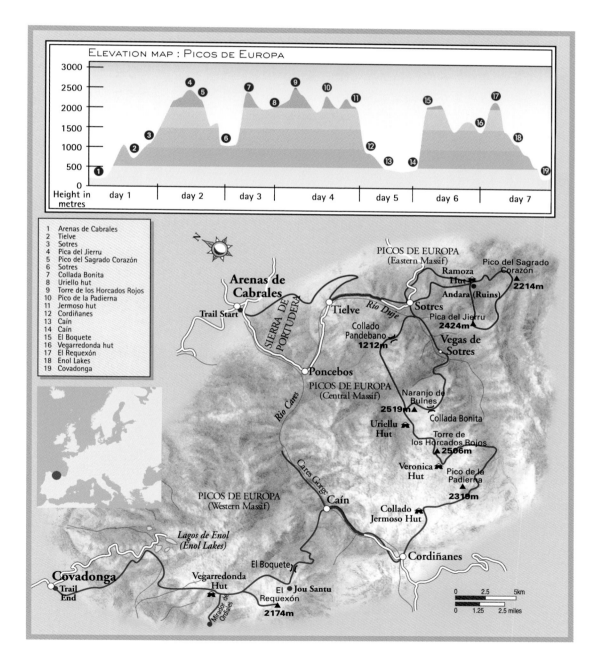

ELEVATION MAP : PICOS DE EUROPA

1 Arenas de Cabrales
2 Tielve
3 Sotres
4 Pica del Jierru
5 Pico del Sagrado Corazón
6 Sotres
7 Collada Bonita
8 Uriello hut
9 Torre de los Horcados Rojos
10 Pico de la Padierna
11 Jermoso hut
12 Cordiñanes
13 Caín
14 Caín
15 El Boquete
16 Vegarredonda hut
17 El Requexón
18 Enol Lakes
19 Covadonga

## PINNACLES AND LIMESTONE BOULDERFIELD

To start the trek, Arenas de Cabrales is reached by bus from the Atlantic coast road. It has *pensiones*, a camping ground, and shops. The first day over the Sierra de Portudera to the village of Sotres is technically straightforward, but strenuous. Start early to escape the heat. A cobbled path, reputedly Roman, rises for 1000m (3300ft) through sweet chestnuts to a bleak area of rock and pasture. Waymarks are sparse, but incorrect routes are recognizable by their thornscrub and scree. At the Collado Posadoiro pass, the jagged skyline of the Picos appears with heart-stopping suddenness across the deep green hollow of the Rio (River) Duje.

The village of Tielve has dirt streets and ancient tiled houses, with a tiny café; and 'Would you like the ordinary cheese – or would you like the Cabrales cheese?' Of course we chose the Cabrales. The first bite was interesting; the next one was challenging. The following few bites were bearable, just. The rest we had to 'keep till later' and discreetly throw away among the thorn scrub. And for rest of the trip, cheese – any sort of cheese – was something we couldn't bear to look at. But do the good people of Tielve actually enjoy the stuff? Or was it perhaps a special lump, two years past its sell-by date, kept for the teasing of tourists?

A road leads up the valley towards Sotres; an old mule-path up on the left offers a more interesting way. This pre-

liminary day can be cut out altogether by taking a bus or local taxi.

The second day is a circular tour of the Eastern Massif, so the heavy backpacks can stay at Sotres. And you'll be very glad not to have them, as you're in for a scramble along a ridge of sun-warmed rock with an eagle floating by and a heat-hazed valley an awful long way below your right-hand boot.

You can start this day's hike two ways. The first alternative is straight up: the forest track above Sotres leads over Picu Boru for some serious, airy scrambling over Pico Valdominguero. Here you work along a knife-edge crest, with drops on the left into the Jou Sin Tierre or 'Bottomless Pit'. Actually, the drops on the right, to the Rio Duje, are twice as deep as the supposedly bottomless ones on the left. The second, less terrifying, alternative is to follow tracks and roads to Jito de Escarandi, for a rough path up Canal de la Jazuca. This leads through interesting old lead mines, and past the primitive cave shelters of the early miners as well as the more comfortable and modern Ramoza hut.

Either way, after Collado Valdominguero you embark on a superb rocky ridge walk and scramble, with no real difficulty. Robin Walker's guidebook indicates a rock-climbing descent into the col before the 2424m (7953ft) Pica del Jierru, but there is an easier way slightly left of the crest. The circuit continues sometimes on old mule paths, but more often over bare rock slabs that are warm or even hot under the hand,

and along a sharp rock ridge. On the right is a drop of about 1800m (6000ft) into the blue haze that fills the Valdebano. Final summit is Pico del Sagrado Corazón (the peak of the sacred heart). In keeping with the peak's name, the summit cairn consists of a statue of Jesus.

## COWS IN THE MIST

The third day heads up a pathless, rock-floored valley to a tiny pass between two pinnacles and through to the high Uriello hut. This needs very careful route-finding. 'If the mist comes down, just grab onto a cow and let it lead you out of the mountains' is how they'd advised me in Bilbao. But the terrain of the Moñetas is such that there's no

ABOVE *The summer herdsmen's village at Vegas de Sotres marks the start of the challenging ascent into the Central Massif.*

grass, so there would be no cows in the first place, and even if there were, they'd have already broken their ankles among the rocks and so be of little value as guides. Accordingly, my advice to my nephews for Day Three of the trek was simpler: 'If it's misty, take the easy alternative route.'

But who listens to uncles? The bottom of the Valle de los Moñetas is obvious enough, rising above the flower meadows and summer huts of Vegas de Sotres. And all they had to do was head up to find the marked path that runs across the top. However, waymarks of wind-blasted yellow paint, or tiny grey cairns, are not obvious in a grey world of mist. The grassland gives way to chunks and ripples of twisted rock. Patches of black between the boulders can be caverns penetrating deep into the underground. For several hours they searched for the upper path, or even for a cow to cling to. Then they started looking for something softer than angular boulders on which to spend the night.

Just in time, the cloud slumped slightly; enough to show them the exit high above. Golden evening sun shone on the 10m-wide (33ft) notch between two rock needles – Collada Bonita, whose entirely apt translation is 'lovely little pass'. As you step into the gap, on the opposite side stands the giant's tombstone of Naranjo de Bulnes. This is particularly spectacular, say my nephews, at sunset. But it's not a good idea to find out, since the descent into

Jou Tras El Pico is very nasty indeed in the dark as it drops steeply over stones or old snow, into a gully of scree and boulders. It then works around the base of Naranjo de Bulnes, to reach an inexpensive supper of soup and sausage at the Uriello hut.

The alternative route for this day from Sotres to Uriello is an undemanding one along tracks and paths by way of the Collado Pandebano.

On day four, the route continues southwards through two distinctive limestone hollows, the Jou Sin Tierre (another 'bottomless hole') and Jou de los Boches. A section of easy scrambling, assisted by a fixed cable, leads to the Horcados Rojos pass. Leave backpacks here for a straightforward, but airy, ascent of 2506m (8222ft) Torre de los Horcados Rojos.

The distinctive Veronica hut is the turret from a World War II aircraft carrier, brought in by helicopter. It serves refreshments and sleeps three. But an even finer nightspot is ahead. First comes a stony mule track where the worst obstacle is a cowpat – or you may have to stand aside for the cows themselves. A short side-trip leads to Pico de la Padierna – a scree walk, but with a 300m (1000ft) drop to a grassy meadow on the other side. The path continues across a stony plateau, then suddenly descends over the edge, to where an astonishing ledge runs along halfway up a precipice. And at its end is the Collado Jermoso hut, perched on a scrap of meadow high above the Cares gorge.

ABOVE *From the Vegarredonda hut, the final morning can be spent on this exposed scramble of El Requexón. Behind, cloud lies over the lowlands all the way to the Atlantic.*

On the following day, the 1200m (4000ft) descent to Cordiñanes takes much longer than you expect. Even so, you should reach Caín early enough for a side trip down the mighty Cares gorge. This is the one part of the trip that could be called a stroll, on a wide path through tunnels carved out of the rock wall. However, it has 100m (300ft) drops, no handrails, and bridges that even the Spanish admit are a bit dubious. You won't have time to follow the spectacular gorge all the way – it eventually emerges on the southern side of the range. Return to Caín for its *pensiones*, camping field and useful shop.

By day six you should be fit enough to face the 1500m (5000ft) climb into the Western Massif. A zigzag path takes you up steep meadows and between crags to the narrow entrance called El Boquete. Once through this 'little mouth' you're swallowed up by the hugest of the limestone hollows, the Jou Santu. It leads through the Western Massif's high peaks to the Vegarredonda hut.

How you spend your final morning will depend on your energy levels. Two hours away there's El Requexón at 2174m (7133ft), which offers a short but exposed rock scramble. Once up its rough, sunny limestone you linger above tremendous empty spaces. In one direction, the jagged silhouette of the mountains resembles the cardiogram of an agitated scrambler; in the other, grey rock foreground fades into blue, then green, reaching halfway to Santiago.

Alternatively, you can visit Mirador (viewpoint) de Ordiales, which has a vista that's half as spectacular – the sheer drop is on one side, rather than both – but involves no rock scrambling. Or you could simply lie around in meadows of Christmas roses, occasionally buying another beer from the hut...

The journey ends with a wander down to the Enol lakes (Lagos de Enol), then across the cow meadows of Vega las Traviesas and down through woodland to Covadonga. The sacred capital of Spain, it has a cathedral, a cave waterfall, and a chapel tucked under an overhang like a swallow's nest. It's as surprising, and inspiring, as the Picos themselves.

# WAY OF ST JAMES

## By Paddy Dillon

The Camino (literally, the way) was designated the First European Cultural Itinerary, and is essentially a pilgrim trail. Links from all over Europe lead the faithful onto a final long trek through northern Spain. Thus the ideal of European unity was forged along its length. It has been walked for a thousand years and has recently seen a revival. Those interested in history, art and architecture find it an immensely satisfying route. Although most walkers are Spanish, up to a dozen nationalities can be encountered along the way. It is well marked, very busy in summer, and is a cultural and historical extravaganza from start to finish. Most people walk the route, and are known as *peregrinos* – but many cycle and a few go on horseback. All are heading for Santiago, where St James the Apostle lies buried. The Way of St James isn't a difficult walk, but it is long and very hot and crowded in summer. Spring or autumn are quieter seasons, while winter travel is awkward, since many facilities are closed and the higher parts are snowbound.

### SCALLOP SHELL ICON

Much of the way leads along clear tracks and paths, with some parts along roads. Hard surfaces mean you should give some thought to your footwear – blistered feet are common. Think light and comfortable, and adopt the same for your backpack. Route markings are clear; employing a scallop shell icon (the symbol of St James) or flashes of yellow paint. A detailed route description is unnecessary, but a commentary about features of interest and facilities along the way is useful. While a knowledge of Spanish is an advantage, it is not essential. The local people know why you are here, where you are going and what you need. They have successfully dealt with travellers for a thousand years, establishing a system of *refugios*, or pilgrim refuges, that can be used by anyone carrying a *credencial*,

**ABOVE** *The village of Cirauqui, in the province of Navarra, lies huddled on a hilltop so that the surrounding land remains available for cultivation. The Camino leaves it along a well-preserved Roman road.*

or pilgrim 'passport'. Taking the Camino a province at a time, the route passes through Navarra in the Basque country, then crosses the wine-growing region of La Rioja. The more arid province of Burgos gives way to Palencia and León. The provinces of Lugo and A Coruña are in the mountainous region of Galicia, where the route continues to its conclusion in the city of Santiago de Compostela.

RIGHT *Cyclists prepare to overtake walkers on the 'Mulekiller Hill' near the village of Hornillos in the province of Burgos. This is one of the high and dry* meseta *sections of the Camino.*

## PROVINCE OF NAVARRA

Though some walkers cross the Pyrenees from St Jean Pied-de-Port in France, the Way of St James is usually started in Roncesvalles, at the foot of the Pyrenees. In Navarra, Basque country, the route runs from village to village among forested hills, then follows the Río Arga. Pamplona, famous for the 'running of the bulls', is the first city. There is a gentle climb over the Sierra del Perdon, then tracks lead to Puente la Reina (*puente* is a bridge).

Once the fine stone-arched bridge is crossed, the route heads for the hilltop village of Cirauqui. From here, it follows an old Roman road, linking with other tracks to reach Estella. At Irache, pilgrims can

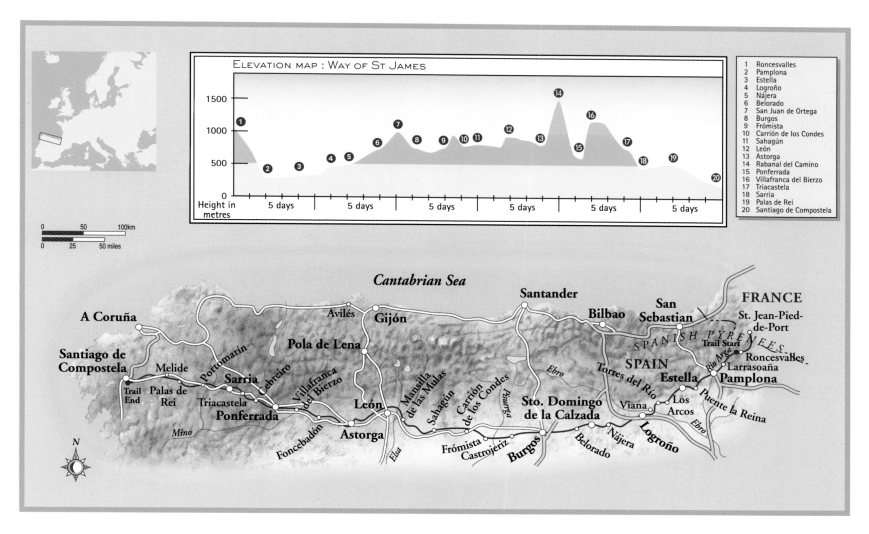

ELEVATION MAP : WAY OF ST JAMES

1  Roncesvalles
2  Pamplona
3  Estella
4  Logroño
5  Nájera
6  Belorado
7  San Juan de Ortega
8  Burgos
9  Frómista
10  Carrión de los Condes
11  Sahagún
12  León
13  Astorga
14  Rabanal del Camino
15  Ponferrada
16  Villafranca del Bierzo
17  Triacastela
18  Sarria
19  Palas de Rei
20  Santiago de Compostela

**ABOVE** *The Romanesque architecture of the church of St Martin at Frómista in the province of Palencia. One of the attractions of the Camino is the architecture along the way.*

indulge at a public wine fountain. A long, dry track leads from Villamayor to Los Arcos, from where tracks run through fields, vineyards and olive groves, passing the hilltop village of Torres del Río on the way to the ancient Viana. Arid country is crossed to reach the city of Logroño.

## PROVINCE OF LA RIOJA

Although the centre of Logroño is old and full of character, the sprawling suburbs take time to clear. The Camino passes a nature reserve, where the reservoir of Pantano de la Grajera attracts wildfowl, on the way to the hillside town of Navarette. Vineyards abound here; La Rioja is where the best wines in Spain are produced. An unpleasant stretch along a road is followed by scenic tracks in rolling hill country on the way to Nájera, which nestles at the base of a red sandstone cliff. The trail

passes through a breach in the rock face and easy tracks lead across cultivated countryside to Santo Domingo de la Calzada, named after the man who assisted pilgrims by building a causeway and bridges. The cathedral in this town is a treasure house of carved stone and woodwork, richly ornamented, coloured and gilded. There are two stretches of road between Santo Domingo and Belorado.

## PROVINCE OF BURGOS

Good paths and tracks beyond Belorado pass many charming villages. Leaving Villafranca, the route crosses the Montes de Oca, passing though oakwoods and pine forest before dropping to San Juan de Ortega. A follower of Santo Domingo, San Juan also built bridges, roads and hospitals for pilgrims. The route wends past villages surrounded by wheatfields, before reach-

ing limestone uplands that offer views towards Burgos. It takes a while to get through the suburbs of Burgos, but the city centre has a splendid cathedral.

Beyond Burgos is a *meseta* – a high, dry plateau with wheatfields. Shade from the blazing sun is limited. Carry plenty of water and check the availability of more water ahead, as it takes hours to get from village to village. Hornillos and Hontanas offer shade and refreshments. Castrojeriz, crowned by a ruined medieval castle, is the only large town. You cross another high *meseta* before reaching a fine old bridge that spans the Río Pisuerga.

## PROVINCE OF PALENCIA

The green countryside on the banks of the Río Pisuerga gives way to another dry and barren *meseta* before the Camino reaches Frómista. Here, the church of San Martín is a Romanesque gem. A good path runs alongside a road through the region called Los Campos, and fine villages are passed on the way to Carrión de los Condes, where several historic buildings may be visited. Then a lengthy track crosses wideopen country between Carrión and Calzadilla de la Cueza. There are several villages, but not all offer food, drink or lodgings, so it is useful to know what's available in advance. Sahagún is the next town that offers a full range of facilities.

## PROVINCE OF LEÓN

Three churches in Sahagún are classed as national monuments. The route continues as a pilgrim path and a long line of plane trees stretches into the distance;

specially planted to provide shade. The villages of Bercianos, El Burgo Ranero and Reliegos are oases, offering refreshment and shade. After the town of Mansilla de las Mulas, the landscape becomes more varied as the Camino continues to the city of León. Here, be sure to admire the extravagant stained-glass windows of the cathedral.

As the trail leaves the city it follows quiet tracks across a bleak *paramo* – an arid, scrubby plain where panoramic views can be enjoyed. The *paramo* gives way to cultivated countryside when the Camino crosses a long pilgrim bridge – the Paso Honoroso – to Hospital de Órbigo. Small villages are passed on the way to Astorga. Here, there's a fine cathedral and an interesting Museum of the Ways that details the history of the Camino.

A few villages are passed on the wild, scrubby Maragatería. Mountains rise ahead and the climb leads through Rabanal, where the 'English Hostel' is one of the best pilgrim refuges.

After the ruined village of Foncebadón comes Cruz de Hierro; the highest point on the Way of St. James at 1504m (4934ft). The route crosses a ridge to descend via the village of El Acebo, then runs through mountain country to Molinaseca, followed by the grim, industrial Ponferrada. Several farming villages are passed on the way to Villafranca del Bierzo, where there is a choice of mountain routes; a winding road or a simple track. They join again at Trabadelo, from where there is a climb to the village of O Cebreiro at 1300m (4265ft) in the mountains of Galicia.

**ABOVE** *The descent towards the village of El Acebo after crossing the highest part of the Camino, at 1504m (4934ft), on the Cruz de Hierro. This part of the route can be cut off by snow in winter.*

**TOP** *Most of the Camino is marked with simple yellow flash paintings or signs bearing a scallop shell in honour of St James. This marker near Sahagún is more elaborate.*

## PROVINCE OF LUGO

Don Elias Sampedro, the person responsible for reviving interest in the Way of St James, ministered at O Cebreiro in the mid-20th century. The route uses tracks and paths to descend to Triacastela, with Monte Caldeiron dominating the scene. A choice of routes (left via Samos or right via San Xil) meet again in the hilltop town of Sarria, beyond which lie several small villages. Here confusion reigns as names on signposts, maps and guidebooks disagree! Wonderful winding *corredoiras* (cart tracks) weave between stone-walled fields. A bridge crosses a reservoir to reach Portomarín. The route leaves again by quiet roads over the rugged Sierra Ligonde to Palas de Rei.

## PROVINCE OF A CORUÑA

The green countryside between Palas de Rei and Melide is dotted with little villages and the Camino frequently crosses a main road that runs from Melide to Santiago. Nonetheless there are quiet stretches along tracks and paths through eucalyptus forest. Villages are small and simple. Then the trail runs around the airport at Lavacolla to a pilgrim monument on Monte del Gozo.

The final stage is through the suburbs of Santiago, into the ancient city centre and to the imposing cathedral. Enter it via the Portico del Gloria, walk up to a statue of St James and give it a hug, as millions of pilgrims have done before. Then descend to the crypt where a silver casket holds the bones of the saint. Be sure to visit the Dean's House to obtain your *compostela*, a certificate granted to successful pilgrims since the 14th century.

# TOUR OF THE MATTERHORN

## By Hilary Sharp

The 4478m (14,692ft) Matterhorn, or Mont Cervin in French or Monte Cervino as the Italians call it, is probably the most famous mountain in the world. Even if people don't know its name, they've seen its shape replicated on anything from chocolate boxes to corporate adverts. Ask children to draw a mountain and that's what they'll draw – a pointed pyramid. It's interesting to imagine what the long-ago first inhabitants of the region thought about this summit as they strove to make a living in the high alpine pastures that butt up against its base. Could they imagine that one day people would stand on its summit? Did they worship it? Believe it to be the source of evil and danger? In fact, the first ascent of the

Matterhorn by British alpinist Edward Whymper and his friends in 1865 caused much controversy, especially when it ended in tragedy: four of the group fell to their deaths during the descent. Even in this age when we are bombarded with extreme images on a daily basis, the Matterhorn remains an arresting sight, especially when seen from Zermatt.

The Tour of the Matterhorn is regarded as new because it has been documented only in the last few years. The paths, however, are often ancient ways over passes leading from one valley to another. People have walked these paths over centuries for trading, transhumance (seasonal movement of livestock to suitable grazing), and migrating or fleeing from enemies.

Each pass provides wonderful new vistas, peaks and unknown valleys beckoning you onwards. The expedition is varied and rewarding: not only will you see the Matterhorn from all sides, but also many of the other high summits of the region. Two countries, Switzerland and Italy, and thus two very different cultures, are visited. You will also encounter the fascinating Walser people – who fled from Germany long ago to settle in the high Italian valleys and have maintained not only their culture, but also their language.

This trek includes two glacier crossings and the chance to ascend the Breithorn, a summit which exceeds 4000m (13,123ft) by 164m (538ft) and dominates Zermatt. The only downside to this trek is that it passes

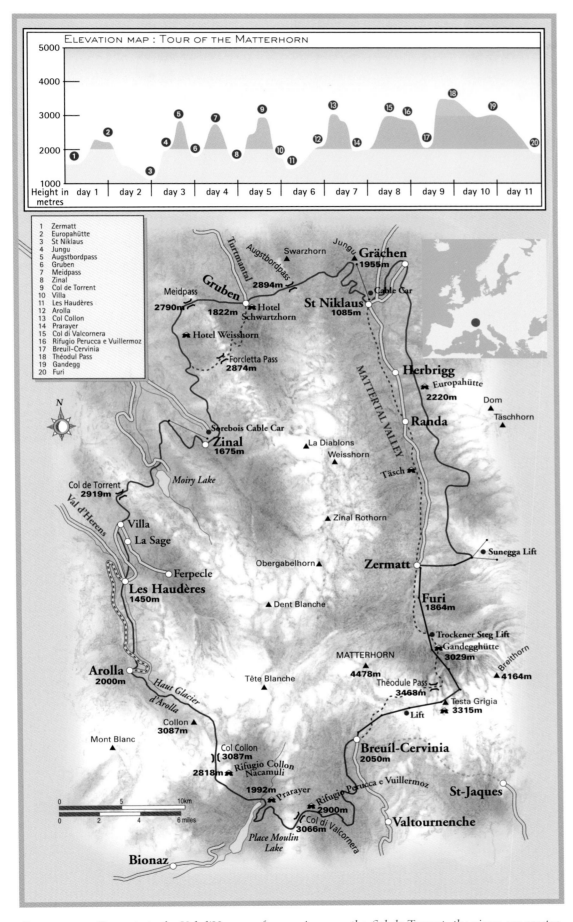

**Elevation map : Tour of the Matterhorn**

| Height in metres | day 1 | day 2 | day 3 | day 4 | day 5 | day 6 | day 7 | day 8 | day 9 | day 10 | day 11 |
|---|---|---|---|---|---|---|---|---|---|---|---|

1 Zermatt
2 Europahütte
3 St Niklaus
4 Jungu
5 Augstbordpass
6 Gruben
7 Meidpass
8 Zinal
9 Col de Torrent
10 Villa
11 Les Haudères
12 Arolla
13 Col Collon
14 Prarayer
15 Col di Valcornera
16 Rifugio Perucca e Vuillermoz
17 Breuil-Cervinia
18 Théodul Pass
19 Gandegg
20 Furi

OPPOSITE *En route to the Val d'Herens, after passing over the Col de Torrent, the views are spectacular in all directions.*

through the major ski areas of Cervinia and Zermatt. If there is plenty of snow cover then these areas will be quite pretty, but be warned: towards the end of the season there are a few places that look more like building sites – notably Trockener Steg above Zermatt. There it's better to concentrate very hard on the fantastic views of the surrounding peaks and ignore all the mess that surrounds the lift and ski slopes. Don't let this put you off, however – it's a small blip, which is more than compensated for by the beauty of the rest of the trek and the feeling of achievement as you return to Zermatt after completing the tour.

Since it's a circular tour, theoretically it can be started anywhere along its length, but some places are more accessible than others. It is usually best to start and finish where you can leave excess gear, buy picnic food and celebrate at the end. Also, it's good to start and finish this tour with views of the Matterhorn since that is what you're walking around, so I'm going to describe it from Zermatt.

It is generally done anticlockwise and that's what I've described. This way the highest altitude on the trek comes at the end when you're most acclimatized.

The trail leaves the fleshpots of Zermatt to head down the Mattertal valley towards St Niklaus 1085m (3560ft), a delightful town with a characteristic onion-shaped church tower. There are various ways of getting to St Niklaus: one is to take the high level path, Europaweg, which leaves from the top of Zermatt's Sunegga lift at 2288m (7507ft). This is a spectacular trail, contouring high above the valley with amazing

ABOVE *The village of Jungu enjoys a wonderful position high above the Mattertal. The cable car access to the village provides an exciting alternative to the steep climb.*

views, notably of the fine sculpted snowy faces of the Weisshorn. It takes two days from Zermatt, with a night in the well-positioned Europahütte at 2220m (7283ft), to reach the village of Grächen. From there a bus goes down to St Niklaus. A shorter alternative is to take the wooded footpath from Zermatt to Täsch, then continue on back roads though the villages of Randa (scene of a huge landslide in 1991) and Herbrigg to reach St Niklaus in an easy day.

A not-to-be-missed spectacular cable car ride leads up to the wonderfully positioned hamlet of Jungu 1955m (6414ft), with its gleaming white church and flower-filled meadows. An old trail heads away from the traditional wooden chalets and up into the mountains past a huge cairn that marks the best place to stop and view the surrounding peaks. Pride of place is taken by the Dom, the Täschhorn and the Weisshorn. Rocky terrain leads to the Augstbordpass 2894m (9495ft), an ancient crossing used to reach the Turtmantal valley. This first part of the trek coincides with the Chamonix–Zermatt Walkers' Haute Route so you're likely to meet plenty of fellow walkers here. Haute Route candidates are nearing the end of their route and this is their last col so they'll either be overjoyed, relieved or sad.

## PICTURESQUE VILLAGES

Gruben, at 1822m (5978ft), a small village in the beautiful and relatively unspoilt Turtmantal is the next stop. All visitors stay at the rather grand Hotel Schwartzhorn, whose size and style reflect an earlier age of alpine travel. Take the time to stroll up the road past the old houses and the picture-book church.

The Val d'Anniviers is the next objective and two options present themselves. If you want to sample the traditional old Victo-

rian Hotel Weisshorn then the Meidpass at 2790m (9154ft) is the col to aim for. Otherwise the Forcletta pass at 2874m (9429ft) is a shorter option. Both lead onto a beautiful traversing trail that wanders along high above the valley with fantastic views of the glaciated mountains – the Dent Blanche, Zinal Rothorn, Obergabelhorn and, if you're lucky, the Matterhorn – before plunging down into the forest to quickly deposit you in Zinal at 1675m (5495ft). The old part of Zinal is a delight – old houses built of red larch and stone set in pretty gardens and cultivated fields.

If you don't want to walk, you can take the Sorebois cable car from town. The way onwards from the cable car up bulldozed ski pistes to the Sorebois pass at 2438m (7999ft) is not a beautiful walk, but on the other side of the col is a great vista – the blue waters of the artificial Moiry Lake and, beyond, the next objective: the Col de Torrent at 2919m (9577ft). From here you walk through meadows, down gentle pastoral slopes, perhaps past the odd chamois, all the way down to the Val d'Herens and the hamlets of Villa and La Sage. The valley leads to Les Haudères at 1450m (4757ft), another picturesque village with old larch chalets and flowery window boxes.

To reach Arolla at 2000m (6562ft) you can either take the bus or walk. A tiny village with a big reputation, Arolla was famous before cable cars for giving access to lots of big peaks. From here you head for the high mountains – up the Haut Glacier d'Arolla, a more-or-less icy, crevassed slope, to reach the Col Collon at 3087m (10,128ft). In my experience you need to carry crampons for this section, and when there is snow on the ice you certainly need a rope – it's a glacier and they generally have holes in them. The glacier abruptly ends at the col from where views in all directions are superb. Stop for a moment here as you bid Switzerland farewell and walk into Italy. Stony ground leads past the Rifugio Collon Nacamuli, perched on rocks at 2818m (9245ft), and on down into the grassy meadows bordering the huge blue lake of Place Moulin at 1968m (6457ft). The level track along this lake provides a perfect day out for young and old and so expect to see plenty of Italian families walking the *bambinos* and the grandparents. Prarayer, at 1992m (6535ft), is at the far end of the lake and a good place to spend the night.

The next hurdle, the Col di Valcornera at 3066m (10,059ft) is not glaciated, but it can nevertheless be a difficult ascent. It is steep and rocky and névé sometimes remains well into the season, but it is the northeasterly slope on the far side that is to be respected the most. Again crampons could be useful. Further down, the Rifugio Perucca e Vuillermoz at 2900m (9514ft) is a good place to spend the night before carrying on down to the dubious joys of Breuil-Cervinia at 2050m (6726ft). The route down is through grassy meadows surrounded by waterfalls.

From Breuil-Cervinia there is a triple cable car ride that goes all the way up to Testa Grigia at 3315m (10,876ft). You can either take this or walk from town up to the neighbouring Théodule Pass at 3468m (11,378ft). This pass has been used since time began – artefacts have been found

**ABOVE** *The view from Zermatt of the distinctive Matterhorn, also known as Mont Cervin in French or Monte Cervino in Italian.*

from Roman times attesting to the fact that the climate was indeed considerably warmer then. There is even an old chapel, the Capelle Bontadini, en route, where travellers would pray for protection from the elements before embarking on the final stage of their climb. However, this area is an example of the worst ravages of winter tourism – lifts abound, along with the associated junk and destruction of the slopes. I strongly advise taking the lifts up to the Testa Grigia from where a short walk down snowy slopes leads to the Théodule-hütte next to its col. There is also accommodation at the Rifugio Guide del Cervino at Testa Grigia itself. Once you raise your eyes above the nearby lifts and summer ski slopes the mountains are stunning – best of all, of course, the Matterhorn, soon to be seen from its Swiss side again.

An ascent of the Breithorn, for which guides can be hired at either of the two huts, is possible before descending to Zermatt. For this summit, and for the descent from here down to the top of the Trockener Steg lift at 2939m (9642ft) you will be walking on glaciers. Views of the Matterhorn are superb as you descend. It's worth breaking away from the piste lower down to go to Gandegg hut at 3029m (9938ft). There is a fine restaurant with a terrace facing all the Zermatt peaks – the Breithorn, Pollux, Castor, Lyskamm and the many summits of Monte Rosa.

Walk or take the lift down to Furi at 1864m (6115ft) then walk the last part through larch forest past picture-perfect wooden chalets into the madness of Zermatt high street.

All huts in the Alps that have a warden will provide mattresses, blankets and a cooked food service. Sometimes you can cook your own food, but not always. So you only need to carry regular walking gear with some extra clothes for the night. There are also unguarded huts and bivouac huts. These are not used in the Alpine treks described here. However, even these usually have mattresses and blankets and a stove with gas. Most hut wardens will allow camping within the vicinity of the hut, but why bother when it means carrying far more gear? The beauty of the hut system in the Alps is that you can travel light and live in relative luxury.

# ALTA VIA 2 – THE DOLOMITES

*By Hilary Sharp*

Situated at the eastern end of the Alpine chain, the Dolomites form part of the region of South Tyrol. The Tyrol overlaps Austria and Italy. Until the First World War, the South Tyrol was part of the Austro-Hungarian Empire. In 1918 The Treaty of Versailles gave the South Tyrol to Italy, but its population remained predominantly German-speaking. It seems that in this region of Italy the people still feel more Austrian than Italian. If there's one thing you must know before going to the Dolomites, it's that everywhere has two names – an Italian one and an Austrian one – which are usually quite dissimilar. The town of Bressanone is also known as Brixen, the Rifugio Genova is the Schluterhütte... get used to this peculiarity.

It is thought that the Dolomites is named after the Marquis of Dolomieu, a French geologist who, in the 18th century, analyzed the unusual rock of the region. However, the original name, Monti Pallidi (Pale Mountains), is more descriptive of the limestone spires for which this area is known. The presence of magnesium in the rock gives it a rosy tinge, making sunrise and sunset quite spectacular.

## VIA FERRATA

Many fierce and drawn-out battles were fought in this mountain range between Austria and Italy during World War I. The troops often overcame rocky obstacles on these harsh peaks by means of cables, metal rungs and other ironware ham-mered into the rocks. These equipped scrambles, called *via ferrata* (iron way) have become a Dolomites tradition and today many have been set up to allow the rocks to be climbed for pleasure.

Nevertheless, despite the barren, rugged scenery, the Dolomite trekker will be surprised to also walk through flower-strewn meadows and pastoral, green valleys. The area is hiker-friendly, with vast networks of beautifully maintained, well-marked (usually!) footpaths. There are several *alta via* (high routes) traversing the region, one

**ABOVE** *Nearing the Rifugio Boé from the Passo Gardena. The lunar plateau, surrounded by towers, is typical of the Dolomites.*

of the best being the Alta Via 2, a part of which is described here.

Beginning in the northwestern corner of the region, the route heads towards the southern extremity of the Dolomites, crossing many of the massifs (or groups as they are called here) en route: a week's trek doing part of the Alta Via can take in the Odle, Puez, Sella and Marmolada massifs.

The trek begins in Bressanone, also known as Brixen, at 550m (1804ft). An elegant and charming town whose history dates back more than a thousand years, Bressanone has interesting cobbled streets with narrow alleys and arches. It offers the essence of the Austrian Tyrol, with leather breeches and *Apfelstrudel* in abundance.

The first day out of town involves quite a long slog up to the Rifugio Plose at 2447m (8028ft). This is in the ski area and is accessible by lift, by car or a good footpath. Most people choose not to spend the night here, preferring to take the local bus and then the ski lift, before heading for the

Rifugio Genova, also known as the Schluterhütte. From there you need to get to the cable car. There's a bus service from town or you can walk up the road, but I prefer to take a taxi.

Leaving the cable car the views towards the Odle range are spectacular. The summit of Sass de Putia is visible among the spiky peaks. The path bordered by juniper and blueberry bushes is pretty and provides a good warm-up as far as the Passo Rodella at 1866m (6122ft). After that a steep climb gives a first taste of real trekking in the Dolomites. The well-made path winds up initially through pine forests before emerging onto rocks and scree. Although beautifully maintained, the path is just the wrong incline and is surprisingly tiring. Walkers are generally glad to reach the Forcella della Putia at 2357m (7703ft) for a well-earned rest.

Given adequate time and energy it is highly recommended to continue up the excellent trail to the 2875m (9432ft) Sass de Putia, a fine peak, with a short via ferrata to attain the final summit. All the vie ferrate mentioned here can be done without equipment, but that doesn't mean that they are risk-free. On this peak a fall in the wrong direction would take you over the steep west face; and in bad weather the rock quickly becomes very slippery.

Back to the pass and a quick half-hour walk takes you to the Rifugio Genova at 2301m (7549ft). The second day begins gently, with superb views – ahead to the Piz Duleda and, looking back, the Sass de Putia. The next objective, the Forcella della Roa, at 2616m (8583ft), is rather too

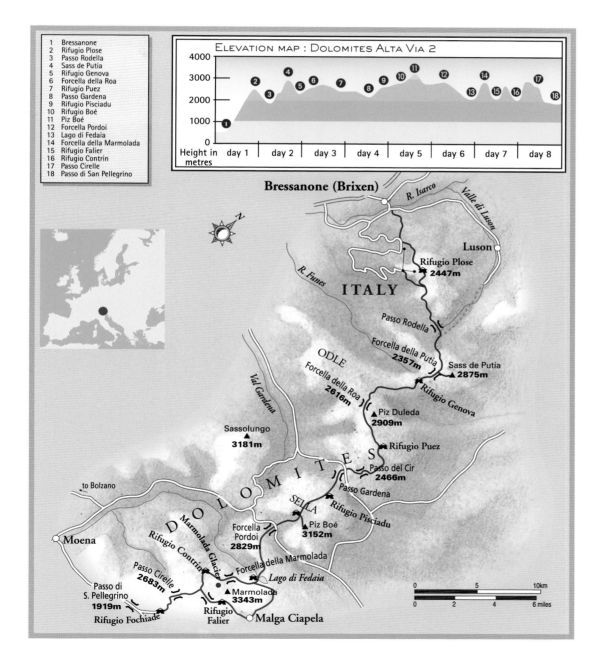

1  Bressanone
2  Rifugio Plose
3  Passo Rodella
4  Sass de Putia
5  Rifugio Genova
6  Forcella della Roa
7  Rifugio Puez
8  Passo Gardena
9  Rifugio Pisciadu
10 Rifugio Boé
11 Piz Boé
12 Forcella Pordoi
13 Lago di Fedaia
14 Forcella della Marmolada
15 Rifugio Falier
16 Rifugio Contrin
17 Passo Cirelle
18 Passo di San Pellegrino

ELEVATION MAP : DOLOMITES ALTA VIA 2

Height in metres

day 1 | day 2 | day 3 | day 4 | day 5 | day 6 | day 7 | day 8

LEFT *Most people breathe a sigh of relief when they reach the top of the steep Val Setus on the final stages of the via ferrata.*

includes a few cables on the steep parts and arrives on the ridge under the Piz Duleda, which can provide a pleasant diversion. There follows a stroll along slopes studded with tiny alpine flowers such as toadflax, glacier crowsfoot and rock jasmine. An impressive drop to the Vallunga offers views of the Sella group and the solid-looking summit of the 3181m (10,436ft) Sassolungo. The trail takes you quickly to the Rifugio Puez at 2475m (8120ft). This easily accessible hut attracts an impressive lunchtime trade (in Italy lunch is a serious business), but most of these visitors will return to the valley later in the day, leaving the hut and its environs tranquil for the night.

From Puez the trail south is a delight in the early morning, with the welcome rays of the sun and faraway views of the glistening snowy summits of the Ötztal Alps. Ahead is the Sella group – your objective – reached by descending from the Passo del Cir at 2466m (8091ft) through a forest of unusual red and orange limestone spires. The Passo Gardena at 2137m (7011ft) provides civilization, of sorts (prepare for chaos in the summer). Basic provisions can be bought here, as well as refreshments provided by several cafés.

A well-signed path tempts many walkers up the Val Setus. Rather dauntingly numbered 666, the trail zigzags relentlessly up scree to a via ferrata which exits onto a

obvious – a deep notch up ahead that looks steep and hard to get to. For now, enjoy the pastoral surroundings and look out for early morning chamois grazing the slopes. The Forcella is reached by a

steep, but mercifully short, scree slope and, of course, the views are fabulous. To reach the Puez Alp from this point you need to cross the ridge. There are at least two possible routes. The most direct

rocky plateau by the lake and Rifugio Pisciadu at 2583m (8474ft). Staying here would give time to ascend the Cima Pisciadu at 2985m (9793ft), just above. Continuing up steep scree gives access to a barren plateau and a lunar landscape. The cabin on top of the Piz Boé at 3152m (10,341ft) is obvious, while the more tempting Rifugio Boé at 2773m (9098ft) is at the base of the peak and provides a good overnight stop.

## THE JOYS OF SCREE

From the hut take the time for a quick, steep ascent of Piz Boé, which includes a short via ferrata. The summit is unlike any other I've visited, with its hut and strange square aerial, rather like a drive-in movie screen. Not a place to linger, but the views are stunning, nevertheless. Either return to the hut at Rifugio Boé or traverse the peak to reach the bleak Forcella Pordoi at 2829m (9281ft), where there is another hut.

The way down from here takes a narrow couloir of scree, very steep and quite intimidating. It's like looking down a snow slope just before you launch off on skis. Some rather odd chap took to skiing scree slopes in the Dolomites in the early 80s and it's almost possible to see why. Nowadays scree-running this slope is frowned upon and a good path has been constructed. If too many people run down the scree, all the small stones are gradually pushed down to the bottom of the slope, leaving bare ground. Descending this severe slope you'll feel just a little bit sorry for the people toiling up, but then that comes down to bad planning, I guess!

ABOVE *Edelweiss are common in the higher meadows of the Dolomites, preferring, as they do, limestone soil.*

The Passo Pordoi at 2242m (7354ft) provides another brief glimpse of holiday tourism. Supplies are available and again the chance to sample some Italian cafés before setting off along the famous Via del Pan – the Grain Route, used for smuggling in the 17th century. This path gets busy – very – partly for its views of the Marmolada, at 3343m (10,965ft) the highest summit in the Dolomites, and because it is flat. Nevertheless, the views of the Marmolada glacier and the imposing rocky summit of the neighbouring Gran Vernal, and the numerous alpine flowers found here, such as gentians, anemones, edelweiss and vanilla orchids, make for a memorable walk – even more so if you leave the main trail for the ridge above. But beware, this is very treacherous in the rain.

The night can be spent at one of the hotels on the shores of the Lago di Fedaia at 2050m (6726ft), under the glaciated slopes of the north face of the Marmolada.

The Marmolada formed the Austro-Italian frontier before 1919 and consequently saw a lot of fighting. As the Marmolada glacier recedes, tunnels carved in rock and the remains of wooden shelters are emerging at 3000m (9800ft) and above, testament to the sheer effort put in by the troops who had to fight here. Two options exist to cross the Marmolada. The glacier itself can be crossed, via the Forcella della Marmolada at 2910m (9547ft), after which a steep descent and via ferrata lead to the Rifugio Contrin at 2016m (6614ft). The alternative is a long, but very scenic, route circumnavigating the mountain via Malga Ciapela and up past the Rifugio Falier at 2080m (6824ft). It is situated under the orange and grey walls of the Marmolada's south face, an important rock climbing venue. The Passo di Ombretta 2702m (8863ft), with its bright red bivouac hut, is reached after a long ascent, from where meadows of edelweiss, field gentians and houseleeks lead down to the Rifugio Contrin. It is a big and interesting building owned by the Italian Army, in a fine setting below the Cima Ombretta at 2931m (9616ft).

A pleasant path climbs through alps then into the usual rockier terrain, past remnants of barbed wire and tin cans, a poignant reminder of the war, to the Passo Cirelle at 2683m (8802ft) and an endless vista of misty mountains. The descent to the Rifugio Fochiade at 1982m (6503ft) allows a last wild jaunt down a steep trail before lunch at the hut. From there the Passo di San Pellegrino at 1919m (6296ft) is just a stroll away.

# JULIAN ALPS, TRIGLAV

*By Ronald Turnbull*

Slovenia isn't quite the real Alps. Nothing even hits the 3000m (9843ft) contour, and the last ice field was wiped out by global warming a few years ago. Rather, the Julian Alps have the atmosphere of an old story. It could be a tale from the Brothers Grimm, illustrated with woodcuts of droopy fir trees, dangling precipices, and deep, green river gorges. Slovenian mountain huts offer abundant soups of bean, cabbage and garlic: if that doesn't sound too tasty, it will once you've walked up there through the droopy firs in a thunderstorm. Slovenian huts have beer, and blankets, and cosy, shapeless slippers. They have green porcelain stoves the size of a camper van, which will dry the thunderstorm out of your breeches ready for

the next thunderstorm tomorrow. And in some ways, the Julian Alps are as comfortable as those sloppy hut slippers. Red paint waymarks lead, every four hours or so, to a mountain hut. The ascent out of the valley is never much more than 1000m (3300ft), and neither is the descent back down again. The rucksack, provided you left behind the unneeded sleeping bag and the spare shoes, is only moderately heavy. Beech trees below, larch and dwarf pine above, shade you from the heat of the sun.

But there is one difference. The slippers may be soft and shapeless: the mountains are not. They rise as limestone towers, pinnacles, and crags that shut out the sky. But the paths go up there anyway, equipped with wire ropes, and iron footholds, so

that ordinary walkers can experience the thrill, normally reserved for serious Alpine climbers, of having a quarter-mile of empty air below our boot-soles.

The star of the Julian Alps is Triglav, the Three-headed One. At 2864m (9396ft) it is the high point of Slovenia, and every Slovenian has a duty to get up it at least once; so, to my mind, should everybody else. It's a rock mountain, with an approach ridge that's about half a metre (20 in) wide with a drop on either side of 1000m (3300ft) or more. The rock is firm and well-trodden,

**ABOVE** *A walker approaches Rodica on the ridge that runs eastward from Črna prst. It gives the trek a long, but otherwise easy, first day.*

and (without thunderstorms) warm and rough to the touch. To make things slightly less scary, there is a wire handrail, with security chains to clip into on the steep bits. And to distract you from the 1000m (3300ft) drop, there is a view across Austria and Italy almost to the Mediterranean.

The Slovenians take their patriotic duties seriously. There are quiet, remote spots in the Julian Alps, but the summit ridge of Triglav is not one of them. Whole families, from grannies to kids, scramble up the fixed wires. The crowd is comforting, in the event that the 1000m (3300ft) drops make you feel at all queasy. And the hold-ups give you time to appreciate the valleys dropping to a haze of forest far below, and mountains rising in jagged lines beyond, right out to the blue horizon.

The summit of Triglav is a busy and friendly place for eating the summit sandwiches. You can try spotting the various nationalities by their equipment. Compared with Eastern Europeans, walkers from the West may feel somewhat over-dressed in waterproofs that are, indeed, waterproof; a bit of rope and a karabiner for not falling off; rucksacks rather than plastic bags.

We were glad enough of our karabiner, though, when our choice of descent path led onto a face of little scree ledges that dropped away vertically, with the hut visible just beyond our toes but still 300m (1000ft) below. It was a place that inspired exhilaration and anxiety in rough balance.

An afternoon up to the hut, and a couple of hours the next morning, will get you to the top of Triglav. But whereas Triglav may be the high point of a trip to the Julian Alps, it is not the whole point. So we came in by a more contemplative way, making full use of the simple but comfortable huts, the forests and the occasional tiny lakes, the less demanding foothills and the well-marked paths. From Bohinjska Bistrica we ascended through forest to Črna prst with its summit hut at 1844m (6050ft).

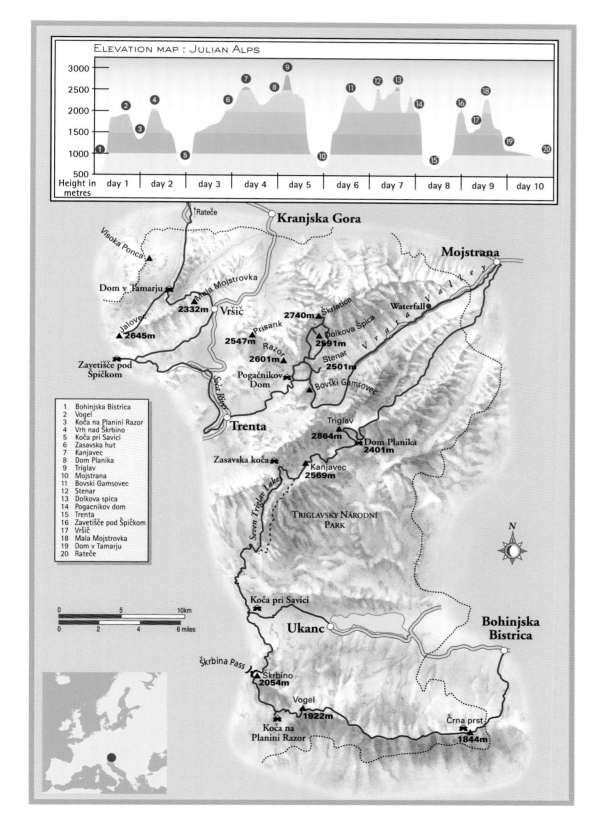

ELEVATION MAP : JULIAN ALPS

1 Bohinjska Bistrica
2 Vogel
3 Koča na Planini Razor
4 Vrh nad Škrbino
5 Koča pri Savici
6 Zasavska hut
7 Kanjavec
8 Dom Planika
9 Triglav
10 Mojstrana
11 Bovski Gamsovec
12 Stenar
13 Dolkova spica
14 Pogacnikov dom
15 Trenta
16 Zavetišče pod Špičkom
17 Vršič
18 Mala Mojstrovka
19 Dom v Tamarju
20 Rateče

ABOVE *The second day crosses Vrh nad Škrbino. From here the peak gets higher, and slightly harder, up to day five's chained scrambling on Triglav.*

across the night, below some particularly pointy summits, a single light gleamed. It was the Pogačnikov Dom, an overnight stop still three days of walking away.

The next night saw us at Dom Planika nestled under the face of Triglav. This hut is huge: we thought we might suffer from altitude sickness just by climbing the four storeys of ladders to our bunk. Its facilities were less impressive. We'd passed the last running water 10 hours earlier. The bathing facilities for 120 guests were in the basement and consisted of a single tap, from which trickled meltwater, funnelled off the roof. The mountain winds would have to keep us sweet.

## SPIRITUAL HIGH POINT

In terms of mountain endeavour, Triglav was the spiritual and geographical high point. Sun-warmed rock, blue distances, and scrambling with rough, grippy rock, chains and wires for protection, and superbly scary drops in all directions.

But real mountain atmosphere has hailstones in it. And equally memorable was the approach day before Triglav over the 2569m (8428ft) Kanjavec, where faded waymarks led to the top of a chain, not recently maintained, which dangled into the mist and disappeared. After Triglav we descended over slippery tree-roots to the village of Mojstrana and returned by the Vrata valley, which has one of those freefall waterfalls you can walk behind. A chained path, less serious than Triglav, but with full packs serious enough, led over Bovški Gamsovec. The name means 'chamois', and indeed we spotted chamois

From there an untechnical but long ridgeline runs west, through dwarf pine and over bare limestone, on paths that are always high (occasionally with wires to assist at short exposed sections). That evening we dropped from Vogel at 1922m (6306ft) to a woodland hut, Koča na Planini Razor.

The next day we chose a slightly serious mountain: the 2054m (6739ft) Vrh nad Škrbino has half an hour of rocky scrambling, mostly protected with chains and occasional metal rungs. Any threat of thunder, or a desire for a quieter life, would have taken us on a path over a pass, called Škrbina, just to the west. The afternoon was a wander through contorted tree-covered limestone; ground torn up, says tradition, by the rootling tusks of

Zlatorog. A well-marked path allowed us to enjoy the effects of that primordial pig, as well as the forest gentians. A descent through a truly beautiful beech wood led to a supply point and huts at Ukanc.

The pretty way up Triglav is by the Valley of the Seven Triglav Lakes. The lakes are very small, but they are surrounded by spruce trees, wild flowers, and decorative mountain huts selling herbal tea. However, in the sky above the treetops hang towers of limestone. And by the top of the valley we were up there with them. Trees give way to a scene of stones rising to a skyline hut, the Zasavska koča, and behind the hut the ground drops 600m (2000ft) into the valley of the Soča River. As night fell the limestone towers turned pink, then black against a greenish sky. Kilometres away

and also ibex in the wild ground leading to Pogačnikov Dom. From this hut, a scrambling day-tour of the 2501m (8205ft) Stenar and Dolkova Spiča could also have taken in the serious, chained ascent of the 2740m (8989ft) Škrlatica.

## FIGHTING GROUND

On our eighth day, bad weather ruled out the classic crossing of the 2601m (8533ft) Razor and Prisank. Instead we descended between dripping pines to a valley obscured behind grey curtains of rain. We wandered the banks of the green-gravelled Soča river, and explored Mlinarica gorge that's so deep and narrow as to almost qualify as caving. Because we'd been seeing scraps of barbed wire and ancient concrete pillboxes, we visited the museum at Trenta (and also because it wasn't raining in there) to discover that this had been a fighting ground of the World War I. Then called the Isonzo, and the border between Austria and Italy, its 12 battles saw half a million people lose their lives.

That day ended with a walk up through scrub and bare limestone with thunder echoing from all directions. The Zavetišče pod Špičkom hut, when we found it, was full of soggy Austrians from under all the various storms; and lightning flickered through the windows all night.

The path out ran along the steep valley wall dodging in and out of forest, or around the sides of high scree hollows. Little black salamanders emerged from underground and posed on pathside boulders, pretending to be something from the age of the dinosaurs. The salamander is, in fact, an amphibian, occupying some biological middle ground between lizard and toad. You see it in those puzzling drawings by Escher, but it's just as odd in real life. The larger Fire Salamander is decorated with bright orange flashes like a 1970s lampshade.

We bundled down an easy peak called Mala Mojstrovka with lightning striking the summit behind us; and arrived at the busy bus stop of Vršič to find the place deserted. Stream washout had blocked the road, and cafés with seats for 50 were occupied by a few wet walkers. The worst storms in many years had taken out our path, leaving

us to clamber across new gravel gullies. The crags dripped, the pine trees thrashed in the wind, and the waterfall filled the valley with its roar.

All night, rain on the roof of Dom v Tamarju hut indicated that our final day wasn't going to be a romp up the 2645m (8678ft) Jalovec, a chain-assisted summit that's a degree more serious than Triglav. Instead, a gravel track ran down the Planica valley and into a wide puddle. We tried the other track, but its puddle was even wider. So we splashed through the puddle and, when we lost the track, found ourselves wading thigh-deep between the trees. A large river that, according to the map, didn't exist at all, emerged from a cave mouth on the opposite side and turned our valley into a warm, greenish lake. Ordinary, over-ground streams came down the slope in a brown froth, with a rattling noise of stones and boulders being carried along their beds in the flow.

Technically speaking, this end of our holiday was a wash-out. So why were we having so much fun? After several hours we saw a deserted ski resort: grey concrete, rain streaming down colourful billboards with vivid skiers and pristine snow. We entered a car park tollbooth, drained our waterproofs, and squeezed out our trousers. Then we went back out into the rain. On the main road, the only traffic was tractors. Standing ankle-deep in water, I practised my Slovenian on a bus driver.

'Kranjska Gora: problema? Ne problema?'

'Problema.'

We set out hitch-hiking and splashing towards the airport.

# HIGH TATRAS

## By Ronald Turnbull

The Carpathians: for most trekkers, the name may mean a rumour of brown bears and perhaps of bandits and vampires. In fact it's the eastern European range that takes over where the Alps leave off, bending through five countries to the Black Sea. Most of the range is tree-covered and, yes, there are bears. But along the border of Poland with Slovakia, the Carpathians become seriously craggy, with granite towers, green lakes, and sharp ridges textured with dwarf pine and boulderfields. This is the Tatras.

With a good path system, a good hut system, and a row of Communist-era spa resorts running along the top of the treeline, this could be a place for a week of high-level walking among spectacular scenery. But this trek reaches further up into that spectacular scenery and clambers about on top of it. It starts in Slovakia, crosses the frontier at the highest point of Poland, and reaches a climax high above the valley of the Polish Lakes. The Orla Perć, or Eagle's Perch, is 5km (3 miles) of granite knife-edge protected by fixed chains.

The trek starts at Ždiar, near the Polish border, for a crossing of the White Tatras (Belianske Tatry). This limestone range is a nature reserve, covered in lush forest and limestone-type wildflowers. But after a shady and scented half-day, you emerge at a pass (Široké sedlo) where everything ahead is jagged granite. Here the well-waymarked paths turn busy; for the Tatras are the only real rock for about 1000km (620 miles) and the Poles, Slovaks and Czechs do enjoy their mountain walking. The path winds through waist-high dwarf pines, and past stony tarns, its junctions marked with twisty-branch signposts. We soon learnt, if we wanted to get to the hut quickly, not to try our few words of Slovakian – for they would prompt a reply in perfect English followed by a friendly and long conversation. And we did want to get to the hut: for the sun was shining and there was a must-do mountain above.

TOP *The hut at the Przedni Staw Polski in the valley of the five Polish lakes, base for the exposed and demanding traverse of the Orla Perć.*

The Slovakian *chata* is whimsically translated as 'cottage' – but the more correct 'mountain hut' is just as misleading. *Chata pri Zelenom plese* (the Cottage by Green Lake) is a multi-storey pinewood palace, with red-checked bedspreads and wide balconies. It has a view across a little lake and several miles of spruce, steeply downhill, and then over the Poprad plains in the direction of Romania. We dumped our gear, and scampered up a boulder path above the lake, a little chain-assisted scrambling, and some exciting ledges to catch the last light on the 2230m (7317ft) Jahňací štit.

The next day follows the Tatranská Magistrála (Tatra master-path) high above the tree line along the southern flank of the range. Muggy haze meant that we saw across the lowlands for only about 10km (6 miles). But we turned up into the mountains for a new sort of scenery: the high Malá Studená dolina (valley). Its boulder floor was dotted with a few random pools, and on all sides rose spiky ridges of bare granite. There seemed to be no way out.

But then the path zigzagged up boulder scree to the bottom of a rock wall and the way out suddenly became all too obvious. A ribbon of brightly coloured climbers lay

like a trailing prayer flag up the face. We'd timed our ascent to the Priečne sedlo (*sedlo* means col) with the early afternoon rush.

The ascent is spectacular even without its decoration of happy wanderers sitting on every ledge, hauling themselves hand-over-hand up the protecting chains, and (those of them that were dogs) peering anxiously out of rucksack tops at the 200m (700ft) drops below. Alongside the chained way was firm rock with good holds, and by diverting onto this we overtook a school outing and some middle-aged ladies ascending on their knees with closed eyes; to reach the tiny notch in the ridge above.

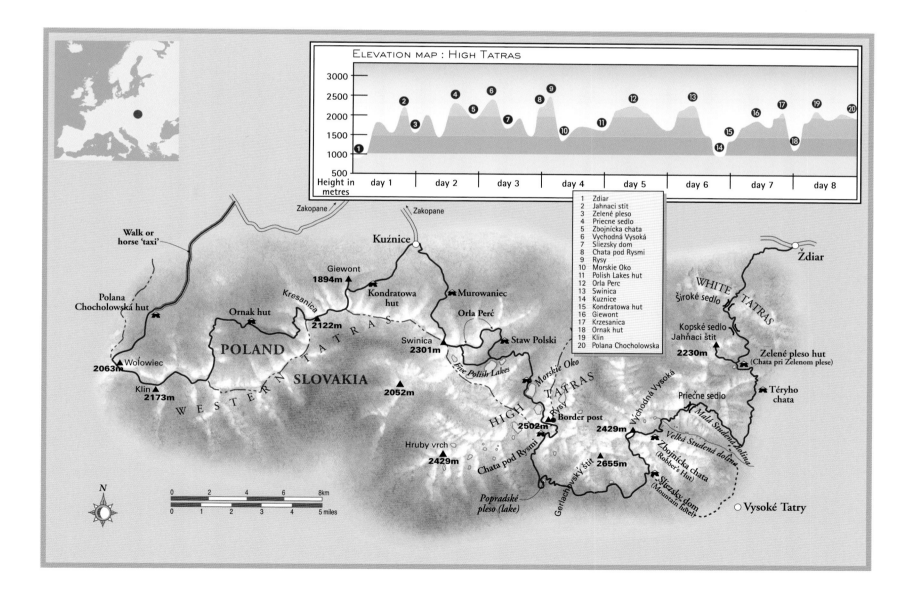

Elevation map: High Tatras

| | Height in metres | day 1 | day 2 | day 3 | day 4 | day 5 | day 6 | day 7 | day 8 |
|---|---|---|---|---|---|---|---|---|---|

1 Zdiar
2 Jahnaci stit
3 Zelené pleso
4 Priecne sedlo
5 Zbojnicka chata
6 Vychodná Vysoká
7 Sliezsky dom
8 Chata pod Rysmi
9 Rysy
10 Morskie Oko
11 Polish Lakes hut
12 Orla Perc
13 Swinica
14 Kuznice
15 Kondratowa hut
16 Giewont
17 Krzesanica
18 Ornak hut
19 Klin
20 Polana Chocholowska

ABOVE *Štrbské pleso (lake), looking up to the High Tatras. Their highest point, Gerlachovský štit, is immediately above the communist-era hotel. It may only be climbed with a guide*

Such crowds are uncommon. After a night at Zbojnícka chata (robbers' hut), you'll probably find yourselves alone again on Východná Vysoká 2429m (7969ft). A little rough scrambling gets you up, and at the top are row upon row of granite skylines one behind the other. The middle of day three should see you at the mountain hotel Sliezsky dom. For members of recognized climbing clubs, or those who have pre-arranged a local guide, this is the leap-off for a day trip up Gerlachovský štit. At 2655m (8711ft) it is Slovakia's high point, reached by a fairly demanding chained scramble.

The high huts of Slovakia are supplied not by helicopter but by human beings. At Popradské pleso (lake) was a pile of coal and a sign promising free tea all evening if we put 5kg (11 lb) of it into our rucksacks and carried it up. But the tea at the Rysy hut really isn't that expensive… Above the Žabie lakes, just below the rocky section with the fixed chains, we passed one of these hauliers, with a pack frame loaded with soft drinks stretching high above his head. When he rested his load on a boulder I asked him what it weighed.

'A small one. Eighty kilos.' (176 lb).

This wasn't a joke. Carrying these loads is a profession, but also a competitive sport. The record for a rocky path with 1000m (3281ft) of ascent is 180kg (397lb).

The Chata pod Rysmi (hut under Rysy) is the last stop in Slovakia. It nestles in a high stony hollow about 200m (700ft) below the summit. The beds are wooden shelves, sometimes occupied by a pair of intimate friends pretending to be a single sleeper. The menu is whatever you want, provided it's garlic soup followed by goulash. Outside, the sanitation is a simple wooden hut with a hole in the floor and stones below: one of Europe's most squalid, but at the same time most splendid, toilets, it stands proud and stinking before a spiky skyline that fades through red and purple into darkness.

## INTERNATIONAL LANGUAGE

The hut's dayroom, later to become an overflow dormitory, was crowded and cheerful. Five different nationalities sat at our table – although there were only four seats. Speech was English and German, and a sort of fallback Slavic that is spoken wherever Poles, Slovaks and Czechs assemble: but alcohol is an international language as the slivovitz passes around.

The summit above boasted a blue Slovak border marker, and a yellow Polish one. Even though both countries joined the European Union in 2004, this is still the only legal border crossing in the entire Tatras, and frontier guards stamp passports during office hours (except during thunderstorms). Although the frontier markers are on the 2499.6m (8201ft) high-point of Poland, the actual summit, a few steps to the south, reaches up to 2502m (8209ft). A rugged path leads down to Morskie Oko, a beautiful tarn whose name means 'Eye of the Sea'. Despite being a freshwater lake at 1395m (4577ft) altitude, it was thought to be fed from the sea by mysterious channels. Its hut was one of the favourite places of the Polish pope

John Paul II. It's a large and busy one. Much to the dismay of trekkers there is even an asphalt track leading to the lake these days, so we hurried around the spur to the Five Polish Lakes.

The Staw Polski hut is delightful at the edge of a small lake, among thickets of dwarf pine. At evening you can wander up the path and see the ibex clattering across the scree. At midday you can lounge on the terrace, listening to the lake waters, enjoying the hot sun and the scent of the pine. It's a place to relax and be very quiet. However, the mountain edge that rises above the dwarf pines and the stones, drives out any calm feelings extremely quickly.

The Orla Perć is a chain-protected way along four high, steep-sided granite peaks. On scree sections the path is made by squared blocks supported on spikes driven into the rubble. But it's mostly bare rock. From the gap between two mountains, ledges lead round out-of-balance bulges until there's lots of drop below, and then the red flashes take you straight up the rock face. There are plenty of holds, including stapled iron rungs. There is an iron chain and, if you're Polish, you simply grab and haul up. We thought this technique inelegant – besides, we'd noticed some of the attachments dangling loose.

At the top you come out of shadows, lie in the sun, and try not to look at the view, which consists of an uncomfortable expanse of empty air. And you wonder how you're going to get down. According to one encouraging fellow in the hut, people at this point get out their mobile phones and call the helicopter. He also told

*High above the Polish lakes, a scrambler demonstrates the inelegant hand-over-hand technique on the chains of Orla Perć*

us that on average, one person a week died on this ridge. He was just trying to make it more exciting for us foreigners – actual mortality rates are less than 20 a year for the whole Polish Tatras.

## GETTING DOWN

Getting down is perfectly easy. There is a ladder, at the foot of which you have to step carefully sideways. Directly below is 500m (1600ft) of space. And then comes another notch, and another clamber up, and a slab down on the left-hand side of it all. The slab has large sloping holds, and its bottom edge is outlined against scrub pine and boulders of the valley floor. 'I like that in mist particularly,' said the chap in the

hut: 'below the bottom edge you see absolutely nothing at all.' All we'd asked him was to translate the menu board…

We had to cross the ridge again, but this time with our packs. And this time not with sun, but in cloud and rain. The 2301m (7549ft) Swinica may be named 'the Pig' but is an easier mountain, with only short sections of chain and iron rungs. And on its ridge, the cloud parted occasionally to show us some particularly sharp sections of the Orla Perć in vignette, like the end-paper of an old mountain manual. We came down out of the mountains in a thunderstorm that sent brown water ankle-deep along the path.

Kuźnice ends the granite of the High Tatras, and the high-scrambling trek. But it is also the start of the Western Tatras. These shale mountains would seem tame after the cragged and sharp-edged granite.

If, however, instead of a high-scrambling route, you have been doing a high-walking route, bypassing the Priečne sedlo and leaving out the day on Orla Perć, you'll be here in five days rather than six. And for high walking, the Western Tatras are magnificent. So resupply at the small shop and continue to the Kondratowa hut. The next day a fairly easy chained scramble visits the airy summit of Giewont, or the Sleeping Knight, at 1894m (6214ft). This summit is small but spectacular; one of Poland's most popular peaks. Quieter paths continue over Kresanica 2122m (6962ft) to the woodland Ornak hut. A final day of high narrow ridges, again with good paths, leads over the 2172m (7126ft) Klin and Wołowiec to the Polana Chochołowska hut.

# KUNGSLEDEN

*By Chris Townsend*

L apland in northern Sweden is a land of rugged mountains; 1000km (600 miles) of them running north-wards across the Arctic Circle and rising to 2117m (6946ft) on Kebnekaise, the highest mountain in Sweden and Arctic Scandi-navia. These ancient mountains are geologically linked to the Scottish High-lands and the Appalachian Mountains of North America, all once part of the huge Caledonian Mountain chain. It split apart some 65 million years ago, and the gap was filled by the Atlantic Ocean. Arctic tundra sweeps round the mountains and over the lower summits while the valleys are filled with a boreal forest of birch and pine. The whole area is a huge unspoilt wilderness, the largest by far left in Western Europe.

The Kungsleden, the King's Trail, winds through this wild land from south to north, passing through four national parks – Pieljekaise, Sarek, Stora Sjöfallets and Abisko – as well as Vindelfjällens nature reserve, at 4800km² (1853 square miles) the largest in Europe. The Kungsleden was cre-ated by the Swedish Touring Association (Svenska Turistföreningen, or STF) in the early years of the 20th century after the railway line reached Abisko at the northern end of the trail. The original route went from Abisko to Kvikkjokk, which is still by far the most popular section, and was later extended south to Hemavan.

The trail is marked with cairns or large upright stones, each topped with red paint. In places the trail runs through pairs of these stones, making an avenue that you feel ought to lead to a giant megalithic monument, though one never appears. In winter and spring red crosses on tall poles or tree branches mark the line of the trail through the snow, across frozen lakes and rivers. In summer the deeper rivers are bridged, but the lakes have to be crossed, either by rowing yourself across in the boat provided or on the small ferries run by local people. These usually run once or twice a day and there is a small charge. Rowing across requires some skill – the

**ABOVE** *There are hikers' huts all along the Kungsleden, like these in the magnificent Tjäktja valley below the highest mountains in Sweden.*

lakes can be several kilometres wide and are often windswept, making the water choppy. If in doubt, pay the ferryman. When using a rowing boat note that there are three boats for each crossing and that there must be at least one on each side to ensure availability to walkers coming from either direction. That means that if there's only one boat you should row across, then row back towing another boat to leave at your start point, and then row across

again. At high points on the trail there are basic wind shelters for protection from the weather. Boggy sections of the trail have duckboards laid across them.

Crossing the grain of the land, the trail undulates as it climbs over high ridges and passes then descends back down into forest and lake-filled valleys. This makes for a great deal of ascent, but the reward is a variety of scenery, from deep forest to arctic tundra.

## FIRST WILDERNESS SITE

In the south, the Kungsleden starts in the little ski resort of Hemavan, a rather inauspicious beginning among ski tows and bare pistes. However, the trail soon crosses an open hillside and descends gently into the long Syterskalet valley, with steep dark hills rising up on both sides. This is an exhilarating place to be in a storm: the scenery dramatic and mysterious with hints of big mountains in the swirling mists. After 11km (7 miles) the first STF lodge appears, little Viterskalet. However, I pitched my tent right at the head of Syterskalet, with a view straight back down the valley; the first of many wilderness sites along the Kungsleden. Even in the rain I wouldn't have swapped it for a night in a lodge.

Beyond Syterskalet the trail winds on through the Vindelfjällen nature reserve, crossing the marshy end of Tärnasjön lake by way of long board-walks and twisting bridges, slipping through dense green birch woods and traversing open, lake-dotted tundra. There are four more lodges in this initial section – Syter, Tärnasjö, Serve and Aigert. After 70km (43 miles) the trail reaches the small village of Ammarnäs.

After Ammarnäs there are no lodges on the 67km (42 mile) section to the next village, Adolfström, necessitating either camping or a very, very long day of hiking. From Ammarnäs the Kungsleden climbs on to the rolling tundra of Bjorkfjället where there are small lakes and long whale-backed hills edged with small broken crags. Dwarf birch dots the ground. This is empty country, a wide open landscape under a big expansive sky. Any hills are distant lines on the horizon. It's the loneliest part of the Kungsleden. I only met a couple of walkers on the whole 180km (112 mile) stretch between Ammarnäs and Kvikkjokk. I didn't mind. It was good to be alone in the vastness. Solitude is best if you want to see wildlife too. Reindeer are abundant in places, though they aren't really wild, all of them belonging to the Sami people. There are many birds including long-tailed skuas, golden eagles, capercaillie, willow grouse, ptarmigan and bluethroat. A pair of light-weight binoculars is worth carrying by anyone interested in wildlife.

From the high tundra the trail descends through birch woods and the occasional pines to reach the hamlet of Adolfström, where there is a restaurant, a store and cabins to rent, and then climbs back up through forest to Lutaure lake and Pielje-kaise National Park, which mainly consists of unspoilt mountain birch forest. There is one cabin for walkers in the park, Pielje-stugan, with gas lighting and a wood stove. However, since it is only 22km (14 miles) from Adolfström to the next hamlet, Jåkkvik, it is not essential. The next section of 99km (61-mile) is the longest on the

tortuous as the little open boat twists around marshy promontories on Riebnes lake. A 340m (1115ft) climb then leads through woods and across a lake-strewn basin to the wide, high Barturte ridge. Once across this exposed plateau a descent leads to more forest walking below the shattered, disintegrating, black rock face of Kabtapakte. There are bridges across the end of Tjeggelvas lake and a final ferry across Saggat to tiny Kvikkjokk on the wild Kamajåkkå river, at 350m (1148ft) the lowest point on the Kungsleden and roughly halfway along the trail. Kvikkjokk is very remote, situated at the end of a 40km (25 mile) one-way road, but there is a bus service, a store and also the Kvikkjokk Fjällstation, the first STF accommodation since Ammarnäs. There are STF lodges all the way to the finish now. Kvikkjokk is an old settlement, founded in the 1600s when silver was discovered nearby.

On the descent to Saggat lake the peaks of Sarek National Park, higher and sharper than the flat-topped tundra hills along the route so far, can be seen to the north, lifting the heart and inspiring you to keep going. The best really is still to come. The scenery north of Kvikkjokk is more impressive than that further south with real glacier-clad mountains replacing the rounded hills. Immediately north of Kvikkjokk the trail cuts through the edge of Sarek, a wild and beautiful area worthy of extended exploration.

TOP *The Kungsleden crosses many long lakes. Here on Teusajaure rowing boats are supplied for hikers. There are also ferries across the lakes for those not confident about their rowing skills.*

ABOVE *Tjäktjavagge is a beautiful upland valley between splendid mountains, including Kebnekaise, the highest peak in Sweden. The trail leads up Tjäktjavagge to a narrow pass at its head.*

Kungsleden without any STF lodges, although there are a few tiny shelters.

At Jåkkvik the first ferry on the route takes you on a circuitous route across Hornavan lake. The next big lake comes after only a few hours and an ascent and descent across the broad southeast ridge of Riebnekaise, during which you cross the invisible, but symbolic and emotive, Arctic Circle. It is marked by a crude wooden sign labelled Polecirclen. You are now truly in the arctic. The next lake crossing is again

## HEART OF THE MOUNTAINS

From Kvikkjokk gentle birch and pine wood walking leads past Stuor-Tata and

Stabtjakjaure lakes to the small Pårte lodge. Rugged walking lies ahead as the trail climbs through rockier terrain and passes between two craggy knolls called Faunåive and Huornatj to traverse open hillside with views to distant peaks. As the trail drops back into the trees the scene is dominated by the steep rock wall of Tjakkeli rising to the north.

Soon you reach Laitaure lake where a ferry or a rowing boat is needed to cross to Aktse lodge on the far side. There is a small shelter at the lake if you have to wait for the ferry during inclement weather. At Aktse it is worth taking a day off to make the ascent of the 1179m (3868ft) Skierfe, a splendid viewpoint perched right on the edge of the cliffs. It overlooks the wide marshy Rapadalen valley, from where you can look into the heart of the Sarek mountains.

There are also good views of Sarek from the mountain shoulder of Njunjes, which you cross after leaving Aktse. After descending to Sitojaure lake you again have to wait for the ferry or row across to the lodge of the same name.

A fine section of trail lies beyond Sitojaure as it runs high on the side of the wild valley of Autsutvagge with the cliffs of Sjäksjo rising above you. You leave the valley to descend into birch woods before reaching the large Saltoluokta Fjällstation on the shores of long Langas lake. A large ferry runs from Saltoluokta across Langas. On the far side a major road cuts through the wilds, the only one encountered on the whole route. The Kungsleden is broken here and you need to catch a bus for the 25km (15 miles) to Vakkotavare lodge to the west. To make up for the ease of the

**ABOVE** *Reindeer range throughout northern Sweden and are likely to be seen by hikers. They are semi-wild and are owned by the Sami people.*

bus journey there's a steep climb from Vakkotavare to cross a high ridge from which the trail descends to the lovely Teusajaure lake, crossed by rowing boat or ferry to the eponymous lodge.

Beyond Teusajaure steep slopes begin to close in around the trail as it reaches the beautiful 32km (20 mile) valley of Tjäktjavagge. Mountains of every shape and size – spires, domes, ridges, rock walls, snow slopes, and glaciers – lie to either side. There are two lodges in Tjäktjavagge, Singi and Sälka. From the first an ascent can be made of Kebnekaise, which can be seen from the Kungsleden. This is a worthwhile detour and no more than a steep, rough walk. The views from the tiny, exposed summit are superb.

You leave Tjäktjavagge by going up the narrow, windswept, Tjäktja pass, at 1150m

(3773ft) the highest point on the Kungsleden. From here the trail descends to the Tjäktja lodge and then into the Alisvaggi valley, which has the Alesgätno river meandering through it, and Alesjaure lodge.

From this lodge the Kungsleden winds past three scenic lakes and then descends again into narrow Gardenvaggi valley, hemmed in by steep Kartinvare and Siellanjunnji. The Kungsleden leaves the high mountains at this point and the path continues descending past the last lodge, Abiskojaure, before reaching Abisko National Park. A final relaxing walk through glorious birch woods beside the wide Abiskojåkka river leads to the trail's end in Abisko on the shores of the huge Torneträsk lake. The comfortable Abisko Fjällstation is a fine place to celebrate your completion of a magnificent trail.

# NORTH PINDOS – ANCIENT MULE PATHS

*By Judy Armstrong*

Forming the central spine of mainland Greece, the Pindos mountains stretch southward from Mount Grammos on the northwest border with Albania to the Gulf of Corinth. From above, this highland range resembles an extravagantly wrinkled tablecloth dotted with stone villages, wooded forest, limestone towers, deep gorges, and some of Greece's highest mountains. In the days before roads were built, the mountains were so remote that even the Ottoman tax collectors avoided the region!

Within the vast tracts of the Pindos, the best-known area for trekking is in the north, in the district of Zagoria, where trails, including several international long-distance paths, have been waymarked.

Zagoria, which directly translates as 'the place behind the mountains', has been inhabited since the ninth century BC. Because of its early isolation, it became wealthy and autonomous, a situation that prevailed until the 20th century, when wars and economic migration caused the decline of many villages.

Today, a sensitive approach to ecotourism is helping to revive many villages, yet the area remains remote. In 1990 the Vikos National Park was created within the Pindos range. It is home to European bear, wild boar, lynx and wolves, but these animals are elusive and rarely seen.

A six-day trek takes in the best parts of the North Pindos, including a breathtaking walk down the world's deepest gorge and exploring an alpine plateau – which can provide more excitement than you bargained for! Two ethnic groups, the Vlachs and the Sarakatsani, traditionally graze their sheep on the high mountain meadows; their dogs are large and loud – and trained to protect their flocks at all costs.

The trek can be reduced to four days if ascents of the Gamila and Astraka peaks and the walk to the historical village of Vradheto are excluded.

Distances each day are short so that time can be spent absorbing the wonderful

**ABOVE** *Arched Zagorian bridges, which date primarily from the 18th and 19th centuries, are a visual delight in this region.*

views and dozing in the shade. This leaves plenty of scope for side excursions, and for sampling the menus of the village tavernas. Each village has one or two guesthouses which offer, besides their excellent food, friendly hospitality (a Greek-English phrasebook will be a useful addition to your luggage).

The best starting point for this trek is the timeless village of Vitsa or its neighbour, Monodendri. Like most Zagorian villages, they are built almost entirely of local stone: the softer white rock comes from quarries, the harder black stone from rivers.

## SECRET CAVES

Monodendri, on the lip of the Vikos gorge, is home to the uninhabited monastery of Ayias Paraskevis and secret caves where hermits and persecuted Christians laid low in centuries past. Today, the monastery offers both serenity and wide-angle views into the gorge. The descent into Vikos gorge passes a Guinness Book of Records sign informing trekkers that this 'deepest gorge in the world', is 980m (3215ft) deep and 1650m (5414ft) wide. The track down to and along the gorge was greatly improved in 1998 and waymarked lavishly; it is now virtually impossible to get lost. It is delightful walking through maple and walnut woodland, along tracks fringed with wild thyme, and over gigantic boulders on dry sections of the Voidhomatis riverbed. Wildflowers bloom, cicadas rasp and tortoises amble slowly across the track. As the gorge sweeps around bends, views change constantly, with skyward-soaring cliffs.

## COBBLED MULE TRACKS

The climb to Vikos village (called Vitsiko on some maps) follows the switchbacks of an ancient *kalderimi*, or cobbled mule track, up the gorge side. Once the sole domain of mules and their drivers, the maintenance of these amazing tracks now benefits from European Union grants.

The village of Vikos is perched on a breeze-cooled saddle, with sweeping panoramas on all sides. Watching the sun set outside the Pension Vikos guesthouse, eating baked feta cheese and rich meatballs washed down with local Mythos beer, is paradise indeed.

The next day's route follows the hairpin bends of the *kalderimi* on its way to the village of Mikro Papingo and twists back to the river. It passes a white chapel before reaching the Voidhomatis spring. Here, ice-cold water takes a week to drain 1300m

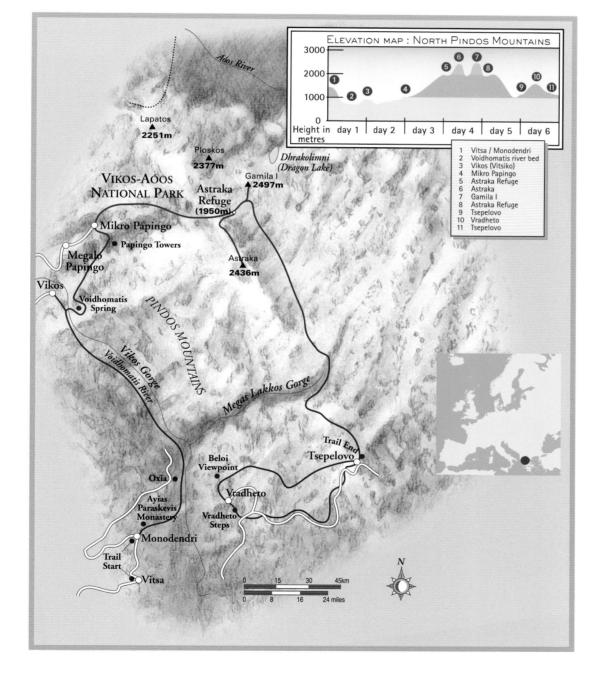

(4265ft) through the cliffs. Once over the river, the climb up to Mikro Papingo is steady for about two hours, with far-reaching views and glimpses of caves. Wild strawberries grow on banks and green lizards sunbathe on pebbles.

Nearer the village, your eyes are drawn upward to the Pirgi, or Papingo Towers, which loom like giants over the track. Like most of the Zagorian villages, Mikro (small) Papingo and its sister Megalo (big) Papingo, have the status of protected traditional communities, meaning that their architectural integrity should be maintained. This is certainly true in Mikro Papingo, with its narrow cobbled lanes, tightly packed stone houses and stone-flag roofs. Walking from here to Megalo over the old Zagorian arched bridge, an architectural delight in a limestone gorge, includes an opportunity to swim in the deep, natural pools of the river. Back at the Pension Dias, a very comfortable, if quirky, guesthouse, you can eat marinated olives and drink local white wine, watching the village goats being herded home for the night along quiet, cobbled streets.

On day three, the morning's climb from Mikro Papingo soon moves above the tree line, with rural Greece spread below. The Astraka cliffs, striped with snow gullies well into June, dominate the view. It's a three- or four-hour hike up to the Astraka Refuge, a white building on a windy pass at 1950m (6397ft). The refuge, owned by the Hellenic Alpine Club, was extensively renovated in 2004 and offers dormitory accommodation in magnificent surroundings. From the terrace a path runs down a bouldered bank, skirts a pond and huts used by shepherds in summer, crosses an alpine meadow, then climbs to Dhrakolimni – 'dragon lake'. According to legend a guardian dragon lives in its bottomless depths. Vivid blue gentian flowers grow on the lakeshore, and the surrounding cliffs are reflected in the cold, deep water.

## REMOTE AND TIMELESS

Next day there is some real height gain, up the 2497m (8192ft) Gamila I or the 2436m (7992ft) Astraka peak. Of the several approaches to Gamila, the shortest follows a thin trail across a limestone plateau at the

ABOVE *Long-legged mountain sheep graze on the high plateau near Astraka Refuge. They are protected by large, loud dogs. Hikers beware!*

foot of the Astraka cliffs. The mountains visible on the left are the 2377m (7799ft) Ploskos, Gamila I and Gamila II. A lone tree shows where to turn left into a shallow valley which leads up to Gamila I. A steady hike up its broad flank leads to the flat, rocky summit, with views across the Aóos River valley to the 2637m (8651ft) Mount Smolikas, the second highest in Greece.

Climbing Astraka involves backtracking from the huts toward Papingo, then weaving left around the cliff edges while following cairns to the summit. The wilderness appears enormous, remote and timeless – an indication of the extent of Greece's uninhabitable land.

Setting out on the fifth day from the Astraka Refuge, the trail passes Gamila, skirts little lakes, crosses alpine meadows and files down bands of limestone rock. At this point the upper reaches of the Megas Lakkos gorge are visible and the path drops into the gorge. It then climbs up the left bank, under steep cliffs and past banks of wild iris. It looks as though eagles should live here – and apparently they do. Well waymarked, the path climbs out of the gorge when the walls narrow in anticipation of its meeting the Vikos gorge. The path then crosses grassy hilltops and streambeds before descending a meadow to the village of Tsepelovo. This is a stone enclave on the edge of the mountains, snowbound in winter and a cool haven in summer. Men gather in the main square to play backgammon, while the women stay indoors. Pension Alexis Gouris is a hub for visitors to Tspelevo, with its balconies, courtyard and friendly welcome.

The final day's walk to the village of Vradheto and back starts on a poorly maintained *kalderimi* leading up the right side of a deep ravine. It is the old route to the village which, until recently, was only accessible on foot. The climb is steep, through limestone bands and across grassy bowls. It arrives, suddenly, on a shiny new road – only the final 4km (2½ miles) of the ancient track to Vradheto has been closed off. Luckily, a track leaves this road, heading for the Beloi viewpoint over the pancake rock stacks of the Vikos gorge. With Monodendri behind your left shoulder, you can look along the length of the gorge, Vikos village faintly represented as a

clutch of grey buildings. The scale is terrific and it's a treat to see the entire route. Vradheto itself, just half an hour away, is a small village with a taverna. It is famed for a *kalderimi* called the Vradheto Steps. This plunges through a rock palisade in a series of twists and turns to a Zagorian bridge – and the modern road back to Tsepelovo.

LEFT *The rugged Astraka cliffs soar skyward as walkers climb toward a windy pass and the welcome sight of Astraka Refuge.*

BELOW *The Vradheto Steps are a beautiful example of kalderimi, the cobbled mule tracks that wind through the Pindos region.*

# NORTH AMERICA

BY JACK JACKSON

Long-distance, self-guided walking and backpacking may have started in Europe, but North America is where it grew up. With conditions varying from the heat of the deserts through canyons and high mountains to some of the worst weather in the world in the far north, North America has it all. With the widest possible range of trails, you can find a trek with a suitable climate at any time of year. Vast areas of North America are preserved as national parks. The great diversity of landscapes in the west of the US is thought by many to be some of the most spectacular in the world.

**Legend**

■ Major city    ⬤ Featured Trek

● City    - - - International Boundary

0             1000 km

0         500 miles

RUSSIA

Cape Lisburne

Bering Strait

Arctic Circle

*Beaufort Sea*

Point Barrow

Prince Patrick Island

Melville Island

Banks Island

Cape Bathurst

North Magnetic Pole

Parry Islands

Devon Island

Somerset Island

**(Greenland)**

Kong Frederik VI Kyst

*Greenland Sea*

Nuuk (Godthåb)

Nunap Isua (Kap Farvel)

*Baffin Bay*

Prince of Wales Island

Boothia Peninsula

Baffin Island

*Davis Strait*

**Alaska**
(U.S.A.)

Brooks Range

*Alaska Range*

Anchorage

*Gulf of Alaska*

ALASKA ON FOOT

Mackenzie Mountains

Victoria Island

Melville Peninsula

*Foxe Basin*

Cape Chidley

*Labrador Sea*

Cape Bauld

Alexander Archipelago

Queen Charlotte Islands

*Coast Mountains*

*Rocky Mountains*

*Great Plains*

Southampton Island

*Hudson Strait*

*Peninsule d'Ungava*

Newfoundland

**CANADA**

*Hudson Bay*

Labrador

Belcher Islands

Cape Breton Island

Île d'Anticosti

*Gulf of St. Lawrence*

Fraser Plateau

CONTINENTAL DIVIDE TRAIL

Edmonton

Calgary

Saskatoon

Regina

Winnipeg

James Bay

Vancouver Island

**Vancouver**

**Seattle**

Victoria

Tacoma

Olympia

Spokane

Duluth

Quebec

**Montreal**

Halifax

**Portland**

Salem

SAWTOOTH TRAVERSE

Boise

St. Paul

**Minneapolis**

**Milwaukee**

Madison

**OTTAWA**

**Toronto**

Rochester

Mt. Albany

**Boston**

Hartford

Providence

Kitchener

Grand Rapids

Flint

London

Buffalo

Erie

Newark

**New York**

JOHN MUIR TRAIL

**Sacramento**

Oakland

**San Francisco**

Reno

Carson City

**Salt Lake City**

Great Basin

HIGHLINE TRAIL

Cheyenne

*Great Plains*

Ohama

Des Moines

**Chicago**

Toledo

Gary

**Detroit**

**Cleveland**

Youngstown

**Pittsburgh**

**Philadelphia**

**Baltimore**

Trenton

*Sierra Nevada*

EVOLUTION LOOP

**Denver**

Aurora

Lincoln

Peoria

**Indianapolis**

**Columbus**

**Cincinnati**

Frankfort

Charleston

Richmond

**WASHINGTON**

Las Vegas

**UNITED STATES**

Colorado Springs

Pueblo

Topeka

**Kansas City**

**Saint Louis**

Springfield

Louisville

Knoxville

**Norfolk**

Bakersfield

Albuquerque

**Los Angeles**

**San Diego**

Tijuana

Mexicali

**Phoenix**

Tucson

Amarillo

**Oklahoma City**

Tulsa

**Wichita**

**Nashville**

**Memphis**

Chattanooga

Huntsville

**Charlotte**

Greensboro

Raleigh

Columbia

Cape Fear

GRAND CANYON

El Paso

Ciudad Juárez

**Fort Worth**

**Dallas**

Waco

Shreveport

Jackson

Birmingham

**Atlanta**

Macon

Montgomery

Mobile

Baton Rouge

APPALACHIAN TRAIL

*Appalachian Mts.*

**ATLANTIC OCEAN**

Bermuda Islands (U.K.)

Isla Guadalupe (Mex.)

Hermosillo

Ciudad Obregón

**Chihuahua**

Austin

**San Antonio**

**Houston**

Beaumont

**New Orleans**

Corpus Christi

**Orlando**

**Tampa**

St. Petersburg

West Palm Beach

**Fort Lauderdale**

**Miami**

Indias Occidentales (West Indies)

Tropic of Cancer

*Baja California*

Los Mochis

Torreón

Culiacán

Durango

Monclova

Nuevo Laredo

Reynosa

Matamoros

*Gulf of Mexico*

**Monterrey**

NASSAU

**THE BAHAMAS**

Turks and Caicos Islands (U.K.)

**DOMINICAN REPUBLIC**

*Sierra Madre Occidental*

*Golfo de California*

Cabo San Lucas

Mazatlán

**MEXICO**

Ciudad Victoria

Ciudad Madero

**Tampico**

Tropic of Cancer

**LA HABANA**

Marianao

Matanzas

**CUBA**

Pinar del Río

Cienfuegos

Camagüey

Holguín

Santiago

Puerto Rico (U.S.A.)

Aguascalientes

San Luis Potosí

Tepic

**León**

Irapuato

**Guadalajara**

*Sierra Madre Oriental*

Mérida

Cancún

Cayman Islands (U.K.)

Bayamo

Guantánamo

Santiago de Cuba

**PORT-AU-PRINCE**

**SANTO DOMINGO**

Islas Revillagigedo (Mex.)

**MÉXICO**

**Puebla**

Veracruz

Campeche

**Yucatan Peninsula**

**HAITI**

**KINGSTON**

**JAMAICA**

Antillas Mayores (Greater Antilles)

Uruapan

**Toluca**

Cuernavaca

Orizaba

Minatitlán

Coatzacoalcos

Villahermosa

**BELIZE**

**BELMOPAN**

*Caribbean Sea*

Acapulco

Oaxaca

Istmo de Tehuantepec

Tuxtla Gutiérrez

**GUATEMALA**

San Pedro Sula

**HONDURAS**

**TEGUCIGALPA**

Punta Gallinas

Alaska is one of the world's great wildernesses. With 5000 glaciers and large areas with no habitation, its total area is over a million square kilometres (386,100 square miles), yet there are only about 500,000 permanent residents. It is by far the largest state in the US, and includes vast, empty tundra, high mountains, glaciers, rivers, lakes and forests. Some trails are open to various kinds of activity including mechanized transport while others, or parts of others, especially the National Scenic Trails, are dedicated to travel on foot. Some trails have huts at suitable intervals along the way. Many of the backpacking trails are so long that they traverse many states and take months to complete. It is rare for trekkers to cover the longer trails in one go: they either trek the routes in sections or pick out bits that are considered exceptional. Backpackers should be able to manage shorter sections and then move out to the nearest town, but for longer sections they will have to arrange fresh supplies along the way.

Supplies can be addressed to oneself care of a nearby post office en route with a note on the outside of the package explaining that the post-person should hold onto it for you. However, getting from the trail to a town and back again may add days to the route. Alternatively, there are companies that resupply backpackers with fresh food etc., at convenient locations on popular trails. Some will provide a solar shower as well as carrying out your garbage and surplus gear and mailing any surplus gear, letters and exposed film back to your home.

In Canada, they are putting together a Trans Canada Trail, which will be the longest trail in the world when it is completed.

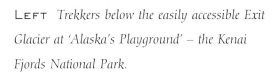

**LEFT** *Trekkers below the easily accessible Exit Glacier at 'Alaska's Playground' – the Kenai Fjords National Park.*

**PREVIOUS PAGE LEFT** *A trekker surveys the Bob Marshall Wilderness, Montana – often referred to as the crown jewel of America's wilderness areas.*

**PREVIOUS PAGE RIGHT** *A close shot of rhododendrons in bloom.*

The Trans Canada Trail is a registered charity, which raises funds for construction and negotiates rights of way for a recreational trail that will wind through every province in Canada. Individual Canadians 'symbolically' purchase metres of the trail and the purchaser's name, or the name of anyone that they designate, is inscribed in one of many distinctive Trail Pavilions along the route. There will be over 2000 bilingual information panels featuring topics on local flora, fauna or geography. Canadian Military Engineers are building bridges and various organizations have donated land including former rail routes.

In the US, the non-profit North Country Trail Association is working in partnership with the National Park Service to build, maintain, and promote the North Country National Scenic Trail. When complete this will be the longest off-road walking trail in the country.

There are a few problems that trekkers would not normally consider for such a destination so you need to check up on these before you go:

• *Giardia lamblia*, which causes Giardiasis (Beaver Fever) and cryptosporidia, are present in most American water supplies. Both cause diarrhoea so treat all water taken from wilderness sources before ingesting it – either with chlorine or, better still, iodine in combination with a water filter, or boil it.

• If you trek through brushy vegetation, you can be bitten by ticks, which can spread a number of diseases, including Lyme Disease, Rocky Mountain Spotted Fever, Relapsing Fever, and Colorado Tick Fever. Peak infection times are in the spring and summer during the nymph portion of the tick's two-year life cycle. The most effective way to combat tick-borne diseases is to take measures to prevent them from attaching themselves to your body. And learn how to remove a tick if it does attach itself to your body.

• Poison ivy, poison oak, and poison sumac can cause an allergic reaction (a red, itchy rash) on contact with the oily resin in these native American plants. The urushiol resin remains stable in dead or dried plants, so they are equally dangerous in winter or summer. The resin can be carried by smoke and infect the lungs if the plant is burned. There are treatments, but it is best to learn to identify the plants and avoid them.

• Mosquitoes can be a major problem in the north and bears can be a problem in some areas so you have to stay alert and follow local instructions on making a noise, cooking and storing food.

## FINDING THE WAY

The first US long-distance trail, Vermont's Long Trail, and the Appalachian Trail were initially blazed (waymarked) by cutting marks on trees, but these cuts healed quickly. Also, when the Appalachian Trail first opened much of it was on private land and roads. A less destructive waymark for trails was required. Various markers from stone cairns to plastic panels were tried, but many were vandalized or taken as souvenirs so painted blazes or waymarks were adopted, since they are easy to maintain. Painted blazes come in various geometric shapes and colours so that where trails cross each other, a given trail can be easily distinguished. Blazes in the US do not incorporate words.

**ABOVE** *The John Muir Trail passes the 181m (594ft) Nevada Fall, which is itself dwarfed by Liberty Cap in this view from Glacier Point, Yosemite National Park, California.*

# CONTINENTAL DIVIDE TRAIL

*By Chris Townsend*

The concept of the Continental Divide Trail (CDT) is of a trail stretching all the way down the watershed of the USA from Canada to Mexico. About 5000km (3100 miles) long (rerouting and new trail sections change the exact length every year), the CDT takes in a great sweep of the American West. It encompasses the dark, remote conifer forests and dramatic mountains of the Northern Rockies, then runs through the desert heart of Wyoming to the rolling heights of the Colorado Rockies and the multi-coloured desert mesas of New Mexico. A difference of nearly 20 degrees in latitude between the northern and southern trailheads results in a noticeable difference in climate and ecosystems. In Montana the

timber line is 2700m (8800ft), in New Mexico it is 3600m (11,800ft). Most of the trail is above 2000m (6500ft) with the highest section in Colorado, where it lies above 3000m (10,000ft) for many miles. Much of the route lies in pristine wilderness, but it also passes through ranch land, logging and mining areas and Indian reservations. Along the way much history unfolds, from the tracks of westbound wagon trains on the Oregon Trail in Wyoming to Anasazi ruins and Mogollon cliff dwellings in New Mexico.

The first Europeans to cross the northern part of the Divide were Meriwether Lewis and William Clark in 1805 on their famous expedition across the continent to the Pacific Ocean. The southern Divide was reached much earlier – Spanish explorers

left inscriptions in the soft sandstone of El Morro (Inscription Rock, New Mexico) in the 1500s. The length and rugged, remote nature of much of the terrain make a through-hike of the CDT a major undertaking. Snow is likely in the mountains at some point – southbound trekkers will probably have to deal with it at the start in Glacier National Park and possibly again in southern Colorado where those heading northwards are even more likely to encounter snow. Northbound trekkers also have to hope they can make it through the

TOP *The Highland Mary Lakes lie just below the Continental Divide in the Weminuche Wilderness, the largest in Colorado.*

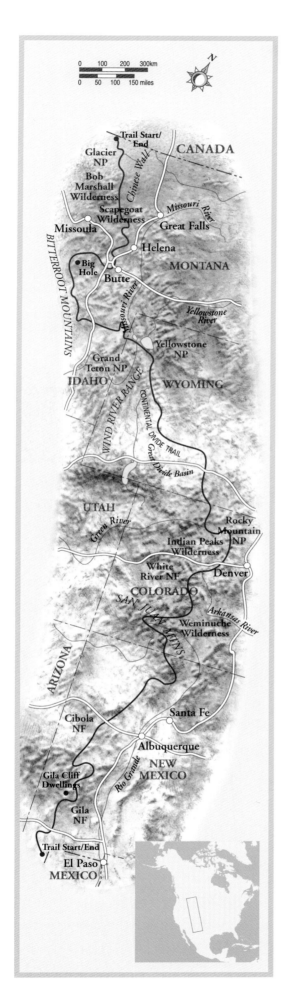

Northern Rockies before the autumn snows set in. Where to start is a key question. Northbound hikers have the easy, fairly flat terrain of New Mexico first while those heading south start in some of the most rugged terrain along the whole trail. However, New Mexico can be hiked late in the year, unlike the Northern Rockies. Overall, walking south is probably the easier direction. Jim Wolf's excellent guidebooks describe the route this way. It is also the direction I took and describe here.

## GLACIER NATIONAL PARK

The northern terminus of the CDT is on the Canadian border in Glacier National Park; a very rugged, spectacular part of the Northern Rockies where snow lies much of the year and grizzly bears roam the wilderness. The trail here runs high on steep mountain slopes, below the jagged crest of the Divide itself. South of Glacier the CDT enters the largest roadless area in the USA outside Alaska, where it winds and twists through the Bob Marshall and Scapegoat Wilderness Areas. In the former, named for one of the great pioneers of wilderness preservation, the trail runs below the impressive Chinese Wall, a great limestone cliff that stretches for mile after mile, towering 300m (1000 feet) above the forest. Most of the walking here is in woods and there are many creek fords, which can be difficult and potentially dangerous early in the season when the spring thaw of the snow from the previous winter is still coming down. The Scapegoat Wilderness is drier and more open and allows easier progress.

South of the wilderness areas the terrain

**ABOVE** *Magnificent symbols of the wilderness, grizzly bears inhabit the Northern Rockies, especially Glacier and Yellowstone national parks.*

is gentler and in central Montana the trail often runs along the Divide itself, following the crest of a line of rounded hills. Once past the old copper mining town of Butte the CDT changes direction and heads west as it begins a loop around the Big Hole, the westernmost valley of the huge Mississippi-Missouri river system. Here the landscape changes as the trail enters the beautiful alpine country of the Anaconda-Pintler Wilderness with its many scenic timber-line lakes.

The route turns back south at Lost Trail Pass, on the border with Idaho, where Lewis and Clark crossed the Divide. The next section through the splendid Bitterroot Mountains is tough and resupply points are far apart and a long way from the trail, but the scenic rewards are great in this

pristine wilderness with its alpine peaks, crystal-clear lakes and flower meadows.

The terrain eases off as the route turns eastwards, following the Divide across rolling hills grazed by large herds of cattle. The grassland eventually gives way to the Centennial Mountains, a sloping tableland of sedimentary rock cliffs, meadows and forest groves.

Beyond the Centennials the trail reaches Wyoming and the world-famous Yellowstone, the first-ever national park. Here the route leads through gently undulating lodgepole pine forest where bubbling hot pools, geysers and other volcanic thermal features add surprise and interest to the walk.

The landscape becomes more exciting as Yellowstone is left for the Teton Wilderness, a region of deep, glaciated valleys rimmed by massive, brightly coloured cliffs. A highlight here is the Parting of the Waters, where small North Two Ocean Creek splits, the eastern branch running some 5600km (3500 miles) to the Atlantic Ocean and the western branch 2200km (1350 miles) to the Pacific. Higher mountains are then reached in the magnificent Wind River Range, the final glorious flourish of the Northern Rockies, where the trail lies mostly above 3050m (10,000 feet).

## ROCKIES FAUNA AND FLORA

In the Montana and Wyoming Rockies the trail is usually high in the mountains, running through montane and subalpine zones. Below the timber line there are huge coniferous forests where lodgepole pine dominates, with stands of massive Douglas fir in shady places. As you approach the timber line, the

ABOVE *Aspen grow at lower levels of the Rockies, giving spectacular autumn colours.*

forest consists mostly of Engelmann spruce, subalpine fir and the occasional stand of subalpine larch, which turns a glorious orange in autumn. At lower levels quaking aspen can be found – another tree that gives spectacular autumn colours – along with black cottonwoods beside water.

Alders, willows, cherries, maples and a mass of other small trees and shrubs grow in clearings and avalanche paths. These are attractive, especially when in flower or autumn colours, but if you lose the trail and have to fight your way through the tangled bush you'll end up cursing them. Many wildflowers grow in the mountains and if you are hiking in July or August a flower guide would come in handy.

Around 60 species of mammals live in the Northern Rockies but most are shy and stay well away from hikers. Of the larger

ones only deer are likely to be seen. A small pair of binoculars is useful for observing wild animals from a safe distance. In the southern part of the region moose, those ungainly looking beasts that are the largest members of the deer family, inhabit the damper areas and can be seen in marshes and shallow lakes at dawn and dusk. Above the timber line shaggy, white mountain goats live on the cliffs, while bighorn sheep roam the high meadows.

The most dramatic animals are, of course, bears. Black bears are found throughout the Rockies, while grizzlies are found in Glacier and Yellowstone national parks and the Bob Marshall and Teton Wilderness Areas. Wolves are found in the Montana Rockies and were reintroduced into Yellowstone in 1996. Their eerie howling, evocative of the wilderness, can sometimes be heard at dusk and lucky hikers could see them running through a meadow. Their smaller relative, the coyote, is found throughout the Rockies and may be heard yipping and yelping at dawn and dusk.

Red squirrels are common throughout the forests and often chatter loudly at passing hikers. Various ground squirrels and chipmunks may also be spotted. In boulderfields hoary marmots, the largest ground squirrels, sunbathe on rocks and whistle loudly when alarmed, as do the smaller pikas that also live in rock piles. Porcupines live in the forest and sometimes wander into camps where, attracted by the salt, they may try and chew on boots, rucksack straps and items of sweaty clothing. A trekking pole is useful for driving them away – you don't want to get too close! Beavers are seldom seen but their dams and lodges, built of sticks, are found on many slow-moving creeks and rivers.

Although many birds live in the Rockies they mostly stay hidden in the forest. Noisy Clark's nutcrackers and gray jays, sometimes called camp robbers, can be seen searching for food scraps. Spruce grouse and various woodpeckers, finches and sparrows are common and likely to be seen. In the skies above ravens may be seen soaring along with red-tailed hawks and, maybe, a golden eagle.

## THE GREAT DIVIDE BASIN

South of the Wind River Range there's a sudden and dramatic change as the route descends through sagebrush country to the Great Divide Basin. Here, the Divide splits to embrace this waterless desert. The route currently follows the eastern edge of the Basin, mostly on roads. The Great Divide Basin is home to wild horses and the fast-running pronghorn, a graceful deer-like animal.

South of the Great Divide Basin the trail climbs slowly through the Sierra Madre mountains, out of Wyoming and into the Colorado Rockies, a complex tangle of small, high mountain ranges. The trail is marked and well maintained through most of Colorado. From the Mount Zirkel Wilderness the CDT runs through the Park, Rabbits Ears and Never Summer ranges, touches the edge of Rocky Mountain National Park and then continues south through the Indian Peaks Wilderness and along the crest of the Front Range, the highest part of the whole CDT where it reaches 4081m (13,390ft) on the summit of

Parry Peak. Next comes the Sawatch Range containing the highest mountains in the Rockies, the 4399m (14,433ft) Mount Elbert and the 4396m (14,423ft) Mount Massive, Both lie close to the trail and can be easily climbed on side trips. The CDT in Colorado finishes with a long circuit round the head of the Rio Grande river valley in the superb rugged San Juan Mountains and the Weminuche Wilderness.

The fauna and flora of the Colorado Rockies is similar to those of the Northern Rockies although grizzly bears and wolves have been exterminated. In early summer, meadows put on rich displays of wildflowers, while in autumn aspen trees and various shrubs glow bright yellow and red against the dark green of the conifers.

Coming down from the San Juan Mountains the CDT finally leaves the Rockies and enters its last state, New Mexico, where the

walking is mostly across open sagebrush-dotted desert with expansive vistas and huge skyscapes. Much of the route is on dirt roads here. Highlights are the massive Chaco Mesa, a plateau rimmed by steep cliffs, the wooded ridges of the Zuni Mountains and El Morro National Monument, with inscriptions dating back to the 1500s .

Nor far from the southern terminus of the trail the terrain changes again as the CDT climbs into the Gila National Forest. A worthwhile variation goes via the Gila Cliff Dwellings, cut high into a cliff face. South of the Gila National Forest, dirt roads lead across the final stretch of desert to either Antelope Wells, the official finish point, or Columbus. Once at the border you can turn and stare northwards over the desert, imagine the Divide stretching out to Canada, and remember the exquisite landscapes and adventures along the way.

**ABOVE** *Halfmoon Creek lies between Mounts Massive and Elbert, the highest peaks in the Rocky Mountains, in Colorado's Swatch Range. The Continental Divide Trail runs beside the creek.*

# HIGHLINE TRAIL

*By Ralph Storer*

If there is one mountain range that encapsulates the rugged beauty and wild grandeur of the Rocky Mountains of northwest USA, it is Wyoming's Wind River Range, known to its devotees simply as the Winds. Here, in a landscape protected from development, is nearly one million acres of designated wilderness, uncrossed by paved road for 180km (110 miles) from south to north and 65km (40 miles) from east to west.

Within this rough rectangle are 23 'thirteeners' – mountains over 13,000ft (3950m), seven of the ten largest glaciers in the USA outside Alaska, over 110 *cirques*, 1300 lakes and more than 1100km (700 miles) of hiking trails. It is truly spectacular mountain country, the peaks characterized by

immense rock walls towering over achingly beautiful lakes. Seen from the west, they form a stunning frieze of bare rock between yellow-green sagebrush and blue sky.

Two features make the Winds unique as a hiking destination. Firstly, during construction, the mountains were raised in stages, with pause enough in-between for erosion to reduce the mountain flanks to plains, which were then raised during the next stage of mountain building. The result is that the spine of the Winds, especially on the west, is separated from the Wyoming plains by a series of benches. The largest of these runs along the length of the range at a height of 3050m (10,000ft) and more. In places it is over 16km (10 miles) wide. This makes access to the heart of the range from high

trailheads technically easy, but also causes hikers to underestimate altitude problems.

The second unique feature of the Winds is the series of ancient fault lines that run south to north beside the crest, which here forms the Continental Divide. Many of the river and valley systems run along these faults, parallel to the crest rather than away from it, for many miles. The benches and valleys combine to provide the Winds trekker with an opportunity to travel in high mountain country close to the spine of the range itself.

TOP *The rock and lake patchwork at the heart of beautiful Indian Basin, with Ellingwood Peak on the left, Elephant Head on the right.*

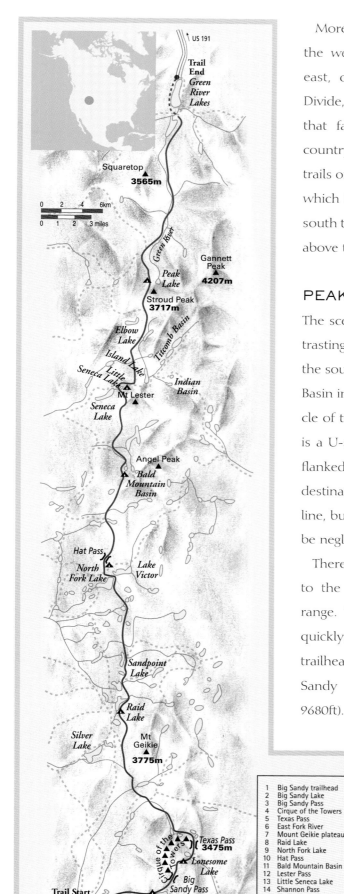

More than 800km (500 miles) of trail on the west and 300km (200 miles) on the east, connected via high passes on the Divide, form an extensive trail network that facilitates exploration of the back-country. The ultimate trek links the highest trails on the west side to form the Highline, which follows the spine of the range from south to north along its entire length, often above the timber line.

## PEAKS AND LAKES

The scenery reaches its zenith at two contrasting spots: The Cirque of the Towers in the southern part of the range and Titcomb Basin in the north. The former is a semicircle of teetering rock peaks, while the latter is a U-shaped trench filled with lakes and flanked by great rock walls and spires. Both destinations require detours from the Highline, but to omit them from the trip would be negligence bordering on criminal.

There are several possible starting points to the trek at the southern end of the range. To reach spectacular high country quickly, begin at the popular Big Sandy trailhead and take the forest trail beside Big Sandy River to Big Sandy Lake (2950m; 9680ft). The 10km (6-mile) walk, climbing

**ABOVE** *A spectacular camp site at Big Sandy Pass beneath the massive rock peak of Warbonnet only 13km (8 miles) from the trail head.*

only 200m (660ft), makes an easy opener, while a two-night camp at the lake aids acclimatization and enables a packless day-hike to nearby Deep Lake Cirque.

The scenery around Deep Lake gives a taste of the spectacle to come later in the trek. The sweeping mile-long rock wall of

1 Big Sandy trailhead
2 Big Sandy Lake
3 Big Sandy Pass
4 Cirque of the Towers
5 Texas Pass
6 East Fork River
7 Mount Geikie plateau
8 Raid Lake
9 North Fork Lake
10 Hat Pass
11 Bald Mountain Basin
12 Lester Pass
13 Little Seneca Lake
14 Shannon Pass
15 Peak Lake
16 Green River Lakes trailhead

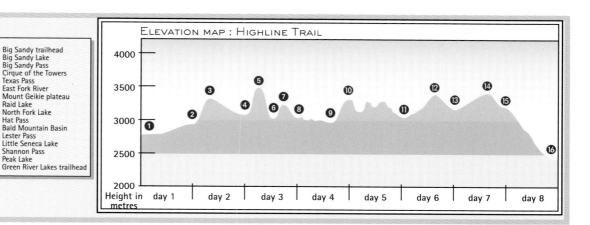

ELEVATION MAP : HIGHLINE TRAIL

**A CIRQUE** is a semi-circular high mountain basin, where snow collects and flows out as a glacier. If the glacier is long gone, it might have left a lake. Cirque is a French alpine term. In Scotland they are called corries, in Wales they're cwms. The Alps, Rockies and other glaciated mountains are full of them.

**A STONE SHOOT** is a gully filled with loose rocks and stones. They come in all shapes and sizes. The one mentioned at Texas Pass has a path of sorts and is easy enough to negotiate. There is no danger of rock fall and no helmet is required.

**A BENCH** is a Rocky Mountain term. Think of it as a long, broad shelf half-way up a mountain. The biggest in the Wind Rivers is 16km (10 miles) wide at a height of 3000m (10,000ft). As explained in the text, a bench is formed when a flat plain is uplifted by mountain building, to form a high-level flat area that makes for good high-altitude trekking.

Haystack Peak contrasts with the rock spires of Steeple Peak, Lost Temple Spire and East Temple Peak, while lakeside slabs turn streams into a series of pools and waterslides. A return via Temple Lake in the adjacent cirque completes a memorable day out.

From Big Sandy Lake, detour from the Highline to cross Big Sandy Pass and reach Lonesome Lake at the heart of the Cirque of the Towers on the east side of the Divide. Although only 5km (3 miles) long, the trail is undulating, but the scenery more than compensates. Sundance Pinnacle hovers over the ascent and the enormous face of Warbonnet overhangs the pass itself. To prolong the view, you may elect to camp at the pass rather than at Lonesome Lake, using snowmelt for water.

Warbonnet is the first of the famed Towers that form a semi-circle of jagged 3660m (12,000ft) peaks around the lake. Others include the Warriors, Watch Tower, Sharks Nose, Overhanging Tower, Wolfs Head and the awesome symmetrical Pingora Peak.

After a night at Lonesome Lake, exit the cirque on the north side to recross the Divide at Texas Pass, the trek's high point at 3475m (11,400ft). More direct routes out of the cirque are difficult to negotiate and are best avoided. Texas Pass is higher than Big Sandy Pass, but easier to cross in season, with any late-lying snow easy-angled and easily crossed. Note, however, that the stone shoot on the far side carries only traces of a path and requires care. Lower down, a better trail descends past a series of lakes into the valley of Washakie Creek.

If the crossing of Texas Pass seems too much at the beginning of the trip, you can avoid the Cirque of the Towers altogether by staying on the Highline at Big Sandy Lake and following it northwards through forest, staying west of the Divide. The Texas Pass route rejoins the Highline near Washakie Creek's confluence with the East Fork River, then heads northwestwards across an open plateau below Mount Geikie.

At a height of 3200m (10,500ft), this plateau makes a scenic camp site, with the southern part of the Winds spread out before you and the Towers glowing a ghostly white at sunset. An ascent of the 3775m (12,378ft) Mount Geikie makes an easy and scenic side trip.

Continuing northwards across the central part of the range, several ridges jutting westwards from the spine give the hiker no option but to detour further west, below the timber line. There are many trail options. The shortest route follows the Old Highline Trail and then the Fremont Trail, heading northwards from Raid Lake to North Fork Lake. Numerous other lakes add interest to this section, but you may prefer to cross it in a long single day's trek in anticipation of more exciting scenery ahead.

## DETOURS AND SIDE TRAILS

Beyond North Fork Lake the Fremont Trail emerges from the forest and enters the northern part of the range at Hat Pass (3306m; 10,846ft). Another couple of easy passes follow, then suddenly you are in breathtaking high country once again as you rejoin the Highline in lake-studded Bald Mountain Basin, with pointed Angel Peak prominent on the right. After exiting the basin at Lester Pass, you next reach Little Seneca Lake, a crossroads in the wilderness where the Highline crosses the side-trail to Titcomb Basin.

As noted above, it would be inexcusable not to take at least a day-hike detour, if not a two- or three-day add-on backpack, to visit this supreme example of Wind River mountain sculpture. If you do not have the

**ABOVE** *The trail to Titcomb Basin approaches the 'Aegean coastline' environs of Island Lake, backed by the 'thirteeners' of Fremont Peak and Jackson Peak.*

time or energy, at least down your pack and climb onto the northwest ridge of Mount Lester for a view into the basin that will haunt you for evermore.

The side-trail into the basin crosses two low passes to reach Island Lake, which guards the entrance. As you follow the trail around the shoreline, numerous islands, rocky headlands and sandy bays give the appearance of an Aegean coastline, making it difficult to believe you are at 3050m (10,000ft) in the Rocky Mountains.

Beyond Island Lake, Titcomb Basin penetrates a further 10km (6 miles) into the highest peaks in the range, including Gannett Peak – at 4207m (13,804ft) the highest mountain in Wyoming. The best camp site is beside Pothole Lake, the first of the ribbon of lakes in the basin itself, from where

you can explore the area, packless, to your heart's content. A good trail continues to Upper Lake, then the trench narrows between The Buttress and Mount Helen, where easy walking on boilerplate slabs enables you to reach the remote cirque of rock spires further along.

## ROCK AND LAKE SYSTEMS

Another spectacular side-trail climbs above Pothole Lake into beautiful Indian Basin, whose heart is an amazing patchwork of rock and complex lake systems surrounded by fascinating 'thirteeners' such as pinnacled Ellingwood Peak and the rocky stump of Elephant Head.

Back at Little Seneca Lake, the Highline continues northwards up the valley of Fremont Creek, passing lovely lakes, tumbling

streams, snow patches and more shapely spires. After reaching Shannon Pass at the head of the valley, the landscape becomes more intricately rocky and the trail threads a satisfying route down past rock bluffs and picturesque lakelets to emerge at Peak Lake.

By now you'll be running out of adjectives to describe the spectacle all around, but Peak Lake Cirque demands yet more superlatives. Much smaller than the Cirque of the Towers, it has the air of a secret mountain sanctuary, where great rock peaks such as Split Mountain, Sulphur Peak and Stroud Peak seem to hang overhead. Their sunset reflection in the lake is other-worldly.

You may wish to take another day out here to climb Stroud Peak. Amazingly, the summit can be reached fairly easily by a little scramble up the south ridge. The ascent ends satisfyingly on huge granite blocks, where you can lie down and peer over the edge at the lake directly below.

Peak Lake Cirque marks the end of the high country. Continuing northwards, the Highline crosses the easy Vista Pass and heads for civilization down the Green River valley. It's a long walk out to Green River Lakes trailhead, but the pack is lighter now and the enormous truncated rock pillar of the 3565m (11,695ft) Squaretop adds scenic interest. This mountain has become the symbol of the range, because it is one of the few Wind River mountains that can be seen easily from afar. You are permitted a (brief) moment of smugness in the knowledge that you have become one of the privileged few who have seen even more spectacular sights in the interior.

# SAWTOOTH TRAVERSE

*By Ralph Storer*

The jagged Sawtooth Mountains are part of the Rocky Mountain system of northwest USA. They are protected as the 89,707ha (221,671 acre) Sawtooth Wilderness, which constitutes the core of the 305,000ha (754,000 acre) Sawtooth National Recreation Area (SNRA). The SNRA was formed in 1972 as a conservation measure, in preference to a national park, in order to prevent tourist overdevelopment and maintain the area's wilderness appeal.

The granite of which the Sawtooths are composed fractures easily, and this has enabled glaciation to carve the mountains into fantastic splintered ridges and rock formations with evocative names such as Fishhook Spire, Leaning Tower of Pisa, Fin-

ger of Fate and the Arrowhead. The retreating glaciers have also left behind ice-scoured cirques filled by around 200 beautiful high mountain lakes. Rarely has glaciation been more artistic.

In size the tooths, as they are known to those who love them, are about 50km (31 miles) long by 32km (20 miles) wide, large and complex enough to tempt backpackers into their rugged interior but less overwhelming than other wilderness areas of northwest America. The spine of the range runs in a north-south line from the 3005m (9860ft) McGown Peak to the 3245m (10,651ft) Snowyside Peak. Long, high side ridges branch off to east and west, enclosing deep cirques and long valleys. It is these side ridges that give the

range a greater topographical complexity than would normally be expected in an area this size and make the range such a delight to explore. The side ridges contain some of the most interesting formations and the highest peak – the 3277m (10,751ft) Thompson Peak. Altogether there are 33 peaks over 3050m (10,000ft).

The east side of the range is more popular than the west side, which abuts against the blanket forest that covers much of Idaho. Western valleys are generally deeper, trailheads are about 450m

TOP *In this view of the Sawtooths from Red-fish Lake, Grand Mogul and Heyburn Mountains are prominent.*

(1500ft) lower and harder to reach, and approach trails to the high country are longer. The east side is more cleanly demarcated by the Sawtooth Valley, a broad grassy depression that carries the great Salmon River, beloved of whitewater rafters. Also on the east side is to be found the greatest concentration of lakes and the most compelling scenery, with access roads from the Sawtooth Valley leading to a series of large lakes at around the 2100m (7000ft) mark.

In an open basin at the north end of the valley lies the tiny settlement of Stanley, which has become the main base for exploration of the range and buzzes with activity during the summer season. The view from here of the mighty east wall of the Sawtooths is breathtaking. Many of the craggy summits are the preserve of rock climbers, so it is no surprise that since the 1930s they have become the home of Idaho mountaineering. But there are also sufficient easy passes between the peaks for a 480km (300-mile) network of good trails to have been laid out.

The classic Sawtooth trek is the north-to-south or south-to-north traverse of the range, an 82km (51-mile) trip that crosses five passes and stays on the east side of the main crest for most of its length. The intricate topography produces an ever-changing landscape in which vistas change dramatically from one moment to the next, making for wonderfully scenic back-packing, mostly above the timber line.

Camp sites are typically located beside lakes in high cirques. The progress of the trek is dictated by the positioning of these cirques. A typical day involves crossing an intervening ridge to move from one cirque to the next, producing trek stages that are generally well-defined and shorter than in other ranges. For this reason, the trek is best described on a day-by-day basis. It can

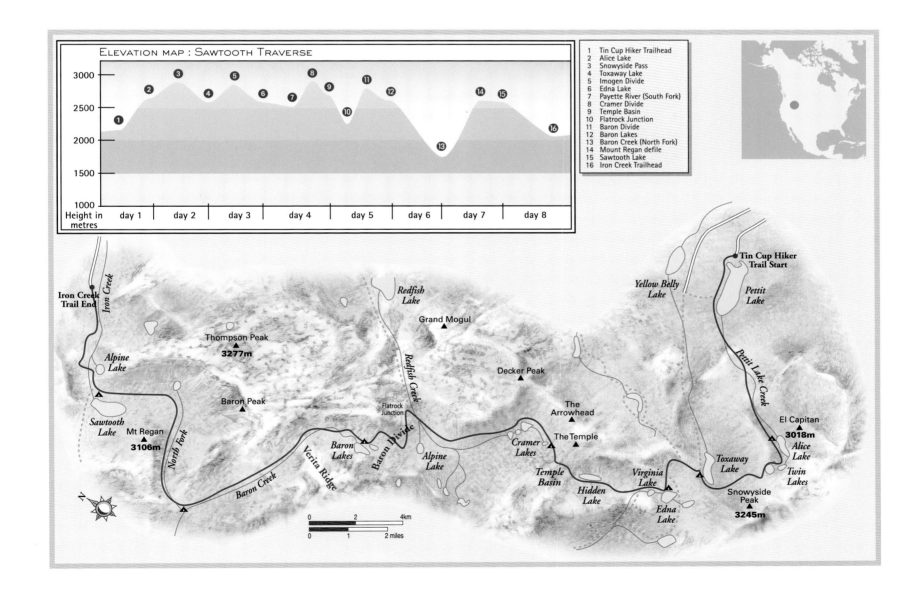

ELEVATION MAP : SAWTOOTH TRAVERSE

1  Tin Cup Hiker Trailhead
2  Alice Lake
3  Snowyside Pass
4  Toxaway Lake
5  Imogen Divide
6  Edna Lake
7  Payette River (South Fork)
8  Cramer Divide
9  Temple Basin
10 Flatrock Junction
11 Baron Divide
12 Baron Lakes
13 Baron Creek (North Fork)
14 Mount Regan defile
15 Sawtooth Lake
16 Iron Creek Trailhead

Height in metres

day 1 | day 2 | day 3 | day 4 | day 5 | day 6 | day 7 | day 8

ABOVE *After a hard day's trek, the 'flower garden' shores of Toxaway Lake promise perfect camping at the foot of Snowyside Peak.*

be done in either direction, but a south-to-north trip gives a gentler introduction and leaves the toughest days until you have become fitter.

## TIN CUP HIKER TRAILHEAD

The first day covers 10km (6 miles) and climbs about 485m (1600ft). It begins at Tin Cup Hiker trailhead on Pettit Lake and climbs the canyon of Pettit Lake Creek to Alice Lake Cirque at 2620m (8600ft). The ascent, though mostly through forest of Douglas fir and lodgepole pine, is never without interest. Along the way there are numerous waterfalls and a number of river crossings, which may require fording. The scenery becomes increasingly impressive, with the approach to Alice Lake itself dominated by the great prow of the 3018m (9901ft) El Capitan. Two ponds

that reflect the surrounding rock walls signal your arrival at the lake, whose beautifully wooded peninsulas and soaring rock peaks make it, perhaps, the most picturesque of all Sawtooth lakes. Pitch camp and settle in to watch the sunset show on El Capitan.

The second day covers 8km (5 miles) and climbs about 250m (800ft). Above Alice Lake the scenery is dominated by the 3245m (10,651ft) Snowyside Peak. This second stage of the trek crosses Snowyside Pass at 2865m (9400ft), east of the mountain, to reach the next cirque to the north. The trail climbs gently to Twin Lakes, then rises about 150m (500ft) in a mile to the pass itself. To add to the interest, the final section has been re-routed from its former course and carved out of the rock. On the far side of the pass the trail continues down

to another beautiful campsite beside the 'flower garden' shores of Toxaway Lake.

The third day covers 7km (4.5 miles) and climbs about 270m (900ft). A narrow pass north of Toxaway Lake enables the trail to cross the Imogen Divide and reach Edna Lake, one of a series of lakes clustered in the next cirque. The switchbacking ascent to the 2830m (9280ft) pass is easy, but the descent is steeper. Days 2 and 3 could be combined into a single, longer hike, but why rush amid such scenery?

Day four covers 10km (6 miles) and climbs about 400m (1300ft). On a more varied day of trekking, the trail continues its descent through the forest beyond Edna Lake, passing Virginia Lake and reaching the South Fork of the Payette River, which must be forded. The landscape then becomes more rugged as the trail climbs past Hidden Lake and above the timber line once more to reach the Cramer Divide at 2890m (9480ft) at the foot of the northwest ridge of the Temple. Note the precariously perched rock that tops the summit.

From this high point of the trek, the trail descends about 210m (700ft) of scree (and maybe snow) into the heart of Temple Basin. This wonderfully wild bowl of rock is tucked beneath the Temple's splintered northwest ridge and boasts a perfectly positioned little lake that reflects the towers of the Temple. Hovering further round the cirque is the improbable blade of rock called the Arrowhead, one of the strangest rock formations in the entire range. The ever-changing patterns of light in the basin may well persuade you to spend a rest day here. Alternatively, if you prefer your scenery less austere, you may wish to camp further down at the picturesque Cramer Lakes, which also reduces the length of the following day's hike.

## LUSH ROCK GARDENS

Day five covers 16km (10 miles) and climbs 550m (1800ft). On another varied day of trekking, the trail first descends to the timber line at the three Cramer Lakes, where it passes a fine waterfall and crosses beautiful open parkland where there are some fine campsites. Continuing down through the forest, the route eventually reaches Redfish Creek at Flatrock Junction, a popular picnic spot and day-hike destination from Redfish Lake 6km (3½ miles) down a side canyon. The river is forded on the flat slabs that give the place its name, then the day's ascent begins, up via switchbacks through lush rock gardens where you will see Indian paintbrush, Wyoming's state flower.

After passing Alpine Lake, with ever-widening views back to Temple Basin, the climb ends at a gap in the main ridge known as the Baron Divide at about 2790m (9160ft). From here the three Baron Lakes can be seen below, cupped in a remote basin between the main ridge and the climbers' playground of the Verita Ridge. To the west is the giant thumb of Big Baron Spire (also known as 'Old Smoothie'), while Verita Ridge itself is crested with amazing rock formations such as El Pima, Damocles and the Leaning Tower of Pisa. Follow the trail down into the basin, camp beside one of the lakes and wonder at the splendour towering above you.

Day six covers 12km (7.5 miles). This easy trekking day is unusual in that it requires no uphill effort; instead the trail descends about 850m (2800ft) beside tumbling Baron Creek to its junction with the North Fork of Baron Creek. The 1735m (5700ft) junction is much lower than either the starting or finishing trailheads and has several campsites among the trees.

Day seven covers 11km (7 miles) and climbs about 850m (2800ft). A tough ascent with one river crossing regains the height lost on the previous day, as the trail makes a long climb through luxurious vegetation beside the North Fork of Baron Creek. If the bushes are wet, expect to receive a drenching as you push through them. Eventually you reach a rugged defile east of the 3106m (10,190ft) Mt Regan, beyond which lies Sawtooth Lake, the day's destination and a welcome sight. When approached from Iron Creek trailhead, the picturesque lake is a 'popular' day-hike destination by Idaho standards. It lies in a rocky bowl beneath the imposing north face of Mount Regan and is the largest high lake in the Sawtooths. Ice floes can still be seen here in July.

On day eight, over 8km (5 miles), the trail bids a sad farewell to the high country with another easy day that consists entirely of a descent beside Iron Creek, Sawtooth Lake's outlet stream. In a series of switchbacks, the trail twists steeply down to the timber line at Alpine Lake (not the same as Day 5's namesake), then continues more sedately down the curving Iron Creek valley. On the north side of the valley is one final, typically impressive 'tooth' ridge before the trail exits the mountains amid lodgepole pine forest at Iron Creek trailhead.

LEFT *The last camp of the trek is beside Sawtooth Lake, which reflects the majestic north face of Mount Regan.*

# GRAND CANYON

*By David Emblidge*

Most treks take us to new heights. Paradoxically, a walk into the Grand Canyon takes us down – to new discoveries in a world so beautiful that the superlatives of everyday language do not suffice. Indeed, 'Grand' is a modest name for one of the world's natural wonders. Proclaimed a World Heritage Site in 1979, a trek here leaves an indelible impression – also sore feet and knees, parched throats and sunburnt skin. The canyon's climate is harsh, with intense heat, dry air, and steep, relentless descents and ascents. The rewards are commensurate, however, especially for those who come prepared to cope well with the elements and who can appreciate the silent, haunting beauty of ancient wind- and

water-carved rocks, of feisty plant life in the desert environment, and of ever-changing light shows as sunshine and shadows inch through the canyon.

The geological history of the Grand Canyon stretches back 1.84 billion years. At first glance, the dry canyon may seem frozen in time, but imperceptibly it grows wider and deeper. In the beginning, volcanic eruptions pushed up mountains that eroded and reformed again over long periods. The first mountain-building event, the one that helped form the basement rocks, was caused by a continental mass colliding with island arcs. Sediments from the erosion were compressed and, under heat, they metamorphosed into the base rocks we see today, deep in the canyon.

In a mere six million years the river, now called the Colorado, eroded the canyon. Rainwater erosion carved and reshaped the canyon's towering walls. Wind plays a minor role in the process. A mile deep and 30km (18 miles) wide at some points, the sheer scope of the Grand Canyon is hard to take in visually or emotionally.

Human habitation here began long before the first European explorers arrived. There were villages, trading and some agriculture. A drought in the 13th century forced a move away from the canyon and other

TOP *A mule supply train serves Phantom Ranch in the bottom of the Grand Canyon. Some trekkers also use mules.*

native Americans, such as the Cerbats, replaced the Anasazi. The oldest evidence of human occupation in the area dates back roughly 10,000 years. No name has been assigned to these early peoples. The 'ancestral Puebloans' arrived about AD500. Until the mid-13th century they shared the canyon with the Cohonina Indians.

Spanish explorer Garcia Lopez de Cardenas was the first European to see the Grand Canyon, in 1540. However, the earliest documented exploration stems from the intrepid John Wesley Powell, a one-armed Civil War veteran who led an expedition by boat down the raging Colorado in 1869. Powell's colourful account of his two trips set the tourism and prospecting ball rolling. When the Santa Fe Railroad finished laying track around 1900, tourism became big business. The railroad arrived at the South Rim in September, 1901. Grand Canyon Village, on the South Rim, took shape shortly after the railroad's arrival and is still the trailhead for most trekking.

## FIRST GLIMPSE

Your first glimpse down into and across the void will take your breath away. Early mornings and sunsets in particular reveal the canyon in its richest light. The South Rim, at Grand Canyon Village, is intensely busy, clogged with auto and RV traffic as well as tourist buses throughout the summer. Do not despair. The North Rim gets only 10 per cent as many visitors.

A traverse of the canyon can go either south to north, or north to south. In either case, transportation arrangements to or from the North Rim are the big problem. Highway access to the canyon itself is far easier from the south. The northern access road closes in winter and is a long haul through vacant territory in summer. From Grand Canyon Village, it can take a full day to reach the North Rim trailheads on 350km (215 miles) of park service roads in your own car or by rented vehicle. Trekkers who have the time and resources to position cars on both rims before hiking have more choices, but most will arrive at the South Rim, stay a

night in lodgings there, then head down with the crowd into the canyon on Bright Angel Trail (the most popular) or on South Kaibab Trail for a more isolated walk. There is a rim-to-rim shuttle that operates mid-May to mid-October. It makes one trip each way, daily. A couple of hours down into the canyon, where fatigue and heat will have persuaded most day hikers to return to the top, trekkers will have the place mostly to themselves, depending on the season.

Starting at the South Rim lets you walk away from civilization rather than back into it. However, the North Rim is more than 305m (1000ft) higher than the South Rim, a factor that persuades many hikers to start on the North Rim. The trek described here uses the South Kaibab Trail, whose Yaki Point Trailhead is accessible by shuttle bus from Grand Canyon Village. The panorama from Yaki is superb and the drop-off a challenge. Pray that your hiking boots fit well – you are about to descend 1460m (4800ft) to the Colorado River, steep most of the way, over the next 10km (6 miles).

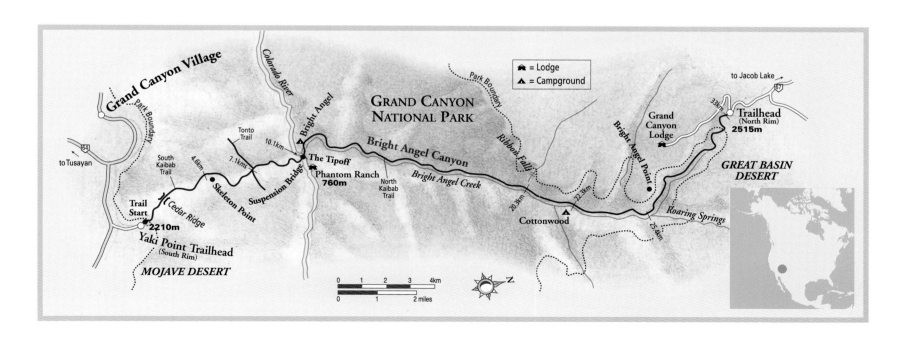

There is almost no shade and there is no drinking water available on the South Kaibab Trail once you leave the trailhead. Carry a map and use it. Although the path is easy to follow, keeping track of where you are by distance and time requires concentration, especially in the heat and glaring sunshine, which may make even the fittest hikers light-headed. Avoid hiking in the heat of the day. Summer temperatures in the bottom of the canyon frequently exceed 40°C (104°F). Hiking alone is not recommended.

Cedar Ridge is just 2.4km (1.5 miles) down the path, one of several ridges followed by this zigzagging path (most trails use side canyons). The trail actually follows the same ridge from the rim to just before The Tipoff. Cedar Ridge is just a place name along that ridge. A place, ominously named Skeleton Point, is reached at 4.6km (2.9 miles). Vast Redwall Formation (largely limestone) hosts about a mile of South Kaibab Trail as it meanders downward on huge switchbacks.

Though steep-sided, much of the Grand Canyon is actually desert, lying on the borders of three deserts, the hot Mojave and the cold Great Basin, with a bit of the Sonoran thrown in for good measure. The most striking fact is dryness, of soil and air. Desert plant life is a marvel of adaptation. Blackbrush, the dominant shrub, sprouts small, hairy leaves. The hairs capture a thin layer of still air that retards evaporation from the leaves. In times of drought, the plant turns deciduous and essentially shuts down its metabolism. About once every decade a blooming spring of desert plants appears, with abundant brittle bush, trailing four o'clock, globe mallow, and prickly pear cactus.

## THE FINAL PLUNGE

Tonto Trail Junction, at 7km (4.4 miles), is followed shortly by The Tipoff, the final plunge into the Colorado River Gorge. By this time, you will hear the river if not see it. Upon reaching the Colorado, you will have walked more than 9km (6 miles) and may well feel like taking a swim. Don't. The

**ABOVE** *The descent from the South Rim on the South Kaibab Trail affords sweeping views of the remarkable geological features of the canyon.*

current is vicious and the water is numbingly cold. Cross the suspension bridge and carry on to either Bright Angel Campground or Phantom Ranch, where a soak for tired feet in a quiet brook will be safer. The ranch is reachable only on foot, horseback, or by river raft. Set amid cottonwood trees beside singing Bright Angel Creek, this is a canyon oasis that feels, and is, far from the outside world. While water supplies can be replenished here, there are no groceries for sale. The ranch is not a spa, conditions are Spartan, but the privilege of staying here leaves a luxury of good memories.

The Colorado River is a matter of endless political debate. Built in 1963, Glen Canyon Dam, some 140km (90 miles) upstream, changed the ecology of the river basin in unanticipated ways, and some people now argue that the dam should be breached. Sediment flow that formerly carved the canyon has been stalled. Seasonal fluctuations in water flows have been eliminated, and the water temperature has stabilized at a relatively cold level. Fish adapted to living in muddy water varying in temperature from just above freezing to more than 18°C (65°F) with spring floods and winter ebbs, now struggle to survive in clear, cold, constant flows. Streamside vegetation has increased, since seedlings are not washed away each spring. One plant that has taken root, however, is tamarisk, an alien species. Some animals benefit from the dam. Rainbow trout, another exotic species, thrives, to the detriment of indigenous fishes. Waterfowl have increased, as have the peregrine falcons that feed on them. Rafters are divided on the effects of

**ABOVE** *Prickly pear cacti put on majestic shows of yellow, pink and magenta flowers from April through June. These hardy succulents are profuse on the lower, hotter, sections of the Kaibab Trail.*

the dam. The regulated flows provide for a longer rafting season with predictable and thrilling whitewater conditions. Far downstream, the states of Arizona, Nevada and California siphon off most of the Colorado's water. Mexico is guaranteed 1.5 million acre-foot (1850 million cubic metre) a year of Colorado River water by treaty. (Acre-foot is the amount of water required to cover one acre of ground to a depth of one foot.) That flow is siphoned off mostly for farming so that in many years the river ends nearly dry at the sea.

Hiking out to the North Rim on North Kaibab Trail through Bright Angel Canyon is a long climb that is best broken into two parts. At 10.2km (6.3 miles) up from the Colorado River, there is a respite at Ribbon Falls. A night at Cottonwood Campground at 12.2km (7.6 miles) requires carrying in all equipment and food and carrying out all

garbage. The effort is worth it, however, both to extend your stay in the Grand Canyon and because climbing the north side of the canyon in one fell swoop is more than most hikers can manage.

Roaring Springs/Bright Angel Creek Junction at 15.3km (9.5 miles) is the next major landmark, but there are still 7.6km (4.7 miles) to go before the trailhead. Grand Canyon Lodge lies about 3km (2 miles) beyond the trailhead, and by the time you have hiked that far you will be ready for an overnight rest in a bed before driving out. Chances are – blisters, parched throat, and sore muscles notwithstanding – you will have trouble tearing yourself away from views back down into and across the Grand Canyon from the North Rim. By then, you will know you have walked through a true natural wonder.

# Appalachian Trail

*By David Emblidge*

Grandfather of North America's long footpaths, the Appalachian Trail (AT) is also its most well trodden. At 3488km (2167 miles), traversing 11 states through a variety of landscapes and climates near the United States' Atlantic coast, the trail serves an estimated 4,000,000 walkers each year. A hardy few attempt to through-hike. Each year about 2500 start out; and barely 10 per cent make it to the other end, four to six months later.

Most AT trekkers are day hikers, weekend backpackers, and those on expeditions of a week or two. Despite heavy use in some favoured sections within easy reach of seaboard cities, vast stretches of the track pass through protected wilderness areas offering extreme solitude and backpacking challenges between resupply points.

Forested by a colourful mix of deciduous trees and conifers, the Appalachian region is home to hundreds of bird species and scores of mammals, including black bear and moose. Many AT miles in southern and northern states offer superb vistas, alpine flora, wild weather and exciting above-the-tree-line hiking.

Winter (December to March or April) closes most of the trail in the northern states, and even in the southern states at higher elevations. Major storms can dump several feet of snow. In winter, certain sections of the AT are used for snowshoeing and cross-country skiing. Some hardy outdoors people enjoy winter camping along the trail while an elite, and occasionally foolhardy, few try to traverse the highest peaks in New Hampshire during the frozen months. Each year, due to falls, avalanches, or hypothermia, a number of people die on the AT in winter.

The trek generally follows the crest line of the Appalachian Mountains, arcing from the southern state of Georgia into New England, culminating in the rugged back-country areas of New Hampshire and

TOP *From atop Little Calf Mountain, a peak in the Blue Ridge Mountains in Shenandoah National Park, a lone hiker gazes down at the at the twinkling lights of Waynesboro, Virginia.*

Maine. Great Smoky Mountains and Shenandoah national parks, as well as a number of state parks, play host to the meandering track. A northern extension is under construction – the International Appalachian Trail – which will reach into Canada and the Gaspé Peninsula.

The AT is not, as many believe, a Native American footpath. It was the brainchild of hiking enthusiasts in the late 19th and early 20th centuries. Boston's Appalachian Mountain Club and Vermont's Green Mountain Club began trail building in New England during the 1880s when the expansion of railroads into mountain areas first brought tourists to the wilderness.

During the Depression, a government work-relief programme for unemployed urban young men – the Civilian Conservation Corps (CCC) – built many trail sections, camps and lodges. Credit for the first through-hike, in 1948, goes to Earl Shaffer.

The trail came under the authority of the National Park Service in 1968 which purchased property to create a minimum 300m (1000ft) wide trail corridor.

In many places the corridor is several miles wide. Environmentalists and legislators are engaged in debates over environmental impact concerns (wear and tear, sustainability) and hiker management issues (overuse, low-impact camping and safety).

The typical AT through-hiker walks northwards, starting out, between March and April, at Springer Mountain, Georgia, after a robust climb to the peak through Amicalola Falls State Park. In the early weeks of through-hiking season, about 2500 people start out from here. Only about 10% of them will reach the goal in northern Maine, several months later. Southbound through-hikers, far fewer in number, usually start in late May or as far into the summer as July if the northern New England snow pack lingers. Their starting point is atop Maine's windswept Mt Katahdin. It is reached after a steep, day-long climb to the alpine zone, above the tree line, in Baxter State Park, a day-long drive from the nearest city.

Although the highest peak on the trail is in the deep south, the southern Appalachians are not rugged mountains, and much of the walking is easy, once you're on the trail. Heat and springtime insects may be the *bêtes noires* of trekkers here, but hiking amidst crowds of eager, but often inexperienced or inconsiderate, early starters can also be discouraging for northbound hikers. However, starting from Mt Katahdin in Maine means that the first month or more through Maine and New Hampshire, will be severely rugged, dangerous due to wild weather above the tree line and, in Maine especially, deeply isolated in impenetrable woods. At some points the trail is a full week's walk away from even the smallest town. Springtime black flies in the north can be hellish.

## SECTION HIKERS

'Section hikers' trek for a week or more, then come back to the AT at other times to cover new sections. A few eventually complete the entire trek. Most of the estimated four million trail users per year stick close

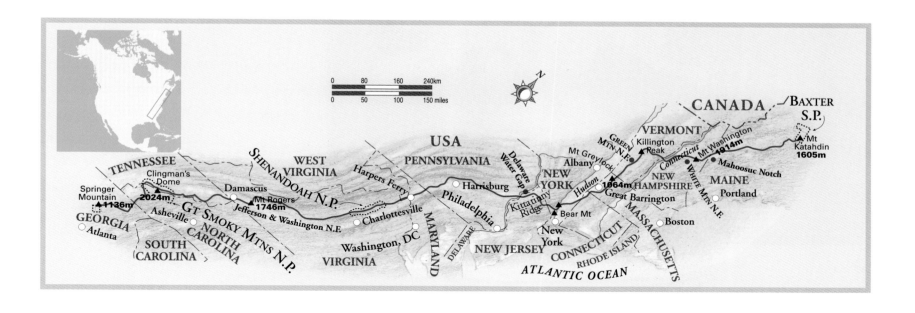

to home, which is easy to do, because much of the AT is within a day's drive of the heavily populated east coast of the United States. The trail is a narrow, often rugged and rocky footpath, usually traversing the highest peaks and most delightful valleys. Rivers are bridged but many streams require fording.

In the southern states of Georgia, North Carolina and Tennessee, the trail runs through several national forests. It spends 110km (70 miles) in Great Smoky Mountains (GSM) National Park, where it crosses Clingman's Dome, at 2024m (6642ft), the trail's highest point. However, it is somewhat marred by the nearby road development and resulting crowds. Except in the first wave of the through-hiking season, this southernmost territory on the trail is largely empty. Expect certain ironies, however – GSM National Park is the busiest

in the country and near its major crossing highways, the trail is heavily used. A mile or so away, crowds mercifully disappear.

Heat, humidity, abundant rain and the latitude favour a varied forest of soft- and hardwoods, with wildflowers, birdsong and frequent sightings of black bear. Evidence of the impact of acid rain (from coal-fired industrial plants to the west) appears in numerous dead stands of trees. Blights wiped out the American chestnut and elm, and the woolly adelgid attacks the balsam firs. The southern Appalachians are steep, though less rugged than New England and the area remains a botanist's paradise. Rhododendron, dogwood, trillium and countless other flowering plants grace the footpath – drawing crowds of day-hikers during peak bloom season.

Some of the highest southern peaks – in the GSM region of Georgia, North Carolina

and Tennessee – are rounded (these are very old mountains), with large open areas, called the balds, offering spectacular vistas across endless ridges and valleys. No one understands the phenomenon. Despite their 1500m (5000ft) elevation, they are not above the tree line, thanks to the warm climate. Native American myths say the gods burned off the mountain tops to keep a clear view of human activity in the valleys. Botanists know that some native people and early white settlers grazed cattle on the balds, but the explanation is incomplete.

## VIRGINIA

Over 640km (400 miles) of the trail goes through Virginia, more trail miles than through any other state. Damascus, Virginia, hosts Trail Days in May to celebrate the passing tide of annual northbound through-hikers. The southern Virginia Highlands rise above 1500m (5000ft). It passes through Jefferson and Washington national forests en route to the second national park on the trail, Shenandoah, near the northern state border. Proximity to Washington, DC, and Baltimore, Maryland, and an easy, level trail make northern trail sections in Virginia busy. Summer in Virginia can be beastly hot, but fall hiking here is long and glorious. A photogenic spot is McAfee Knob, a promontory in central Virginia affording views westwards off a giant overhanging rock.

A few miles of trail pass through neighbouring West Virginia into a National Historical Park at the village of Harpers Ferry where the Appalachian Trail Conference headquarters welcomes all hikers and

**ABOVE** *Vivid rhododendron blooms draw hundreds of hikers to the southern sections of the Appalachian Trail in late spring.*

provides abundant trail information. Across the wide Potomac River, the path takes a 60km (40-mile) hop through Maryland before crossing the Pennsylvania border. This is the culturally significant Mason Dixon Line, a relic of the mid-19th-century Civil War that separates southern Confederate (pro-slavery) states from northern Union (anti-slavery) states.

The AT's mid-point is just north of Pennsylvania's southern border. Accents, cuisine, climate and architecture change noticeably. Pennsylvania's Appalachians curve gently northeastwards, but the walking is tough in 'Rocksylvania'. Long ridges, often treeless (from logging and harsh soils), are littered with sharp-edged rocks thrust upwards by colliding tectonic plates and stirred into disarray by glaciers. Compensating factors on the Pennsylvania section of trail are Civil War historical sites and sweeping pastoral views. The state's northern edge is a mighty river set in a handsome gorge, the Delaware Water Gap National Recreation Area.

## NEW JERSEY

New Jersey, another of the densely populated states, offers segments of the AT along popular Kittatinny Ridge which – at midweek – are quiet and beautiful. These New Jersey 'Skylands,' as they are called, top out at a mere 520m (1700ft) with no distinct peaks, but occasional gems such as Sunfish Pond are rewarding. The trail skirts a corner of New York State about 80km (50 miles) north of the Big Apple, managing to find stunning views in Bear Mountain and Harrison and Hudson Highlands state

**ABOVE** *Harpers Ferry, West Virginia, seen from Loudon Heights, encompassing Maryland and West Virginia on opposite sides of the Potomac and the confluence of the Shenandoah River.*

parks on opposite sides of the Hudson River. Skyscrapers in Manhattan can be seen from Bear Mountain. Isolation is harder to come by here, but you can see the vistas painted by Hudson River School artists of the 19th century who defined the American Romantic view of nature as both sublime and fearsome.

## CONNECTICUT

Entering Connecticut in rolling hill country, the trail is finally in New England, its last distinct region en route north, but there are still five states and hundreds of miles to go – plus most of the climbing. New England villages make the AT's most charming stopovers as the footpath wends its way through remarkably lovely countryside. Increasingly, the trail climbs the first real mountains since Virginia. Connecticut's northwest uplands are the Litchfield

Hills, where the trail roller coasters from ridge tops to valleys, keeping close to the Housatonic River. Between gentrified Salisbury and southern Berkshire County in neighbouring Massachusetts, the track navigates a forest and ridgeline path on the Taconic Range in contiguous state parks, passing through Sage's Ravine – a naturalist's paradise, with waterfalls – and peaking at the 793m (2602ft) Mount Everett.

Crossing the Housatonic River, the trail passes near Great Barrington, Massachusetts, a bustling, upscale market town, then rises onto the Berkshire Massif for most of this state's 130km (80 miles) of trail. Trekkers with a yen for cultural entertainment off-trail will enjoy the Berkshires where towns boast everything from the Boston Symphony Orchestra to the Jacob's Pillow Dance Festival, theatres and superb museums. Mt Greylock in Massachusetts'

**ABOVE** *Black bears can be spotted in any of the forested regions of the trail between Georgia and Maine, but they rarely approach humans and, unless threatened, are not a serious danger.*

northwest corner, at 1064m (3491ft) southern New England's tallest peak, is the first where wild weather may pose a threat. Bascom Lodge, atop Greylock, offers pricey but welcome bunks.

## VERMONT

Green Mountain National Forest hosts most of the trail's length in Vermont, here heading almost due north. Vermont's Long Trail is contiguous with the AT from Massachusetts to Killington Peak, mid-state. The Long Trail predates the AT and has its own legendary through-hikers who walk to Quebec, Canada. Federal wilderness areas in Vermont, within the national forest, remain untouched by mechanized equipment, have few roads, and offer a chance to escape even the amenities of established camp sites. A surprise awaits trekkers at Vermont's popular mountains – the 1200m (4000ft) Stratton and the 1293m (4241ft)

Killington – where ski lifts hoist crowds to the peaks. Stratton Pond, with shelters and tent sites scattered around pristine waters, is magically isolated.

North of Killington, the AT turns east, leaves the Long Trail, and heads down towards the Connecticut River Valley. It takes 80km (50 miles) to get there, in undistinguished rolling forest, on rarely used trail, passing near only one interesting town, Woodstock, brimming with boutiques and elegant Federal period mansions. Dartmouth College, Hanover, New Hampshire, a venerable Ivy League university, lies on the AT. Resupply and rest are easy to arrange here for through-hikers, though purists may find the town too busy and pricey.

## ALPINE ZONE

After lowland rambling northeast of Hanover, the AT begins its toughest ascents

and descents, through White Mountain National Forest. The 1464m (4802ft) Mount Moosilauke takes the trail above the tree line into the alpine zone for the first time. A superb series of high mountain lodges, managed by the Appalachian Mountain Club (AMC), provides respite from the powerful winds common in the White Mountains above the tree line. The ascent to Franconia Ridge is spectacular, leading to a dozen or more miles in the Pemigewasset Wilderness, untouched by machinery and uncrossed by roads. A harrowing descent into Zealand Notch tests everyone's knees and mettle. At Crawford Notch the AMC runs an excellent lodge and education centre.

## PRESIDENTIAL RANGE

Then, abruptly, the trail rises even higher onto the Presidential Range for the longest alpine walk in eastern America, certainly the finest views and undoubtedly the most dangerous weather. The 1914m (6280ft) Mt Washington is the trail's second highest point, but offers greatest exposure to the elements. A bizarre state park concession building mars the treeless peak (19th-century tourism developers carved a road to the top). No camping is permitted in the extremely fragile alpine zone where diapensia, Lapland rosebay, alpine azalea and lichens cling to the rocks, surviving by means of astonishing adaptive chemistry. The only plant ever to have been removed from the US government's list of endangered species – *Potentilla robbinsiana*, or Robbins cinquefoil – survives here, too, thanks to the efforts of AMC and others.

Trekkers not using the AMC huts, which are expensive and booked months in advance, generally must descend significantly to reach tent sites. A trek across the Presidential Range requires careful expedition planning and attention to safety. Several people die there every year due to lightning, fierce winds, rock slides, avalanches and falls. Hiker's Mecca is Pinkham Notch, in the valley below the Presidentials, where AMC runs a lodge, restaurant, bookstore, natural history programmes, and a shuttle service to dozens of trailheads, attracting crowds ranging from mountaineers to hiking neophytes.

The trail rises sharply again, crosses into Maine and encounters infamous Mahoosuc Notch, the 'toughest mile on the AT', a jumble of colossal boulders and twisted, dark passages too tight for full backpacks. A few more peaks in western Maine rise briefly into the alpine zone and the trail passes a busy ski resort, Sugarloaf. However, soon elevations drop off and a week-long trek through the most isolated wilderness in eastern America begins.

## MAINE WOODS

Hours from any city in the USA or Canada, the Maine woods are home to logging companies and hunting and fishing camps and not much else. Pristine glacial lakes dot the rolling landscape, with moose grazing in the wetlands and black bear roaming freely. The 100-Mile Wilderness, along the AT, requires full provisioning. Stream and river crossings in Maine are treacherous. At the Kennebec River, where fording hikers have drowned, the Maine Appalachian Trail Club provides a canoe-ferry service.

But the Maine wilderness is changing and, most agree, for the better. Vast stretches of previously unprotected land have recently been purchased for recreational use by AMC, most notably 15,000 hectare (37,000 acres) surrounding Gulf Hagas. Backwoods lodges, more AT access points, and a year-round program, including skiing and snowshoeing, promise to make the Maine section of the AT more feasible for northeasterners who find New Hampshire's trails too busy.

Baxter State Park, a vast territory in north central Maine, brings the story to a fitting close with Mount Katahdin, which means 'greatest mountain' in Abenaki.

At 1605m (5267ft), Katahdin is the most isolated alpine peak on the trail, with no roads, no mountainside shelters, and no protection from the elements. Snow and ice linger well into May, returning in early or mid-October. The AT spends its last northbound hours well above the tree line, with a rousing finish at Baxter Peak where many a champagne bottle cork has been popped by through-hikers and day-hikers, though often in a chilly fog and bone-rattling winds.

On a clear day a descent on the mountain's northern side (starting from the AT terminus at the peak), after crossing the Knife Edge with its precipitous adrenaline-rush drop-offs, provides the trekker with a big bonus – if the knees will tolerate it. Most hikers return to 'base camp', southwards on the AT. However, all trekkers who have reached this far, go home with a sense of satisfaction and closure. If you have walked all the way from Georgia to Maine, you have now passed through the gates of the AT's hall of fame.

**ABOVE** *New Hampshire's windswept Mt Washington, above Lake of the Clouds. The highest peak in New England, it affords spectacular White Mountains views.*

# EVOLUTION LOOP

*By Ralph Storer*

The incomparable Sierra Nevada (Spanish for Snowy Mountains) is one of the world's most beautiful hikable mountain ranges. It is formed of the largest continuous block of granite in the world, measuring 675km (420 miles) long and 95–125km (60–80 miles) wide. The block is tilted to the west so that the imposing eastern front towers 3050m (10,000ft) and more over the Owens Valley to form one of the great escarpments of the world. On the west the mountains fade into forested rolling hills, with some surprisingly spectacular scenery where ice has carved dramatic canyons, such as Yosemite, deep into the high country.

The central part of the range, known as the High Sierra, is a hikers' paradise

uncrossed by road for about 250km (160 miles). Finely sculpted mountains, 500 of them higher than 3650m (12,000ft) and 11 'fourteeners' (mountains over 14,000ft, or 4270m), pierce the blue sky above enchanting lakes, alpine meadows and basins. Monarch of the range is Mt Whitney, at 4418m (14,495ft) the highest mountain in the US outside Alaska, with a trail all the way to its summit.

As if the scenery were not enough, the Sierra has the mildest, sunniest climate of any of the world's major mountain ranges. Only five per cent of the annual average precipitation falls between the beginning of July and the end of September, with only an occasional afternoon thunderstorm or day or two of rain. Average summer

midday temperature at 3050m (10,000ft) is 16°C (60°F). Despite occasional high-altitude cold spells, sunburn can be more of a problem than hypothermia.

The range encompasses three national parks, 17 wildernesses and eight national forests. Yosemite and Kings Canyon national parks are centred around the two most spectacular canyons, while Sequoia National Park celebrates the giant sequoia trees for which the range is famous. Outside the national parks there is equally

**ABOVE** *Looking west across Wanda Lake towards the silhouetted peaks of Mount McGee, sunset colours are reflected in tranquil pools of water between ice floes.*

beautiful country that gives incomparable high-elevation hiking opportunities far from the crowds.

The classic High Sierra trek is the John Muir Trail (see p116), which runs for 339km (210 miles) along the length of the range, from the summit of Mt Whitney in the south to Yosemite in the north. However, the complete trip is a major undertaking that requires two to three weeks. Owing to time constraints, most vacationing backpackers will be content to sample the trail, and there is no finer introduction than the Evolution Loop. This magnificent circular trip begins at a high trailhead on the east side of the Sierra crest and uses three 3350m (11,000ft) passes to loop over to the west side and follow a

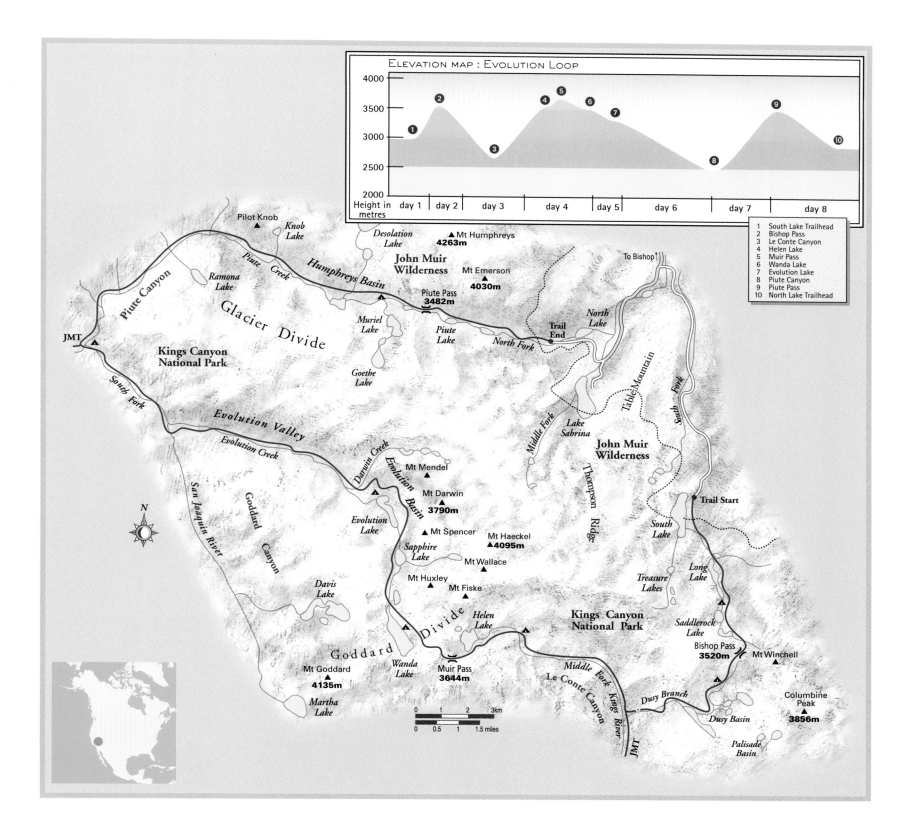

Elevation map : Evolution Loop

| | | | | |
|---|---|---|---|---|
| 1 | South Lake Trailhead |
| 2 | Bishop Pass |
| 3 | Le Conte Canyon |
| 4 | Helen Lake |
| 5 | Muir Pass |
| 6 | Wanda Lake |
| 7 | Evolution Lake |
| 8 | Piute Canyon |
| 9 | Piute Pass |
| 10 | North Lake Trailhead |

section of the John Muir Trail through some of the loveliest parts of the range. The complexity of the terrain makes for adventurous cross-country travel, while the beautiful meadows and lakes above the timber line provide idyllic camping in high country basins. John Muir called these high meadows 'sky gardens'.

The highlight of the trek is Evolution Basin in a remote part of the High Sierra between Kings Canyon and Yosemite. The basin is so named because the peaks surrounding it are named after early advocates of evolution: Darwin, Mendel, Huxley, Spencer, Haeckel, Wallace and Fiske.

## SOUTH LAKE TRAILHEAD

The route begins at South Lake trailhead (2973m; 9755ft) above Bishop and begins with a 10km (6-mile) climb past numerous lakes to reach the Sierra crest at Bishop Pass (3520m; 11,550ft). When planned from the comfort of an armchair, it may not seem like a long first day, but unless you are already acclimatized to the altitude, you may well opt to make a first camp near one of these lakes.

At the pass, the trail crosses the Sierra crest from east to west and enters the great, wide-open spaces of picturesque Dusy Basin, where strings of lakes lie at the foot of Mount Winchell. It is worth taking a day out here to hike across the basin to Knapsack Pass and scramble up the 3856m (12,652ft) Columbine Peak. The summit affords stunning views across neighbouring Palisade Basin to the Palisades, the Sierra's most alpine of mountains. It is also home to its largest glaciers and five of its

eleven 'fourteeners' (the other six are in the Mt Whitney area further south). From Dusy Basin the trail makes a long switchbacking descent beside the tumbling Dusy Branch into the forested confines of Le Conte Canyon, where it joins the John Muir Trail at a backcountry ranger station. On the way down you pass picturesque lakes, waterfalls and a huge waterslide that flows over granite slabs for hundreds of feet.

Once on the John Muir Trail, height is regained on a correspondingly long ascent that climbs Le Conte Canyon to its head, where the Goddard Divide is crossed at the

**ABOVE** *Approaching Bishop Pass from the east. In the basin below, the convoluted shorelines of Bishop Lake and Ledger Lake form part of a complex lake system.*

trek's 3644m (11,955ft) high point, Muir Pass. The length of this climb, the numerous stream crossings and the increasing altitude may well prompt you into an overnight camp before tackling the pass itself. In addition, the final stretch, even in high summer, is often a broad snowfield dimpled with deep snow cups. These are caused by uneven thawing and make for tiring going.

## ICE-SCOURED AND NAKED

Helen Lake on the near side of the pass and Wanda Lake on the far side are named after John Muir's daughters and make wonderfully desolate, if chilly, camp sites. Early in the season, ice floes sculpt the surface of each lake and the even higher Lake McDermand just over the pass. At a height of 3490m (11,452ft), Wanda Lake, especially, is gloriously colourful at dawn and sunset. At the summit of the pass is Muir Hut, a stone hut erected as a memorial to the man himself. This provides shelter in foul weather or an emergency, but makes a less attractive overnight base than a lakeside camp.

Wanda Lake heralds the start of the most spectacular and rewarding part of the trek – a descending stroll through Evolution Basin. At first the land is ice-scoured and naked, and feels even higher and more remote than it is. At the lake's outflow, the trail fords Evolution Creek and enters the stunning lower basin, whose flanking rock peaks tower overhead as you saunter from lake to lake. Every turn in the trail affords yet another flawless photographic composition. First into view are the impressive

**ABOVE** *From above the timber line in Dusy Basin the trail descends in long switchbacks beside the stream, into forested Le Conte Canyon, passing a waterslide of hundreds of feet of granite.*

rock faces of arrow-like Mounts Huxley and Fiske. A corner is turned and the pointed Mt Spencer soars above Sapphire Lake. Finally you reach Evolution Lake, dwarfed by the 900m (3000ft) wall of Mounts Mendel and Darwin.

The far end of Evolution Lake at the foot of the basin has a few pine trees to soften the landscape and may well be the most captivating camp site. Viewed from here, the 3792m (12,440ft) pyramid of Mt Spencer catches the setting sun and glows an unearthly red, as if it were on fire. Its summit is a wonderful perch from which to view the surrounding country, and the easy scramble up the granite slabs of the southeast ridge makes a rewarding day-hike.

After bidding a reluctant farewell to Evolution Basin, and promising one day to return, it is time to quit the high country temporarily. Beyond Evolution Lake the trail plunges in switchbacks into forested Evolution Valley, which is followed down to its junction with Goddard Canyon. The valley's beautiful but fragile meadows suffered from years of trampling before the decision was taken finally to reroute the trail around them to allow them to recover. Another backcountry ranger station is situated halfway along the valley.

## CANYONS AND LAKES

In Goddard Canyon the trail continues ever downwards beside the South Fork of the San Joaquin River to the junction with Piute Canyon – at 2454m (8050ft) the low point of the trek. The river surges between high, narrow walls, but thankfully all river crossings are bridged. The day's trek ends at Piute Canyon, where there are lovely camp sites hidden among tall pine trees beside the boiling river. Since it is downhill all the way, the 20km (12.5 mile) hike from Evolution Lake to here can easily be completed in a single day.

The canyon junction marks the point where the John Muir Trail is left to complete the Evolution Loop. Piute Canyon is a side canyon that leads back to the Sierra crest and so to the east side where you began the trek. The climb begins with a steep ascent, then levels off to a fork beneath Pilot Knob in Hutchison Meadow, where French Canyon branches to the left. The Piute Pass trail stays right of Pilot Knob, fords French Creek and climbs above the timber line into Humphreys Basin, a vast featureless bowl backed by monolithic Mt Humphreys. The trail traverses high above the Trout Lakes, Muriel Lake and numerous others to reach Piute Pass at 3482m (11,423ft) just beyond Summit Lake.

The 19km (12 mile) ascent can be broken with a high camp in Humphreys Basin, which gives one last night at altitude before crossing Piute Pass the following day. On the far side of the pass the trail descends past Piute Lake and Loch Leven to re-enter civilization at North Lake trailhead. From here it is some 19km (12 miles) along the road to South Lake trailhead. You can get there by a shuttle service or by walking or hitchhiking. Alternatively, you can hike the connecting trail that climbs about 760m (2500ft) across intervening Table Mountain, but be assured that this option will require more determination than any you have evinced so far!

# JOHN MUIR TRAIL

## By Hilary Sharp

The John Muir Trail (JMT) passes through the unspoilt wilderness of three of western America's National Parks – Yosemite, Kings Canyon and Sequoia. The route of the trek runs through the high Sierra Nevada mountains of California, from the world-renowned soaring granite walls of Yosemite to the summit of Mt Whitney, the highest summit in the USA outside of Alaska.

John Muir, after whom this trek is named, was a famous explorer of the back country and is considered the founding father of the national parks system. The John Muir Trail embodies his adventurous spirit as it takes the hiker into the back country wilderness on a route of great beauty and variety. This is the stuff of

dreams, where the pleasure of being surrounded by breathtaking peaks and deep clear lakes is enhanced by the joy of self-sufficient travel, the only constraint being to find a camp site for the night.

The trail usually takes about three weeks to complete and requires considerable organization. There are neither hostels nor huts en route, just a few lodges in the northern half of the trail. Walkers need to carry a tent and food for several nights at a time. Add to that the fact that most of the trail is above 2700m (8858ft), and crosses high passes on most days, and you have the makings of a serious adventure.

During the high-summer season many people hike this route, but camaraderie on the trail only adds to the joys of being in

such splendid scenery. The trail is generally well-maintained and waymarked, with no difficult parts. Water is plentiful, although it must be sterilized for drinking, and good camp sites abound. In summer, park rangers are often on hand to give advice.

The trek can be undertaken in either direction but the most popular is north to south and this way the ascent of Mt Whitney is right at the end – a fitting finale for tired but well-acclimatized hikers.

It's difficult to imagine a more inspiring starting point for any trek than Yosemite.

ABOVE *Yosemite Valley, start of the trail, viewed from the precarious summit of Half Dome, an optional extra on the JMT.*

YOSEMITE NP Cathedral Peak
**3326m**
Cathedral Pass Visitor Centre
**2957m** Tuolomne Meadows
Half Dome Columbia Finger
**2693m** Lyell Canyon ANSEL ADAMS
Nevada Falls WILDERNESS
Happy Isles Donohue Pass
Nature Centre **3370m**
**1230m**
*Thousand Island Lake*
Banner Peak Bridge Island Pass
Mount Ritter **3110m**
*Emerald Lake*
*Garnet Lake*
*Shadow Lake* Soda Springs
Devil's Postpile Reds Meadow
Mammoth Lakes
*Duck Lake*
*Purple Lake* Pass
*Virginia Lake*
Waterfall Silver Pass
TO VERMILLION RESORT **3322m**
*Edison Lake* Ferry
*Bear Ridge* INYO
NATIONAL
Rosemarie Meadows FOREST
Mount Hooper
**3763m** Selden Pass
**3313m**
Muir Trail Ranch
SIERRA
NATIONAL Evolution *Evolution Lake*
FOREST Meadows
Sapphire Lake Helen Lake
Wanda Lake Le Conte
Muir Pass Canyon
**3644m**
*Palisade Lakes*
Mather Pass
KINGS CANYON NP **3682m**
Pinchot Pass
**3697m** *Wood*
Bridge *Creek*
*Dollar Lake*
Fin Dome *Rae Lakes*
Glen Pass
**3651m**
Independence
SEQUOIA NP Forester Pass Center
**4017m** Peak
Tyndall Creek Junction Peak
Ranger Station
Mt Whitney
Three **4418m**
Rivers Crabtree Meadows
*Guitar Lake* Whitney
Portal
Lone Pine
Whitney Trail
Junction
**4115m**

0   10   20   30km
0   5   10   15 miles

Even the most seasoned traveller could not fail to be moved by the first sight of the impossibly sheer granite walls of El Capitan, at around 1000m (3300ft), the tallest monolithic granite face in North America, the goal of rock climbers worldwide. Huge waterfalls cascade down the walls of the valley, carved thousands of years ago from the rock by long gone glaciers, while the lower slopes host forests of pine, fir and manzanita bushes.

## RANGE OF LIGHT

Long ago inhabited by the Ahwahneechee Indians, who found shelter from the severe Sierra Nevada climate in this lush valley, Yosemite was discovered by white people in 1833. John Muir first visited Yosemite in 1868 and he named this mountain chain the Range of Light. Muir spent his life exploring the Sierra Nevada and was one of the first environmentalists, recognizing the potentially disastrous effects of the actions of man. Much of his time and energy was spent trying to conserve the wilderness. Later generations of Sierra explorers formed the Sierra Club and finally conceived this route in his memory. The region is also blessed with an

exceptionally mild and sunny climate. While rain is not uncommon, and snow plentiful in winter, the precipitation often only lasts a few hours.

## HAPPY ISLES

The trailhead for the trek is Happy Isles 1230m (4035ft) at the east end of the valley. This is a popular starting point for many hikes so the first few hours of climbing up out of the valley are generally quite social.

The crowds on the trail thin out after the spectacular sight of the Nevada Falls, cascading down in one sheer sweep to the valley floor far below. Soon after, the south face of Half Dome comes into view and this summit is the objective for many day hikers. Its east face is equipped with a fixed cableway, – two thick steel cables about 91cm (3ft) apart – which allows the steep and slippery granite face to be ascended by anyone with a good head for heights.

The trail onwards to Tuolomne Meadows goes over the rocky and beautiful Cathedral Pass at 2957m (9700ft), from where Cathedral Peak can be seen to great advantage. This Pass and the lakes nearby are a taste of what's to come, before a long descent finally leads to the comforts of Tuolomne

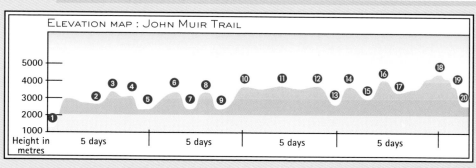

ELEVATION MAP : JOHN MUIR TRAIL

5000
4000
3000
2000
1000
Height in
metres

5 days      5 days      5 days      5 days

1   Happy Isles
2   Tuolomne Meadows
3   Donohue Pass
4   Island Pass
5   Reds Meadow campsite
6   Silver Pass
7   Vermillion Resort
8   Selden Pass
9   Muir Trail Ranch
10  Muir Pass
11  Mather Pass
12  Pinchot Pass
13  Wood Creek campsite
14  Glen Pass
15  Vidette Meadow
16  Forester Pass
17  Tyndall Creek campsite
18  Mount Whitney
19  Trail Camp
20  Whitney Portal

ABOVE *En route to the John Muir Pass, Wanda Lake, named after one of John Muir's daughters, provides a most welcome and beautiful spot for a rest.*

Meadows, where there is a lodge and store. Lyell Canyon is a grassy valley, formed by a clear, flowing river popular with fishermen, hikers and bears. The going is fairly flat all the way to its upper reaches where it gives way to more typical rocky terrain. The Donohue Pass is the first high col on the trek and this height of 3370m (11,056ft) will not be attained again until well into the second part of the trek.

## ANSEL ADAMS WILDERNESS

At Donohue Pass you leave the Yosemite National Park and enter the Ansel Adams Wilderness. This is a region of crystal clear lakes, high peaks and grassy meadows. Island Pass, at 3110m (10,203ft), leads to Thousand Island Lake, surrounded by the high peaks of Mounts Ritter and Banner. The next few hours of hiking continue to overload the visual senses: Emerald Lake,

Garnet Lake, Shadow Lake and Gladys Lake. The descent to the national monument of Devil's Postpile is long and somewhat dull, while the Postpile itself, a cliff of basalt columns of volcanic origin, is rather overrated. Far more exciting are the natural thermal baths at Reds Meadow resort and camp site.

Purple Lake and Virginia Lake provide yet more reflections en route to Silver Pass 3322m (10,900ft), an important landmark on the trail, since it gives access to Edison Lake. Just before the lake the JMT heads off southeast towards Bear Ridge. However, it's advisable to take a rest day at Vermillion Resort, one of the most important resupply posts on the trek. A ferry runs from the resort along the lake twice a day so it's worth taking this unless you feel in need of the extra 6.7km (4.2-mile) walk alongside the lake. This is the last place

where you can sleep in a room with a shower and eat a meal other than trail food. However, be sure to go armed with your plastic card – such luxury does not come cheap.

Back on the trail, Bear Ridge is reached by a fine series of switchbacks and from where you look down wooded valleys towards Muir Trail Ranch and ahead to Mt Hooper: a view of meadows interspersed with high mountain lakes as the route goes over the 3313m (10,870ft) Selden Pass and down past the multiple Sallie Keyes lakes. The Muir Trail Ranch is reached by a short detour from the path, but the main trail veers off left just above to descend to the River Joaquin. An unusual rocky gorge gives access to the Sequoia and Kings Canyon Wilderness and the Evolution Lake area with Evolution Lake, Sapphire Lake and Wanda Lake, named after one of John Muir's daughters. The latter is situated at 3,483m (11,426ft), just below the 3,644m (11,955ft) Muir Pass and the only shelter on the trek. This circular structure, built by the Sierra Club in 1930 for emergency use in bad weather, beckons the tired hiker for the last grind up to the col.

The final few days of the trek take us further and further into the wilderness, among soaring, pointed peaks, far, very far, from regular life – at least two day's walking to the nearest trailhead and then many miles along unfrequented roads to reach civilization.

Below the Muir Pass is Helen Lake, named for Muir's other daughter, and beyond is LeConte Canyon, framed on both sides by numerous granite cliffs.

Mather Pass, at 3682m (12,080ft), is the highest so far and is reached by the Golden Stairs, a section of trail hewn from the rock in the usual multi-zigzag style of this route. The Palisade Lakes give welcome flat terrain before the rigours of the final ascent to the col.

The 3697m (12,130ft) Pinchot Pass is an easy climb, since not too much altitude is lost from the preceding pass. From this point there remain three big climbs to reach the top of Mt Whitney. But first a pleasant break is had by descending to Wood Creek, which is crossed by its fine new suspension bridge. Onwards lies Glen Pass, lower than some at 3651m (11,978ft) but quite a climb, culminating in a steep and improbable trail manufactured into the hillside. En route are passed the rather gloomy Dollar Lake and then the attractive double Rae Lakes, crossed by an unusual isthmus.

Vidette Meadow offers the last escape route – itself at least a day and a half of walking – before entering the committing final stages of the JMT.

## MT WHITNEY

The route up to the 4017m (13,180ft) Forester Pass is dominated by the huge rocky summits of Center Peak and Junction Peak. The pass itself is attained by a pleasant meandering route, but the very steep south face is breached by yet another hewn path, which zigzags carefully down to flatter lake-strewn ground below. From here you have your first sight of Mt Whitney – the end of this adventure.

After a night camping at Tyndall Creek, next to an unusual reed-filled lake, the trail to Guitar Lake is easy after days of high passes. Crabtree Meadows is particularly tempting for a few hours lying in the sun before heading past Timberline Lake and

up to Guitar Lake, under the west face of Mt Whitney. A final night is spent here. As the sun sets on the nearby cliffs of Mt Russell and you hover at the lakeside to get that perfect reflection photograph, you will feel somewhat sad to know you will soon be leaving this land of dramatic views, perfect trails and fabulous wilderness.

The track to Whitney Trail Junction at 4115m (13,500ft) is as well-made as the rest of the JMT. Here a left turn takes you to the summit of the 4418m (14,496ft) Mt Whitney. The panorama is 360° and so you can look back the way you've come and ahead towards the Owens Valley far below in the lowlands. The summit has a shelter for emergency use and a toilet. The summit is also where the JMT officially ends. Clearly this is a rather daft end for a trek as, generally treks have to end where you can get back to civilization. So, back to Trail Junction and then up a hundred more feet to Trail Crest at 4145m (13,600ft) where you'll meet the hordes of people who, every day during summer, climb to America's highest summit outside of Alaska.

Prepare your knees here – there are allegedly 97 switchbacks from Trail Crest to Trail Camp at 3670m (12,040ft). This is a scruffy camp area and will be a shock after those nights spent in splendid isolation on the trail. There is another camp site lower down at Outpost Camp and lower down still at Lone Pine Lake. Maybe you'll stop or maybe the stomach groans will win over and you'll stagger all the way down to Whitney Portal, which may not be the official end of the JMT but serves as such for all practical purposes.

ABOVE *Trekkers approach the summit of Mt Whitney. The highest peak in the contiguous US, the trail to its summit is a popular hike.*

# ALASKA ON FOOT

## By Dean James

Across the mirrored lake, the haunting call of the Common Loon broke the evening's silence. Like the eerie call of the wolf, this bird's lonesome cry emphasized the true wilderness around us. As night fell the deep forest that surrounded us seemed to close in even further. In the growing darkness we all felt the timeless spirit of Alaska, a peculiar mix of awe for this untamed land and an almost primeval fear of its vast emptiness.

Our group of seven had arrived in Alaska, the most northerly state of the USA, some days earlier via the scenic flight from Seattle to Anchorage. Backpackers from the 'Lower 48', as the rest of the US is known in Alaska, seldom travel north-

wards to their last true wilderness. Directly south of Anchorage across the Cook Inlet, the Kenai Peninsula juts out into the cold northern Pacific Ocean. Despite lying in the backyard of Alaska's main city, the Kenai has maintained its 'last frontier' atmosphere. The mountainous, heavily forested peninsula still boasts its original array of wildlife: black and brown bear, wolf, moose, caribou, and wolverine. The Kenai has an extensive trail system and probably the best known trek in Alaska is along the Resurrection Trail System, made up of three connecting trails, The Resurrection Pass Trail, Russian Lakes Trail and the Resurrection River Trail. The 116km (72 mile) trek traverses the whole Kenai Peninsula from north to south along its eastern side.

The trail follows old abandoned routes blazed by the legion of gold prospectors who swarmed into the area during the Turnagain Arm Gold Rush of the 1890s. It starts near Hope, a small town that had its halcyon days during the gold rush.

### CARIBOU CREEK

Our first day was a short leg through deep spruce forest. It was late August and the short Alaskan summer was rapidly reaching its end, with the occasional hint of autumn colour in the trees and a lack of

**ABOVE** *Crossing the cold, clear, and possibly gold-laden waters, of a river in the Kenai Mountains.*

mosquitoes. These are Alaska's smallest but meanest residents, and are jokingly referred to as Alaska's National Bird. The occasional bear droppings reminded us we we were not the only users of this remote track! The first night's wild camp was in a shaded forest beside Caribou Creek. We spent the evening eating and drinking around a campfire. Gill, soon touched by gold fever, volunteered for dishwashing duties since, after the cleaning chores she

would try her hand at gold panning. Using the lid of the cooking pot, she would sluice some river gravel, looking for gold. That night was a cold, crystal clear one. The chill in the air whispered the near onset of winter. Between the dark, tall trees that surrounded our camp, patches of the night sky were brightly illuminated by innumerable stars. I peered upwards for what seemed like an eternity, before catching a fleeting glimpse of the fabled aurora bore-

alis. The dark nights of early September are one of the best times to catch this display, though it normally appears around the unearthly time of two in the morning.

## LONE WOLF

Our second day's trek led us higher, following the headwaters of Resurrection Creek. In the crystal clear morning, we had grand views through gradually thinning forest to the surrounding Kenai Mountains. As we gained altitude the individual trees became more and more stunted until we reached the tree line. In unusually sunny weather for the area it was wonderful to leave the claustrophobic forest behind and stride out over the open moorland of alpine tundra. We made our way up to the main watershed at Resurrection Pass (792m; 2600ft), which was carpeted in juniper berries and fiery Indian paintbrush. On each side of the pass were numerous small, beaver-dammed lakes, each displaying disused beaver dens,

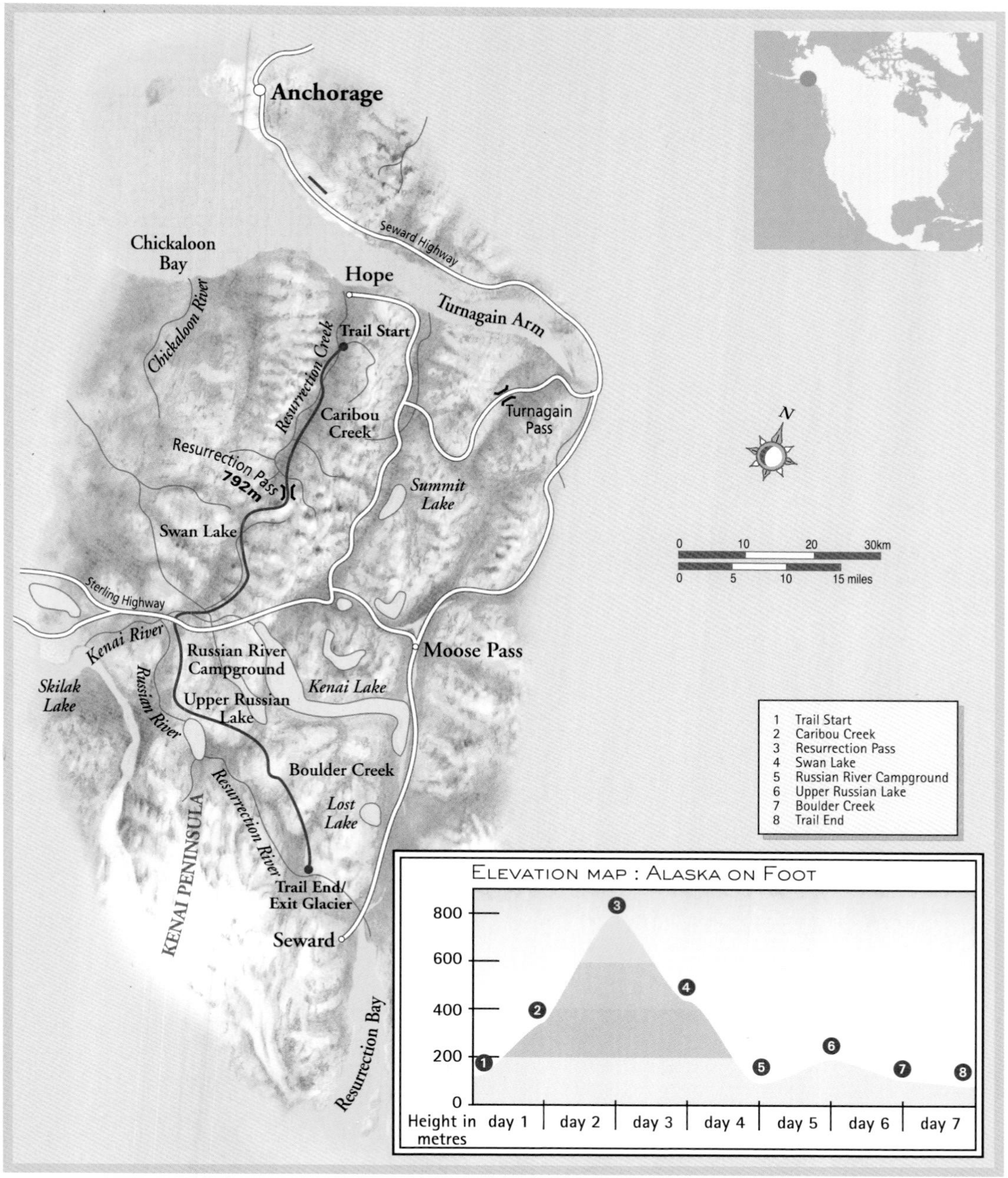

Map legend:
1 Trail Start
2 Caribou Creek
3 Resurrection Pass
4 Swan Lake
5 Russian River Campground
6 Upper Russian Lake
7 Boulder Creek
8 Trail End

ELEVATION MAP : ALASKA ON FOOT

### MOSQUITOES

These come very large hereabouts and are often referred to as the National Bird of Alaska. They are around from May to the first frosts of September/October, but peak around late June. During late August and early September you should not have too much trouble with them. Take some insect repellent with a high percentage of Deet (diethyltoluamide).

which meant we did not get to see these big-toothed characters. The 1000m (4000ft) mountains that flank the pass were covered in white reindeer moss, appearing like fresh snow on the hillsides. We camped at the top of the pass, surrounded by hordes of noisy, whistling marmots and were treated to a rare sighting of a small herd of the Kenai upland caribou. Our tents were pitched on a comfortable spot carpeted with the soft reindeer moss – you hardly needed a sleeping mat with this natural spongy mattress.

That evening three of the group walked to a small lake and came across a lone wolf who had come down to drink. For just a moment they were quite close and the animal looked directly at them with those intense, intelligent eyes. A rare experience even for the Alaskan wilderness.

Over the next couple of days we descended from Resurrection Pass into and along the Juneau Creek Valley with its tree-lined lakes. One night we camped in an idyllic position on the banks of Swan Lake near the head of the valley. The shal-

low sides of the lake were choked with dead or dying sockeye salmon who, after an arduous journey from the ocean and up the creek's rapids, had arrived back at the lake to spawn.

That evening, as the last colours faded and darkness fell, a large female moose quietly left the forest and entered the lake. She looked down her long, almost comical, nose at us for quite some time before lifting her long legs to splash across the lake and into the night. Soon it was totally dark and our imagination turned to the

OPPOSITE *The devil's club with its inch-long thorny spines. Alaska's early explorers and gold prospectors had epic struggles through whole forests of this infamous plant.*

BELOW *The wilderness peaks of the Kenai Mountains rising into an azure early morning sky above a forest shrouded in a damp, quiet mist.*

fresh bear droppings, huge paw prints, and claw marks on trees we had seen earlier in the day. Slightly nervous, we made our last toilet stops before retiring to our tents.

## DEEP FOREST

Descending the Juneau Creek Valley we again entered the deep forest and came across large areas of the infamous devil's club. This forest shrub, growing up to 2m (6½ft) in height, forms impenetrable undergrowth, especially along riverbanks. Its nutritious leaves are protected by 1cm (½-inch) long brittle spines that break off if brushed against and easily penetrate the skin. Stories of exploration in Alaska are littered with epics concerning this plant. Occasionally we came across the bright red berries of the infamous baneberry. This small, innocuous looking plant is highly poisonous and the ingestion of as few as six of its berries has been fatal.

Eventually the Juneau Creek Valley opened out into the impressive Kenai Valley. We crossed the deep turquoise Kenai River where it was bridged by the Sterling Highway. It felt quite strange to emerge from the solitude of the forest and stride out onto the wide, hard tarmac. The large pick-up trucks and motor homes whizzing past made us feel like weird, scruffy intruders. On the south side of the Kenai River we booked into the official Russian River Campground where, as previously arranged, a transit van turned up from Anchorage with our supplies for the next leg of our trip.

The next morning we again headed southwards into the wilderness, now fol-

### Bears

Like all wild animals, bears are only dangerous if taken by surprise or attracted by food. While travelling in bear country be alert at all times. Make noise, particularly where visibility is limited: this will warn the bears of your approach. (We normally bang a big wooden spoon on a cooking pot.) If you spot a bear, never approach it. The minimum safe distance from any bear is at least 100m (300ft), especially from a sow with young. Sleep in a tent rather than in the open. When camping, separate your cooking (food storage) and sleeping areas by distances of at least 100m (300ft). Either store food in bear-resistant containers (can be purchased in Anchorage) or suspend it in trees at least 3m (10ft) above the ground, using a heavy-duty stuff sack and a length of thin rope.

lowing the Russian Lakes Trail. Moose loomed out of the banks of valley cloud, which shrouded the forest in a damp, quiet mist. That night we camped on the wild shore of the Upper Russian Lake.

As we turned in for the night, dark sinister clouds were rolling in from the vast Harding Icefield to the south. The wind picked up and churned the lake into a mass of mare's tails and the forest swayed and creaked ominously. Only two of us remained outside the tents as the twilight faded. Just then, a wolverine quite nonchalantly sauntered directly through our camp, not even bothering to look sideways at us. We were frozen to the spot. Some claim that this badger-sized weasel is the only animal to which even the grizzlies will give way on a trail.

## GRIZZLY VISIT

Apprehensively we said goodnight and retired to our tents. We lay there listening to the wind until we heard the distinct noise of one of our cook pots moving outside. Through the slightest gap in the flysheet door, I peered out into the blackness, and there, very close to the tent, was the unmistakable hump-backed silhouette of a grizzly. The huge jet-black form moved through camp and out to the lakeside from where you could still hear the frantic splashing of the spawning salmon. After what seemed like an age of holding our breaths, the bear moved away, probably far more interested in the protein-rich salmon meal on hand.

The last leg of our walk was along the Resurrection River. This was the hardest

part of the trek as the trail is intentionally neglected by the authorities. Various bridges had been washed away leaving potentially awkward river crossings; and innumerable trees had fallen across the track, forming difficult barriers especially when backpacking.

## GOLDEN LEGENDS

In this wild, untamed landscape I constantly marvelled at the journeys into the unknown undertaken by the former gold miners. Legends abound concerning these wild 'sourdoughs' as they tirelessly explored the harsh country in search of the 'mother lode'. The old miners' trails became the mail routes to inland towns, when dog teams would pull the weekly mail from the 'Outside'. In 1924 the bush plane superseded the old reliable dog teams for mail transportation, but the huskies were to have their final most famous flourish. In 1925 a diphtheria epidemic threatened Nome, which was low on serum to inoculate the boomtown's population. Planes were sent out, but were turned back due to the harsh weather. In the end a relay of dog teams and their 'mushers' carried the urgent serum through to Nome in just over five days. These men and their dogs became heroes. Some of them, including Balto, the lead dog of the finishing team, became international celebrities. For nearly half a century

### RIVER CROSSINGS

It is best to cross in the early morning when the glacier-fed rivers are at their lowest. Loosen straps and undo the waist belt so that you can drop your rucksack if you fall. Always wear shoes or boots. Don't cross in bare legs. Use ski sticks for stability and cross as a group, linking arms or holding a ski stick horizontally, facing upstream. Keep something warm and dry to put on at the other shore.

ABOVE *Screen trekking alongside the mirror-like Juneau Lake, one of a number of tranquil lakes that line the Juneau Creek Valley.*

RIGHT  *Two lonely tents, a classic wilderness camp in the deserted heart of the Kenai Mountains.*
BELOW RIGHT  *Bull moose (Alces alces). Generally solitary animals, they may gather in small groups during winter months. They feed on low-growing and aquatic plants.*

the Iditarod Trail and the sled dog faded into history, but then in 1973 the first official 'Iditarod Trail Sled Dog Race' was run between Anchorage and Nome. The race has become known internationally as 'The Last Great Race on Earth'.

My meditations were rudely interrupted by what appeared to be a large bush moving off to the side of us. This turned out to be a set of impressive, velvety antlers belonging to an oversized bull moose. As we gingerly passed nearby, it lifted its weighty head and eyed us directly. The bull moose in its early autumn magnificence is a large, scary animal.

The small trail we followed wandered through stately conifers mixed with birches in autumn colours. The trees were slung with long drapes of old man's beard moss and the sun-dappled forest floor was carpeted with all sorts of colourful berries and golden ferns. In this enchanted forest I expected to run into hobbits at any time. The forest, touched by delicate autumn colours, contrasted wonderfully with the high peaks' shrouds of the first winter snow. In this great north land the change of seasons is a magical time.

It was with some relief that we crossed the last major creek on our trek by way of

a log-jam and again emerged from the forest onto the gravel Exit Glacier Road. As we ambled contentedly down this road towards the snout of the Exit Glacier and the end of our trip, I stared off into the wilderness of mountains and forest that led away from the edge of the gravel highway. Except for the thin, nearly overgrown

trail we had followed, the area was a pristine wilderness. Out in that vast forest, God knows how many wild animals were foraging. We had fleetingly passed their way and now it was as it should be: we were leaving for home. The land would soon be locked into the winter's big freeze and the forest would become even quieter.

# SOUTH AMERICA

BY JACK JACKSON

**S**outh America is a diverse region with mysterious civilizations, breathtaking

mountain scenery, colourful people, beautiful landscapes, tropical rain-

forests and abundant wildlife. Most trekkers know about Machu Picchu and

the Inca Trail, but the great variety includes volcanoes, mountains, glaciers and lakes as you

head south to 'the end of the world'.

Santa Ana
SAN SALVADOR  Leon
EL SALVADOR  TEGUCIGALPA
MANAGUA
**COSTA RICA**

Isla del Coco
(Costa Rica)

Islas Galápagos
(Archipiélago de Colón)
(Ecuador)

Equator
Isla Fernandina
Isla Isabela
San Salvador
Isla Santa Cruz
San Cristóbal

N

Tropic of Capricorn

P A C I F I C

O C E A N

ABOVE  *Quenual tree, Cordillera Blanca, Peru. Only found at high altitudes, these endangered trees form the world's highest forests.*

PREVIOUS PAGE LEFT  *Local girls from Pisac, Sacred Valley, Peru. The picturesque Andean village northeast of Cuzco is best known for its Sunday market.*

PREVIOUS PAGE RIGHT  *A church on the Altiplano, Bolivia. The Altiplano is the most extensive area of high plateau on earth outside of Tibet.*

## PERU

Peru is now recovering from the bloody, political upheaval with the Maoist guerrillas of the Shining Path during the 1980s and the early 1990s. People think of the country as mountainous, but there are a wide variety of ecosystems. The Andes range divides an immense desert coastline from a large belt of cloud forest, rich in flora and fauna, and a vast area of lowland Amazon jungle that covers nearly half the country.

The best time to visit Peru's various regions is complicated by the country's physical geography, with three main zones known as La Costa (the coast), La Sierra (the mountains) and La Selva (the jungle). The climate in the Sierra and Selva regions can be divided into a wet season (October to April) and a dry season (May to September). Some rain occurs during the dry season, but it is much heavier and more frequent in the wet season. Generally, summer along the desert coast is hot and sunny from December to March, and cooler with a frequent hazy mist from April to November. In the Andes, there are heavy rains from December to March, though usually these are worst between January and March. The Inca Trail is usually closed for these months due to the possibility of landslides or mudslides (*huaycos*). The best time for trekking is the relatively dry period from June to September. It is hot and humid all year in the jungle.

If you want to visit several different regions of Peru in one trip, it is best to travel in the middle of the dry season between June and September. If you have flown to Cuzco, 'the navel of the world', you must set aside time for acclimatization to avoid altitude sickness. The altitude averages 3500m (11,483ft) with Cuzco at 3360m (11,024ft) and Machu Picchu at 2400m (7874ft).

As in other parts of the world where too many trekkers on popular routes are causing erosion, litter, damage to trees etc., many areas in South America have introduced park fees, regulations, and limits on numbers. At the time of writing, the Inca Trail leading to Machu Picchu in Peru's Machu Picchu Sanctuary, a protected area managed by the Peru National Institute of Natural Resources (INRENA), only allows 500 people per day. This 500 includes guides, porters and helpers so it equates to around 150 tourists. Add the fact that permits must be applied for together with passport numbers in advance and independent trekkers who do not book through an overseas agent will find it difficult to obtain a permit. As with everything else in South America, regulations change often so check with the relevant authorities before you go.

## PATAGONIA

The Patagonian region, which includes parts of Argentina and Chile, has mountains, lakes, forests and glaciers.

Chile's Laguna San Rafael National Park was created on 17 June 1959, and was declared a UNESCO Biosphere Reserve in 1979. It is the largest National Park in the region of Aisén.

Created in 1937 and declared a UNESCO World Heritage Site in 1981, the vast Los

**ABOVE** *The Cuernos del Paine (Horns of Paine) across Lake Pehoe in the Torres del Paine National Park, Patagonia, Chile, make one of the most wonderful mountain views in the world.*

Glaciares National Park (Parque Nacional Los Glaciares) is home to the largest icecap outside of the polar regions. The northern part contains Cerro Fitzroy (called Mount Chaltel in Chile) and Cerro Torre, while the southern part has glaciers.

First created in 1959, but the current area was established at the beginning of the 1970s, the Torres del Paine National Park in Chilean Patagonia was declared a UNESCO Biosphere Reserve in 1978. It is beautiful, unspoiled and remote with craggy, near-vertical peaks that are among the most spectacular in the world. The park is open all year round but winter visitors should be prepared for severe weather. The park contains both the Cuernos del Paine (Paine horns) and the even more famous majestic

pink and white granite towers – the Torres del Paine (Towers of Paine).

Spring and summer (October to March) are considered the best time for visiting these southern regions, but flexibility in your itinerary is nevertheless recommended. Be prepared for constant wind. In summer, the average temperature is 11°C (52°F) and there are 18 hours of daylight.

A major problem in South America is theft. Put it down and look the other way, and it is likely to disappear, even in remote places. The danger is to property, not the person, so always be alert. You can buy an adjustable Steel-mesh net to cover rucksacks against theft, which will guard against thieves who slash rucksacks with a knife while it is on your back.

# INCA TRAIL

*By Dave Wynne-Jones and Chris Hooker*

The Machu Picchu Historical Sanctuary, in the Cordillera Vilcabamba mountain range, lies in a remote corner of southeast Peru, to the north of Cuzco and east of the Andean watershed. Its 325km² (125 square miles) contain a mix of subtropical forest and towering snow peaks, and a plethora of jungle-covered ruins linked together by Inca paths. The sanctuary was designated a UNESCO World Heritage Site in 1983.

In the early 20th century Hiram Bingham, a Yale historian, scoured this area in search of the fabled 'lost city' of Vilcabamba, a jungle redoubt where the last Incas had exiled themselves post-Spanish Conquest 400 years earlier. Discovering the jungle-covered ruins of Machu Picchu

in 1911, Bingham believed he had found Vilcabamba, an easy mistake to make given the circumstances. So if not Vilcabamba, what is Machu Picchu? Let the enigma fire your imagination; and develop your own theories.

## BRILLIANTLY ENGINEERED PATH

Trekking access to Machu Picchu is via the Inca Trail, a brilliantly engineered path traversing an extreme, densely forested topography. The trail, rediscovered after Machu Picchu, is the best-known trekking route in South America. After Bingham's team had cleared Machu Picchu, they traced the trail back to other settlements. Further discoveries on the trail were made by Paul Frejos in 1940.

Although it represented a mere fraction of the overall Inca road network, the trail was undoubtedly important: the quality of religious architecture at Machu Picchu and along the Inca Trail suggests as much, and it is likely that the trail served as a sacred pilgrimage route, probably related to the veneration of natural and celestial phenomena. But no contemporary written evidence exists – the Incas had no writing – and the Spanish chronicles make no mention of Machu Picchu, so it's all conjecture. However, we can assume that any memory

**ABOVE** *The beautiful complex of Wiñay Wayna, with its sacred terraces and temples, perches high above the Urubamba River.*

of its existence had gone by 1531 (the year of the Spanish Conquest); indeed the good condition of its structures suggests the Spanish never found it.

The sanctuary ranges in altitude from the 6271m (20,575ft) summit of Salkantay to forest valleys lying just above 1700m (5600ft). It has 10 life zones, ranging from alpine tundra on peaks like Salkantay and the 5917m (19,413) Humantay to steaming jungle. On the Inca Trail, a rapid succession of habitats are encountered, including sub-alpine *puna* (paramo) and seven forest types, each with its own flora and fauna. The trail is a paradise for botanists (there are 60 genera of orchids alone) and bird-watchers, with its 380 recorded species.

Although set in a wilderness region, the weight of trekker numbers and patrolling park rangers means the trek cannot be termed a wilderness experience; rather, it is an adventure of the mind and body, with a rich combination of natural environments and sacred ruins reachable only on foot. While it is big enough to absorb large numbers of trekkers, some camp sites become overcrowded in high season. By starting at Km 77 you have increased flexibility to avoid bottlenecks.

## SACRED VALLEY

The three-hour drive from Cuzco to the trailhead crosses rolling plains and descends dramatically to the Sacred Valley. The impressive ruins at Ollantaytambo – the region's most authentic 'Inca' town – should be visited before continuing on a rutted track along the Urubamba River to the settlement of Chilca (known as Km 77) at 2900m (9515ft). From here you cross the bridge and follow a dusty trail downstream through dry scrub of cactus and agave, with the majestic 5822m (19,100ft) Nevado Veronica looming large to the east. At Km 82 (2850m; 9351ft), an alternative starting point, trekkers cross to the east bank for a ticket check and re-cross to continue above the roaring Urubamba. About 3½ hours from Chilca the path climbs to a plateau. The Kusichaca Valley lies 100m (328ft) below at 2800m (9187ft), with the Llactapata ruins, ancient supply point for the Inca Trail. The path drops steeply to the valley, turns left (west) and ascends the agricultural valley a short distance to a camp site.

The path from Km 88 joins the trail at Llactapata. Trekkers coming from the railway stop cross the Urubamba, turn left (south) and walk through a stand of euca-lyptus to the Llactapata ruins.

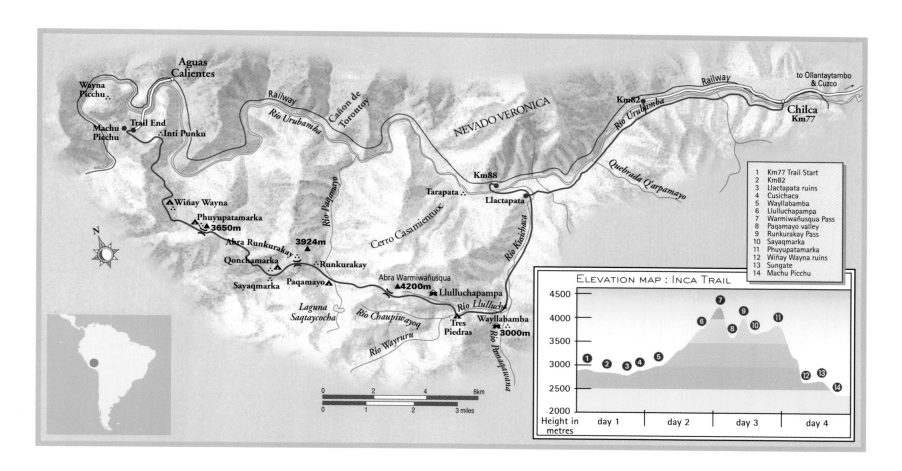

Screeching parakeets are often heard as you ascend the temperate Kusichaca. After 1½ hours, you reach Wayllabamba at 3000m (9843ft), the trail's last settlement, with shops selling basic provisions. Most trekkers camp here so by passing through mid-morning, you avoid the hordes. Wayllabamba is also a crossroads: trekkers joining from the Salkanatay Trail approach from the west, but the classic Inca Trail doglegs to the right (north) and begins a gruelling 1200m (3937ft) ascent towards Dead Woman's Pass (Abra Warmiwañusca). You pass Tres Piedras camp after one hour and, 30 minutes later, on a high bend, there is another camp. The steep path ascends into shady quenual (*polylepis sericea*) forest, an ideal habitat for many flower and bird species. Finally, following the Llullucha stream to the Llulluchapampa hanging valley at 3800m (12,468ft), forest gives way to *puna*. The camp site is relatively quiet, boasts great views of Nevado Huayanay and breaks up the long ascent to Warmiwañusca at 4200m (13,780ft),

Lack of oxygen takes its toll on the body for the final 400m (1312ft) of stiff, stepped ascent. From Abra Warmiwañusca a stepped path descends to the forested floor of the Paqamayo valley. The busy camp site at 3600m (11,812ft) is best avoided. The trail climbs to Runkurakay, Egg Fort; the views from this neat oval ruin would qualify it as a lookout post, though it may once have been a *tambo* (rest-house), or both.

The trail skirts two tarns before reaching the second pass, Abra Runkurakay at 3924m (12,800ft), from which the glaciers of the 6070m (19,915ft) Pumasillo are

**ABOVE** *Weavers from the Pisac area, Sacred Valley of the Incas, spin their wool.*

**OPPOSITE** *A view over Machu Picchu from the trail end, as the morning mist rises.*

seen glistening in the distance. The gradients and rugged terrain have by now made it clear why the Incas never developed the wheel! The path drops in tight zigzags then sweeps above Lake Yanacocha, suddenly revealing Sayaqmarka (Inaccessible Place) – a lookout with ritual functions or a fortress? – perched on a sharp spur ahead. Its ancient buildings look over two deep gorges which run into the Lower Urubamba.

The trail, with original paving and overhung now with vines, descends through hairpin bends and humid forest to river level and the restored Qonchamarka tambo. It ascends gradually, crossing a dry lake before traversing the length of a steep-sided valley and disappearing into a tunnel. By now the cloud forest is more luxuriant and gnarled trees, swathed in mosses and lichen, support bromeliads, giant ferns and

orchids. Hummingbirds and butterflies are also seen. The trail itself, an awesome example of engineering, is terraced into the valley side. Be careful here: what looks like a grassy mound beside the track may be only a patch of moss over an abyss!

## MAZE OF TEMPLES

The trail traverses to Abra Phuyupatamarka at 3650m (11,976ft), a spectacular viewpoint and the trail's best situated camp site. The breathtaking views take in forested mountains, the distant Pumasillo snow peaks and, 1800m (5906ft) below, the meandering Urubamba River. Don't miss the dawn views of Salkantay to the west. Just over the pass is Phuyupatamarka, or Town at Cloud Level, with its puzzling maze of temples and balconies. It has a chain of ritual baths (a feature of all sites from Sayaqmarka to Machu Picchu) and a reproduction of the Southern Cross constellation drilled into the rock. From a west-facing sacred platform 50m (164ft) above, you can see how this constellation dominates the night sky as it rises and sets over Salkantay!

The original route traversing the mountainside has fallen into disuse, so a huge flight of brilliantly-engineered Inca steps is now used. It plunges for about 1000m (3300ft) through increasingly dense forest, which is home to many bird species. The path twists through another short tunnel before dropping via dusty zigzags (the original trail briefly disappears here) to a complex of buildings, including a bunkhouse, known as Wiñay Wayna. This, the last camp site before Machu

Picchu, gets extremely busy and witnesses a mass daily pre-dawn exodus to the Sun Gate for sunrise. (Not only does it get crowded, but morning cloud often obscures Machu Picchu. Tranquility and a clear view are more likely in the afternoon). Ten minutes from the hostel is the sanctuary of Wiñay Wayna (Forever Young, named after an orchid), featuring ingeniously irrigated terracing and ritual baths. A work of art, it harmonizes with the landscape. It is also possible to reach the lower entrance of Wiñay Wayna in three hours via a trail from Km 104, where the 'backpacker' train stops beside the Urubamba River 700m (2297ft) below.

From Wiñay Wayna it is 1½ hours to Inti Punku (the Sun Gate). The trail, cut into the vertical Machu Picchu mountainside, undulates through steaming cloud forest, then cuts up to Inti Punku at 2700m (8859ft). Early afternoon is a good time to get here, since the Sun Gate and site should both be relatively peaceful. It is from here that you get the first stunning views of Machu Picchu a few hundred metres away; a panorama that will leave you in awe and convinced that every step has been worth it!

The site, straddling a ridge about 400m (1300ft) above the roaring Urubamba River, is surrounded by steep forest-clad mountains. If Machu Picchu was an astronomical observatory, as some believe, then the setting would make some sense. But how and why was it kept a secret?

The descent to the site at 2400m (7874ft) takes 45 minutes. Large backpacks must be checked at the lower entrance before you roam the ruins, which by mid-afternoon will be unencumbered by the masses who descend after lunchtime for their return train to Cuzco. It's a further 30 minutes by bus to Aguas Calientes at 2000m (6562ft) for your afternoon train. However, a second day at Machu Picchu is recommended, with an early start to maximize exploration time before the trains arrive. Side trips include the summits of the 2700m (8859ft) Wayna Picchu, a 1½ hour round trip, or the 3000m (9843ft) Puticusi (2½ hours). Both are reached by dramatic Inca paths.

Leave time to catch your train to Cuzco – one of the world's great railway journeys.

# HUAYHUASH CIRCUIT

*By Chris Hooker*

The compact Cordillera Huayhuash looks insignificant on most maps of Peru, yet it is one of the Andean chain's most magnificent ranges. One of 20 glaciated *cordilleras* (mountain ranges) in Peru, the Huayhuash soars dramatically from rolling grasslands some 50km (31 miles) south of the Cordillera Blanca. Its profile, seen from a distance, resembles that of a giant saw. A dozen ice-clad summits line its serrated ridge, with the 6635m (21,768ft) Yerupajá, the second highest peak in Peru, standing out above the rest.

The heart of the Huayhuash is a pristine wilderness. Fissured glaciers and moranic screes, vast U-shaped valleys, carpeted with *puna* (paramo grasslands) and adorned with sparkling lakes, stretch away towards the horizon. Occasional forests of quenual (*polylepis sericea*) punctuate the slopes of the western cordillera, though this tree is not found on the range's eastern flanks. The elusive vicuña – wild progenitor of the alpaca – is occasionally sighted, but more common on the bleak mountainsides are cattle, brought up by families of seasonal graziers whose crofts dot the *puna* landscape. This is the setting for the 190km (118-mile) Huayhuash Circuit which, over 10 to 13 days, loops the entire cordillera, crossing 10 high passes, nine of them above 4500m (14,700ft).

Ancient Andean people imbued their local mountain with great powers. In times of drought, famine or war, the *apu* (mountain spirit) might need appeasing through rituals and, even today, Andean farmers often pay homage to their local *apu* and weather creator at planting time. Archaeological discoveries have demonstrated that Inca priests occasionally performed sacrifices on sacred peaks at over 6000m (19,700ft), possibly making them the first humans to reach such altitudes. Many peaks remain sacred to the local community, but there is no evidence of ancient mountaineering exploits in the Huayhuash; not surprising, given the no-nonsense verticality and technical difficulty of its peaks.

ABOVE *Trekkers negotiate a cushion grass-covered plateau en route from Carhuacocha to Huayhuash*

The Austrian geographic team of Schneider and Awerzger made the first-known important ascent in the Huayhuash, reaching the summit of the 6344m (20,815ft) Siulá Grande in 1936, with Schneider going on to solo the 6017m (19,742ft) Rasac. Yerupajá was first climbed in 1950 by Americans David Harrah and Jim Maxwell. The best known epic in Huayhuash climbing annals is a singular feat of survival on the unclimbed west face of Siulá Grande in 1986, and recounted in British climber Joe Simpson's book, *Touching the Void*. He was badly injured after a fall near the summit and his partner, Simon Yates, started lowering him. In a blizzard, and with light failing, Yates unknowingly lowered Simpson over a precipice. Yates started to slip and had to cut the rope, leaving Simpson to plummet into a crevasse where he was left for dead. Despite several broken bones, he dragged himself out of the crevasse and then for miles across the glacier and moraine to safety. The Huayhuash Circuit trek does not require such extraordinary grit, but a degree of perseverance certainly comes in handy!

Recent road building has made Llamac an ideal start and finish point for the trekking circuit. Llamac can be reached by public transport from Huaraz (a two-leg journey via Chiquián). Alternatively, a vehicle can be hired in Huaraz for the whole journey. Approached by road, the massif is first glimpsed in the distance on the descent to the 3400m (11,1152ft) Chiquián, three hours from Huaraz. From there a rough country road zigzags down into the hot, dry Pativilca Valley 500m (1640ft) below, turns east and traverses a cactus-and-scrub environment. The road turns into the more fertile Llamac Valley, passing stands of eucalyptus, the odd walnut and a variety of blooms, including red, trumpet-shaped cantuta flowers (national flower of Peru and sacred flower of the Inca). Llamac (3200m; 10,500ft), one of only two villages encountered on the circuit, lies some two hours' drive from Chiquián. This agricultural village offers camping on its football field, basic hostel accommodation (no electricity yet) and donkey hire. Its several small shops are the last encountered for over a week.

## HOME OF THE PUMA

On the first full day of walking, a well-trodden trail is taken from the east side of the village. It climbs high above the Llamac valley, goes through a series of switchbacks and after about three hours, reaches a col at 3900m (12,796ft). On this ascent – steep in parts – the first effects of altitude might be felt. It is important to avoid overexertion and adapt pace to steepness and scarcity of oxygen. At the higher passes on the circuit, the body has only 60 per cent of the oxygen available at sea level. The trail

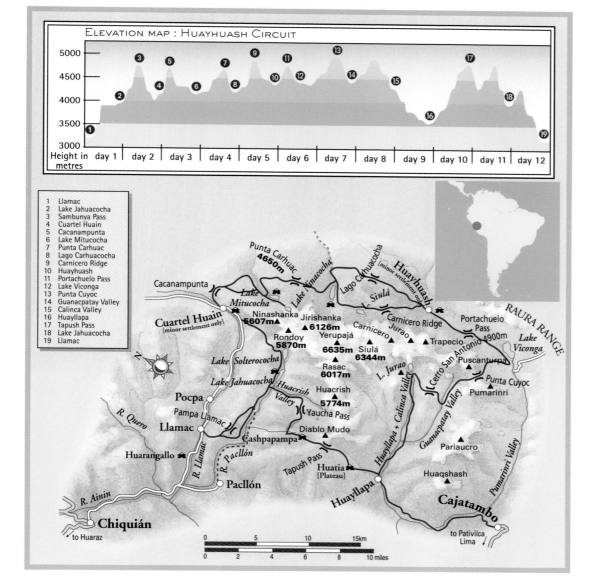

ELEVATION MAP: HUAYHUASH CIRCUIT

1  Llamac
2  Lake Jahuacocha
3  Sambunya Pass
4  Cuartel Huain
5  Cacanampunta
6  Lake Mitucocha
7  Punta Carhuac
8  Lago Carhuacocha
9  Carnicero Ridge
10 Huayhuash
11 Portachuelo Pass
12 Lake Viconga
13 Punta Cuyoc
14 Guanacpatay Valley
15 Calinca Valley
16 Huayllapa
17 Tapush Pass
18 Lake Jahuacocha
19 Llamac

RIGHT *The glacier lakes of Quesillococha and Siulá, beneath the towering Jirishanka and Jirishanka Chico peaks.*

traverses east, high above the Achin river and, reaching a spur, offers the first clear views of Huayhuash peaks: the 5870m (19,259ft) Rondoy, the 6126m (20,098ft) Jirishanka and Yerupajá.

The trail rounds several more spurs before meeting the river at about 3800m (12,400ft). Here, pale, coarse *ichu* grass predominates, while patches of dark quenual forest mark the valley sides. This copper-barked species, endemic to the Andes, thrives at up to 4800m (15,700ft) and is prolific hereabouts. Mammal species such as the elusive puma and Andean mountain cat shelter here. But the landscape is dominated by the looming, glacier-encrusted peaks of the cordillera. There is good camping in the shadow of these peaks, beside Lake Jahuacocha at 4050m (13,288ft).

A dramatic sector of the trek begins on the approach to the range's glaciated flanks via the north shore of the lake. As it zigzags up northwards towards the 4750m (15,585ft) Sambunya pass, the trail reveals ever more impressive panoramas of turquoise Laguna Solterococha and the colossal glaciers and peaks beyond, including Yerupajá. Beyond the pass, the first of nine above 4600m (15,093ft), there is a long descent to the Quebrada Rondoy (*quebrada* means valley) and on to the broad Quebrada Cuncush, where a vehicle track leads gently right and up towards the night's

camp near a tiny scattering of *chozas* (grazier crofts) known as Matacancha, or Cuartel Huain. At 4150m (13,615ft) Cuartel Huain also affords views to the southeast of the 5870m (19,260ft) Rondoy and the 5607m (18,397ft) Ninashanka. With clear skies,

early morning temperatures can drop to -4°C (25°F), providing a taste of what's to come: from here on the circuit descends only once below 4000m (13,000ft).

Giant condors may be spotted circling on the ascent to the Cacanampunta pass at

4700m (15,400ft). Flora is varied and features several medicinal plants, notably *wamanripa* (for pneumonia) and *anqush* (an expectorant). The pass marks the Continental Divide and transition from 'dry' to 'rainy' *puna*. An hour and a half after the pass there are views over Lake Mitucocha to several towering snow peaks – now seen from the east. Camp at Mitucocha, from where the twin summits of the 6126m (20,098ft) Jirishanka stand out crisply in the sharp light. There is a three-hour side trip to the lateral moraine above Laguna Ninacocha. To resume the circuit, skirt the southern edge of the boggy Janca Plain until 45 minutes from Mitucocha, then cut south up a relatively narrow valley and ascend gently to Punta Carhuac at 4650m (15,266ft). From here the towering form of Yerupajá stands out among a rank of gigantic peaks. Descend to Laguna Carhuacocha at about 4200m (13,700ft), where there are several camp sites with a backdrop of the 5960m (19,554ft) Carnicero, the 6344m (20,815ft) Siulá Grande, Yerupajá and Yerupajá Chico.

Resuming the loop, there is a choice of two routes to Huayhuash. The most interesting is via Laguna Siulá, cutting steeply up to the 4850m (15,912ft) Carnicero ridge. The ascent offers vistas to the north to match any on the trek. With luck and patience, vicuña may be sighted on the descent. In the shadow of Carnicero, the 5600m (18,373ft) Jurao and the 5644m (18,528ft) Trapecio, a vast expanse of cushion grass covers the flooded valley floor. It is surprisingly easy to hop, cushion by cushion, right across the valley! Two-house Huayhuash at 4350m (14,270ft) provides good camping.

The roughly 400m (1300ft) ascent to the Portachuelo pass is gentle. From the pass, the spectacular Raura range comes into view. Large herds of alpaca are often seen between here and Laguna Viconga at 4450m (14,600ft), situated at the end of the descent. A soak in the nearby al fresco thermal bath provides welcome muscular relief before tackling the 4950m (16,240ft) Punta Cuyoc next day. The three to four-hour ascent to the trek's highest point forks half way: go left for the more spectacular views of the southern peaks of the Huayhuash as well as those of the Raura to the east. The steep, scree descent back to the west side of the range leads into the long Guanacpatay Valley and camp at some 4,400m (14,436ft).

## FLUTED ICE WALL

From nearby, a rarely-trodden path leads to a remote corner of the cordillera. The route heads north up a spur abutting Cerro San Antonio to the ridge-top 4900m (16,077ft), where there is a view of the south faces of Yerupajá, Siulá Grande, Sarapo and Rasac, as well as the west faces of Jurau and Carnicero. The rather loose descent beyond leads to the upper end of Quebrada Calinca at 4300m (14,108ft) where camping options are plentiful. (Donkeys usually take a longer, but more straightforward route to the camp, descending the Quebrada Guanacpatay, then turning up the Calinca valley).

This is an excellent area for a free day, allowing exploration of the Quebrada Sarapococha, scene of Joe Simpson's dramatic retreat from the west face of Siulá Grande.

Its famous fluted ice wall is one of several fantastic landmarks that can be appreciated from the valley. The retreat from Sarapococha follows the Quebrada Calinca downstream. The trail drops below 4000m (13,124ft) for the first time since day one, passing below an impressive 200m (656ft) high waterfall and following the temperate, agricultural Quebrada Huayllapa to the village of Huayllapa at 3550m (11,648ft). Some supplies are available here and camping is permitted on the football pitch and at the hacienda across the river.

The 1250m (4100ft) ascent to the Tapush Pass is steep in places, but eases off after the Huatia plateau at about 4300m (14,000ft), where there is good camping, and ends after five hours. It's then an hour down to the Cashpapampa plateau and another half-hour to the junction with the Yaucha Valley. Heading east, a two-hour ascent culminates in a scree traverse to the Yaucha Pass at 4800m (15,700ft). On a clear day, the 6017m (19,742ft) razorback ridge of Rasac dominates the skyline.

A two-hour descent via the Huacrish Valley ends on the shores of Lake Jahuacocha at 4050m (13,288ft) for the second time, where a line of magnificent snow peaks forms the perfect backdrop for an overnight stop.

The final pass, Pampa Llamac at about 4300m (14,000ft), is reached in about three hours on an undulating path through quenual forest. It's a dusty, two-hour descent to Llamac. Public transport to Chiquián normally leaves late morning, and from Chiquián there is onward transport to Huaraz or Lima.

# ALPAMAYO CIRCUIT

*By Kathy Jarvis and Chris Hooker*

The Alpamayo Circuit is set in the extreme north of the Cordillera Blanca, the largest of 20 glaciated mountain ranges in the Peruvian Andes, and within the 340,000ha (840,000 acre) Huascarán National Park. A World Heritage site since 1985, the park straddles the continental divide; its 41 rivers draining either west to the Pacific Ocean, or east to the Amazon basin and Atlantic Ocean. The Blanca range boasts 29 snow peaks above 6000m (20,000ft) – including Peru's highest, the 6768m (22,205ft) Huascarán – making it the world's highest tropical mountain range, with the greatest concentration of tropical zone glaciers (663 in all).

The broad Santa Valley – or Callejón de Huaylas – flanks the Cordillera Blanca to the west. In its teeming produce markets, colourfully dressed villagers buy, sell and barter their highland produce, including guinea pigs, *cuchuru* (an edible highland algae) and potatoes in a variety of shapes and colours. Huaraz, Carhuaz and Yungay, all towns founded in the colonial era, boast very few colonial buildings because an earthquake on 31 May 1970 levelled much of the Callejón. While Huaraz and Carhuaz were able to rise from the rubble, Yungay was less fortunate: the violent quake had also shaken loose a vast section of glacier from the flanks of Huascarán, producing a cataclysmic mud-slide. Yungay's 25,000 inhabitants, with only seconds to react, were inundated by a sea of mud, ice and boulders. Since 1970 they and their town

have remained interred under several metres of earth. Meanwhile, the new town of Yungay thrives just a few kilometres further along the road.

### FIRST MOUNTAINEERS

Mountaineering records for the Blanca begin in 1903 when an Englishman, C.R. Enoch, in the area to establish a trading route across the cordillera, was drawn to the huge Huascarán massif. With a small team of locals he attempted to scale it, but gave up at about 5100m (16,733ft). A few

TOP *The view of the snow and ice-capped peaks of Santa Cruz and Caraz, is just one of many mountain vistas in the Cordillera Blanca.*

years later, and after several failed attempts, a diminutive American woman called Annie Peck became the first person to summit Huascarán.

After 1932 a number of Austro-German expeditions came to the region, with Dr Hans Kinzl and Erwin Schneider the prime movers. In 1936 they photographed Alpamayo, with Kinzl returning in 1939 to summit several unclimbed 6000m (20,000ft) peaks. Soon the Cordillera Blanca – and especially Alpamayo, which now boasted the soubriquet 'world's most beautiful mountain'– was attracting some

of the world's top climbers. The first attempt on Alpamayo was made in 1948, via the north ridge, by a Swiss team. They failed when a cornice collapsed on them, but miraculously all survived. The north ridge next received climbers in 1951, but poor visibility stopped the Franco-Belgian expedition short of the summit – by a mere 75m (250ft)! Alpamayo was finally summited in 1957 – via the south ridge – by a German expedition. A later Italian team established today's standard 'Ferrari' route on the southwest face, and the north ridge was eventually conquered in 1966 by a

British expedition. Since the sixties, countless serious ascents have been made throughout the range as the Blanca gained world recognition as a centre for both mountaineering and high-altitude trekking.

## ANCIENT CULTURES

For millenia the Blanca region was settled by ethnic groups, as witnessed by ruins at Gekosh, Willcahuain, and Jonkapampa. The most ancient cultures developed in the northern part of the park – the cave remains at the Cueva del Guitarrero near Yungay date back some 5000 years. The region's major archaeological site, and one of the most important in Peru, is Chavín de Huantar, situated to the east of the Blanca. In its heyday 3000 years ago it served as the ceremonial centre of a pan-Andean cult of feline worship.

## TRAILHEAD

To reach the Alpamayo Circuit's trailhead, leave Huaraz early for the four-hour journey to Hualcayán. The drive along the agricultural Callejón de Huaylas is on tarmac and provides tantalizing views of some of the Cordillera Blanca's most impressive peaks, including the 6188m (20,303ft) Copa, the 6768m (22,206ft) Huascarán and Huandoy's three jagged summits, of which the highest is 6359m (20,864ft). Hualcayán village, at 3000m (9843ft) is two hours on from Caraz, at the end of a dirt road. Here burros (donkeys) and arrieros (donkey drivers) can be hired (take enough extra food for your arriero).

The path ascends in sweeping zigzags, offering superb views over the Callejón.

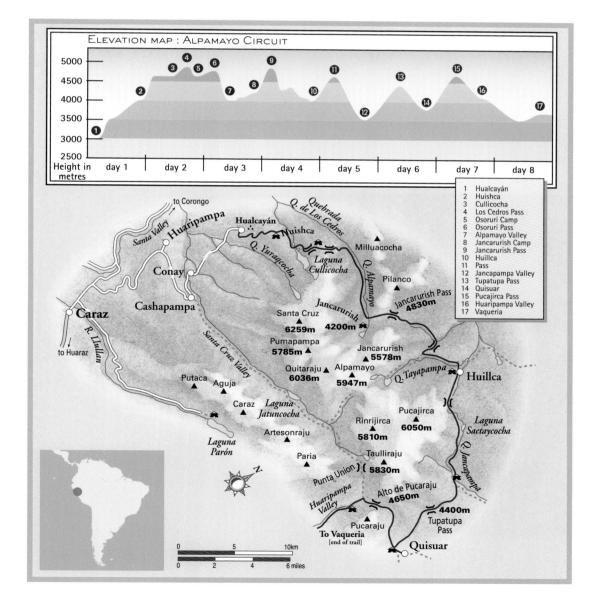

ELEVATION MAP : ALPAMAYO CIRCUIT

1 Hualcayán
2 Huishca
3 Cullicocha
4 Los Cedros Pass
5 Osoruri Camp
6 Osoruri Pass
7 Alpamayo Valley
8 Jancarurish Camp
9 Jancarurish Pass
10 Huillca
11 Pass
12 Jancapampa Valley
13 Tupatupa Pass
14 Quisuar
15 Pucajirca Pass
16 Huaripampa Valley
17 Vaqueria

The first camping option is on a 4000m (13,124ft) plateau at Huishca, some four hours from Hualcayán. Nearby, the Quebrada de Los Cedros gorge plunges away, with copper-barked quenual trees (*Polylepis sericea*) lining its sides. The trail climbs on until it meets a water channel carved into the sheer mountainside, which it follows upstream to Laguna Cullicocha at 4600m (15,093ft), some four hours from Huishca. The lake shore offers camping near the guardian's hut, as well as the first close quarters view of the three magnificent ice peaks of Santa Cruz Norte, Chico and Grande (6241m; 20,476ft), with their sheer flutings and immense cornices. Spectacular mountain views continue as the path climbs north above the lake.

The first pass, Paso de Los Cedros at 4850m (15,910ft) is the highest on the trek. Rabbit-like *viscacha* are often seen scurrying among the moraine debris hereabouts. From Hualcayán to this point, there has been virtually no let-up in the ascent, and the descent to Osoruri at 4600m (15,100ft) comes as a relief. Osoruri offers camping on a sometimes boggy plateau. A 45-minute ascent takes you over the 4750m (15,580ft) Osoruri Pass and into a steep two-hour descent to the floor of the Quebrada Alpamayo, where a small farming hamlet of straw-roofed houses nestles.

## TERRACED FIELDS

Terraced potato and bean fields perch on the high valley sides where goats, tended by young children, also graze. Turning right, you follow the Los Cedros River upstream, where camping options abound. Across the valley to the north, waterfalls tumble off the glaciers of Milluacocha, as a dramatic panorama of snow peaks up ahead also begins to unfold. Alpamayo appears during this approach 'as all that can be expected of the perfect ice-peak' as Kinzl and Schneider wrote in their book *Cordillera Blanca (Peru)*. The gentle ascent culminates at Jancarurish camp (4200m; 13,780ft) beneath the distinctive form of the 5947m (19,512ft) Alpamayo. It soars spectacularly as two sharp summits separated by a corniced razor ridge. Although smaller than its neighbours, it is extremely graceful and its profile is unmistakable. However, it is probably true to say that the mountain obtained its unofficial title of 'the most beautiful mountain in the world' from the view of its southwest flank as seen from the adjacent 6036m (19,804ft) Nevado Quitaraju. From this angle, Alpamayo appears as a perfect, steep trapezoid of fluted ice.

## OPAQUE TURQUOISE LAKES

Moving on, the Los Cedros River has to be forded and a *bofedal* (marsh) negotiated before you take on the gruelling ascent to Abra Jancarurish pass at 4830m (15,850ft). The views back across bleak moranic moonscapes and opaque turquoise lakes towards the glaciers and peaks of Alpamayo, the 5578m (18,301ft) Jancarurish, Quitaraju and the 5785m (18,980ft) Pumapampa are awesome. From the pass, which marks the continental divide, the glaciers of the 6050m (19,850ft) Nevado Pucajirca's triple peaks to the southeast cleave the clear blue sky. The trail descends steeply to a green valley, the rolling landscapes roundabout reminiscent of the Scottish highlands.

**ABOVE** *Loaded donkeys carrying trekkers' kit. Each* arriero *(donkey driver) is in charge of a maximum of five donkeys.*

Crossing the narrow valley, you ascend briefly to a low pass to the right and descend to the Quebrada Tayapampa. Here, a rutted track leads down to the tiny settlement of Huillca at 4000m (13,124ft), with good camping nearby. Under an agreement with the national park, local people rear alpacas on the broad Huillca plain. From Huillca, the trail southeast climbs a steep, narrow valley. From the 4600m (15,093ft) pass, a surprisingly verdant panorama unfolds to the east, and Nevado Pucajirca to the south. The trail descends toward the enchanting Laguna Sactaycocha. The scattered quenual forests are home to indigenous species such as the elusive *oso de anteojos* (spectacled bear) and puma, as well as the *taruga* (mountain deer). Other mammal species recorded in the national park include mountain cat and vicuña, all of which have been heavily hunted. A total of 112 bird species have been recorded, including the Andean condor, giant hummingbird and ornate tinamou.

## WOODEN PLOUGHS

The trail descends for several hours, initially through subalpine *puna* (paramo) and then through lush green landscapes, including humid montane forest – you should spot bromeliads and, with luck, some mountain orchids. In the broad Jancapampa valley (3500m; 11,483ft), at the foot of the 5810m (19,060ft) Rinrijirca, there is good camping and dramatic views to the west of waterfalls cascading from a vast, glacier-encrusted cirque. Farming communities dot the nearby slopes. An estimated 74 families live within the park, and

**ABOVE** *The lakes of Orconcocha and Chinancocha in the Llanganuco valley, best appreciated from the Portachuelo de Llanganuco pass, where the road crosses the Andes on the drive back to Huaraz.*

encountering the scattered crofts of grazier and farming communities is a highlight of the trek. The climb south leads through a community where local Quechua-speaking Indians, aided only by oxen and wooden ploughs, cultivate nutritious native crops such as *chocho* (edible lupin seeds).

The Tupatupa pass at 4400m (14,400ft) is reached after four hours. From here, a stunning panorama, encompassing several summits of the northern Cordillera, reveals itself. This dramatic backdrop remains for much of the descent to Quisuar at 3800m (12,465ft), where there are good camp sites. The path up to the 4650m (15,260ft) Alto de Pucaraju pass is steep. From the top, another breathtaking view unfolds, with the jagged profile of the 5830m (19,128ft) Taulliraju looming large to the northwest. Andean condors might be spotted as they soar on thermals.

The rocky path drops to Quebrada Huaripampa and meets the main valley path coming from the north. Turn left and follow the trail south, threading in and out of forest and crossing the occasional clearing (most provide camping possibilities).

The final section of the trek comprises a gentle descent via the tiny village of Huaripampa. To the north is a dramatic view of Nevado Chacraraju's east ridge (6112m; 20,052ft). There is a final steep ascent to the road head at Vaqueria. Here it is possible to find public – and sometimes private – transport for the memorable five-hour return journey to Huaraz. The mountain road re-crosses the Andean watershed at the Portachuelo de Llanganuco pass (4767m; 15,640ft), offering postcard views of the Llanganuco Lakes, Huascarán, Huandoy (6356m; 20,853ft) and a host of other peaks.

# TORRES DEL PAINE

## By Chris Hooker

The Parque Nacional Torres del Paine lies in the wilds of southern Chile, sandwiched between the windswept Patagonian steppe to the east and the vast Continental Icecap to the north and west. To the southwest are the fjords and islands of the Chilean Archipelago. The Paine, one of South America's most spectacular national parks, is a wonder of natural sculpture. Its 2422km² (935 square miles) display many of the typical natural features of southern Patagonia, including soaring granite peaks, vast glaciers, jewel-like lakes and dense Magellanic forest. Paine's various life zones harbour many endemic bird and mammal species and it was granted World Heritage status in 1978.

The weirdly contoured Paine massif, which surges dramatically skyward from a low-lying plateau, is the centrepiece of the park and the hub of the great Paine trekking circuit. This demanding 10-day loop takes trekkers to the pristine heart of one of the world's most breathtaking wildernesses. The ferocious westerly winds that buffet this region throughout the trekking season are part and parcel of the Paine experience. They are due largely to the nearby South Patagonian Icefield, an anomaly given the moderate latitude – some 50 degrees south. Relatively recently (in geological terms), this entire area was choked with ice; the colossal glaciers that snake into the park today are a legacy of this era.

The breathtaking Paine range is first viewed from afar on the approach by vehicle from Puerto Natales, its various features coming into focus on rounding the east shore of Lago Sarmiento. The monolithic Cerro Paine Grande dominates its western flank, with the aptly named Cuernos (horns) thrusting skyward to the right. The bulky Cerro Almirante Nieto forms the eastern shoulder of the massif, obscuring from view the Torres – these three frost-polished columns of pink granite first appear in the distance when you

**ABOVE** *The view south over Lago Nordenskjöld from the trail between Refugio Los Cuernos and the Ascensio Valley.*

approach the Laguna Amarga gate from the east. Entering the park, grey *coiron* (bunch-grass) gives way to lush, rolling pre-Andean heath, one of Paine's four floral communities. This is guanaco country, and close encounters with groups of the wild camelid – once on the brink of extinction – are commonplace.

The dirt road to Lago Pehoe winds through a zone characterized in spring by bright yellow *calafate* (burberry) flowers and blazing red *notro* (firebush). The route veers west and passes high above turquoise Lago Nordenskjöld, sparkling at the base of the massif. Here, for the first time, the scale of the landscape hits home: the lake lies a mere 60m (197ft) above sea level while the peaks beyond soar to 3000m (9843ft). The Pudeto boat jetty and ranger post is located in the northeastern inlet of Lago Pehoe, some three hours from Natales by bus. Strong winds can turn the lake into a seething cauldron of whitecaps, but with benign conditions and clear skies, the half-hour catamaran crossing to Refugio Pehoe bunkhouse and private camp site (on the northwest shore) is a pleasure.

## GEOLOGICAL ORIGINS

To the north, the Cuernos rise to 2600m (8531ft). Their unusual stratification and teat-shaped crowns are the result of dark, crumbly shale overlying their granite base. The Cuernos, indeed the whole massif, have their geological origins a mere 12 million years ago in a tectonic convulsion that thrust a large body of intruded igneous rock upward. (This compact range does not, strictly, belong to the much older Andean range, whose median lies to the west.) Since then, frost action and glacial erosion have cracked and polished the batholith to its current profile.

Heading west, the boat is soon in the shadow of the frequently cloud-bound Cerro Paine Grande. Refugio Pehoe's setting is spectacular and exposed. The camp site has windbreaks, but gales can shred a badly pitched tent in minutes. The anti-clockwise circuit begins here, with an undulating walk towards the Cuernos through mixed grassland and sparse forest, passing two large tarns occupied by ducks and coots. After two hours, the trail reaches the Valle Francés and crosses the river by a suspension bridge. On the far side is the free Campamento Italiano, consisting of several clearings within deciduous Magellanic forest.

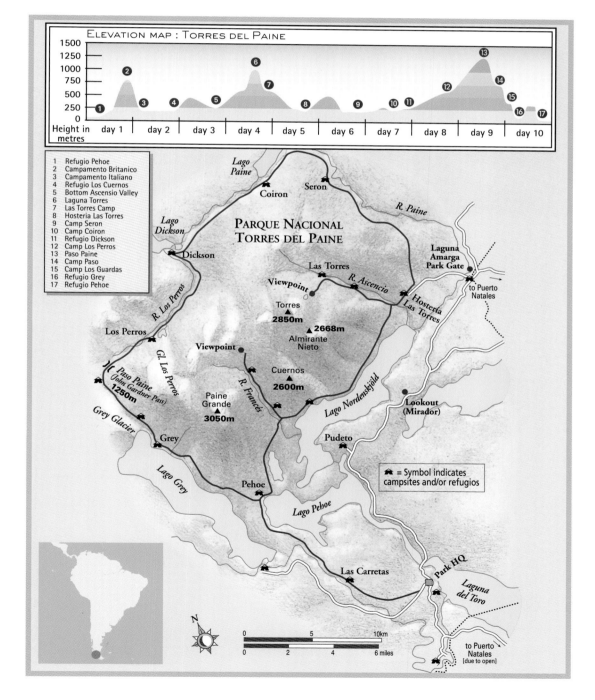

ELEVATION MAP : TORRES DEL PAINE

1 Refugio Pehoe
2 Campamento Britanico
3 Campamento Italiano
4 Refugio Los Cuernos
5 Bottom Ascensio Valley
6 Laguna Torres
7 Las Torres Camp
8 Hosteria Las Torres
9 Camp Seron
10 Camp Coiron
11 Refugio Dickson
12 Camp Los Perros
13 Paso Paine
14 Camp Paso
15 Camp Los Guardas
16 Refugio Grey
17 Refugio Pehoe

PARQUE NACIONAL TORRES DEL PAINE

= Symbol indicates campsites and/or refugios

The first side trip, steep in places, begins here, ascending the dramatic Valle Francés through *lenga* (southern beech) forest, which becomes more stunted with every metre gained. Early on, the trail requires a few short, steep clambers on moraine boulders. Periodic ear-splitting cracks announce the calving of ice from hanging glaciers on the sheer east face of Paine Grande to the left. The disintegrating glaciers are usually clear of cloud since the valley lies in the lee of the mountain.

## ICE MUSHROOMS

When weather conditions permit and Paine Grande's summit ridge is in view, ice mushrooms – typical of southern Patagonian snow peaks – can be seen. The ascent continues to a wind-buffeted moraine ridge. Some bog land has to be negotiated before the Campamento Británico is reached after two hours. A rickety hut, used by pioneering British climbers, stands in a clearing and a viewpoint just beyond affords stunning panoramas of the Cuernos to the east. To the north, a sheer wall of shale-capped granite has been sculpted by ice and wind into several improbable shapes including the Aleta de Tiburon (Shark's Fin). The walk back to Campamento Italiano takes about 1½ hours.

The trail continues around the north shore of Lago Nordenskjöld, reaching the Refugio Los Cuernos bunkhouse and camp site after two hours. A long, exposed slog follows as the trail heads northeast for five more hours across open, undulating terrain before emerging onto grazing plains near the outlet of the Rio Ascensio. The Las

**ABOVE** *A stream cascading towards Lago Nordenskjöld, with the Cuernos del Paine in the background.*

Torres hotel, bunkhouse and private camp site are a little beyond, but you can – time and energy permitting – turn left and push on up the Ascencio Valley. The steep, zigzagging path climbs northeast, turns into a ravine high above the foaming river and drops to river level at the Refugio Chileno bunkhouse and camp site after an hour. It is a further 1½ hours uphill to the Torres camp site, involving two stream crossings. You may spot (or hear) one of Patagonia's extrovert forest-dwelling bird species, such as the screeching Austral parakeet (southernmost parrot species in

the world), flame crested Magellanic woodpecker or mottled Chilean flicker.

The path emerges onto a sandy slope above the concealed woodland camp site. Waymarks lead left to a broad, steep boulder slope and up to the Laguna Torre *mirador* (lookout). Aim to be there in the morning for ideal light conditions. A final clamber over boulders ends at the moraine lip (1000m; 3300ft), with dramatic views of the three pillars soaring above the glacier-encrusted cirque. The descent to the Las Torres hotel, bunkhouse and private camp site takes three hours, and the circuit trail continues anticlockwise to the private Campamento Seron camp site. Hooting buff-necked ibis and the dive-bombing southern lapwing abound in the eastern sector of the park. Pairs of upland goose are also commonplace. The track follows the Rio Paine, crossing flower-filled meadows. Stands of skeletal *lenga* are the legacy of ranchers' slash-and-burn farming methods. This, the most sheltered sector of the park, only obtained protected status in 1975.

## HOUSE-SIZED ICEBERGS

An hour on from Seron, the trail climbs left to a shoulder and descends westward, revealing new panoramas to the north. Two hours further on is the free Campamento Coiron camp site, then a level, three-hour trail across boggy floodplain ends at Refugio Dickson bunkhouse and private camp site. House-sized icebergs cross Lago Dickson, the source of the park's hydrological system. In this, the remotest sector of the park, far fewer trekkers are seen. The roughly 1000m (3300ft) ascent beginning at the Refugio Dickson is the circuit's toughest. The path follows the Los Perros torrent through dense forest and five hours on reaches iceberg-filled Laguna Los Perros, and the dramatically located Los Perros camp site. Above the tree line, the final few hundred metres are on bare rock. Careful route finding is required in poor visibility or when snow is deep. Also beware severe winds at and near the Paso John Gardner, also known as Paso Paine (1250m; 4101ft). If conditions are clear, an awesome

panorama unfolds, with the immense blue Grey Glacier 1000m (3300ft) below and the ice field beyond it filling the view.

The marked track drops to the tree line, where it continues through grotesquely-knotted, branch-strewn forest. The going is very slippery when wet. The first camp site, the free Campamento Paso, is two hours from the pass and Campamento Los Guardas (also free) a further three hours on. The trail improves for the final forest section down to the popular Refugio Grey bunkhouse and private camp site, sited near the fast-receding glacial snout.

On the final four-hour leg to Refugio Pehoe, trekking activity is relatively frenetic. After an hour of steady and then steep ascent, there is a great view back to the forest-fringed Grey Glacier. In autumn, when the *lenga*'s leaves turn a dramatic red, the spectacle is stunning. A little further on the iceberg-cluttered southern end of Lago Grey comes briefly into view. Finally, the path crosses a low ridge, veers southeast and descends for an hour to Refugio Pehoe, the starting point. Exit is either via park HQ at Lago Toro (a six-hour walk), or back across Lago Pehoe by boat.

ABOVE *A trekker stands on the moraine boulders above Laguna Torre, admiring the three frost-polished Torres del Paine and the Nido de Condores (at right). The Torre Central (second left) was first summited by Chris Bonnington and Don Whillans in 1963. Its east face measures well over 1000m (3300ft).*

# ILLAMPU CIRCUIT

*By Kathy Jarvis*

The Cordillera Real rises from the eastern shores of Lake Titicaca on the Bolivian high plains known as the Altiplano. This range of icy peaks is a part of the Andes chain, which runs over 7000km (4300 miles), the full length of the South American continent. The Cordillera Real stretches 150km (93 miles) from Illimani just southeast of Bolivia's largest city, La Paz, to the massif of the 6368m (20,893ft) Illampu and the 6427m (21,087ft) Ancohuma to the northwest. Several ancient paved paths cross the range, evidence of pre-Colombian civilizations. These laboriously constructed roads run from the high Altiplano to the fertile tropical lowlands of the eastern Andean slopes and are usually attributed to the Incas, who ruled most of Bolivia and Peru in the 15th and 16th centuries. It is thought that much of the Inca gold in the ancient capital of Cuzco came from the Tipuani area on the eastern side of the Andes. Gold is still mined in this area.

## STONE ROADS

Stone roads were needed for the movement of Inca armies as they expanded their empire. A network of routes was also developed for trade and the transportation of minerals such as gold and silver. This labyrinth of paths provides remote Indian villages with their only line of communication to the outside world. The Illampu Circuit follows these well-trodden trails over seven days as it takes trekkers high around the flanks of the Illampu-Ancohuma massif. This is a tough trek that starts and finishes in subtropical Sorata at 2695m (8842ft), in between taking trekkers over four passes higher than 4,000m (13,000ft). The fourth and highest one, Abra de La Calzada, takes you up to a heart-pounding 5045m (16,552ft). There is a total of almost 4500m (14,400ft) of ascent and descent, so a high degree of fitness and acclimatization is required. The regular circuit may even be lengthened by taking

**ABOVE** *The distinctive shape of the Condoriri massif dominates the skyline on the drive along the edge of the Cordillera Real to the start of the Illampu trek.*

time to trek high above Sorata to Laguna Chillata at 4204m (13,793ft) and Laguna Glaciar. There are superb views on the trek up of the western slopes of Ancohuma and Illampu, and over the Rio San Cristobal valley far below. At a breathtaking 5038m (16,530ft) Laguna Glaciar is fed directly from the glaciers of Illampu, and usually boasts a few icebergs. This area is sacred to the local Aymara Indians and it is highly recommended to take a local guide on this three to four day diversion.

The main Illampu trail passes through isolated settlements, traversing various vegetation zones, from lush subtropical palm trees through semi-arid valleys terraced and cultivated for thousands of years, to elfin forest of stunted, gnarled *polylepis* trees. The trail finally emerges in stark alpine-type *puna* (a high, cold, dry plateau), where only a few well-adapted plants cling to barren, permanently frozen ground. Throughout the trek there is a variety of animal life: vicuña, the shy mem-

bers of the camelid family, graze warily, once hunted almost to extinction for their fine coats; *viscachas* (rabbit-like rodents) scuttle to and fro among the boulders; Andean geese and other water birds populate the many lakes. The Andean condor soars overhead in search of its next meal.

## GUIDE AND DONKEYS

Sorata, the start and finish point of the trek, is a small colonial town with a semi-tropical climate, lush vegetation and views of the snowcapped peaks of the 6368m (20,892ft) Illampu and the 6427m (21,086ft) Ancohuma.

Leaving behind the waving palms of balmy Sorata, the track heads steeply up out of town on Calle Sucre then Calle Illampu before getting onto a wide path heading southeast. Shortly after leaving town, take the path to the left winding along above the Lakathiya River valley towards the small village of Quilambaya. Route-finding at this early stage can be tricky, so take a guide and donkeys, at least on this first day. It is a good idea to do so throughout – to lighten your load and to provide an insight into local life. At Quilambaya go left at the fork through an avenue of tall cacti and continue climbing steeply. The path levels out and contours left, then sharply right to cross a bridge over the Lakathiya River. Climb the winding track ahead to reach the village of Lakathiya. Walking through the village, keep an eye out to the left for the point where two branches of the river meet. Follow the left bank of the left branch, crossing the river on a small stone bridge.

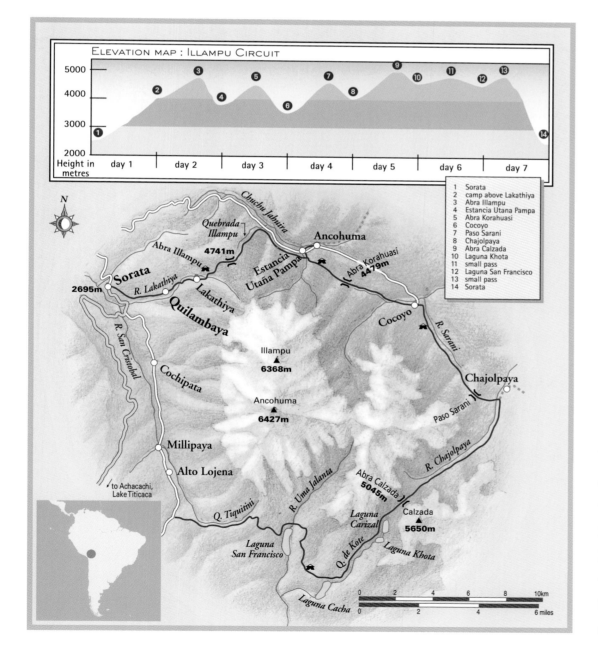

Head on up the track until the valley widens out and there are good grassy camping areas, where you will be sleeping at 4000m (13,100ft). This first leg is a good four to five hour trek from Sorata.

The next day the climb continues. As the valley widens, the route swings to the north alongside a stream. The track steepens, zigzagging almost vertically to the first pass on the trek, Abra Illampu at 4741m (15,555ft). Herds of llamas lift their heads from grazing the tough *ichu* grass, seemingly to admire the magnificent view, oblivious to tired trekkers. Ahead is the glacier-covered Illampu peak. Deep-green valleys plunge away behind, and the vast inland sea of Lake Titicaca shimmers in the far distance.

## UNCHANGED WAY OF LIFE

From the pass, the track descends the grassy valley of Quebrada Illampu to the river Chuchu Jahuira and the dirt road from Sorata to Ancohuma and Cocoyo. Follow the road gently downwards before heading southeast at the small hamlet of Estancia Utaña Pampa. Ancient-looking stone houses with thatched roofs have walled-in plots, ploughed and planted with native crops. Quinoa, a high-protein cereal crop with distinctive red fronds, is widely grown. It makes the most delicious soup. Look out for potatoes spread out on the ground being freeze-dried into *chuño*, to be stored and later reconstituted in stews. Broad beans and tubers such as oca, are commonly grown for food. Life has changed little over the centuries in these far-flung valleys. Cross the Anco Huma

**ABOVE** Viscachas, *strange rabbit-like creatures, are often seen warming themselves in the sun on boulders along the route.*

**OPPOSITE** *Vast, shimmering Lake Titicaca fills the view as trekkers descend to Sorata from Abra Calzada.*

Jahuira River on a stone bridge and continue up the valley. You soon come to some good overnight camping spots.

Next day, walk steeply southeast, keeping to the left side of the valley, up into the hanging valley below Abra Korahuasi at 4479m (14,696ft), the second pass, two hours from the valley floor. Once over the pass, follow the path down through luxuriant vegetation, dropping 1000m (3300ft) to the flat-bottomed, green valley with the village of Cocoyo ahead. It may be possible to buy fresh trout from local children tending llama herds and fishing in the stream that meanders through the valley. Cocoyo is a village of llama herders and miners, with few trekkers passing through. Giggling, inquisitive children often peek nervously from behind corners. There are a couple of small shops here that stock only the most basic provisions. Turn left after crossing the river and first right past the school, following the banks of the

thundering waters of the Sarani River, keeping the river on the left. There are many excellent camping spots within half an hour of the village. Four hours of gentle climbing from Cocoyo bring you to Paso Sarani at 4600m (15,090ft). The path follows the right bank of the Sarani River, crossing at a huge boulder just two hours from Cocoyo. On reaching a few thatched stone houses the path climbs steeply out of the Sarani Valley. Ahead, water cascades dramatically into the boggy pampa at the top end of the valley. There is good camping next to two abandoned houses half an hour above the thatched houses. Watch for condors overhead and *viscachas* on the boulders on the way up the pass.

Over the pass, the trail descends steeply towards the remote village of Chajolpaya where there are several houses, but little sign of life other than llamas and sheep. There are camping spots by the river with views of the Negruni group, the Chajowara group and La Calzada. Aymara is the only language spoken here and the nearest shops are two days' walk away in the town of Achacachi far beyond Abra Calzada.

After passing through the village turn immediately right up the valley skirting the boggy ground bordering the river Chajolpaya. From here it is five hours of steady climbing to the highest pass on the trek, Abra Calzada at 5045m (16,552ft).

Spectacular views over Lake Titicaca, and of the deep blue-green lakes of Carrizal and Khota reward trekkers for the long, steady climb to Abra Calzada. There are abundant camping spots on the way up and even a few at the top, rubbing shoulders with the glaciers, rugged icy peaks towering above. The pass itself is broad and almost barren, with the ubiquitous *ichu* and just a few other hardy plants clinging to the earth, struggling for survival amid ice-scraped boulders and meltwater lakes.

The initial descent from the pass is steep and tricky for donkeys. The track winds through large boulders, but soon levels out and passes close to lakes Carizal and Khota, crossing a scree slope of dark red rock. From Laguna Khota, the route becomes less distinct, but head towards Laguna San Francisco across the grassy pampa of the Quebrada de Kote, and on to the grassy ridge up to the right. From the top of the ridge, an impressive 360-degree panorama unfolds; the vast inland ocean of Lake Titicaca to the west, the high peaks of the Cordillera behind. The colour of the landscape, accentuated in the light over the Altiplano, is unsurpassably beautiful. There are several places to camp before reaching Laguna San Francisco, although it is best not to camp within sight of houses, since local farmers are not friendly. A local guide will advise of the best place to overnight.

## CLOSING THE CIRCLE

Finding a way across the silted streams flowing into the Laguna San Francisco isn't easy, except with the help of local children who may come running. Avoid getting wet feet by heading north up the valley at the head of the lake to find a place to cross. Look out for the large black-and-white Andean geese often feeding along the lakeshore. The trail heads for a rocky cairn at 4867m (15,969ft) with superb views. From here the route is cross-country, with little evidence of a track of any sort. Traverse the next small valley before turning west, down across the pampa and past the head of the valley of Quebrada Tiquitini until you reach a path. Follow this until it joins a dirt road that goes to the village of Alto Lojena. Sorata is a day's walk down the road, through the small village of Millipaya, although you could catch a truck. There are good camping spots on the way: try just beyond the old mine, one hour from Millipaya before the village of Cochipata.

The landscape changes dramatically as you descend from the stark grassy *puna* of high mountain passes to cultivated fields and small colourful villages. There are still fabulous views of the towering glaciated massif of Ancohuma and Illampu above, meltwater cascading down deep gullies towards the valley bottom. Vegetation becomes prolific, the temperature rises and birdsong is abundant as you approach Sorata.

# ASIA

By Jack Jackson

S tretching from Assam in eastern India and west to Afghanistan, the

Himalayas, the 'abode of snows', are the highest and youngest mountains in

the world. Since ancient times, merchants have crossed them for trade and

ascetics have climbed into them in search of peace. Long before commercial trekking had

been thought of, pilgrimages were established to places like Mount Kailash and Man-

sarovar Lake in Tibet, Thyengboche in Nepal, and Badrinath, Kedarnath, Yamunotri,

Gangotri Amarnath (Kashmir), and Hemis (Ladakh) in India.

## NUMBERED ON MAP

① Kaçkar of the Pontic Alps

② Lukpe La

③ Biafo-Hispar Traverse

④ Ladakh and Zanskar

⑤ Zanskar River

⑥ Manaslu and Annapurna Circuit

■ Major city     ● Featured Trek

● City     --- International Boundary

| 0 | 1500 km |
| 0 | 800 miles |

Arctic Circle

SWEDEN

FINLAND (SUOMI)

Severnaya Zemlya

More Laptevykh

International Date Line

Petrozavodsk

Sankt Peterburg

MOSKVA

Nizhniy Novgorod

Kirov

Perm'

Izhevsk

Kazan'

Serov

Nizhniy Tagil

Tyumen

Surgut

Sredne Sibirskoye

Ploskogor'ye

Verkhoyanskiy Khrebet

Khrebet Kolymskiy

Sredinnyy Khrebet

Ostrova

Petropavlovsk-Kamchatskiy

Poluostrov Kamchatka

Okhotskoye More

RUSSIA

Zapadno-Sibirskaya Ravnina

Samara

Ufa

Orenburg

Yekaterinburg

Chelyabinsk

Magnitogorsk

Orsk

Novosibirsk

Tomsk

Krasnoyarsk

Bratsk

Kemerovo

Prokop'yevsk

Novoaltaysk

Angarsk

Irkutsk

Chita

Khabarovsk

Komsomol'sk-na-Amure

Ostrov Sakhalin

Kuril'skye Ostrova

Valgograd

Astrakhan'

Pavlodar

Barnaul

Ulan-Ude

Asahikawa

Hokkaidō

Sapporo

Hakodate

Aomori

Ural Mtns.

KAZAKHSTAN

ASTANA

Qaraghandy

Semey

Öskemen

Ulaan-Ude

Altay Shan

ULAANBAATAR

Qiqihar

Jiamusi

Jixi

Mudanjiang

Vladivostok

Akita

Sendai

Kōriyama

BAKI

Astrakhan'

Aqtöbe

Üstirt

TURK-MENISTAN

ASGABAT (ASHKHABAD)

UZBEKISTAN

TOSHKENT

Samarqand

Almaty (Alma-Ata)

BISHKEK

KYRGYZSTAN

Ürümqi

Tian Shan

MONGOLIA

Gobi Desert

Harbin

Changchun

Shenyang

Jilin

Fushun

Anshan

N. KOREA

PYONGYANG

Sea of Japan

Niigata

JAPAN

TOKYO

Yokohama

Mashhad

TAJIKISTAN

DUSJANBE

CHINA

Huhhot

BEIJING (PEKING)

Baotou

Datong

Taiyuan

Andong

S. KOREA

SŎUL

Taejŏn

Pusan

Taegu

Kyōto

Nagoya

Osaka

Hiroshima

Kitakyūshū

Fukuoka

② Lukpe La

③

KÂBUL

Hindu Kush

ISLAMABAD

Rawalpindi

Srinagar

Gondokoro La–Hushe to Concordia

④ Kangchenjunga

Handan

Jinan

Qingdao

Lianyungang

Xuzhou

Zhengzhou

Luoyang

Xianyang

Xi'an

Nanjing

Zhenjiang

Wuxi

Shanghai

Hangzhou

East China Sea

Ryukyu Islands

Naha

Nagasaki

Kagoshima

AFGHAN-ISTAN

Lahore

Faisalabad

Amritsar

Multan

Ludhiana

⑤

Singalila to Kangchenjunga

Himalayas

Chengdu

Huainan

Nanchang

PACIFIC OCEAN

Tropic of Cancer

PAKISTAN

Sukkur

Delhi

Jumla to Mount Kailas

NEPAL

Lucknow

Tiger's Lair and Chomolhari

BHUTAN

The Snowman Trek

Luzhou

Zunyi

Hengyang

Xiamen

T'AIPEI

TAIWAN

Karachi

Jodhpur

Kanpur

Patna

⑥

BANGLA-DESH

DHAKA

Liuzhou

Guangzhou

Kowloon

Kaohsiung

T'ainan

Dhaulagiri Circuit

Arabian Sea

Vadodara

Surat

Nagpur

Kolkata (Calcutta)

Chittagong

Mandalay

HA NÔI

Hai Phong

Zhanjiang

Hainan Doa

Hong Kong

Macau

Nanning

Luzon

Quezon City

Mumbai

Pune

Hyderabad

Bhubaneshwar

MYANMAR

YANGON

LAOS

VIETNAM

VIANGCHAN

Da Nang

Paracel Is. (China)

MANILA

PHILIPPINES

Sholapur

Kolhapur

INDIA

Vishakhapatnam

Bay of Bengal

BANGKOK (KRUNG THEP)

Mindoro

Cebu

Leyte

Dharwar

Vijayawada

Andaman Islands

Thon Buri

THAILAND

Bangalore

Mysore

Chennai

CAMBODIA

PHNUM PENH

Ho Chi Minh (Saigon)

South China Sea

Palawan

Negros

Zamboanga

Mindanao

Davao

PALAU

Calicut

Salem

Laccadive Islands

Cochin

Tiruchchirappalli

Madurai

Andaman Sea

Nicobar Islands (India)

Sulu Sea

BANDAR SERI BEGAWAN

BRUNEI

Celebes Sea

Halmahera

Equator

Trivandrum

SRI LANKA

Colombo

Sri Jayewardenepura Kotte

MALE

MALDIVES

George Town

MALAYSIA

Ipoh

KUALA LUMPUR

PUTRAJAYA

Medan

Nias

Sumatra

MALAYSIA

SINGAPORE

Borneo

Sulawesi (Celebes)

Buru

Seram (Ceram)

Maluku (Mollucas)

Aru

New Guinea

Kepulauan Tanimbar

INDONESIA

INDIAN OCEAN

British Indian Ocean Territory

Bangka

Palembang

Banjarmasin

Ujung Pandang

JAKARTA

Bandung

Java

Yogyakarta

Semarang

Surakarta

Surabaya

Malang

Bali

Sumbawa

Sumba

Flores

DILI

EAST TIMOR

Timor

Timor Sea

AUSTRALIA

Although organized trekking as we now know it began in Nepal, it soon spread to nearby mountainous areas in the Himalayas such as India, and including Ladakh, Bhutan, Pakistan, Russian and ex-Russian states, Sikkim, and Tibet.

When operators realized that trekking was popular and could make them a profit, it spread to almost anywhere that travelling on foot was advisable due to lack of roads. Asia is a large area with a great diversity of terrain and climate and soon people were trekking among exotic animals, birds and plants in Southeast Asia's rainforests, remote hill-tribe minorities, and in mountainous desert areas such as those in Israel, Jordan, Oman, and Yemen.

As roads and *pistes* (dirt-tracks) were developed, some 'treks' were no longer viable, but new treks became possible, particularly in very dry areas where four-wheel drive vehicles could resupply trekkers with water at prearranged locations en route. Trekking has now been established for so long that hardened trekkers have done most of the well-known routes and are looking further afield – Asia can be colourful, exotic and mystic and has the advantage that many of its local people can speak some English. Even China is opening up like never before.

## LOCAL POPULATION

Most Himalayan valleys have rural settlements but the population density thins out with rise in altitude. Local people have well-developed routes from one village to another, to and between mountain pastures and across high-altitude passes. They travel from one valley to another for trade, festivals, religious activities and intermarriage.

Only Nepal has enough local population on popular trekking routes to make it possible to stay overnight at teahouses or lodges every night. However, when trekking among the hill-tribes you will be able to overnight with them. In Nepal, you can usually camp near a supply of water but on the minus side, leeches can be a problem at or below the tree line. The rainforests of Southeast Asia also have leeches and in Borneo there are overhanging rattans with sharp spines across the trail which, as I found to my cost, are not easy to spot. If you wish to include Mt Kinabalu 4125m (13,533ft), local regulations insist that you employ a guide. The route is easy, well-marked and equipped with thick, fixed ropes where deemed necessary, but trekkers still manage to get lost in the mist.

Peninsular Malaysia even has 'Air-trekking' – travelling from point to point along steel cables up to 30m (98ft) above the ground in the tree canopy. You don a climbing harness that is attached to runners on the cables.

Bhutan is unique in that it intentionally keeps trekking numbers down in order to manage tourism in a sustainable way by charging a high minimum fee. At the time of writing this fee, at peak periods, is US$200 per person per day. Individuals

LEFT *Women in local traditional dress of the Nyinba Valley attending the Jethi Purna festival at Ralling Gompah, Humla in Nepal.*
PREVIOUS PAGE LEFT *Young girl in traditional dress, Laya village, the second highest village in Bhutan*
PREVIOUS PAGE RIGHT *The peak of the 8156m (26,758ft) Manaslu towers above the roofs of Sama Gompah.*

*The Annapurna region is famous for its colourful Rhododendrons. These are in the Modi Khola valley, which leads to the Annapurna sanctuary.*

travelling in groups of four or less pay an additional fee of US$20 each per day and those travelling alone pay an additional fee of US$40 each per day.

While it is possible to organize your own trek in most Asian countries, in some it is difficult without the help of a local agency, particularly in the ex-Russian states. These were well developed during Soviet times when they were cheap travel destinations for trekkers from Eastern Europe and the former Soviet Union, but nowadays little remains of their infrastructure.

## BEST TIMES

In many parts of Asia, the best times for trekking are dictated by the monsoon rains, which vary from region to region and will be different depending on whether you are on the east or west side of a large landmass. In Nepal, for instance, most trekking is done in mid-October and November and then in February, March and April. The best time to see rhododendrons in flower is March and April, but one advantage of going soon after the monsoon rains is that there is no dust in the atmosphere, so the visibility and conditions for good photography are better.

At the time of writing, Nepal's Maoist rebels, who want to replace Nepal's monarchy with a communist state, have stepped up their campaign in protest against King Gyanendra's decision to dismiss the government and suspend civil liberties. Although a few trekkers have been robbed, most have been politely asked for a small donation (about US$14) to the rebels' cause and issued with a written receipt to show to other Maoist rebels who might stop them later. Make sure that you get the latest information from your foreign office advice unit before you go.

# LYCIAN WAY

*By Kate Clow*

Lycia is the mountainous bump on the south coast of Turkey, where the Taurus range plunges into the Mediterranean. The Lycian Way follows Greek and Roman roads and aqueducts, traditional nomad trails and forest tracks around the coast, over ranges and around deltas. Existing tracks have been linked up to form a continuous walking route which stretches over 509km (320 miles), soars along cliffs, winds through forests, pauses at deserted beaches and takes several detours inland. Old fishing villages, now tourist honeypots such as Kemer, Kaş and Kalkan, offer supplies, accommodation and a break from the solitude of the trail.

Most Turks still work on the land, often as shepherds, trekking up and down the mountains with their flocks on seasonal migrations. But second-generation city-dwellers have now rediscovered their ancestral lands; the Lycian Way marks a new recreational fashion. It was sponsored (and signposted) by a major bank and waymarked in red and white flashes similar to the French Grande Randonnées. Opened in 2000, the route has won awards from the *Sunday Times* (one of the world's ten best walks) and from SKAL International (2003 Ecotourism award). Although the trail is popular with European walkers, in some seasons it's possible to walk for a week without meeting a soul. The most popular section is the diversion to Mount Olympos – the physical and spiritual highpoint of the walk.

The Lycians were originally a client state of the Hittite Empire, established in central Anatolia about 1800BC. Pushed southwards by new invaders, they intermixed with Greek settlers and established an artistic, wealthy culture, supplementing farming and fishing with mercenary warfare – Lycian contingents fought at Troy and Salamis. After Alexander's death (323BC), the Seleucids and then the Romans ruled Anatolia, but allowed the Lycians, now Greek speaking, the freedom to form a unique democratic league. After centuries

ABOVE *The lighthouse at Cape Chelidonia is a good place to see the yachts and dolphins rounding the point.*

of prosperity, by the 6th century most of the population had succumbed to plague and Arab pirates. The Lycian peninsula lay almost deserted until the arrival of the Turks in the 15th century.

The first, and greatest, hero to travel the Lycian Way was the Macedonian king, later ruler of the then-known world, Alexander the Great. With a mission to free the Greek cities of Asia Minor from Persian rule, he entered Lycia at present-day Fethiye, with his army of 10,000 foot soldiers. He traversed the mountain of Baba Dağı en route to the superbly fortified stronghold of Xanthos, where he accepted the surrender of the capital of Lycia. One by one, the other cities submitted; the representatives of Phaselis bringing him a gold crown. Alexander overwintered at Phaselis, and,

seated in the open air theatre, must have contemplated Mount Olympos and the gorges to the north, which blocked his route. After winning local skirmishes, he sent engineers to cut steps for the passage of his army. Alexander himself, with his closest companions and his usual bravado, marched along the beaches, wading around rocky coastal spurs to rendezvous with his army on the plain at Antalya.

## ANCIENT STONES

The trek starts at the much-photographed crescent of golden sand called Ölü Deniz, where a rash of hotels and *pensions* would easily accommodate Alexander's army. The route climbs abruptly up mule trails on the slopes of Baba Dağı, where paragliders soar in the westerly breezes and the waves

pound the rocks far below. The first day's trek descends past a beautifully restored mill house to Faralya, where a friendly village *pension*, offering excellent local cooking, is perched on cliffs above Butterfly Valley. After this comfortable night, you continue winding through farmland and forest, with glimpses of the sea and occasional passing boats. The switchback climb, between strawberry trees and pines, out of Kabak valley is probably the most beautiful track in Turkey. An eccentric *pension* awaits at Kabak, and village headmen at Alınca and Gey will offer you beds and food in their old farmhouses.

The first Lycian city en route is Sidyma, where ancient stones have been adapted to the daily needs of a beekeeping and farming community: a temple doorway supports tumbling cottages, a few inscriptions are incorporated into the mosque walls and a stone sarcophagus has become a toolshed.

A steep downhill coastal track between Sidyma and an ancient fort at Pydnai is a real test for a trekker with a full pack – the track is slippery with loose stones and the ancient kerbstones have long collapsed. The route drops into orchid-filled forest and crosses wheatfields to Gavurağılı, (Christians' enclosure), a village where descendants of the ancient Greeks sheltered their flocks until their return to Greece in the chaos after the first world war. Only a few old people remain in the decaying balconied houses set among olive trees and vegetable gardens.

A climb over a ridge, with views of both coasts, leads to the battlemented fort of

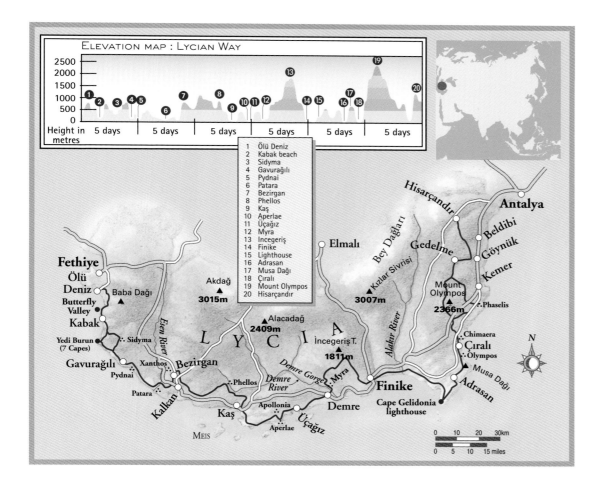

LEFT *Near Kaş, the route runs over sharp, broken limestone pavement – but dipping sore feet in the summer sea can bring relief.*
BELOW LEFT *This beautifully carved, Byzantine-era cross, with acanthus decoration, is now used as a doorstep in the village of Belen.*
OPPOSITE *The romantic Genoese Castle of Kale was built over earlier Lycian ruins; a tiny theatre and rock tombs lie inside the walls.*

On still-used nomad paths through olive groves to the high pastures of Bezirgan, the trail enters a stark world where the season is two months behind the sunny coast below. Wind-rounded rock formations tower over gushing springs and scarlet anemones dot the paths. The hilltop site of Phellos, where a huge relief of a bull shows the skill of ancient sculptors, commands views to the Greek islands. The hairpin descent to the coastal resort town of Kaş passes peregrine nests on the cliff face.

From Kaş the route hugs the coast, winding through thyme-scented maquis to the ruins of Aperlae, where ancient tombs guard a shallow bay. Further along is the flower-filled fishing village of Üçağız, the Genoese castle of Kale, and Myra, a stupendous ruin and legendary home of St Nicholas. You can use the wooden boats to skip sections of the route between Kaş and Myra.

Above Myra, in May, the seasonal migration can be seen first hand – the goats rush eagerly to their upper pastures, spewing spring flowers from chomping jaws. The route climbs past the ruins of a Byzantine church and a hermit's cell to İncegeriş hill at

Pydnai. Past that, a 12km (7½ mile) beach stretches to Patara, once the chief harbour of the Lycia. Sand has half-buried the temples of Artemis and Apollo where Alexander once worshipped. The Lycian Way circles the delta, first through eucalyptus and mimosa planting, then following the courses of the aqueducts which supplied Xanthos and Patara from the hills above. The Patara aqueduct is borne over dry valleys on an impressive siphonic pipeline made of one thousand stone blocks, each weighing 600kg (1300 lb), a 2000-year-old masterpiece of engineering.

1811m (5942ft). The coast, from the islands of Üçağız to the limestone ridge of Cape Chelidonia, is spread like a carpet below. Past the ruin-strewn hill of Dinek Tepe, a steady descent over mule track leads to Finike. Cedars were once dragged down these hills to the Byzantine boatyards below. Now fibreglass yachts fill the harbour, and the hinterland is used for growing oranges. The route leads along a sandy beach and past little coves with names like Korsan Koyu (Pirate Bay) to the southernmost point of Lycia. The Cape is marked by a manned lighthouse. Camp outside and watch the beam sweep across the Milky Way; climb the tower to watch the rising sun paint the world in rose and gold.

## ETERNAL FLAMES

Turning north, the going gets tough. After two energetic days switchbacking over forested ridges, the route divides. One branch turns inland past the eternal flames where Bellerophon, mounted on his horse Pegasus, killed the Chimaera monster. The best food on the route, baked trout and vegetables served with fresh bread, green salads and beer, is served here at Ulupınar, at a trout farm fed by gushing springs. A long and lonely climb leads to the saddle of Mount Olympos, where huge cedars guard the pass at about 1800m (5900ft). For the brave and experienced, there is a chance to reach the summit at 2366m (7763ft) – to be greeted by misty views of rolling ridges silhouetted in deep indigo against the shining sea. The less brave can follow a coastal route passing turtle nesting beaches, old chrome mines, the theatre at

Phaselis where Alexander once sat, and the gorge of the Kemer river. Beyond Mount Olympos, the routes rejoin at the summer village of Gedelme, which now has a *pension* to accommodate trekkers. The route finishes with a descent of a deep, silent valley to Göynük and the sea, and a final

climb to 1500m (5000ft). It emerges on a narrow ridge with a breathtaking drop into a canyon below, and views beyond to the bay and your destination city – Antalya. A couple of hours along the ridge is the nearest village of Hisarçandır, a long walk or a short car ride away from civilization.

# KAÇKAR OF THE PONTIC ALPS

## By Kate Clow

The Pontic Alps, a glaciated, granite mountain range in northern Turkey, hugs the coast of the Black Sea. It sweeps down as a narrow ribbon from the Russian border in the northeast to the Çoruh River in the south. To the west, the Zigana and Ovit passes link the medieval entrepôt of Erzurum – gateway to Persia (Iran) and last defence against Russia – with the ancient Greek colony of Trabzon on the Black Sea. Northern mountains are wooded, with rhododendrons and pines succeeded at lower levels by spruce, chestnut and beech, then with tea plantations and hazelnut groves. In contrast, the dry southern slopes are patched by stone-walled fields and summer pastures where black cattle graze.

The lakes, streams and springs, variety of afforestation up to 2100m (7000ft) and extremes of climate ensure a variety of flora. Before the summer hay is cut, the meadows are a riot of spring flowers, including *dactylorhiza* and *orchis* species in wet patches, anemones, poppies, campanulas and, at lower levels, dusty white umbellifers. At snowmelt level, the minutest treasures await the trekker – delicate crocus or pink merenderia, rich blue grape hyacinth and scilla, and the bells of fritillaria, deep brown outside but with yellow inners. The wildlife, which includes bear, wolf and chamois, is far more secretive, although eagles, vultures, Caspian snow cocks, Caucasian black grouse, partridge and many smaller birds haunt the crags.

Once densely populated and productive, for three short months the valleys still ring to the sound of summer returnees from Istanbul or Germany. The women's clothing, a brilliant contrast to the dour *chador* of Erzurum, is multi-layered and brilliantly colourful. In terms of religious influences, devout Christian worship has been replaced (within living memory) by devout Muslim observance, including temperance – rumours abound of residual Armenian communities. A scattering of abandoned or converted churches, some dating from

TOP *This ancient stone bridge in Davalı Dere links the summer pastures to the lower, winter village.*

the heyday of the Georgian kingdom in the 10th and 11th centuries, are reminders of past glories. The annual Kafkasör festival at Artvin, celebrated with bullfighting and folk dancing, demonstrates the variety of ethnic origins of this region.

The Kaçkar mountains, forming the northern part of the Pontic range, have been inhabited since prehistoric times. In the fourth century BC, Xenophon brought his army of 10,000 Greek mercenary soldiers back from Persia. After fighting his way across Kurdish territory in a bitter, snowy winter, he crossed the Pontic Alps via the Zigana Pass: *'When the men in front reached the summit and caught sight of the sea there was a great shouting. Xenophon and the rearguard heard it and thought that there were some more enemies attacking in front ...So they rode forward to give support and heard the soldiers shouting out "The sea! The sea!" and passing the word down the column. When they all got to the top, the soldiers, with tears in their eyes, embraced each other and their generals and captains.'* – Xenophon, the Persian Expedition.

In 1890, the British explorer, Isabella Bird, was delighted by the snow: *'Villages of chalets with irregular balconies and steep roofs are perched on the rocky heights or nestle among walnuts, with a blue background of pines above which tower spires and peaks of unsullied snow; ridges rise into fantastic forms and mimicries of minarets and castles; pines, filling gigantic ravines with their blue gloom, stand sentinel over torrents silenced for the winter; and colossal heights and colossal depths, an uplifted snow world of ceaseless surprises under a blue sky full of light, make one fancy oneself in Switzerland, 'till a long train of decorated camels or a turbaned party of armed travellers dissipates the dream.'*

## SIX-FINGER SPURS

The Kaçkar were discovered as a climbing paradise in the 1980s. The first commonly available map was drawn in 1988. There are two times of year to trek in the Kaçkar: high summer, when the snow has melted from all but the most sheltered valleys, and late winter, when avalanche risk is over, the snow is crusted and days are lengthening and cloudless. Although the summits are most impressive under snow, all commercial treks are made in summer.

This two-part trek ascends and circles the 3932m (12,900ft) Mount Kaçkar, the fifth highest peak in Turkey, with its descending spurs looking (on a map) like a hand with spread fingers coming out and down from it. The trek then meanders along the ridge of the Altıparmak range with similar spurs (*altıparmak* translates as 'six fingers').

The climb of Kaçkar, using the southern, non-technical route, is the highlight of the trek, which starts at a rambling *pension*

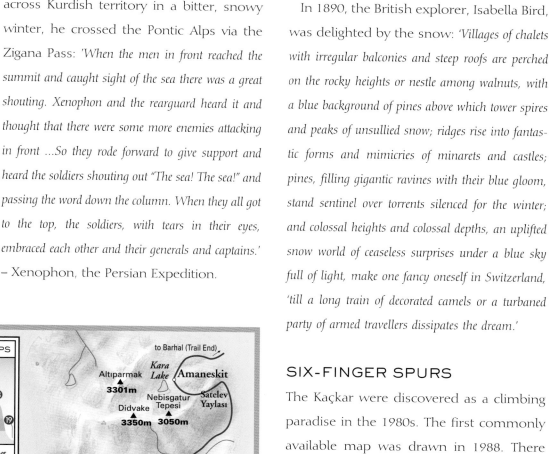

Elevation map : Kaçkar of the Pontic Alps

1 Yaylalar Pension
2 Damla Gölü
3 Davali Yaylası
4 Derebaşı Lake
5 Yukarı Kavron
6 Büyük Deniz Lake
7 Düpedüzü
8 Deniz Lake
9 Summit of Kaçkar
10 Dilberdüzü
11 Olgunlar pension
12 Karamolla
13 Satelev Yaylası
14 Okuz Çayırı Lake
15 Nebisgatur Tepesi
16 Kara Lake
17 Altiparmak
18 Kara Lake
19 Barhal

**ABOVE** *During the long winter only two of Olgunlar's houses are inhabited. Electricity, telephone, food supplies and road access are frequently cut off by snowfalls, so the locals stock up carefully.*

overhanging the dirt road at the entrance to Yaylalar (still known to the locals as Hevek), a stone and timber village on the south bank of the Hevek River. The route rises into the Hevek valley and skirts its cliffs at the western end. From the Hevek pass, the Anatolian plateau is visible, spread like a dusty blanket checked with squares and lines of poplars, stretching to Erzurum. The day ends at a tiny rock encircled lake, Damla Gölü, where the hardy can bathe in sun-warmed snowmelt.

At dawn an easy, dewy descent through long grasses and flowers into the wide Davalı valley ends at a meadow camp site for day two above a primitive *yayla*, or summer pasture, where the hardy black cattle graze.

## LOCAL DELICACIES

Forking right for Kavron pass the following day, the route veers, aiming straight at the summit massif, to dodge between spurs to a narrow, nameless pass opening onto the northern side of the range. Views of the serrated edges of the summit sawing into the sky make the heart stop. Below, rocky spikes and spurs obscure the northern trailhead village of Yukarı Kavron. First comes a steep descent to grassy Derebaşı lake, and an easy contour to Okuz Çayırı Lake – the base camp for technical climbs via the northern glacier of Mount Kaçkar.

A clear path leads steeply down to a gaggle of low houses at a junction of two valleys. Yukarı Kavron is a homely, stone village. Seasonally bustling cafés, two *pensions* and a village shop cater for climbers and trekkers with vast meals of local delicacies such as skewered kebabs, pancakes, fresh yoghurt and helva. When mist shrouds the valley, the villagers light bonfires to guide in benighted trekkers.

A lake, Büyük Deniz (*deniz* literally translates as 'sea'), marks day four's camp site, but it is only three hours away, up the Çaymakur valley. This is Turkey's deepest high-level lake, set in a basin scooped out of flaking rock and fed by glaciers. Nearby are tiny Metenek Lake, and Kara Deniz, all swimmable and with camp sites. From here a good path leads upwards to shady Naletleme pass, topped all year by snowfields, and onwards to a large camp site at Düpedüzü, in the beautiful valley of the same name.

## SUMMIT REGISTER

An almost trackless short-cut crosses a dividing ridge to Dilberdüzü, the southern camp site used as a base for nontechnical climbs of the 3932m (12,900ft) Mt Kaçkar. There is room for a tent or two at Deniz Lake on day six, hidden by scree slopes two hours above, and from here, the summit is four hours away. Climbers circle the lake and climb a snowy valley to pass below the glacier that lies ahead. A climb first over slabs, then scree, leads to the ridge, and a final stiff hour over broken rock leads to the summit, where a cairn and double box hold the summit register. In clear weather, the views are magnificent; the panorama extends from the northern glacier, anticlockwise to the dusty lake at Okuz Çayırı, the ridge and Verçenik peak in the west, and your start point, Deniz Lake below. Two tiny lakes atop the Devil's Rocks lie below, and beyond them the Hevek valley. The descent is by the same route, and, after a night in camp, the return to Yaylalar only takes three or four hours.

## SECOND PART

The second part of the trek, starting on day eight, leads north from Yaylalar to the Altıparmak massif (still part of the Kaçkar range). A delightful mule path leads from an arched stone bridge up a side valley to Karamolla, a permanent village of massive houses with only four winter inhabitants. Next is the *yayla* of Körahmet ('blind Ahmet'), named for an outlaw who took refuge here. Beyond the scattered thorns and birches where partridge feed, the path mounts the right bank to climb to a pass leading to Okuz Çayırı lake, at the start of the Altıparmak range. Past Bulut (meaning 'cloud') *yayla*, into Bulbul ('nightingale') valley, the route aims across the valley to a detached spur, Nebisgatur hill, a lovely point from which to view the range. On the far side of this is Kara Lake – *kara* translates as 'black'. Set in a stony valley above rattling waterfalls, it is the base camp for

climbs on Altıparmak ridge. Serrated ridges ahead invite exploration. There are several routes onward, mostly suitable for day climbs, and rewarded by glimpses of the north side of the range – green and lush below the misty blanket.

After completing your daytrip excursions, the final walk down to Barhal from Kara Lake goes past pretty *yaylas* with water mills and beehives, blooming meadows and apple orchards, then descends into forest on the left bank of the Barhal River. Above the town, nestling in trees next to the school, is a beautiful Georgian 10th-century basilica – the Church of the Four Apostles – the sharp roof echoing the ridges around. Converted to a mosque 40 years ago, the simple dressed-stone exterior is decorated with crosses reminiscent of ancient tombstones, which share with the mountains the name 'Kaçkar'. Look inside at the power of the main piers, set off by carvings of tiny angels, supporting a stone roof. The frescoes survived a thousand years of worship to succumb to a thoughtless coat of whitewash. Arch shapes and stone motifs were later inherited by the conquering Selçuk Turks.

The Pontic Alps always were a wild refuge from powerful rulers, refuge of individuality against conformity. As the sparkling valley leads downhill to the plains, the Kaçkar, behind, lift up their heads to the light and shade of the sky.

LEFT *Cliff-bound Tortum Lake was created by rockfalls damming a major valley – this waterfall now forms the outlet.*

# GONDOKORO LA – HUSHE TO CONCORDIA

*By Steve Razzetti*

Named after an ancient pass across the watershed between the Indian Ocean and Central Asia, the Karakoram is one the most savagely beautiful range of mountains on earth. Extending for some 320km (200 miles) from the Hindu Kush in the west to the Ladakh range and the Greater Himalaya in the east, the peaks of the Karakoram lie on one of the most mobile fault lines on earth, and while tectonic forces push the summits ever skywards, enormous glaciers and tumultuous rivers tear them down again. To travel in the Karakoram is to witness the greatest exhibition of active geology the world has to offer.

Everything about the Karakoram is extreme. Four of the world's 14 peaks

above 8000m (26,000ft) – K2, Broad Peak, Gasherbrum I and Gasherbrum II – tower over one glacial system, the Baltoro. No fewer than 36 summits exceed 7300m (24,000ft), while hundreds exceed 6000m (19,600ft). These are some of the most heavily glaciated mountains outside of the polar regions, and the seven largest glaciers (Biafo, Hispar, Baltoro, Gasherbrum, Chogo Lungma, Siachen and Batura) all cover areas in excess of 350km² (135 square miles). In summer, valley temperatures frequently exceed 40°C (104°F), and the searing rays of the sun melt the glaciers and snowfields above at such a great rate that the rivers, turned raging brown torrents, carry the highest volume of sediment of any rivers on earth. Such is the

power and fury of the water that boulders the size of houses are constantly driven along their beds, crashing and booming as they go. Great chunks of blue ice often drop into the water from the decaying glacier snouts, and can be seen miles down-valley washed up on sandbars to meet their end in the desert heat.

Though Englishman Godfrey Thomas 'Ramrod' Vigne was the first European to actually see the Karakoram, it was Thomas Montgomerie of the Survey of India who first realized their true stature. In 1856, from a rather chilly survey station atop the

Top *Looking up the Vigne glacier towards the Gondokoro La from the centre of the Baltoro.*

distant peak of Haramukh in Kashmir, he triangulated a series of 32 peaks to which he gave the prefix 'K' for Karakoram. When his observations were finally computed in 1858, K2 was found to be the second high-est mountain in the world, and the currently accepted figure for its height is 8611m (28,251ft).

Fellow countryman Henry Haversham Godwin-Austen got the first close look at K2 in 1861. At the end of an epic expedi-tion, during which he discovered the Hispar Glacier on reaching the Nushik La from the head of the Kero Lungma, he made a brief sortie onto the Baltoro Glacier.

**ABOVE** *The trail from Askole to Concordia has been much improved of late, but in summer spate the Braldu is a fierce torrent and river-level traverses like this may only be passable in the morning.*

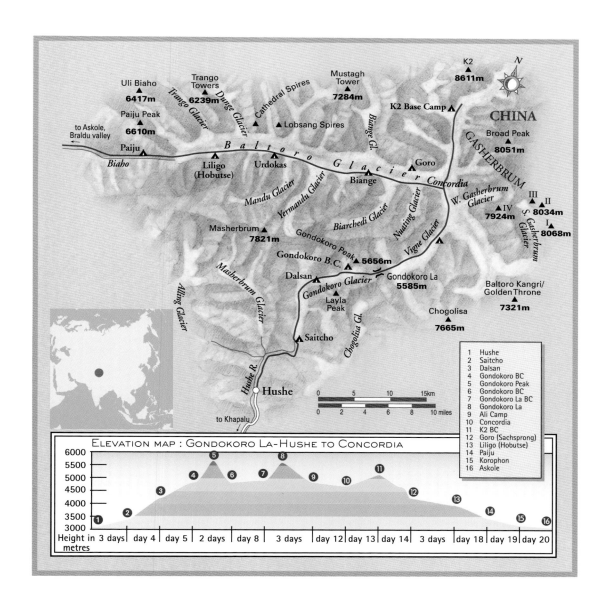

Determined to see K2, he gave up follow-ing the Baltoro and ascended a spur above the camp now known as Urdokas, reach-ing a point where he was able to sketch just the summit of that monstrous pyra-mid towering over the intervening ridges.

## PHOTOGRAPHIC RECORD

The visual record of the Karakoram peaks made by celebrated Italian photographer Vittorio Sella, during the Duke of Abruzzi's expedition in 1909, brought this area to the attention of the mountaineering world. Using a large camera capable of exposing 30x40cm glass plates, Sella made over 800 superlative images during the expedition (developing the plates in his tent at night!). Prints were subsequently acquired by such august bodies as the Royal Geographical Society and the Alpine Club in London, and the National Geographic Society in Wash-ington. Italian interest in K2 never waned,

**ABOVE** *Even at around 5000m (16,000ft), the Karakoram summer sun can melt the surface of the Baltoro at an alarming rate, with torrents like this vanishing beneath the ice down lethal sinkholes.*

and in 1954 Ardito Desio led the expedition that succeeded in making the first ascent.

Trekking to Concordia, the confluence of the Baltoro and Godwin-Austen glaciers at the very heart of the Karakoram, is difficult. The highest of the Karakoram peaks are situated in the Pakistani province of Baltistan, the sleepy capital of which is Skardu. Although it is served by daily scheduled air services from Islamabad, mountain weather is fickle and flights are often cancelled. The alternative is a two-day road journey up the Karakoram Highway, which alone qualifies as an adventure.

## GRUELLING EXPEDITION

Until 1986, those then seeking to approach K2 and its mighty neighbours faced a gruelling expedition, considered among the toughest treks in the world. From Skardu, it was into jeeps for the bumpy ride up the Shigar and Braldu valleys to the roadhead at Dassu. There they embarked on a treacherous journey, the first three days of which were through the infamous Braldu Gorge to the oasis village of Askole. Such were the rigours of this trail, swept sometimes by the tumultuous river, sometimes by stone fall, frequently loose underfoot and always very hot, that many had to recuperate for days at Askole before proceeding. Beyond, the sweltering heat continued by day, with increasingly bitter nights. Hair-raising river crossings, vertical cliffs to traverse, torturous moraines to scramble over, and finally the bare ice of the Baltoro glacier brought them to Concordia, the Throne Room of the Mountain Gods.

Expeditions returned by the same route. Then came a man called Ali Mohammed from the village of Hushe.

His home lies at the head of a previously obscure valley to the south of Masherbrum, visited only briefly by the infamous American travelling couple Fanny Bullock Workman and her husband William Hunter Workman in 1911, and by sporadic expeditions to the south face of Masherbrum until the 1980s.

## TANTALIZING SHORTCUT

The hardy men of Hushe regularly work as high-altitude porters on the Baltoro and, in 1985, Ali Mohammed was employed by an expedition attempting Chogolisa, a 7665m (25,147ft) peak on the upper Baltoro. Looking south across a nearby col from a camp high on the peak, he was amazed to see the unmistakable form of Layla Peak, an elegant spire on the Gondokoro Glacier, just above his village. He decided to attempt to get home via this tantalizing shortcut, succeeded, and thus discovered the Gondokoro La (5585m; 18,324ft).

Hushe was already fast gaining a reputation among trekkers and mountaineers in the mid-1980s. Ali Mohammed's discovery suddenly opened up the possibility of a circuit trek taking in the most picturesque of the four glaciers above Hushe village, a high pass commanding breathtaking views of K2, Broad Peak and the entire Gasherbrum group, and a visit to Concordia, concluded with a walk out down the Baltoro to Askole. Among aficionados of the wild and adventurous, this route has become something of a classic.

**ABOVE** *From the upper slopes of the Gondokoro La, this stupendous view of the Gondokoro glacier is revealed, with Layla Peak dominating the skyline.*

The village of Hushe can be reached by jeep in about 10 hours from Skardu. The men there have organized themselves to cater for trekkers and mountaineers. Calling themselves the Hushe Mountain Rescue Team, at the beginning of each season, in late May, they fix ropes on the difficult sections, place bamboo bridges across crevasses and establish camps at the base of the pass on either side. For a fee they will even guide people across.

This route is certainly not for those without a head for heights, and a level of competence in navigating and traversing glacial terrain is essential. It qualifies as a serious expedition, and for those wishing to experience the joys of mountaineering without actually venturing onto a major peak it is unbeatable. A clue as to the nature of the crossing may be gleaned from the words of the famous mountaineer Reinhold Messner. Looking back to the pass after crossing it, he said 'It is a good way – but not for trekkers!'

Many people acclimatize for the crossing by ascending the technically straightforward Gondokoro Peak (5656m; 18,557ft) above the Gondokoro Glacier and, having crossed to Concordia, spend a few days visiting the base camps of the Gasherbrums, Broad Peak and K2 before heading off down the Baltoro. As a result, one is treated to a jaw-dropping parade of mountains right until the end, with the Mustagh Tower, the north face of Masherbrum, the Trango Towers, Uli Biaho, the Cathedral Spires and Paiju Peak saved as treats for the final few days.

# BIAFO - HISPAR TRAVERSE

*By Steve Razzetti*

K2 and the host of other mighty peaks that look down on Concordia and the upper Baltoro Glacier have long attracted the attention of the world's leading explorers and mountaineers, but one enigma of the Central Karakoram had geographers guessing as to its true identity well into the 20th century: Lukpe Lawo, or 'Snow Lake'. It is a vast névé basin from which the Biafo and Hispar glaciers radiate. It embodies, perhaps more so than any of the region's magnificent mountains, all that is special about the Karakoram.

Cutting an enormous swathe through the very heart of the Central Karakoram between Baltistan in the east and Hunza in the west, the Biafo–Hispar forms one of the longest continuous expanses of glacial ice outside of the polar regions – a total of almost 130km (80 miles). Snow Lake was for years believed to be a genuine ice-cap, and many legends grew around it before its true nature was established. The first explorer to set eyes on the Biafo Glacier was a British sportsman by the name of H Falconer in 1838. Henry Haversham Godwin-Austen discovered the Hispar when he reached the crest of the Nushik La from the south in 1861. However, the true extent of this glacial superhighway was not realized until Englishman Sir Martin Conway's expedition 31 years later.

Travelling from the Hunza side, Conway made the first crossing of the Hispar Pass (5151m; 16,900ft) on 18 July 1892. Though he then traversed the Biafo Glacier to Askole, he made no attempt to survey Snow Lake. This omission, and his tantalizing descriptions of the place, enticed an infamous American couple: Fanny Bullock Workman and her diminutive but resilient husband, William Hunter Workman. Between 1898 and 1908 they made no less than seven major expeditions to the region, and published many lavishly illustrated, self-financed books and articles about their travels. Modest they certainly were not and became known for a haughty

TOP *As the sun dips to the western horizon over Hunza, shadows lengthen eastwards across the Hispar La towards The Ogre.*

attitude and rudeness to their local staff. In 1908 they followed Conway over the Hispar Pass, from which Fanny made her famous ascent of Workman Peak and proclaimed the area of Snow Lake to be in excess of 700km² (270 square miles).

Only in 1939, on the brink of the outbreak of World War II, was this enormous glacial wilderness accurately surveyed, during a phenomenal expedition that represented the climax of the career of Britain's most celebrated and accomplished mountain explorer, Eric Shipton. During the second of his epic trips to the Karakoram, Shipton and his colleagues conducted a survey that was to produce a map of extraordinary accuracy. This work was to be the opening phase of a mammoth 16-month mountain odyssey, but even in

**ABOVE** *Balti porter on the Biafo glacier. Loads are carefully regulated and adequate clothing must be provided for these hard-working men.*

the most remote Karakoram, momentous events cannot be ignored by men of the world. The party had split into several units for the purpose of conducting their work, and, approaching a prearranged rendezvous on Snow Lake, Shipton wrote: *'When at last we were within earshot, Russell shouted out the shattering news that England was at war with Germany. He had heard it on the tiny wireless receiving set we had brought to get time signals for our astronomical work. It was hard to realize the meaning of the disaster. Perhaps the London where we had planned this very venture was a chaos of destruction and terror. How fantastic, how supremely ridiculous it seemed in our remote and lovely world of snow and ice. As if to point the contrast, the mists cleared and for a moment the glacier was bathed in a sunset glow reflected from the high peaks. The great granite spires of the Biafo stood black against a deep blue sky. At*

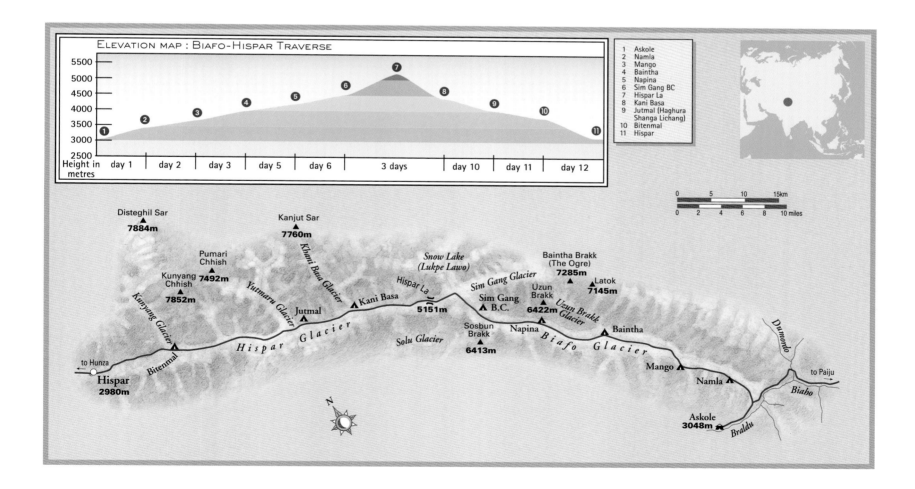

**ABOVE** *Glacier table on the Biafo near Baintha. This is a classic feature of glaciers in the Karakoram, created by the differential rates of ablation (melting/vaporization) that occur between the rock-covered ice and surrounding bare ice.*

least this mountain world, to which I owed so much of life and happiness, would stand above the ruin of human hopes, the heritage of a saner generation of men.' The expedition was abandoned.

For half a century, the lonesome bears and snow-leopards of the Biafo–Hispar had the place almost to themselves, watching the occasional mountaineering expedition that ventured to scale the pinnacles and spires lining these glaciers from solitary vantage points amid this vast and savage mountain landscape. Facts and figures may hint at glacial magnitude, but they utterly fail to convey the impact of the place in terms of sheer grandeur. Disappointingly perhaps, Shipton's survey revealed the area of Snow Lake to be but a tenth of that posited by the Workmans, but, nevertheless, where the Biafo flows south out of Snow Lake it is nearly 5km (3 miles) wide, 1000m (3300ft) deep and moves over 100m

(330ft) a year. Go to sleep in your tent at night on the Biafo, and when you awake in the morning you are 15cm (6 in) closer to Askole! Its cavernous blue crevasses could swallow entire apartment blocks.

## STILL A DAUNTING TREK

Today, scheduled but weather-dependent air services to Gilgit and Skardu, and the wonder that is the Karakoram Highway may have made things easier than in Shipton's time, when expeditions were obliged to set off on foot from Srinagar in Kashmir. Rough jeep tracks may indeed now snake their tentative way into the range's wild and desolate valleys, but the Karakoram are still a daunting proposition for those seeking to travel or climb there. In northern Pakistan the traveller will find few of the creature comforts taken for granted elsewhere, but the kindness and hospitality

of the people encountered at every turn will surely prove disarming. Of all the possibilities for wild and adventurous trekking here, the route described here has been widely acknowledged as the quintessential Karakoram traverse.

Departing from the approach to K2 just beyond the village of Askole, you will not pass another human settlement until the penultimate day, when you reach the village of Hispar. Leaving the comparatively busy mountaineers' trail up the Braldu Valley, the way to the Hispar La turns sharply northwest onto the boulder-strewn lower reaches of the Biafo and instantly enters another world. The tip of this glacier, like all the major ice flows of the Karakoram, is hidden beneath an enormous mass of debris transported from above, and protrudes into the Braldu Valley to such an extent that it almost blocks it. In only a few places is the blackened, pock-marked and rapidly melting ice visible beneath the gravel and rocks, and walking on the surface is a tortuous and energy-consuming business at first. Only on the third day, as the route crosses to the northern flank, does a streak of clean white ice appear in the centre and the going become easier.

Ahead, from very early on in the ascent of the Biafo, a spectacular array of enormous snow-capped peaks appears on the horizon, luring the traveller onward. These are the Latoks and Baintha Brakk (7285m; 23,901ft), given the ominous sobriquet 'The Ogre' by Sir Martin Conway. From the third-stage camp at Baintha, an easy climb can be made to the summit of Baintha Peak (5100m; 16,732ft) for panoramic views of the magnificent mountain architecture that lines the upper Biafo and its tributary, the Uzun Brakk. From the gently angled slopes above this camp, where a rest day is almost mandatory so that your porters can bake bread and feed themselves up for the rigours ahead, the full extent of The Ogre's formidable defences is revealed. The epic first ascent of this mountain was made in 1977, by British mountaineers Doug Scott, Chris Bonington and Mo Antoine, and it was not repeated until the year 2000.

## MENACING PHANTOM

However dramatic the perspective on the south face of The Ogre may be from above Baintha, it is surely surpassed by that on the north face from the Hispar Pass itself, where, given good weather, a camp should be made. A more sensational location could not be imagined, as the angle of the seemingly interminable snow slopes that lead up to the pass gradually eases and imperceptibly the ground begins to descend again to the west. To the east, the vast whiteness of the Sim Gang Basin and Snow Lake is walled in by a host of perpendicular peaks, over which the shadowy north face of The Ogre broods like a menacing phantom. To the west, the convoluted surface of the Hispar disappears into the distance towards Hunza.

RIGHT *Returning to Sim Gang base camp from a reconnaissance of the upper Biafo. Conditions change rapidly, and an hour's scouting can save a day of routefinding through a bad section of crevasses.*

Both sunrise and sunset from this bird's-eye viewpoint can only be described as mind-blowing, yet, unbelievably, the biggest mountains are still to come. The Hispar is a more difficult glacier than the Biafo, and its four enormous northern tributaries descend from a mountain watershed that includes the summits of Kanjut Sar (7760m; 25,459ft), Disteghil Sar (7885m; 25,869ft), Pumari Chhish (7492m;

24,579ft) and Kunyang Chhish (7852m; 25,761ft). Crossing these, and negotiating the almost vertical lateral moraines, is the toughest part of the trip. In consolation, camps at night are made in some of the most idyllic and unexpectedly verdant ablation valleys. By the time you join the tourists relaxing in the comfortable hotels of Karimabad in Hunza you will surely have earned your Karakoram stripes.

# LUKPE LA

*By Steve Razzetti*

At 5700m (18,700ft), the Lukpe La (*la* is a 'pass' in Balti, an ancient form of Tibetan) is the highpoint of this seldom undertaken and seriously committing traverse of the northern Karakoram. From the village of Shimshal in Hunza, to Askole in Baltistan, this is one of the most strenuous treks in Pakistan.

The journey across 260km (160 miles) of spectacularly remote and difficult country will take a fit party three weeks. Few places on the planet today are as inaccessible as these peaks and valleys, and those who would venture here should be aware that, in an emergency, help is a very long way away. All parties should be well versed in the techniques of roped glacier travel, crevasse rescue and mountain navigation. A

degree of expedition medicine and first-aid experience would also be wise. Here you must truly be self-sufficient.

Geographically, this trek is the only way one can legally cross the Karakoram watershed, part of the great Central Asiatic divide. Standing on the vast windswept *pamirs* (grazing grounds) of the Shimshal Pass (4735m; 14,535ft) you look into valleys that drain their waters into the shimmering salt flats of the Takla Makan desert. Behind you, the fearsome gorges carrying the headwaters of the Shimshal River (a section northeast of Shimshal village known as the Pamir-i-Tang) eventually debouch their silt-laden torrents into the Indus. Waters that rise within a kilometre of each other are destined to different fates – either

to evaporate under the furnace-like heat of a desert sun, or languidly travel thousands of kilometres to the Arabian Sea.

Much of the country traversed lies within the Khunjerab and Central Karakoram national parks in Pakistan, founded in 1975 and 1994 respectively, with the primary aim of protecting shrinking populations of

**ABOVE** *The plains of Zhit Badav as seen from a windswept ridge above the Shimshal Pass, with the Braldu valley in the distance to the east.*
**OPPOSITE** *A meltwater stream beneath the snout of the Malangutti glacier. Clear, innocuous and crossed without wetting your feet early in the day, by mid-afternoon they may be silt-laden torrents.*

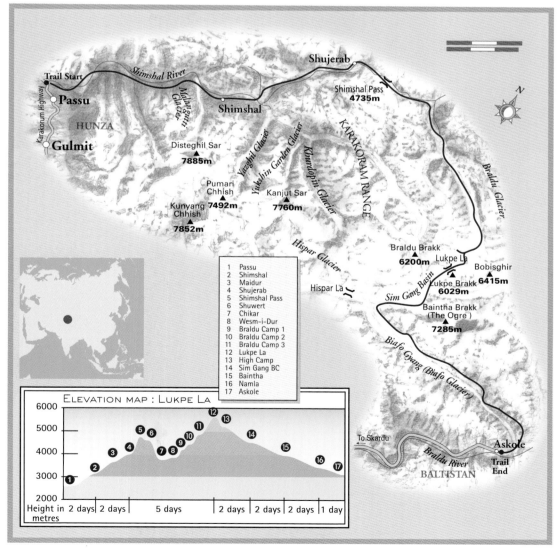

| | |
|---|---|
| 1 | Passu |
| 2 | Shimshal |
| 3 | Maidur |
| 4 | Shujerab |
| 5 | Shimshal Pass |
| 6 | Shuwert |
| 7 | Chikar |
| 8 | Wesm-i-Dur |
| 9 | Braldu Camp 1 |
| 10 | Braldu Camp 2 |
| 11 | Braldu Camp 3 |
| 12 | Lukpe La |
| 13 | High Camp |
| 14 | Sim Gang BC |
| 15 | Baintha |
| 16 | Namla |
| 17 | Askole |

Marco Polo sheep, snow leopard and brown bear. Within their bounds lie some of the most beautiful and rugged tracts of mountainous country on earth. From idyllic orchards, patchwork farmland and the tranquil calm of Ishmaili villages in Hunza – dwarfed by snow-peaks and presenting what British mountaineer Eric Shipton described as 'the ultimate manifestation of mountain grandeur' – this route follows the Shimshal River east to its headwaters below Shimshal Pass, just a few kilometres from the border with China's Xinjang Province. Then it swings south up the Braldu valley to the Lukpe La, Snow Lake (or Lukpe Lawo) and the legendary mountains that surround it.

The first European to cross the Shimshal Pass, from the north in 1889, was one of Britain's great imperial adventurers, Francis Younghusband. Being essentially a player of The Great Game (British secret service), his main concern was Russian expansionism and potential routes of Tsarist incursion into British India. Hence, after a brief look into the top of the Pamir-i-Tang he re-crossed the pass and continued his explorations in what is today Chinese Turkestan.

## GEOGRAPHIC MYSTERIES

The opening decades of the 20th century saw further sporadic exploration of the area by the likes of Kenneth Mason and RCF Schomberg, but it was the members of Eric Shipton's 1937 expedition who finally unravelled the complex geographic mysteries that had for so long shrouded the central Karakoram. At last, the blank on the map was filled in. No one should think of

ABOVE *Shimshal village, of which Schomberg wrote in 1934 'On the whole, I was agreeably surprised at the village, which must be almost the most remote and inaccessible inhabited place in the Indian Empire...'*

OPPOSITE *The gorges of the Pamir-i-Tang (upper Shimshal valley) from the Shashmirt Pass. Every spring the Shimshalis drive their livestock through this inhospitable ravine to reach the rich grazing grounds at the Shimshal Pass.*

a journey here without first reading the accounts of these men, for in these valleys little has changed in the last century.

The necessity of using Shimshali yaks to cross the Braldu River obliges travellers to start from the Hunza side. The domain of the Shimshalis effectively begins immediately across the Hunza River from the village of Passu, and Shimshali men rightly insist on doing any portering into their territory.

This may seem headstrong, but it should not be ignored that many are excellent mountaineers and high-altitude porters.

After more than a decade of wrangling with the Pakistani government and several unilateral attempts by the villagers to build it themselves, there is now a rough 60km (37-mile) jeep road to Shimshal from Passu. Like the one built to Askole, this has removed what was a most challenging and

gruelling three-day walk into the village. The word 'road' is used very loosely hereabouts and, depending on your enthusiasm for death-defying feats of four-wheel-drive bravado, you will either love the journey or wish you had rather walked.

Shimshal village (3200m; 10,499ft) is a skilfully tended and verdant oasis of whitewashed houses, poplar trees and apricot orchards. The surrounding fields cover an area in excess of 250 hectares (618 acres), and these, along with large flocks and herds of grazing livestock support a population of over 1100 people. The community is almost completely self-sufficient in agricultural produce and, considering its physical isolation, the degree of worldliness and level of education among the population is remarkable.

There is a new low-level trail through the Pamir-i-Tang to Shujerab, the summer grazing settlement below Shimshal Pass. Shuwert, the larger settlement right on the pass, used to be three gruelling days from the village. Those wishing to actually see the area should contemplate taking the old route. The trail initially heads north into the desolate valley of Zardgar Bin, but soon climbs away east up steep screes to the Shashmirk La (4160m; 13,648ft), from which the true majesty of the country is revealed. South, across the Shimshal valley, the white ice of Yazghil glacier carves away through barren ranges to the vast mountain wall that forms the Hispar-Shimshal watershed. Disteghil Sar (7885m; 25,870ft), Kunyang Chhish (7852m; 25,760ft), Pumari Chhish (7492m; 24,579ft) and Kanjut Sar (7760m; 25,460ft) are all visible among a snowy sea of lesser summits. Northeast, the fantastic, eroded flanks and ancient river terraces of the Pamir-i-Tang stretch away into the distance.

## VALLEY SEEN BY FEW

Two brutal days of constant ascent and descent on hideously steep and loose trails take you to the pastures at Shujerab, where the gorges finally give way to open country and the Shimshal Pass. A few days' rest here, among the women and children who spend their summers tending huge flocks of sheep, goats and yaks, will both entertain and acclimatize you. The lakes which crown the pass are a stopover for many species of migrating ducks and wading birds, and the nearby plains of Zhit Bhadav

LEFT *The final ascent to the Shimshal Pass leaves the fearsome ravine of the Pamir-i-Tang behind and reaches the col up the broad and grassy valley of Abdullah Khan Maidan.*
BELOW LEFT *Bobisghir and the peaks at the head of the Braldu glacier. The route to the Lukpe La heads through the obvious gap to the right of the peak.*
OPPOSITE *Heading out down the Biafo glacier from the camp at Baintha. Though the terrain is easier here, fresh snow on the glacier can obscure crevasses and holes, making a rope essential.*

Just two days' walk to the north, the Braldu flows into the almost mythical Shaksgam – today in Chinese territory, alas – which rises north of Ladakh and drains the northern slopes of the biggest peaks in the Karakoram: K2, Broad Peak and the Gasherbrum group. South, the valley is almost immediately blocked by the rubble-blackened, convoluted, and thoroughly appalling snout of the Braldu glacier.

## LABYRINTH OF ICE TOWERS

There are no trails or cairns from this point until you leave the snout of the Biafo glacier a couple of hours from Askole, so proficient route-finding is essential. The lower section of the 40km (25-mile) Braldu glacier consists of a labyrinth of ice towers and crevasses. Though the ground above is treacherous and steep, it must be traversed until a safe way onto the smooth tongue of ice – which eventually appears in the centre of the glacier – can be found.

The height of the snow line, and the number and size of crevasses vary from

provide a backdrop of epic proportions. Your Shimshali hosts will arrange yaks to accompany you into the Braldu valley; they carry both men and kit across the river. The possibilities for exploratory hikes and climbs in this area are almost endless, but most travellers will be anxious to press on

to the crux of the trek. Once you are across the Braldu River and your yaks have gone back, you are committed to crossing the Lukpe La. Serious stuff.

Descending east from the Shimshal Pass you enter a valley that has seen but a handful of foreigners in the last century.

season to season; from month to month even. In such a remote location the consequences of an accident could be fatal, so rope up and tread carefully! Available mapping of the upper Braldu is unreliable, but a safe bet is to follow the eastern edge of the medial moraine until the pass appears ahead. Do not be tempted by any of the enormous tributaries coming in from the west. The main glacier eventually sweeps away up westwards to the pass, a very long but gradual ascent.

## BIAFO WALL

Few places on earth today are as truly remote, challenging and spectacular as the Lukpe La. From the crest, a panorama of stupefying magnificence is revealed. Behind you to the north, the icebound Karakoram diminishes into the lifeless brown ravines and deserts of Turkestan. Ahead, the north face of Baintha Brakk, also known as The Ogre (7285m; 23,901ft), rears above the blinding glare of the Sim Gang basin and Snow Lake. The apparently smooth surface of the Sim Gang is far from benign, however: beneath are complex systems of enormous crevasses. Snow conditions are usually terrible after 09:00, so travel early and keep the rope on until you reach the moraines at the head of Biafo glacier.

Distances here are deceptive. Descending the 35km (22 miles) from Lukpe La to the moraine camp, usually referred to as Sim Gang base camp, may look straightforward after the Braldu, but allow 12–14 hours. Though you are still at least three days from Askole and the road out to Skardu, the Biafo is a friendly glacier by Karakoram standards and you may finally relax and enjoy the superb scenery. Spend a day spying out routes on the rock towers of the west Biafo Wall, and another revelling in the sudden verdure of the alpine meadows at Baintha. Ascend Baintha Peak (5300m; 17,388ft) for one last dose of Karakoram magnificence before you make your way to Askole village. This easy summit affords close-up views of the entire Ogre and Latok ranges and is a fitting finale to such an odyssey.

# LADAKH AND ZANSKAR

*By Steve Razzetti*

**Z**anskar and Ladakh are the most remote of all India's Himalayan domains. Secreted among rugged, torrent-filled defiles and stark, barren mountains, the patchwork of irrigated fields that surround villages throughout the region appear like vibrant emerald jewels set in a desolate crown of thorns. Perched atop unlikely spurs and cliffs, often commanding breathtaking views of the surrounding countryside, numerous Buddhist monasteries or *gompahs* add splashes of brilliant white to the soaring browns and greys of the scene. With a landscape that elicits comparisons with the moon, the high mountain deserts of Ladakh are not everyone's idea of bliss, but the area has an undeniable magic.

Bounded in the north and east by the Karakoram and Kailas ranges and in the south by the Great Himalaya, the Ladakh and Zanskar ranges do not attain the great heights of their neighbours. They are, however, just as complex and contain sufficient summits in excess of 6000m (19,600ft) to catch heavy winter snowfall. Being north of the Himalayan rain shadow, Ladakh and Zanskar are not afflicted by the monsoon, but under the fierce summer sun the high snowfields and glaciers melt rapidly, turning the rivers below into raging torrents. Many of the valleys become impassable for this reason, and the major trails often surmount huge ridges in order to avoid dangerous gorges. *Ladakh* means 'land of the passes' in Tibetan, and summer

trekking here often involves hair-raising river crossings, especially on the less frequented routes.

The history of Ladakh is one of conquest and acquisition, with rulers constantly having to fend off Tibetan and Kashmiri designs on their territory. Due to its rich and vigorous Buddhist cultural heritage, Ladakh is often referred to as Little Tibet, but, in truth, it has never been ruled by the Dalai Lama. The forcible conversion of neighbouring Kashmir to Islam in the 13th century effectively brought the separate

ABOVE *The Kagyupa monastery at Lamayuru occupies a dramatic cliff-top position on the Indus (northern) side of the Photu La.*

kingdoms of Ladakh and Zanskar closer together. The zenith of Ladakh's power came in the 17th century, at the beginning of which the king, Senge Namgyal, built a palace at Leh to rival the Potala at Lhasa. Zanskar has effectively been a dependency since that time.

The first European to reach Ladakh was a Portuguese layman by the name of Diogo d'Almeida who spent two years in the vicinity around the year 1600.

He was followed, briefly, by the Jesuit priests Francesco de Azavedo and Giovanni de Oliviero in 1631, and by Ipolito Desideri in 1715 during his epic journey from Srinagar to Lhasa. Another century passed before the influence of the British East

**ABOVE** *The Tibetan poppy (meconopsis aculeata), an endangered species, may be found on the periphery of yak pastures of Zanskar.*

India Company reached Leh, in the persons of William Moorcroft and George Trebeck. They found the Ladakhi authorities most suspicious of their motives and Moorcroft relates how the Khalun (king) of Ladakh had heard that 'it was the practice of the English to appear at first in the guise of merchants, merely to gain a footing in the country, and that, having effected this, they speedily brought it under their authority.' Barely two decades elapsed before the Khalun's apprehensions were borne out.

## TIBETAN CULTURE

Western interest in the history of Zanskar began with a chance meeting between an Englishman and a Hungarian on the caravan route between Srinagar and Leh, in 1822. William Moorcroft was travelling under the auspices of the East India Company, while Alexander De Körös was returning from Leh having failed to get further towards Yarkand in his quest to discover the origins of the Hungarians. Moorcroft aroused De Körös' interest in things Tibetan, and in June 1823 the latter arrived in Zanskar where he spent 16 months compiling a Tibetan grammar for the British Government.

Ladakh may be remote, but Zanskar is both remote and almost inaccessible. Its name translates from the Tibetan Zangsdkar and means white copper, after the precious mineral found in this area. The territory consists essentially of lands drained by the two major tributaries of the Zanskar River, and covers 4800km² (1853 square miles) of extremely mountainous

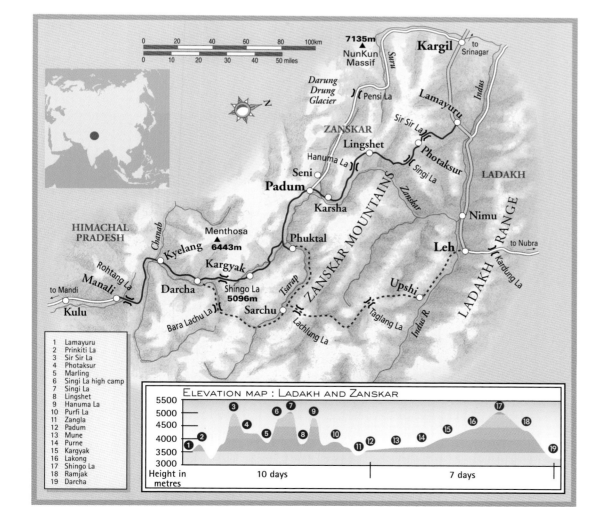

terrain at an average elevation of 4000m (13,000ft). Before the coming of the rough road into Zanskar from Kargil on the Srinagar–Leh 'Beacon Highway', Padum, the tiny capital, was cut off from the outside world for most of the year. Zanskar's isolation and obscurity have served to preserve it as a rare enclave of untrammelled Tibetan culture, carrying its rich heritage of Tantric Buddhism into the 21st century largely intact. The monasteries tucked away among the arid mountainfolds of the country are living repositories of ancient traditions that have been violently obliterated in their Tibetan homeland.

## MEDIEVAL MONASTERY

The mountains and valleys of Ladakh and Zanskar have a network of trails and passes, making the area a paradise for trekkers prepared to ad-lib. Tourists may wander the open areas without permits or other bureaucratic hindrance, but the sparse population and barren land make self-sufficient travel essential. Itineraries can be tailored according to a party's level of fitness and interest in Buddhist culture, but if there is one that combines the best of mountain scenery and monastic splendour it is the traverse of Zanskar from Lamayuru to Darcha. Few treks offer the combined attractions of sustained cultural interest and scenic diversity over such a long and challenging walk.

A few days' acclimatization in and around Leh at 3505m (11,499ft) before setting off is time wisely spent. The journey into Zanskar on foot begins beneath Lamayuru *gompah*, the well-preserved

**ABOVE** *Guardian of the East, chief of the guardians of the four directions often depicted in temple porches. This one is at Thiksey, near Leh.*

medieval buildings of which perch astride a spur amid a bizarre and alien landscape of wind-eroded hillsides and sculpted cliffs. Today, the trail bypasses both the village and the monastery. However, from the monastery one can still follow the ancient caravan route up on foot, past crumbling *mani* walls and disused switch-backs towards the Photu La at 4147m (13,606ft). (*Mani* walls are so called because they are made of stones inscribed with the Tibetan Buddhist mantra *om mani padme hum* which translates as 'hail the jewel in the lotus'.) The Beacon Highway today snakes across the Photu La on its way from Srinagar in Kashmir to Leh. Until 1987, when the Indian government sent in the army to defend its territorial claim to Kashmir against secessionists and insurgents, this was the main road between Ladakh and the outside world.

The way to Zanskar leaves Lamayuru down-valley, before sneaking off south up a dry, stony defile towards the Prinkiti La (3750m; 12,303ft), the first of eight passes between Lamayuru and Padum. Allow at least 10 days to complete this section and be prepared for plenty of tough climbs and knee-crunching descents. Local guides are strongly recommended, since up-to-date route information is essential: trails and bridges are frequently washed away and available mapping is often inaccurate.

## LION PASS

The highlight of this walk into Zanskar is undoubtedly the crossing of the Singi La (Lion Pass) at 5060m (16,600ft). Immediately to the east of the col is a dramatic rocky peak, but it is the vistas back north to the previous pass, the Sirsir La, and ahead southwest towards Lingshet that really take the breath away. The fabulous and remote monastery at Lingshet still lies beyond two slightly lesser passes (the Khupte La and the Niekutse La) from here. The walls of the *gompah* are decorated with exquisite old murals, and today the monks are celebrated mural artists. Many of the recent refurbishments to monasteries in the Leh area have been decorated by artists from Lingshet.

Finally, from the Purfi La, the Zanskar Valley is revealed, and from a point just below the crest on the descent there is an awesome view into the formidable gorges through which the Zanskar River escapes north towards the Indus and Ladakh. For centuries, it was along the frozen surface of this powerful river that the Zanskaris tentatively used to lead their yaks on trading trips to Leh, during the long winter months, when the passes were closed.

The pace of life in Padum has picked up considerably with the coming of the road, but it is still a sleepy, dusty backwater. There are several very important monasteries in the vicinity, however, making a couple of days' rest here more than worthwhile. Opposite the town on a very steep hillside sits Karsha, the largest *gelugpa* (yellow-hat sect) *gompah* in Zanskar and home to 150 monks. Two *du-khangs* (assembly halls) are entered from the main courtyard, but the real treasure is a temple called the Labrang, which is dark and unused today. Entrance is gained by ladder

through a tiny skylight, but a torch reveals the crumbling walls, richly covered with frescoes and murals that are over a thousand years old.

Padum is situated at the confluence of the two major tributaries of the Zanskar River, the Doda and Tsarap Chhu. The trail south to Darcha and Lahaul via the Shingo La initially follows the Tsarap Chhu. Allow a minimum of seven days to reach Darcha. Compared to the intricate ridges and deep gorges traversed on the first half of the route, this section passes through vast, open landscapes of windswept plains and isolated farmsteads. Though it involves a short diversion into the valley of the Biri Chhu, a visit to Phuktal *gompah* should not

be missed. A more dramatic setting for a monastery could not be imagined, with the whitewashed buildings appearing to tumble out of an enormous cave high above the roaring waters of the river.

The last village in Zanskar is Kargyak, and south of this hamlet of 20-odd houses the trail passes beneath the Gumbarajon, a rock over 1000m (3300ft) high that would not look out of place in Yosemite. Beyond lies the Shingo La (5096m; 16,720ft), the only pass to be crossed between Padum and Darcha. This col may be snow-covered at any time of year, and the steep five-hour descent to the tiny camp site at Ramjak will make you thankful you chose to complete the route in this direction.

ABOVE *Phuktal, arguably the most dramatically situated monastery in Zanskar. This beehive building nestles beneath and inside a huge cave above the Biri Chhu, and the earliest buildings date from the 11th century. It is well worth a short diversion from Purne village to see it.*

# SINGALILA TO KANGCHENJUNGA

*By Steve Razzetti*

While the Nepal Himalaya and Tibet were strictly forbidden to European explorers throughout the 19th century and for much of the 20th, the same cannot be said of the tiny mountain principality of Sikkim. British India came to the aid of the beleaguered Maharaja in the face of an attempted invasion by the Tibetans in 1888, precipitating the establishment of Sikkim as a Protected Native State, and it has effectively been a part of India ever since.

By the 1930s, Sikkim was firmly established as a favourite haunt for British mountaineers and naturalists. Government officials from Calcutta flocked to the hill stations of Darjeeling and Kalimpong to escape the oppressive heat and humidity of the Indian monsoon, and touring the mountain districts of Sikkim was definitely *en vogue*. The journals of the Alpine and Himalayan Clubs were crammed with accounts of members' exploits as Sikkim rapidly became one of the best known of all the Himalayan districts. In geographical terms, the country may accurately be described as the catchment area for the Teesta River, bounded in the west by Kangchenjunga and the Singalila Ridge, and in the east by Pauhunri and the Donkya Ridge.

The Indian government no longer grants foreigners quite as much freedom to roam these hills. Few places in the Himalaya require as much bureaucratic manoeuvring to obtain the necessary permits, but do not be discouraged. This route may be the only mountain journey of any substance officially sanctioned today, but it affords magnificent perspectives on the peaks of the Singalila Ridge, Pandim and the east face of Kangchenjunga and reaches the very heart of the Sikkim Himalaya.

In spring, the Singalila Ridge yields only occasional tantalizing glimpses of the glistening white giants ahead, as the trail along its crest heads north through swirling mists and dense cloud forest, crossing entire mountainsides cloaked with enormous

**ABOVE** *Tibetan prayer flags flutter in the icy dawn breeze atop a ridge above Dzong Ri on the final approach to Kangchenjunga.*

azaleas and rhododendrons in full bloom. Exotic orchids flower in dripping grottoes, while luxuriant ferns cloak the ground beneath the trees in a dense tapestry of green. In autumn, the grass is golden underfoot, the frosts hard in the mornings and the snow-capped peaks to the north appear close enough to touch, so clear is the mountain air.

Until 1999, the five-day hike to the Goecha La (4800m; 15,700ft) from the village of Yuksom was usually preceded by a gentle three- to four-day stroll along the Sandakphu section of the Singalila Ridge between Dhodray and Phalut, and an overnight stay at the town of Pemayangtse. Thus two short but enjoyable treks were interspersed with a couple of days' road travel and a night in a rather decrepit hotel.

The second half of the trek started with a steamy slither along leech-infested forest trails in the deep gorge of the Rathong Chhu, followed by the ascent of the steep and seemingly interminable ridge dividing the valleys of the Churong Chhu and Prek Chhu rivers. Emerging from the trees at Dzong Ri, trekkers were confronted with a mountain vista as breathtaking as any in the entire Himalaya. Ahead, the pyramid form of the Kangchenjunga towers over an intervening ridge. To the west, a chain of magnificent peaks forms the northernmost part of the Singalila Ridge itself, rising at last to Kangchenjunga in a series of spectacular snowy steps.

Early in 2000, the Indian authorities opened the previously off-limits section of the Singalila Ridge between Phalut and Dzong Ri. However, it has been closed again, forcing trekkers to endure the frustration of diverting from the ridge-walk at Phalut, just as the most tantalizing and

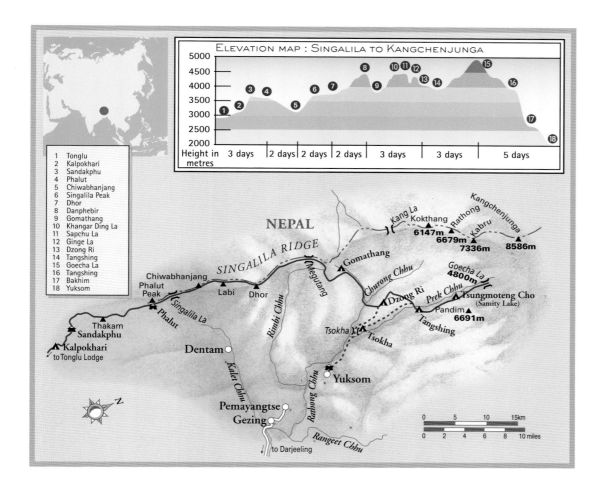

**ABOVE** *Accommodation on the lower part of this route has improved in the last decade, but north of Phalut you must be self-sufficient.*

alluring section becomes visible ahead (see panel opposite). Without the detour, the entire walk from Dhodray to the Goecha La via Dzong Ri could be completed in a sensational 17-day hike, before backtracking for a couple of days and then finishing with the descent to Yuksom.

## ROLLERCOASTER IN THE SKY

North of Phalut, the Singalila really comes into its own. The trail is a roller-coaster in the sky, with panoramic vistas at every turn and increasingly chilly overnight stops as the altitude increases. Though the flanks of the Singalila Ridge are densely wooded, the crest is dotted with idyllic meadows and pasture, to which the locals bring their livestock during the monsoon. Many of these clearings make fantastic camp sites, but as the monsoon recedes and the autumn season progresses, water supplies up here may become an issue. Having a guide or local crew with detailed knowledge of the location of freshwater springs will save you much time and effort in this matter. You may have to descend a very long way to fill your bottles in December.

The 3685m (12,090ft) Singalila La and the 4430m (14,534ft) Danphebir Lekh are best

LEFT *Hiking through Lothlorien – the magical forests on the Singalila Ridge are comprised mainly of giant magnolias and rhododendrons, bamboo, birch and blue pine.*

OPPOSITE *A viewpoint above Thangshing and the upper Prek Chhu valley, from where the final approach to the Goecha La and Kangchenjunga is spectacularly revealed.*

crossed very early in the morning from a camp at 4250m (13,944ft) – the highest on the ridge itself – at the tiny lakes to the west. The views are unforgettable. Dawn light on distant Makalu (8463m; 27,766ft) and Everest (8848m; 29,029ft) to the west will surely have you reaching for that telephoto, while to the north the high peaks of Sikkim – Kangchenjunga, Pandim (6691m; 21,952ft) and Kabru (7317m; 24,006ft) beckon.

## COMPLEX TOPOGRAPHY

Eventually, after crossing the double crest of the Danphebir Lekh, the ridge has to be abandoned, but the trail to Dzong Ri and Kangchenjunga is never less than exhilarating. The intervening ridges have a deceptively complex topography. Several subsidiary passes have to be crossed on this section, giving some fairly long days of

walking, with a feeling of proximity to the snow-peaks. From the camp at Dzong Ri, over which the brooding southeast face of Kangchenjunga peers menacingly, one can gaze into the tantalizing but forbidden Tikip Chhu valley that leads immediately west to the Kang La (5084m; 16,680ft) and Nepal. A pre-dawn hike up to the prayer flags on a snowy rise above Dzong Ri will convince you that you have truly arrived in the heart of the Himalaya. To the north-west, the Singalila Ridge itself takes in the summits of Kokthang (6147m; 20,167ft) Rathong (6679m; 21,913ft), Kabru South (7317m; 24,006ft), Kabru North (7338m; 24,075ft) and Talung (7349m; 24,111ft) before finally culminating at the summit of Kangchenjunga itself. To the north, the Prek Chhu cuts a spectacular cleft hard beneath the jagged ramparts of Pandim and thence to

the Goecha La. Standing on this snowy col three days later, most visitors will lament the modern political constraints that preclude a more complete tour of the sensational Sikkim Himalaya.

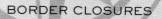

### BORDER CLOSURES

Current political uncertainty has led to temporary closure of the border at Phalut. It is not possible to walk the ridge continuously. Both sections are open, but you have to leave the ridge at Phalut, descend to Rimbik and drive into Sikkim, completing border formalities on the way. You rejoin the ridge 1.5km (1 mile) from Sikkim.

Current permit situation is this:

• Yuksom to Dzong Ri/Goecha La route requires a minimum of two applications for the permit, obtainable at the Sikkim Tourism offices in Delhi, Gangtok, Siliguri. An application form must be filled in and submitted with one passport photo and photocopies of your India visa and passport details page.

• Uttarey (Chitre) – Dzong Ri Ridge route (beyond Phalut): two sets of permits are required, but the application form is the same. Apply for an inner line permit to visit Gangtok, Pelling. Based on this, only the Gangtok Tourist office is authorized to give the second trek permit for the Uttarey – Dzong Ri route. Both application forms require a passport photo and copies of your passport and India visa.

• Lower Singalila Ridge (Darjeeling) from Dhodray to Rimbik: no permit is required. As long as you have a valid India visa, you can go.

# ZANSKAR RIVER

*By Seb Mankelow*

Sandwiched between the Karakoram to the north, the Tibetan Plateau to the east and the Himalaya to the south, India's remote and high altitude desert region of Ladakh endures ferociously cold winters. By early January, the persistently low temperatures begin to choke the region's larger rivers with ice; even the mighty Zanskar River is coerced into winter dormancy. As the swift currents and boiling rapids are calmed they slowly solidify into an icy thoroughfare. The brief annual life of the Zanskar River trek has begun.

Walking on the frozen Zanskar River by day and overnighting in caves and Zanskari homes, this unique winter journey transports trekkers through terrain that for 10 months of the year is only accessible to ibex, snow leopard and the occasional summer rafting party. Draining much of southern Ladakh into the Indus, the Zanskar River has carved a serpentine gorge that in places is over 1000m (3300ft) deep. Confined to the course of the river by steep rock walls and towering peaks, this tough and occasionally hazardous winter route rewards the trekker with stunning scenery, fascinating geology and a privileged glimpse of winter life in Zanskar.

Squashed between the Zanskar Range to the north and India's Greater Himalayan Range to the south, the Zanskar Valley is remote and largely accessible only on foot. During the brief summer, a single thread of road – mostly unsurfaced – links the valley to the rest of the Indian subcontinent. Otherwise, all access is confined to those who trek over the high mountain passes. In winter, both the road and the trekking routes are impassable. Hampered by heavy snow, Zanskar's isolated communities settle into a traditional way of life that has changed relatively little over generations. Winter holds this ancient kingdom captive for up to seven months of every year. Yet, ironically, the bitterly low temperatures do provide Zanskaris with a brief window of escape. Locally referred to as *chaddar*, the

TOP *Enjoying the fine weather and ice conditions, Zanskari porters make quick progress as they start out from Chilling.*

region's frozen rivers effectively act as 'winter roads'. Originally a winter trade route, the Zanskar River is perhaps the greatest of all the *chaddar* journeys. Linking remote Zanskari villages with the Indus Valley and the bazaars in Leh, this route was once used to export the much-prized commodities of Zanskari butter and cheese. More recently it has become a means of transporting children to boarding schools in Leh in time for the spring term. Inevitably, trekkers have also begun to frequent the river, although the extreme cold and arduous nature of the trek deters all but the most determined.

A short flight from New Delhi carries trekkers over the Western Himalaya to Leh. Arriving at 3500m (11,500ft) it is important

to allow time for acclimatization before busying oneself with river-trek preparations. It may even be possible to enjoy one of the several Buddhist festivals scheduled during the winter months. Once fully acclimatized there are provisions to buy, and guide and porters to meet. Undertaking the frozen river trek without an experienced guide is not advisable.

## GENERATIONS OF CRAFTSMEN

From Leh, a cold, and occasionally precipitous, road journey transports the trekker to the start at Chilling. A scatter of dwellings, it is home to some of Ladakh's most famous smiths. Craftsmen in gold, silver, copper and brass, the villagers are descendants of skilled Nepali workers who

were invited in the 16th century by the king of Ladakh to manufacture religious images and objects. (It is possible that 'Zanskar' derives from the Tibetan *zangs-dkar*, referring to white copper).

After spending the night at Chilling, trekkers set foot on the river for the first time. It becomes quickly apparent which ice surfaces offer purchase and which do not. Falling over can become a common occurrence, even for Zanskaris, and unless deemed serious a tumble is usually appreciated with hearty laughter! This is, however, a potentially hazardous trek and from the outset it is prudent for trekkers and guide to travel in a group and negotiate difficult sections together. A surprise dunking is unlikely, but possible. Some

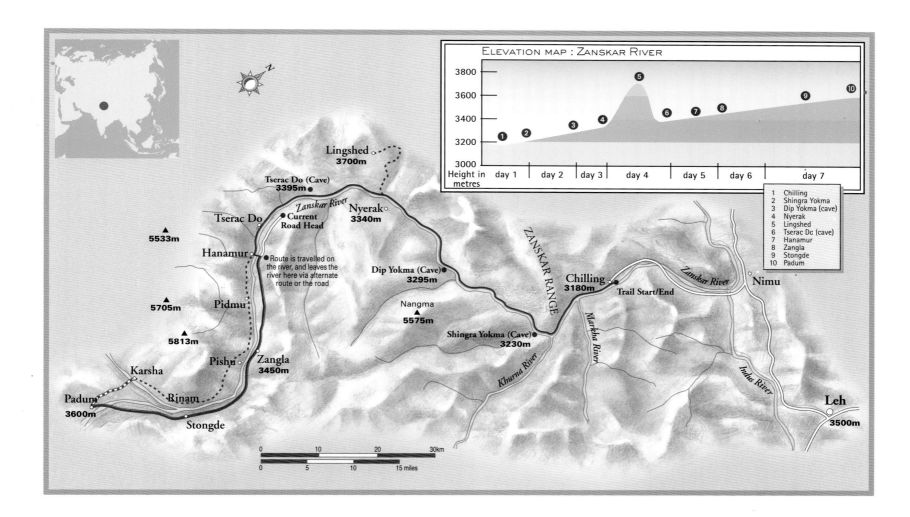

sections of ice are deceptively thin and the river always harbours sections of open water that refuse to freeze. Many of these are easily negotiable; others require sure-footed care.

Nevertheless, the experience of travelling on river-ice entices the trekker to continue around every twist and turn. Several hours from Chilling an impressive rust-red mountain, locally known as Tagmar gongma, dominates the route ahead and from this point the gorge begins to deepen. If ice conditions are favourable, the first night on the river can be spent at Shingra Yokma, a small rocky shelf and beach beneath a conglomerate cliff.

At the end of the trekking day, porters slip into a well-oiled routine and quickly set about collecting wood (usually drift-wood) for a fire. Unfortunately, the growing popularity of this trek has also increased the burden on relatively scarce groves of willow and tamarisk. It is difficult to stem this potential environmental problem. The use of kerosene stoves helps, but it doesn't meet the needs of the less well-equipped Zanskaris, who use the fires for warmth and to dry their woollen clothing.

The next three days of trekking follow a similar routine. An early start combats the insidious morning cold and maximizes the chance of reaching the preferred caves by nightfall. The gorge continues to grow in stature as the route weaves back and forth, unfolding around each river bend. Easy progress, however, is by no means a certainty. In places where river-ice is thin or nonexistent, the trekker has little choice but to scale the rocky sides and traverse

**ABOVE** *Having sprinkled sand to provide extra grip, a Zanskari porter carefully negotiates a narrow section of river ice.*

above the clear turquoise water. If the rock is too steep or featureless, and the water not too deep, then a quick wade may suffice. A handful of rickety walkways are being constructed at sections notorious for being wet, but their state of repair cannot be guaranteed. It may still prove necessary to climb several hundred metres above the river in search of another route: a strenuous alternative to an otherwise lengthy wait for the river to refreeze.

Indeed, fluctuations in temperature constantly modify ice conditions. Sweeping corrugated surfaces track the demise and eventual solidification of river currents, and occasionally the ice is so transparent that boulders are clearly visible on the river-bed below. Temperature also influences the

trekking day and breaks usually coincide with one of the welcome pockets of sunshine that penetrate the shadows of the gorge. Tucked out of the wind it is often warm enough to enjoy a cup of tea and air damp boots. The second day ends far from the sun's warmth at Dip Yokma, a large cave well above the river. The ash floor and soot-blackened roof bears testament to the generations of Zanskaris that have sought shelter here.

## LEGENDARY COOK

Leaving Dip Yokma on the third day, the trekker soon passes the cave known as Gyalpo Skyalzos. Legend tells of one of the kings of Zanskar who was supposedly trapped here for so long that hunger forced him and his party to contemplate eating their cook! Upon realization of the deadly plot the cook tied their remaining belongings together and trailed them in the river overnight. The resulting build-up of ice around the objects created a frozen walkway that eventually allowed the party to escape their predicament the following morning. The cook survived to tell the tale, but to this day the cave has remained an unpopular place to spend the night!

A further hour of walking and the route enters several kilometres of river notorious for poor ice formation. Both brown and white throated dippers enjoy this section, but the pleasure of seeing these aquatic birds is usually offset by some tricky rock scrambling and the fear of joining them in the water! The spacious camp site at Nyerak is, however, not far ahead and trekkers usually spend their third night here. The collection of small stone huts (and accompanying fields if you are camping) between the village and river offer valuable shelter, especially for your guide and porters. The main settlement at Nyerak is perched high above and out of sight from the river. At the end of a long day the prospect of a steep climb to visit these households tends to be not so attractive. However, if one does make the effort at dusk, the climb up and out of the gorge offers a wonderful expanse of star-studded sky.

## TRUE HIMALAYAN WINTER

From Nyerak the tributary stream that marks the trail to the village of Lingshed is only one hour upriver. The trekker is now in Zanskar and the noticeable increase in snow cover suggests the declining influence of Ladakh's rain-shadow and the growing dominance of the true Himalayan winter. The gorge also begins to make a transition and, despite leaving Nyerak through one of the most impressive sections of vertical cliff, the end of the fourth day finds the river-trekker enjoying a slightly more open landscape and a little more sunshine. Again, there is a choice of locations in which to overnight. A small cave perched above the river at Tserac Do provides a breezy shelter, or for those making good time there are several smaller caves and overhanging rocks further upriver. Your guide should know whether it is possible to reach these before nightfall.

An hour or two of walking on day five and the trekker arrives in Sham, or Lower Zanskar. The severity of the gorge is long gone and the river now cuts across the floor of a vast U-shaped valley: the legacy of the immense glaciers that once crept northwards from the Greater Himalaya. There are now plenty of opportunities to leave the river and follow a combination of the snow-packed trails that link Zanskar's villages in winter. Alternatively trekkers can join the new road that is being cut adjacent to the Zanskar River on the true right (east) bank. This new road project – which is intended to follow the course of the Zanskar River – will eventually connect the Zanskar Valley with the road-head at Chilling (and ultimately the Indus Valley). Progress is slow, however, and although construction recommences each summer, building activities at both the Chilling and Zanskar ends have yet to reach the gorge proper.

Depending on the frequency of vehicular traffic and the amount of accumulated

**BELOW** *Trekkers take a short break to appreciate one of the many icefalls that tumble into the Zanskar gorge.*

snow, trekkers wanting to organize transport to Padum (the largest town and administrative capital of Zanskar) may improve their chances by following the road on foot to Zangla. If the road is drivable, an irregular bus service runs several times a week between Zangla and Padum. Other private transport may also be available and this is best coordinated with the help of your guide.

Alternatively, trekkers can avoid the road and the vagaries of securing transport by exiting onto the true left (west) bank of the Zanskar River and continuing to Padum on foot. This route, which takes a further two to three days, goes via a number of interesting settlements, including Karsha, a prosperous village that supports Zanskar's largest Buddhist (*Gelug-pa*) monastery. Your guide and porters will no doubt have relatives and friends in the villages you visit. Organizing a room for the night should not pose a problem and hospitality requires that you sample a little salt tea!

Backed by the lofty peaks of India's Greater Himalayan Range, Padum (3600m; 11,811ft) occupies the southeastern corner of the Zanskar Valley. Stocked with goods brought in the previous summer, the settlement in winter offers a few basic supplies. Arriving in Padum is only the halfway point for most *chaddar* trekkers. It may be 10 years or more before a winter road link exists between Padum and Leh and only with careful forward planning is it possible to charter a helicopter departure. The majority of trekkers indulge once again in the delights of the *chaddar* by retracing the route to Chilling.

# Kangchenjunga

## By Steve Razzetti

Hope Leezum Namgyal, crown princess of Sikkim, was adamant. Seeing my notes pertaining to our travels to Kangchenjunga she exclaimed 'You cannot write the name like that! It means nothing! The mountain's true appellation is the Tibetan *Kang-Chen-Dzong-Nga*, which translates as 'Peak of the Five Great Treasuries of the Snows'. As a matter of politeness we do not anglicize the names of mountains in Wales or Scotland, so why should you those of Sikkim and Tibet?' Kangchendzonga it is then!

Separated from the great peaks of the Khosi section of the Nepal Himalaya by the mightiest of all the country's trans-Himalayan rivers, the Arun, Kangchendzonga is often referred to as part of the Sikkim Himalaya. Unlike the other major summits of the Great Himalaya, this peak does not merely lie on the crest of a ridge-system running east–west, but forms the centre of a giant mountain cross, radiating east, west, north and south from its 8586m (28,168ft) apex. Just 25m (82ft) short of K2, it is the third highest mountain in the world.

The western arm of this monumental intersection terminates at the summit of Jannu (7710m; 25,294ft), itself one of the most spectacular peaks in the entire Himalaya, while the eastern arm descends to the Zemu Gap in Sikkim. To the south, the Singalila Ridge extends for 80km (50 miles) and forms the border between Nepal and Sikkim. To the north, a complex chain of summits leads to the 7473m (24,511ft) Jongsang Peak and the border with Tibet. Rising directly from the plains of India, the Kangchendzonga massif lies east of the protective barrier of the Siwalik Hills, which snare the incoming monsoon clouds before they can unleash their deluge on the rest of the Nepal Himalaya. Consequently, these mountains receive the highest precipitation in Nepal, and their summits are adorned with astoundingly

ABOVE *The north face of Kangchenjunga/ Kangchendzonga from the summit of Drohmo Ri, about 6200m (20,300ft) above Pang Pema.*
OPPOSITE *Lama and novice at the tiny monastery above the Tibetan village of Phole (Phere on some maps) in the Ghunsa Khola valley.*

varied snow formations, while the valleys below are cloaked in impenetrable sub-tropical jungle.

Clearly discernible from the popular hill station of Darjeeling in West Bengal, Kang-chendzonga attracted the attention of explorers long before the rest of Nepal. To this town, the sportsmen, loungers and ladies of the Raj fled to escape the oppres-sive heat and humidity of Calcutta. Nepal and Tibet were both forbidden to foreign-ers during the 19th century, and the first travellers to penetrate their borders did so clandestinely and at considerable risk to themselves and their local guides.

The first explorer to visit the Nepal side of Kangchendzonga was a British botanist, Sir Joseph Hooker. His reports caught the attention of the Royal Geographical Society

and the Survey of India, and the latter dispatched the pundits Sarat Chandra Das and Rinzin Namgyal to find out more. Chandra Das made two journeys into Nepal, one in 1879 and another in 1881, entering on each occasion across Singalila Ridge via the Kang La, but crossing into Tibet via the Jongsang La in 1879 and the Nago La in 1881. In 1883, Rinzin Namgyal also crossed the Kang La from Sikkim, and explored the upper reaches of the Yalung Glacier before retracing his predecessor's footsteps over the Jongsang La.

In 1899, it was the same Rinzin Namgyal whom the Englishman Douglas Freshfield

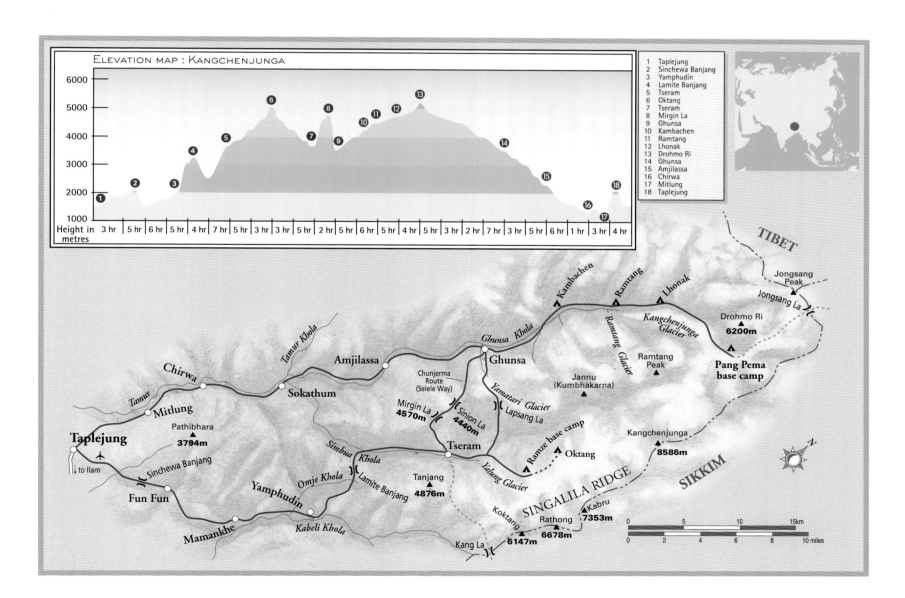

ABOVE *The Hindu shrine at Oktang, on the moraine of the Yalung glacier, with the vast amphitheatre south face of Kangchendzonga beyond.*

OPPOSITE *The north face of Jannu (also known as Kumbhakarna), Sobithongie and Phole and the Jannu glacier, from the mountainside high above Khambachen.*

tiny landing strip at Suketar above the administrative centre of the district, Taplejung. By flying in and out, it is feasible to visit the Yalung Glacier and the south face of Kangchendzonga, cross either of the routes to Ghunsa and trek up to Pang Pema beneath the awesome north face before retreating back to Taplejung in 23 days.

The ideal starting point, however, is Tumlingtar (510m; 1673ft) in the steamy Arun Valley. From here, the trek leads into Taplejung across the Milke Danda ridge, from the crest of which the entire Kangchendzonga group presents itself in all its glory some 64km (40 miles) away. Ramze, the base camp on the Yalung Glacier for the South Face of Kangchendzonga, is an eight-day hike from Taplejung.

## ACROSS THE GRAIN

Totally devoid of tea-houses and lodges, this walk offers a refreshing alternative to the crowded commercialism of the more popular regions of the country. Cutting across the grain of the land, however, it is not an easy undertaking. The first half of the walk-in winds through intensively farmed country, with quaint thatched farmhouses surrounded by lovingly tended gardens and shaded by some of the biggest poinsettia trees you will ever see. Testament to the hard work of the mountain folk of Nepal, the vast expanses of terraced rice paddies hereabouts are without equal. Beyond Yamphudin (2150m; 7052ft), the most remote hamlet passed on this route, the trail enters a region of pure mountain wilderness as it climbs steeply into forests of birch, conifer and rhododendron. It crosses yet more

chose to accompany his multinational party on what was undeniably the most important expedition in the exploration of Kangchendzonga. Setting off from Darjeeling, their aim was to circumambulate the entire massif. Accompanied also by the eminent mountain photographer Vittorio Sella, his brother Erminio and mountain guide Angelo Maquignaz, they entered Nepal illegally across the Jongsang La. Descending to the village of Ghunsa, they were disarmed by the nonchalance of the inhabitants at the sight of a party of pale-faces in their midst, and, fearing they would be caught by the authorities, scurried back east into Sikkim across the Chunjerma and Kang La's.

The first ascent of Kangchendzonga was made in 1955, by a British expedition led by

Charles Evans. On two consecutive days in May, George Band and Joe Brown, followed by Tony Streather and Norman Hardie reached the top. Kanchendzonga is in fact the only 8000m+ peak to have been first climbed by the British, and as a mark of deference to the beliefs of their Sherpa companions they did not actually sully the summit with their footsteps.

Trekkers wishing to visit the Nepal side of Kangchendzonga today will find the Nepalese authorities far more obliging, provided you have the necessary permits and are self-sufficient in food, fuel and accommodation. Due to the extreme remoteness of the region, a thorough tour will occupy the best part of five weeks (30 days' walking). Those with less time at their disposal may consider the daily air services to the

ridges before finally approaching the south side of Kangchendzonga up the picturesque valley of the Simbua Khola. The stunning array of peaks that tower over Ramze (4650m; 15,252ft) is impressive enough, but follow the glacier for another hour – on an easy trail in the ablation valley or on the crest of the lateral moraine – to the Hindu shrine at Oktang for a close encounter with the real giants. On your right are Rathong (6678m; 21,903ft), Kabru (7353m; 24,117ft) and Talung (7349m; 24,104ft), while straight ahead is the sheer south wall of Kangchendzonga itself.

There are two possible routes across the watershed between the Yalung Glacier and the Ghunsa Khola Valley to the north. The Lapsang La (5100m; 16,728ft) is higher and involves traversing steep screes and boulder fields on both sides, but its mountain views are no better. The Chunjerma Route, known locally as the Selele Way after the summer grazing pasture on the Ghunsa side, may be lower, but the trail is far better and stays at higher elevations for much longer. It crosses two passes, the Sinion La (4440m; 14,570ft) and the Mirgin La (4570m; 14,900ft). The steep initial ascent above Tseram on the Yalung side offers superlative panoramas of the entire south side of Kangchendzonga, while from the prayer flags at the crest of the Mirgin La the views west across the Arun and north to the awesome ramparts of Jannu are simply magnificent.

Having walked in to Ramze, spent a day or two there and then crossed north to Ghunsa, you will be sufficiently acclimatized to really enjoy the undisputed climax of this trek – the three-day hike up to the Kangchendzonga Glacier and Pang Pema (5150m; 16,892ft). On this stretch, a new, even more breathtaking vista is revealed at every turn until finally, as the tiny trail above the Kangchendzonga Glacier reaches the base camp at Pang Pema, the awesome North Face of Kangchendzonga is revealed. No mountain prospect on earth is more utterly overpowering, as it soars to the heavens in perpetual shadow – foreboding, intimidating and absolutely amazing. For a bird's-eye view, ascend Drohmo Ri, the 6100m (20,008ft) 'hill' immediately above camp. Retreat to Taplejung takes a further seven days.

# DHAULAGIRI CIRCUIT

*By Steve Razzetti*

British mountaineer and explorer Bill Tilman famously wrote that 'the identification of very distant peaks is a harmless and fascinating amusement so long as the results are not taken seriously.' As a rule, the natives of the high Himalaya do not share the Westerner's obsession with giving things names and, frequently, when asked the name of a particular snowy peak on the horizon the Sherpa innocently replied 'Dhaulagiri, sahib' (White Mountain, sir). In the case of the massif we know today as Dhaulagiri, this simple fact led to considerable early confusion as to the topography of Nepal, and resulted in some imaginative mapping.

Dhaulagiri I (8167m; 26,795ft) is the highest peak of a complex massif that is over 55km (35 miles) across, and includes the six summits of Dhaulagiri and their western outliers, Churen Himal and Putha Hiunchuli, all of which are in excess of 7200m (23,600ft). Tukuche Peak, one of the most spectacular in the group, fails to make the 7000m (23,000ft) mark by a mere 80m (260ft).

Swiss geologist Arnold Heim was the first European to get close to the peaks of central Nepal, while conducting an aerial survey of the region in 1949. One year later, Tilman's party saw Dhaulagiri from Muktinath after crossing the Thorung La from Manang, but it was the Frenchman Maurice Herzog and his expedition that same year who first got really close to this beautiful yet intimidating Himalayan behemoth.

Herzog was the leader of a stellar team, organized under the auspices of the French Alpine Club, which included such seminal alpinists as Gaston Rébuffat, Lionel Terray and Jacques Oudot. Theirs was purely a climbing endeavour, undertaken with the intention of reaching the summit of the first 8000m peak 'for the honour of France'. Dhaulagiri and Annapurna were their selected objectives, and they chose the village of Tukuche in the Kali Gandaki Valley as their base camp. The approaches to both peaks were unknown, and the

**ABOVE** *A view from French Pass into Hidden Valley. On the right are Damphus Peak and the Damphus Pass.*

team was faced with a daunting task of reconnaissance. Electing to concentrate on Dhaulagiri first, they split into small groups and set about finding a way to the mountain. Formulating their strategy according to an erroneous Survey of India map, several abortive forays were made into the Damphus Khola Valley and up the terrifying East Dhaulagiri Glacier before they reached the watershed west of the Kali Gandaki, at what we now know as Damphus or Thapa Pass (5250m; 17,224ft).

The glaciers on the north side of Dhaulagiri remained a mystery, however. Only when Lionel Terray and Jacques Oudot finally succeeded in crossing Hidden Valley, and reached the col overlooking the Chhonbardan Glacier and the North Face of Dhaulagiri, was the problem finally solved. The glacier drained into the fearsome ravines of the Myagdi Khola. Although French Pass is named after that heroic feat, Herzog and his group eventually retreated, proclaiming the peak 'unclimbable'. The

first expedition to approach Dhaulagiri via the Myagdi Khola was led by Swiss mountaineer Bernhard Lauterburg in 1953. With only one photograph (taken by Terray from French Pass in 1950) to go on, the Swiss set about exploring the Chhonbardan Glacier and tried to find a route onto Dhaulagiri itself. A thorough reconnaissance was carried out and an altitude of 7200m (23,600ft) reached on the peak, but while several of the team left via French Pass and Damphus Pass, the difficulty of climbing the north face remained obvious.

In 1960, a second Swiss expedition finally conquered the mountain. They brought with them a single-engined aircraft equipped for glacier landings, complete with veteran pilot and mechanic. After laying on a shuttle service and flying the entire team up to Damphus Pass, pilot Ernst Saxer set a world height record for a glacier landing when he dropped Kurt Diemberger and Ernst Forrer off at the northeast col, from where they commenced their ascent.

## TWO REMOTE PASSES

The basic circuit of Dhaulagiri I remains one of the most challenging and rewarding routes in Nepal. It starts at Beni and finishes across Damphus Pass to rejoin the Kali Gandaki at Tukuche or Marpha, committing you to a long and difficult trek, with two remote passes and the highest camp, Dhaulagiri base camp, right at the end of the trail. Contingency plans should be carefully weighed up. Given fine weather and good snow conditions the French and Damphus Pass crossings are

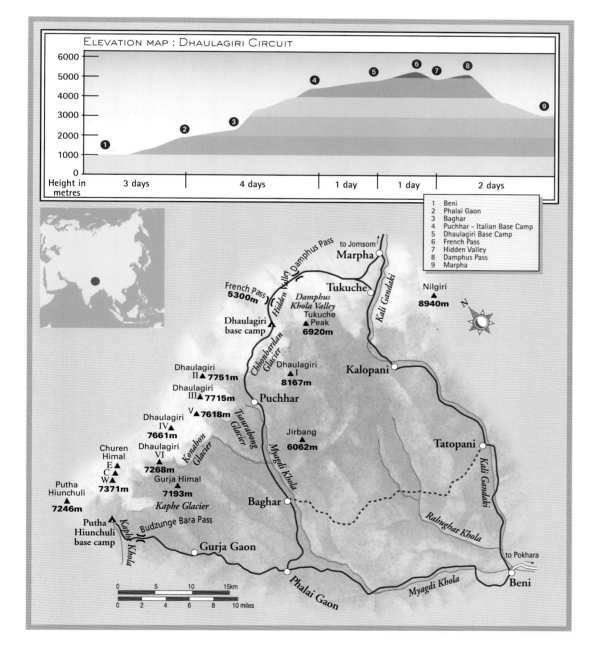

unforgettable, with impressive perspectives gained on the north face of Dhaulagiri, but in a blizzard navigation may prove extremely difficult. Similarly, choosing the correct col when crossing into the Kali Gandaki from Hidden Valley is imperative, since a mistake could lead to dangerously steep ground.

For a party travelling in expedition mode, the basic circuit can be made even more rewarding by beginning with a side trip to the Kaphe Khola Valley and the base camp of Putha Hiunchuli (7246m; 23,766ft). This

peak was first climbed from the north in 1954 by a small British expedition led by Jimmy Roberts, but it was the second and third ascents, both made in 1972 by Japanese teams, that pioneered the route in from Phalai Gaon village in the valley of the Myagdi Khola, via Gurja Gaon and the Budzunge Bara Pass (4590m; 15,055ft).

## WALK IN THE CLOUDS

The roller-coaster trail that constitutes this dramatic ridge walk rises skyward from Darsinge Karka, just beyond the village of

Gurja Gaon, onto the Budzunge Bara. Under snow it would be a most serious proposition, but, given fine weather, a high camp just east of the col is feasible. Tucked right under the south face of the Gurja Himal (7193m; 23,593ft), this spot commands a most spectacular sunset panorama to the east, with Manapati (6380m; 20.932ft), Jirbang (6062m; 19,888ft) Fang (7647m; 25,089ft), Annapurna South (7219m; 23,684ft) and Hiunchuli (6441m; 21,132ft) lined up along the horizon. With no other high ground south, east or west

ABOVE *Looking west across the Kali Gandaki valley from Thulobugin Pass to Dhaulagiri I and Tukuche Peak. The descent route from Damphus Pass to Marpha is on the far right.*

for miles it feels like a walk in the clouds. From the col, both Putha Hiunchuli and Churen Himal (7371m; 24,176ft) are visible. Beyond, the desolate and seldom visited Kaphe Kola valley awaits.

Backtracking to the village of Muri, the route then rejoins the thin trail up the Myagdi Khola. Above the village of Baghar it enters a magical zone of dense primordial jungle. The path zigzags up and down, crossing the tumultuous river on rickety bamboo bridges and surmounting vertical sections of rock by way of bamboo ladders lashed into place with knotted vines, and disappears under enormous, precariously balanced boulders, reappearing over the rotting trunks of gigantic fallen trees.

Only on the fourth day do the deciduous trees give way to conifers, and the claustrophobic valley walls retreat to a more respectable distance. Abruptly, the trail emerges into a clearing and straight ahead is Puchhar. The tiny camp, known as Italian Base Camp (3585m; 11,758ft), is situated in a tiny grassy meadow immediately beneath the west face or Puchhar Wall of Dhaulagiri I. A more awesome and intimidating spot would be hard to imagine. Along with the Rupal Face of Nanga Parbat in Pakistan, this ranks among the highest mountain walls in the world, sweeping skyward over 4600m (15,100ft) above the camp. The now diminutive waters of the Myagdi Khola issue from between the ice-plastered walls of a dark and forbidding gorge to the north, and the savage beauty of the scene is enhanced every evening as the setting sun projects its light-show across the entire face.

Beyond Puchhar the country is serious. Having sneaked through the gorge at dawn to minimize the risk of stone-fall from the mighty precipices above, the route then ascends the Chhonbardan Glacier to Dhaulagiri base camp (4750m; 15,580ft). Although thoughts of beer, dalbat and apple pie may be almost overpowering, the final two-day crossing of the high passes from here to Tukuche should not be undertaken unless the weather is perfect.

**ABOVE** *The south faces of Ghustung and Gurja Himal from a high camp on the Budzunge Bara ridge. When crossing late in the season, carry sufficient water, since sources on the ridge run dry.*

# MANASLU AND ANNAPURNA CIRCUIT

## By Steve Razzetti

The Kingdom of Nepal encompasses 800km (500 miles) of the highest peaks in the Himalayan chain, from east to west, and is 220km (136 miles) north to south at its broadest point. The latest statistics for the number of tourists visiting this mountain realm annually put the figure close to 400,000. Of these, some 80,000 head into the hills on foot, enjoying the magnificent mountain scenery for which the country is justly renowned worldwide. To those who suggest that the country is now over-trekked and *passé*, I would point out that a similar number of people trek in the Torres del Paine national park in Chiléan Patagonia annually.

Nepal first tentatively opened its borders to foreigners in 1949, and trekking as we know it began in the 1960s. The ensuing 40 years have seen dramatic changes in Nepal, unfortunately not all of them positive. Tourism is a mixed blessing. Large numbers of visitors, for whom hot showers, cold beer and apple pie are essential, have contributed to the serious ecological degradation of popular areas, and the rude and arrogant behaviour of a small minority has tarnished the unsophisticated charm of their inhabitants. Thankfully, most Nepalis are resilient enough to resist such insensitivity and there are still countless mysteries to enthrall the discerning explorer.

The central part of the Nepal Himalaya is known as the Gandaki Section, since it comprises mountain ranges drained by the tributaries of the Gandaki River – the Kali

Gandaki, Seti Gandaki, Marsyangdi, Buri Gandaki and Trisuli Gandaki. The highest chain of peaks running east–west throughout Nepal is known as the Great Himalaya, and to the north of this lies a secondary crest zone sometimes referred to as the Ladakh Range. Most of the major rivers predate and cut through the Great Himalaya, while a few drain areas in Tibet north of both chains. The practical result of all this geography is that the Nepal–Tibet

TOP *The panorama westwards at sunrise from Poon Hill, above Ghorepani on the Annapurna circuit. In the sun are (left) the Gurja Himal and (centre) Dhaulagiri I, while still in shadow to the right is Tukuche Peak.*

frontier follows the northern crests in some places, and the Great Himalaya in others. Where the former is the case it is often possible to complete circuits of the highest peaks in the Great Himalaya while remaining within Nepal. So it is with Manaslu and Annapurna.

European exploration of the area started modestly in 1864 when Nain Singh Rawat, the 'Chief Pundit' of Montgomerie's Great Trigonometrical Survey (GTS), visited the upper Buri Gandaki on his way to Tibet. Almost a century passed before the next chapter commenced. In 1950, at the start of

their second expedition to Nepal, British mountaineers Bill Tilman, Jimmy Roberts and their team spent several weeks around Bimtakhoti, the meadows below the western flanks of the Larkya La. Marked on modern maps as Bimthang, this was still an important trading post with Tibet at that time. Tilman's real objective during this expedition was to scout possible approaches to the Annapurnas and Manaslu for future climbing expeditions, but the team also succeeded in mapping the details of what has today become one of the most celebrated stretches of mountain terrain on

earth. Once in Manang, the party split up into pairs and between them explored the upper Marsyangdi Valley, crossed the Thorung La to Muktinath, reached about 7200m (23,600ft) during an attempt to climb Annapurna IV, crossed the Larkya La to Nupri and finally left the area down the awesome defile of the Buri Gandaki Valley.

## REAL BACK-COUNTRY

Today, as a way of experiencing the stupendous revelations that come with crossing remote mountain passes in the heart of the Nepal Himalaya, and appreciating the stark contrast between trekking in real back-country and on the tourist trails, a combination of the Manaslu and Annapurna circuits is unbeatable.

Three of the major tributaries of the Gandaki are featured on this route. In the east, the Buri Gandaki separates the peaks of the Gurkha Himal (Manaslu, Himalchuli and their satellites) from the Ganesh Himal. Next, the Marsyangdi divides the Gurkha Himal from the Annapurnas, and finally the great gorge of the Buri Gandaki cuts between the Annapurnas and Dhaulagiri. North of Manaslu lies Nupri, and north of the Annapurnas lie Manang and Mustang – tracts of barren upland under Nepalese sovereignty but populated by *Bhotias* (people of Tibetan origin).

Those undertaking this journey usually set off from the town of Gorkha (1145m; 3757ft). It was from his durbar here that Prithvi Narayan Shah, an ancestor of today's king, set out to unify the country in 1768. Leaving the chaos of Gorkha's dusty main square and bus terminus, the trail

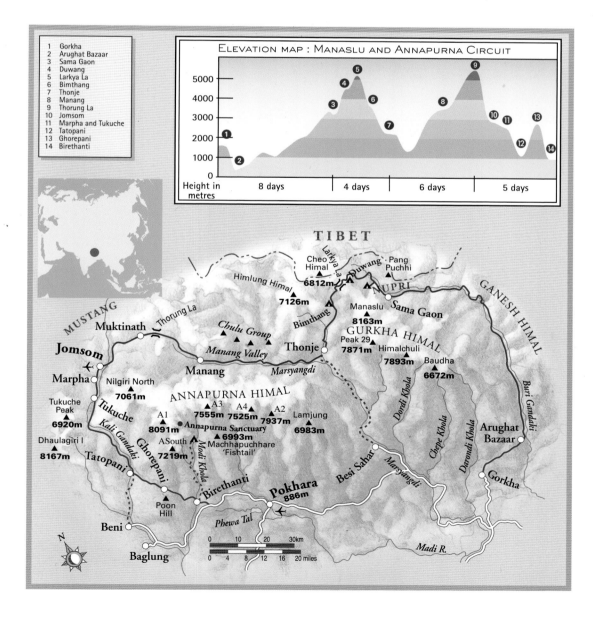

climbs a low ridge to the east before plunging down into the sweltering heat of the Buri Gandaki, reaching the valley floor at the sleepy market town of Arughat Bazaar. The journey north along the river from here into Nupri presents a real challenge, takes eight days and traverses one of the longest and most dramatic trans-Himalayan valleys in Nepal.

Though the trail through the gorges has been in use for centuries as a trade route, it is regularly devastated by the monsoon and certain sections are always difficult. Expect to have to make high, time-consuming diversions and to sweat profusely as you scramble among the twisted debris of avalanche-decimated jungle before reaching the delicious cool air of the upper reaches. Rich rewards await those who venture this way: a host of sensational peaks to ogle; isolated, unspoiled

villages nestling amid pristine forest and precious arable land; monkeys cavorting gymnastically in the trees; tiny, remote *gompahs* (monasteries) where you may drink *chang* (beer) or butter tea with lamas from as far afield as Lhasa and Sikkim.

## OUTLANDISH SPOT

Those with sufficient time will find plenty to keep them entertained in and around the biggest village in Nupri, Sama Gaon. Tucked away in the arid upper reaches of the Buri Gandaki, this truly outlandish spot consists of a tight cluster of medieval Tibetan timber dwellings and boasts a picturesque *gompah*. Nearby ridges command awesome perspectives of the northern and eastern aspects of Manaslu. The ruins of Larkya Bazaar, evidence of a vanished era of prosperity before the coming of the Chinese to Tibet, lie a short distance away to the north.

The Larkya La (5100m; 16,700ft) crossing from Nupri into Manang is straight forward enough in good weather but, like all passes of this height in the Himalaya, it can turn into an epic in the event of a blizzard. The trail sneaks its way over between the Cheo and Manaslu Himalaya, yielding views of the Annapurnas and Himlung Himal ahead and Pang Puchhi and the Ganesh Himal behind. There is a tiny stone shelter at Duwang (4480m; 14,698ft) on the eastern side, and a long, rough and knee-punishingly steep descent from the west across loose boulders to the idyllic grassy meadows at Bimthang. This is a spectacular spot to camp – a flat area sheltered beneath ancient glacial moraines and dwarfed by a cirque of towering Himalayan giants.

As with many of the places described in this book, there is much to be gained by lingering here to explore. Those prepared to devote more time to their wanderings will find plenty of scope for adventure in the vicinity of the Larkya La. Thonje village, the Marsyangdi River and the main Annapurna

LEFT *Hiking through the village of Lata Manang on the main Annapurna Circuit trail.*
OPPOSITE TOP *A wooden panel at the entrance to a temple at Muktinath depicting Yamantaka the Terrible. A Guardian of the Faith, he is a wrathful form of the Bodhisattva of wisdom.*
OPPOSITE BOTTOM *A panoramic view west across the Kali Gandaki towards Dolpo from just below the Thorung La. To the right (north) the valley disappears out of shot into the fabled kingdom of Mustang.*

Circuit trail are two long days away from Bimthang down the valley of the Dudh Khola. This trek could be completed in a couple of days from Thonje by turning south for the roadhead town of Besi Sahar, but it would be a great shame to miss out on the splendours to the north. The Marsyangdi Valley is nowhere as difficult as the Buri Gandaki. Although the path is busy and villages along the trail increasingly pander to the whims of tourists (often presenting a garish spectacle of sun terraces bedecked with beer banners, TV satellite dishes, provision stores and trashy trinket bazaars) the surrounding mountain scenery is scintillating.

Crossing the Thorung La (5400m; 17,700ft) from the cramped lodge at Thorung Phedi certainly will not be a peaceful wilderness experience. As many as 500 trekkers set off in torchlit processions before dawn every morning during peak

season, and there is now even a teashop on the top. The Larkya La is certainly more dramatic and remote, but the contrast between the steep defiles of Manang and the vast, barren vistas of the Kali Gandaki

and Mustang that await you on the Thorung La more than justify its popularity. For sheer mountain magnificence, the outlook on Dhaulagiri and Tukuche peak from the descent is peerless.

Be sure to visit the exquisite temple complex at Muktinath on your way down from the pass. It is one of the holiest sites in Nepal and a popular pilgrimage destination. You can fly out from Jomsom, a day's walk below Muktinath, but why deny yourself the joys of strolling down the Kali Gandaki and savouring the famous hospitality of the Thakali inns in villages such as Marpha and Tukuche? For an unforgettable scenic finale, divert east from Tatopani and head to the road at Birethanti, via Ghorepani and Poon Hill. Rise early and get to the top before dawn. Sunrise panoramas don't come any better, even if you do have to share it with hundreds of others.

# JUMLA TO MOUNT KAILAS

*By Steve Razzetti*

The Himalaya have long been the stuff of myth and legend. When the first wave of Indo-Aryans crossed the Punjab circa 2000BC and saw the Himalaya, there arose among them a cosmography that recognized these distant snow-clad mountains as divine and the rivers that flowed from them as life-giving.

The Hindu, Bon, Buddhist and Jain religions of the Indian subcontinent developed mythologies that focus on the idea that a particular mountain in the Himalaya is the 'world pillar' around which all existence revolves. Jains revere this mountain as Astapada, where they believe Rishaba, the founder of their creed, attained enlightenment. Hindus call this mythical peak Meru, and believe that upon its lofty summit the great god Shiva sits – meditating, consorting with his goddess Parvati and smoking *ganja* (marijuana). Their sacred river – the Ganga (Ganges) – is believed to fall directly from heaven to its summit, where it divides into four streams that flow to the four corners of the earth for its purification.

Time has shown these seemingly fantastic legends to have a surprising basis in geographical fact. North of the main Himalayan chain in the remote western Tibetan province of Ngari there does indeed stand a unique mountain, Kailas, near the base of which rise four of the most significant rivers of the Indian subcontinent – the Indus, Sutlej, Karnali and Tsangpo-Bramaputra. The plains around Kailas form the apex of the Tibetan tableland, and the waters that rise in the vicinity reach the ocean as far apart as the Arabian Sea and the Bay of Bengal.

The ancient pre-Buddhist Bon religion of Tibet saw mountains as power points linking heaven and earth; and Mount Kailas as the Soul Mountain of the kingdom of Zhang Zhung. The struggle for the hearts and minds of Tibetans between traditional Bon and modern Buddhism centred on Kailas, or *Kang Rinpoche*. The story of the contest of

TOP *Rara Lake is the largest body of freshwater in Nepal and nestles among tranquil hills, densely forested with blue pine, juniper, spruce, oak and cypress.*

magic between the Bon deity Naro Bon Chung and the Buddhist saint Milarepa to decide which cult could claim the sacred mountain is still told today. Legend has it that Milarepa won, but was magnanimous enough in victory to bequeath a nearby peak to the Bon-po and agree that they might still circumambulate Kailas.

## WORLD OF RELIGION

Walking the *kora* (circumambulation) of Kailas today, you will find yourself in the company of cheerful gaggles of Tibetan ladies, semi-naked trident-bearing Indian *saddhus* (holy men), and white-robed Jains. You will overtake professional prostrators in leather aprons with blocks of wood attached to their hands, measuring the entire route with the length of their outstretched bodies on behalf of wealthy

**ABOVE** *Mt Kailas from the plains of Barkha near Darchen. The mountain is revered as a crystal pagoda and this is the sapphire face.*

patrons, and pass the odd Bon devotee going in the opposite direction. Kailas is a power place like no other.

The Chinese occupation of Tibet in 1951 resulted in the hermetic sealing of borders with India and Nepal. Subsequent internal unrest, and the devastation wrought on Tibetan monastic culture during the Cultural Revolution has had a profound and disastrous effect. Ancient trading links and pilgrimage routes, once the arteries of cultural life, were instantly abolished and many remote frontier communities were pitched into freefall economic oblivion.

## PILGRIMAGE TO KAILAS

In what was then a remarkably conciliatory gesture, the Chinese agreed to reopen the border on the Humla Karnali in northwest Nepal early in 1993, allowing foreigners to

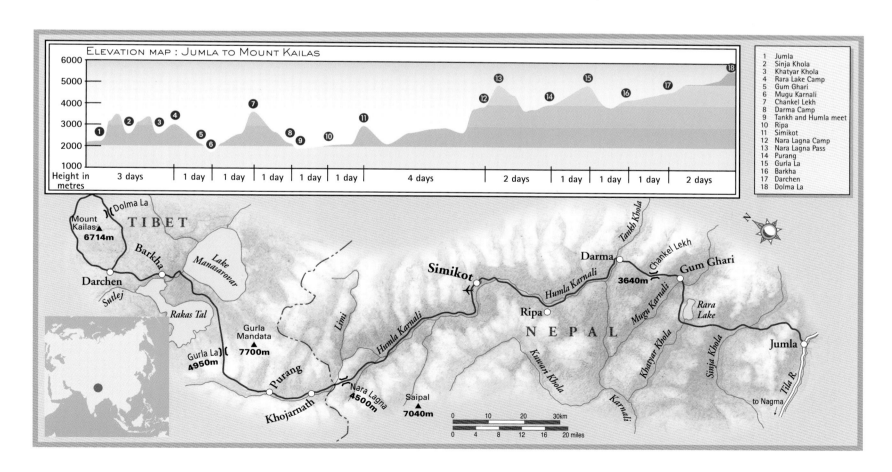

ELEVATION MAP : JUMLA TO MOUNT KAILAS

| 1 | Jumla |
| 2 | Sinja Khola |
| 3 | Khatyar Khola |
| 4 | Rara Lake Camp |
| 5 | Gum Ghari |
| 6 | Mugu Karnali |
| 7 | Chankel Lekh |
| 8 | Darma Camp |
| 9 | Tankh and Humla meet |
| 10 | Ripa |
| 11 | Simikot |
| 12 | Nara Lagna Camp |
| 13 | Nara Lagna Pass |
| 14 | Purang |
| 15 | Gurla La |
| 16 | Barkha |
| 17 | Darchen |
| 18 | Dolma La |

approach Mount Kailas on foot legally for the first time in history. While the historically more significant Mana Pass from India remains firmly closed to all but a strictly limited number of Indian pilgrims, it is now possible to make your own pilgrimage to Kailas through one of the most enchantingly beautiful and unspoiled corners of Nepal. The only alternative is to endure the ordeal of a week-long overland journey from Lhasa. For travellers interested in the ancient history and culture of the Himalaya, this is a unique opportunity.

Most foreigners heading for Kailas today fly into the airstrip at Simikot, the capital of Humla. However, by starting further south at Jumla and following the ancient trade routes north into Humla via Rara Lake (despite the Maoist insurgency in Western Nepal) a hurried visit may be turned into an odyssey befitting the approach to a revered mountain like Kailas.

Rara Lake lies at the heart of the least visited national park in Nepal, its sparkling waters set like a precious jewel amid a wilderness of primeval woodland and rolling hills, and is three tough days from Jumla. The trail is often faint, always strenuous and the countryside traversed sparsely populated, but Rara is a treasure to behold. Leaving Rara National Park northwards, the way to Humla plunges down to cross the Mugu Karnali Valley before starting the long haul up to the Chankel Lekh (3640m; 11,942ft) and approaching Simikot along the valley of the Humla Karnali. Reaching the crest of the Chankel Lekh, the landscape ahead is instantly transformed, with the blue ridges of Humla fading into the arid distance beneath a wall of lofty snow-capped peaks on the border with Tibet.

## PURE TIBETAN CULTURE

Life in Humla continues at a pace unaffected by the schedules and stresses that propel the world beyond. Here the villages are medieval and the lives of their inhabitants intimately entwined with the rhythms of nature. Before you toil up the

LEFT *A Khasa chhetri (Hindu) woman and daughter at the annual Jeth Purni festival at Ralling Gompah in Humla.*

**ABOVE** *Gurla Mandata, known to Tibetans as Naimona'nyi, seen here from the plains of Barkha near Lake Manasarovar.*

steep 1000m (3200ft) climb to Simikot, the subtle yet all-pervasive charm of Humla will have you bewitched.

Though the main trade route follows the spectacular Humla Karnali valley north of Simikot before finally climbing to cross the Nara Lagna (4500m; 14,765ft) into Tibet, there is an even more interesting diversion to be made here. Limi is an impossibly remote enclave of pure Tibetan culture that has survived almost completely unchanged, from the foundation of its monasteries in the sixth century to this day. Economically and culturally it long owed more to the now obliterated west Tibetan kingdom of Guge and, as a repository of the spiritual wealth of that

civilization, it is unique. Trails into this Shangri-la are arduous and the way long. However, it is possible to arrive at the foot of the Tibetan side of the Nara Lagna having come this way.

Formed of the world's highest deposit of tertiary conglomerate, Mount Kailas (6714m; 22,028ft) itself presents an awesome spectacle as it rises dramatically above the desolate plains of Barkha. Travellers approaching the sacred mountain from the south gain their first view of it upon reaching the crest of the Gurla La (4950m; 16,240ft), from where it appears to float on the horizon above the iridescent turquoise lakes of Manasarovar and Rakas Tal. Setting off just after midnight from

the dusty outpost of Darchen, Tibetans complete the 56km (35 miles) *kora* (circumambulation) of Kailas in a single day. Most foreigners take a more leisurely four days, allowing for the extreme altitude, visits to monasteries and a thorough appreciation of the stunning scenery.

The bitter wind howls while the fierce sun beats down through rarified air. Wayside shrines adorn every turn of the path and prayer flags flutter against the deep azure sky above. Against such an austere landscape, and decades of repression, the joyful countenances of the hundreds of Tibetans who complete the *kora* each day are extremely moving; a humbling testament to the resilience of the human spirit.

# TIGER'S LAIR AND SACRED PEAK

*By Judy Armstrong*

Bhutan is a jealously guarded kingdom in the bosom of the Himalaya. The Bhutanese call it Shangri-la and guard its isolation as fiercely as the snow leopard – elusive among the sacred peaks – guards its lair. Squashed between the giants of India and Tibet, Bhutan has for centuries served as a buffer While its borders have been shaped by religion and geography, its soul has remained intact. Bhutan remains a Buddhist stronghold and maintains a hereditary monarchy.

But this tiny kingdom is on the cusp of change. King Jigme Singye Wangchuck has denationalized the tourism industry. This means that the only restriction on tourists entering the country is now based on cost; the old figure of 3000 entry permits per year no longer applies. The nation is rife with anomalies. Roads were built in the 1960s but hill-farmers walk up to five days to reach them. Television was introduced in 1999, but most houses don't have toilets. Astrologers are consulted before doctors, education comes second to hand-harvesting the rice crop.

Bhutanese wear the traditional outfit: *kira* for women (a floor-length dress made from a brightly coloured rectangle of cloth) and *gho* for men (a long robe hoisted to knee-length and worn with a tight belt), but in the temples, monks wear T-shirts under their crimson robes.

Shops in the town of Paro often have no doors, so women, with babies on their backs, climb over ladder-stiles through glassless windows for their shopping. Purchases could be dried yak meat, Nike trainers, bamboo rice strainers or imported glossy lipstick.

The landscape is enormous, yet delicate: Bhutan is on the latitude of Cairo, yet almost a quarter of its area is under permanent snow; jagged, snow-crowned peaks soar behind patchwork fields crammed with crops of rice and potatoes. Churning, glacier-fed rivers become irrigation trickles, broad-hipped monasteries shade tiny temples. Forests of golden larch support

TOP *Backed by the mighty Himalaya, Paro Dzong, one of Bhutan's most impressive fortified monasteries, stands guard over the Paro valley.*

strands of lacy lichen; crested hoopoes hop in the shadow of eagles. Bhutanese culture is founded firmly on Buddhist philosophy and beliefs. The most obvious incarnations are the great white *dzongs*, or fortified monasteries, that guard valleys and towns. Some, such as the Paro and Punakha *dzongs*, are richly decorated with gold and scarlet; others are more subdued. Equally prominent are the *chortens*. These small structures contain religious artefacts

and prayer wheels that are spun to release the blessings inside. They are found on walking tracks, near rivers and mountain passes. Here, too, are prayer flags, long strips of red, white, blue, yellow and green that flap and snap in the wind, sending off with the breeze blessings for luck, and for the deceased.

While many tourists target Bhutan for its festivals and way of life, it is also a haven for trekkers. To minimize the impact on

the environment, there is a restriction on the number of walkers on the trekking routes and every party must hire a guide. Littering is illegal, and no infrastructure exists apart from designated camp sites.

Treks can last for two or three days in the lowlands, and up to 23 days for the high-altitude Snowman trek.

## SACRED PEAKS

The route described here covers the middle ground: a hike up to the camp site of Jangothang (lying at 4090m; 13,420ft), returning the same way or via a different valley. It visits remote valleys to give a glimpse of the sacred peak Chomolhari, but stops short of an altitude where health problems are likely to occur. All peaks are sacred to the Bhutanese – and as a result, serious mountaineering is banned, but Chomolhari, the most sacred of all, is special. The name translates as 'goddess of the mountain'. It is Bhutan's second highest at 7315m (24,001ft).

The best trekking option is to start with a day-hike from Paro valley to the Tiger's Lair monastery, called Taktsang by the Bhutanese. The four-hour walk, ascending 1000m (3300ft) to reach a level of about 3100m (10,200ft), is useful acclimatization for the trek to follow. The track climbs past ricefields, through juniper and pine forests, past prayer flags, and *chortens* (these should be passed in a clockwise direction).

Taktsang monastery, or *goemba*, comprises several building complexes. Taktsang *lhakhang* (temple) is sometimes used too – though this Bhutanese word

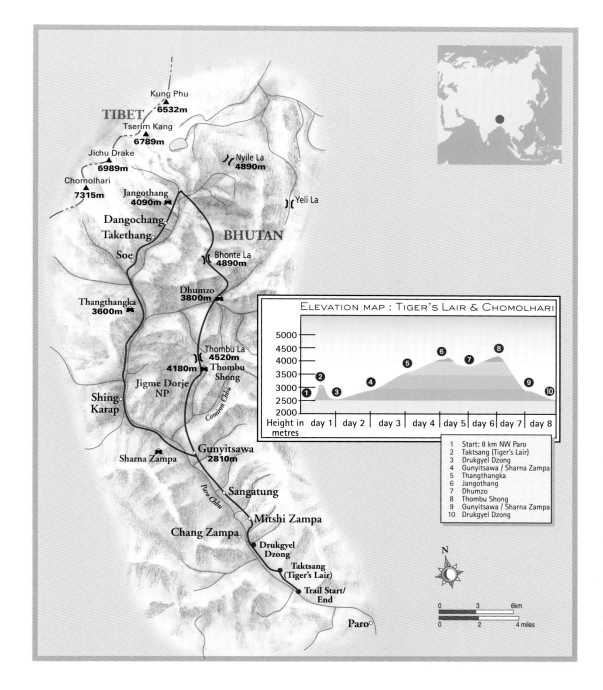

also describes the main shrine within each temple – so the *goemba* contains many *lhakhangs*.)

The best view of Tiger's Lair is from a rocky ledge that runs parallel to the monastery.

This clutch of white buildings clinging to a black cliff was almost destroyed by fire in April 1998. Although the monastery has been rebuilt exactly the way it was, foreigners cannot visit the inner temples unless they hold a special permit. This permit is only granted to practising Buddhists. Exclusion is no hardship: the view is so special, that visitors would be churlish to demand more.

The trek up to Jangothang starts the next day, from the ruined fortress at Drukgyel Dzong (2580m; 8416ft). This is where Tibetan armies were finally forced by the Bhutanese to retreat. A dirt track wanders from the *dzong* up the Paro Chhu valley (*chhu* means 'river' or 'water'), following the line of the Paro river's foaming torrent. The valley is fertile and a crazy patchwork of rice paddies covers every inch of land.

## TRADITIONAL HOUSES

At intervals along the track are traditional houses of stone and mud. They are three storeys high: animals live in the lowest layer, people in the middle, and hay or food is dried under the roof. The houses all have white walls and carved wooden, glassless windows intricately painted with auspicious Buddhist symbols. The raised roofs are made of wooden shingles held down with rocks; there are no chimneys so smoke from the open cooking fires makes its way out through whatever crevices it finds. Soon the ricefields give way to crops of oats, chillies and potatoes. Prayer flags by the river flutter in the breeze, and water-powered prayer wheels spin with the current.

LEFT *Trekking trails are wide enough for people and pack animals. Horses are replaced by yaks above 4000m (13,000ft).*

After passing the army post at Gunyitsawa (2810m; 9219ft), the camp site for the first night is reached. In a peaceful meadow by the river, the trek team will set up tents, folding chairs and tables before serving dinner under the stars.

For the next two days, the track wanders steadily up the valley, crossing and re-crossing the river on wooden cantilever bridges. Waterfalls stream down the steep valley sides and the trees seem to glow in the clear high-altitude air. On the second day from Drukgyel Dzong the track enters the Jigme Dorje National Park. It is Bhutan's largest protected forest area and home to endangered species including snow leopard, red panda and the hairy-coated takin – which looks like a cross between a gnu and a musk deer. Famous biologist George Schaller called it a 'beestung moose' due to its similarity in size to the North American moose – and its humped nose! The wildlife is exotic, with constant sightings of golden birds with long blue tails, cheeky hoopoes with spiky apricot headcrests, and black-and-white butterflies with intricately painted wings.

The second night's camp is at Thang-thangka, a meadow at about 3600m (11,800ft) with a small stone shelter near a cedar grove. Shortly after leaving here in the morning, Chomolhari reveals herself, then disappears again. Anticipation builds, and after the 4000m (13,000ft) mark, the landscape changes. Huge rock amphi-theatres are lined with crashing waterfalls, and glacial debris lies in great lumps on the widening valley floor. This is yak country. These shaggy beasts are used as pack animals – and for meat. Rich and dark, it's four times more expensive than beef. The yak's tail hair is used to make altar brushes. Herds of rare blue sheep (*bharal*) are also likely to be sighted here.

## GIANT ICY PYRAMID

From this point houses are few and far between. Small in size, many have green fodder draped over walls to dry: food for the yaks in winter, since not even these hardy animals can fend for themselves when snow lies as high as the second-storey windows. One house is owned by a Tibetan refugee family. The living layer is a single, large room with thick wooden floorboards, and sliding wooden shutters over the glassless windows. A tall dresser serves as an altar on which seven small bowls full of holy water are placed before a shrine. Black-and-white pictures of their king are pasted onto the walls, and dried meat and chillies hang from a wooden beam. Soon after passing this house, Jangothang base camp, at a height of 4090m (13,420ft), and the giant icy pyramid of Chomolhari come into view. This huge mountain rising immediately behind the camp site is surely one of the most wonderful views in the Himalaya.

From here the choices are multiple: trekkers can continue over the 4890m (16,043ft) pass, Nyile La, toward Thimphu or Laya, turn east over the remote and spectacular Bhonte La or retrace their route along the Paro Chhu. In order to complete a six- to seven-day trek, the quickest way back is the two- or three-day hike down the Paro – but if time, budgets and weather allow, these alternative routes offer spectacular sights into more hidden corners of this mountain paradise.

**ABOVE** *Chillies, a dietary staple, dry in the sun outside a traditional house. In the rural heartland few windows have glass, and ornately painted and carved woodwork is the norm.*

# SNOWMAN TREK

*By Steve Razzetti*

S hangri-la is an epithet ascribed to many places, but if there is one country on earth that deserves such an accolade it is Bhutan. Like many of the lesser principalities bordering Tibet, it has often had to fight for its spiritual and economic independence against its powerful and occasionally aggressive neighbour. This has inculcated a strong sense of pride and cultural awareness and today it is the only country in the world that retains Tantric Buddhism as its state religion. Few nations can claim such a rich cultural heritage, and ancient customs and values continue to inform the daily life of government and people. It has also enjoyed enlightened leadership in the present king, Jigme Singye Wangchuk, and his immediate forebears.

Fleeing persecution in Tibet, Ngawang Namgyal, honoured with the title of Shabdrung (at whose feet one submits), arrived in Bhutan in the 17th century. He succeeded in unifying the 'Land of the Dragon' within 30 years, and created a political and religious establishment that endures to this day. The most celebrated physical manifestations of Shabdrung's legacy are the elegant fortress-like *dzongs* that he built, which today serve the dual functions of administrative centres and monasteries.

The father of modern Bhutan is held to be Jigme Dorje Wangchuk, who reigned from 1952 to 1972. Under his guidance, the long and complete isolation of the country came to an end, and the government adopted a cautious approach to tourism.

Independent travel was not permitted, but limited numbers of foreigners were allowed in provided they travelled on preplanned, prepaid and guided package tours. This situation prevails, and by the year 2000 the number of tourists had reached almost 5500 annually.

Trekking in Bhutan is governed by the same regulations as tourism in general, making exploratory trips almost impossible. Those wishing to travel through Bhutan's pristine and spectacular mountain country

ABOVE *From this airy ridge above the Gangla Karchung La, the majestic peaks of Lunana and the border with Tibet line the horizon. In the centre is Jejekangphu Gang.*

on foot must make all their arrangements through an accredited agency, and travel on one of the fixed itineraries approved by the Tourist Authority of Bhutan. As the current charge for arranging any tourist activity in Bhutan – trekking or otherwise – is US$200 a day, the longer mountain excursions are very expensive. Whatever one's views on this, the appeal of trekking in such unspoiled mountain country cannot be denied. Neither can the fact that of all Bhutan's currently permitted routes, the 400km (250 mile) Snowman Trek is the roughest, toughest, longest and most rewarding. From the ruins of Drukyel Dzong in the Paro Valley to

Bumthang in central Bhutan, this challenging route crosses no less than 11 passes, three of which exceed 5000m (16,400ft). It also takes in the most dramatic mountain scenery in the country, passing both Chomolhari (7315m; 24,001ft), and Gankar Puensum, or Rinchita, (7541m; 24,742ft), the highest unclimbed peak in the world.

## ONCE MIGHTY FORTRESS

Drukyel Dzong, built to commemorate the Shabdrung's victory over marauding Tibetans in 1644, is situated atop a strategic rocky spur some 20km (12 miles) north of Paro airport. Today there is a paved road as far as this once mighty fortress, and on a fine day the imposing summit of Chomolhari towers above the intervening ridges, crowning a scene of quintessential Bhutanese magic. Climbed for the first time in 1937 by Englishman Frank Spencer-Chapman and Nepali Pasang Dawa Lama, Chomolhari is a sacred peak and the actual summit remains untrodden.

Travellers' baggage and equipment is traditionally carried by yaks in Bhutan. After loading these mighty beasts in the shadow of Drukyel Dzong's crumbling ramparts and setting off up the valley of the Paro Chhu, it is an idyllic three-day hike to the base camp of Chomolhari at Jangothang (3960m; 12,990ft). The trails throughout this route are not really difficult, as laden

ABOVE CENTRE *Mural detail at Simthokha Dzong, near Paro, depicting Padmasambhava (the Lotus Born) or Guru Rimpoche (Precious Teacher), the founder of Buddhism in Tibet.*

### ELEVATION MAP : SNOWMAN TREK

Height in metres

5500
5000
4500
4000
3500
3000
2500

5 days | 6 days | 3 days | 4 days | 7 days

1  Drukyel Dzong
2  Jangothang
3  Nyele La
4  Lingshi
5  Lingshi Dzong
6  Gogu La
7  Jhari La
8  Sinche La
9  Laya
10 Rodophu
11 Narithang
12 Gangla Karchung La
13 Tarina
14 Keche La
15 Thanza
16 Gophu La
17 Gangkar Puensum
18 Dhur Tsachu
19 Tsoenchen La
20 Dhur

N

TIBET

Masa Gang
7194m

LUNANA

Jejekangphu Gang
7194m

Zongophu Gang
7094m

Gang Chhen Ta
6794m

Rodophu

Laya

Tarina

Thanza

Gankar Puensum
7541m

Narithang

Gangla Karchung
6395m

Mo Chhu

Pho Chhu

Jitchu Drake
6790m

Kang Bum
6500m

Dhur Tsachu

Chomolhari
7315m

Lingshi

Gangla Karchung La

BUMTHANG

Jangothang

Tashithang

Paro Chhu

**Thimphu**

Drukyel Dzong

Paro

**Punakha**

Wangdi Phodrang

Nikachhu

**Tongsa**

Jakar

0  10  20  30km
0  4  8  12  16  20 miles

yaks require a broad passage, but the valley walls are precipitous, the forests impenetrable, the population sparse and camp sites few and far between. Trekking days in Bhutan are typically longer than in Nepal, and facilities and communications in the mountains are more primitive. The Bhutanese authorities have constructed lodges at the principal camping places on the Chomolhari part of the route, but in practice these are now used by trek crews while their clients sleep in tents.

The valley of the Paro Chhu is an unbridled delight. The turquoise waters of the river flow serenely through a valley wooded with birch and larch trees that provide a magnificent display of autumn colour in late October. Nearing Jangothang, the woods thin out, and branches of bamboo, juniper and rhododendron are silhouetted against the elegant geometry and steep snow-slopes of Jitchu Drake (6790m; 22,280ft) ahead. Chomolhari

remains hidden until just before camp, when the enormous east face suddenly appears at the head of a glaciated valley, the entrance to which is guarded by an ancient but ruined *dzong*. On a day's hike up the grassy slopes immediately north of Jangothang trekkers can easily attain heights in excess of 5000m (16,400ft), achieving excellent acclimatization and revelling in the breathtaking 360-degree panoramas of the surrounding peaks.

## CROSS-BORDER COMMERCE

Continuing northwestwards and parallel to the Tibetan border, the route to Laya and Lunana then crosses a series of high passes, yielding sensational views of Chomolhari, Jitchu Drake, Kang Bum (approximately 6500m; 21,300ft), Gang Chhen Ta (6794m; 22,291ft)) and Masa Gang (7194m; 23,604ft). The only significant settlement passed on the six-day walk between Jangothang and Laya is Lingshi,

where a magnificent whitewashed *dzong* on the crest of a steep ridge above the village presents an unforgettable sight.

At about 3800m (12,500ft), Laya is a large and prosperous village immediately south of Masa Gang, the citizens of which have long traded with their cousins to the north across the passes in Tibet. Agriculture and yak breeding is the mainstay of the local economy, but illicit cross-border commerce is in the men's blood. Many of the houses in the village sport solar panels, and a hunt among them will produce a surprising variety of Chinese and Tibetan goods for sale. The women dress in striking black yak-hair robes, wear distinctive conical bamboo hats and make the *chang* (beer) with which visitors are remorselessly plied.

Beyond Laya, the Snowman Trek continues east over the Gangla Karchung La (5105m; 16,750ft) into the fabulous district of Lunana. Some cross this major watershed in a single day from the high camp at Rodophu (4350m; 14,270ft) to Tarina, but an acclimatized party with sufficient time should consider breaking the journey at Narithang (about 4800m; 15,700ft). Perched on a moraine shelf immediately opposite the fearsome snow-covered northern ramparts of the 6395m (20,982ft) Gangla Karchung, a night here turns the crossing

*LEFT A view east from the Jhari La towards the Jhalethang Chhu valley and Robluthang on the trail from Lingshi to Laya.*

*OPPOSITE A view southwest over Narithang from near the Gangla Karchung La. The climb up to the pass is rewarded with stunning views.*

into two stunning and enjoyable days' trekking instead of one 13-hour marathon. Wending its way between iridescent lakes, over ancient boulder-strewn glacier beds and beneath towering snow-capped peaks, the trail is often thin but always a joy to walk. North of the descent route, a prominent rocky spur can easily be climbed, from which the views of the mountains between Lunana and Tibet are awesome.

From the beautiful Tarina Valley across a series of steep mountain spurs that descend from Jejekangphu Gang (7194m; 23,604ft) to the head waters of the Pho Chhu and Thanza, Lunana is an arcadian land of intense sunlight, scattered medieval hamlets and hardy pastoral folk. Approaching Thanza along the debris-strewn floor of the valley, the colossal south face of Zongophu Gang (7094m;

23,275ft) rears up above the terminal moraines of invisible glaciers beyond. Held back by these unstable piles of rubble are several enormous glacial lakes, from which cataclysmic floods have periodically burst, wreaking destruction as far away as Punakha Dzong.

Thanza, at about 4100m (13,500ft), is cut off from the outside world by deep snow on the passes between November and April. The people live in one of the most inhospitable yet magical places on earth, and represent a genetically significant community. Tall and strong, they are free of Mong's Disease and the deformities of the heart usually associated with people who live their entire lives at such altitude. Naturally, they will be reluctant to take their precious yaks anywhere out of Lunana as the winter snows approach, so careful

logistical planning is required to avoid delays late in the season.

Two possibilities exist for the final part of the Snowman Trek. The westerly route out to Nikachhu from Thanza is high and wild and passes a string of jewel-like lakes, but those anxious to get a closer look at Gankar Puensum will opt for the more rugged eastern route to Bumthang. Both are more strenuous than anything so far encountered and involve camping at over 5000m (16,400ft), but from at least three viewpoints during the seven-day walk out to the road at Dhur in Bumthang, Gankar Puensum presents an absolutely heart-stopping vista. Opportunities abound for side trips, and a soak in Guru Rinpoche's hot tub at Dhur Tsachu perfectly rounds off what many veterans believe is the hardest and most wonderful trek in the world.

# AFRICA

## By Jack Jackson

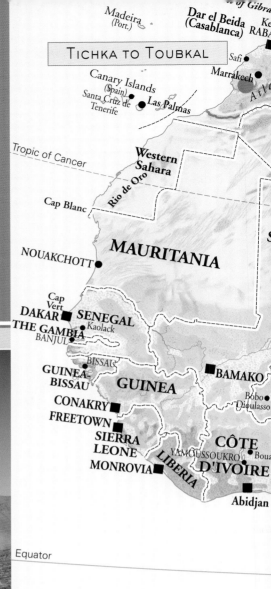

TICHKA TO TOUBKAL

Africa has a wide variety of trekking and many of the hiking and trekking areas are national parks in some form. Particular regions are more accessible than others, and at times local strife can close some. For these reasons, some areas are extremely popular, while others that were popular in the past are now little visited. Many parts of Africa have rock frescoes – cave paintings made by local inhabitants many thousands of years ago, and these are the theme of some treks.

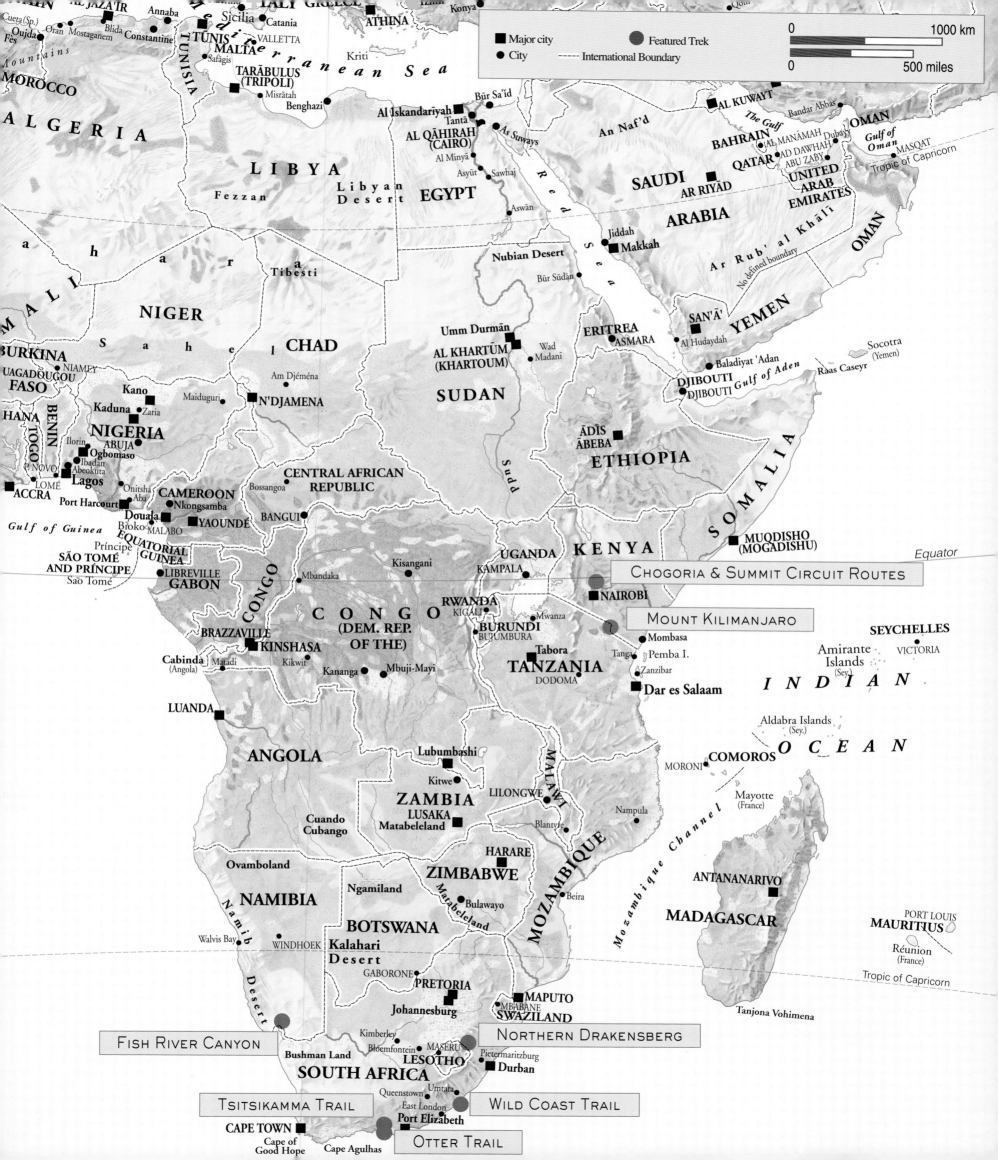

MOROCCO

ALGERIA

Oujda
Oran  Mostaganem
Fès  Blida  Constantine
AL JAZA'IR  Annaba
Mountains

Sicilia  Catania  ITALY  GREECE
TUNIS  MALTA  VALLETTA  ATHINA  Izmir  Konya
Safāqis  VALLETTA  Kriti
TARĀBULUS
(TRIPOLI)  Misrātah
Benghazi

Mediterranean Sea

■ Major city      ● Featured Trek
● City              --- International Boundary

0                    1000 km
0                    500 miles

Bandar Abbas
Būr Sa'īd  AL KUWAYT  Dubayy
BAHRAIN  AL MANĀMAH  MASQAT
Al Iskandarīyah  QATAR  AD DAWHAH  ABU ZABY  Gulf of Oman
Tantā  AD DAWHAH  UNITED  MASQAT
AL QĀHIRAH  As Suways  SAUDI  AR RIYĀD  ARAB
(CAIRO)  Al Minyā  EMIRATES
Asyūt  OMAN
Sawhaj  ARABIA
Aswān  Tropic of Capricorn

LIBYA
Libyan Desert  EGYPT
Fezzan

Sahara

Tibesti

Ar Rub' al Khālī
OMAN
No defined boundary

NIGER  Nubian Desert
Būr Sūdān  Jiddah  SAN'Ā'  YEMEN
Makkah  Al Hudaydah
CHAD  Red Sea  Socotra
(Yemen)
MALI  NIAMEY  Am Djéména  Umm Durmān  ERITREA  Baladiyat 'Adan  Raas Caseyr
BURKINA  Sahel  Wad  ASMARA
UAGADOUGOU  Kano  AL KHARTŪM  Madani  DJIBOUTI
FASO  Kaduna  N'DJAMENA  (KHARTOUM)  DJIBOUTI  Gulf of Aden
Zaria  SUDAN
HANA  NIGERIA  ĀDĪS  ABEBA
TOGO  ABUJA  ETHIOPIA  SOMALIA
P-NOVO  Ilorin  Ogbomaso  CENTRAL AFRICAN
LOMÉ  Ibadan  REPUBLIC  Bossangoa
ACCRA  Lagos  BANGUI  Sudd
Port Harcourt  Onitsha  Aba
CAMEROON  MUQDISHO
Douala  Nkongsamba  BANGUI  (MOGADISHU)
Bioko  YAOUNDÉ  UGANDA  KENYA  Equator
MALABO  EQUATORIAL  KAMPALA  CHOGORIA & SUMMIT CIRCUIT ROUTES
Príncipe  GUINEA  Kisangani
São Tomé  LIBREVILLE  Mbandaka  NAIROBI
SÃO TOMÉ  GABON  CONGO  RWANDA  SEYCHELLES
AND PRÍNCIPE  (DEM. REP.  KIGALI  MOUNT KILIMANJARO  VICTORIA
Gulf of Guinea  OF THE)  BURUNDI  Mwanza
BRAZZAVILLE  BUJUMBURA  Mombasa  Amirante
KINSHASA  Tabora  Tanga  Pemba I.  Islands
Cabinda  Matadi  Kikwit  TANZANIA  Zanzibar  (Sey.)
(Angola)  Kananga  Mbuji-Mayi  DODOMA  INDIAN
Dar es Salaam
LUANDA  Aldabra Islands
(Sey.)
OCEAN
Lubumbashi  MORONI  COMOROS
ANGOLA  Kitwe  Mayotte
LILONGWE  (France)
ZAMBIA  MALAWI  Nampula
Cuando  LUSAKA
Cubango  Matabeleland  Blantyre  MADAGASCAR
MOZAMBIQUE  ANTANANARIVO
Ovamboland  HARARE  Mozambique Channel
ZIMBABWE  Beira  PORT LOUIS
Ngamiland  MAURITIUS
NAMIBIA  Matabeleland  Bulawayo
BOTSWANA  Réunion
Kalahari  (France)
Walvis Bay  Desert  Tropic of Capricorn
WINDHOEK
GABORONE  Tanjona Vohimena
PRETORIA  MAPUTO
Johannesburg  MBABANE
FISH RIVER CANYON  SWAZILAND
Kimberley  NORTHERN DRAKENSBERG
Bushman Land  Bloemfontein  MASERU  Pietermaritzburg
SOUTH AFRICA  LESOTHO  Durban
Queenstown  Umtata
TSITSIKAMMA TRAIL  East London  WILD COAST TRAIL
CAPE TOWN  Port Elizabeth
Cape of  Cape Agulhas  OTTER TRAIL
Good Hope

The Simien and Bale Mountains of Ethiopia, and the highlands of Rwanda, Uganda, Kenya and Tanzania have many features of temperate zones, but with strong influences from their proximity to the equator.

Morocco's Atlas mountains include the 4167m (13,671ft) Djebel (mount) Toubkal, and the 4071m (13,356ft) Irhil M'goun. In Algeria, the Hoggar (or Ahaggar) Mountains, reach 3003m (9852ft) at Djebel Tahat. The Tassili-n-Ajjer, or Tassili N'Ajjer plateau, spreads into Libya and has one of the most important groupings of prehistoric cave art on earth. Over 15,000 drawings and engravings record local people and animals from at least 6000BC. The plateau is mostly over 2000m (6562ft). Chad's Tibesti Massif reaches 3415m (11,204ft) on Emi Koussi. Parts of Sudan and parts of Mali, including the Dogon Escarpment, have good trekking.

Ethiopia is best known for the Simien Mountains and the Bale Mountains to the south, but there are also routes where the Blue Nile plunges over Tissisat Falls downstream from Lake Tana, and others themed on historic sites. The Simien Mountains include Ras Deshen, at 4620m (15,158ft) the highest mountain in Ethiopia and the fourth highest in Africa. The Bale Mountains include Tullu Deemtu, at 4377m (14,360ft), the second-highest mountain in Ethiopia and the 4307m (14,130ft) Mt Batu.

## MOUNTAIN GORILLAS

Uganda has the Ruwenzori Range and the Virunga (Mufumbiro) Mountains. The Ruwenzori Range – thought to be Ptolemy's Mountains of the Moon – reach 5119m (16,795ft) at Margherita Peak, the highest peak of Mt Stanley, and the highest in Uganda. The Ruwenzori Mountains differ from most African snowy peaks, in that they are not of volcanic origin; they are a gigantic ridge of land that has been forced up between faults. The Virunga (volcanoes) Mountains, sometimes spelt Birunga, and also called the Mufumbiro (that which cooks) Mountains, reach 4507m (14,787ft) at Mt Karisimbi in Rwanda. The range reaches 4125m (13,540ft) at Mt Muhavura and 3645m (11,960ft) at Mt Sabinio in Uganda. The few mountain gorillas left in the world are found in the Virunga Mountains and the Bwindi (Impenetrable) Forest of Uganda. Mt Elgon, on the Ugandan border with Kenya, reaches 4321m (14,178ft).

Located on the equator, Mt Kenya's highest peaks, the 5199m (17,057ft) Batian and the 5188m (17,021ft) Nelion, require technical climbing. However, while skirting a small glacier, the third highest peak, the 4985m (16,355ft) satellite summit Point Lenana, is a simple walk. There are huts that can be used on the high-level backpacking summit circuit of the mountain, including one from which Point Lenana can be reached.

With asphalt roads to the towns at the beginnings of the three principal routes up the mountain and four-wheel drive *pistes* (dirt-tracks) leading up to the park gates and higher, it is very easy to gain height too quickly and suffer from the altitude. A high-level circumnavigation of the summit circuit route will help one to acclimatize.

LEFT *Looking across the Atlas Mountains from the summit of Mount Toubkal. This peak is only 65km (40 miles) south of Marrakech.*
PREVIOUS PAGE LEFT *Xhosa woman and child sitting beside their thatch-roofed rondavel (round house) in South Africa.*
PREVIOUS PAGE RIGHT *Ancient trees are common in very dry climates such as the Atlas. This one is near Taghourt in Morocco.*

ABOVE *Giraffes (Giraffa camelopardalis), the world's tallest mamal, with Mt Kilimanjaro in the background, Tanzania.*

In Tanzania, Mt Kilimanjaro – 5895m (19,340ft) at Uhuru (Kibo) Peak, and 5149m (16,893ft) at Mawenzi Peak – stands alongside the smaller, 4565m (14,977ft) Mt Meru on the Tanzanian side of the Kenyan border. In Tanzania, Kibo Peak is known as Uhuru Peak and old Tanganyika maps refer to the peak as Kaiser Spitze. In old maps Mawenzi is referred to as Hans Meyer Peak.

Both mountains are extinct volcanoes. Kilimanjaro is the highest peak in Africa, the highest freestanding peak in the world, one of the world's largest volcanoes and the highest mountain in the world that can be ascended without technical climbing. Only three degrees south of the equator, you hike/trek upward through almost every environment found on earth, while glaciers and snow cover its peak. As with Mt Kenya, it is very easy to gain height too quickly, so be sensible. A minimum of seven days is recommended for the ascent.

The highest recorded flowering plant was a *Helichrysum newii* found at 5670m (18,602ft), close to a fumarole in the Kibo Crater. The carcass of a frozen leopard was found in the summit zone in 1926 and, in 1962, Wilfred Thesiger's party came across a pack of five wild dogs near Mawenzi Peak.

In southern Africa, South Africa and the nearby countries are inundated with top hiking routes, but many are so popular that they are fully-booked up to a year in advance. The Drakensberg is South Africa's highest mountain range, a dramatic escarpment along the Natal-Lesotho border that reaches over 3000m (9843ft). A couple of routes are on steep ground, but the majority of the hiking is on easy trails.

Among South Africa's spectacular routes are the Blyde River Canyon and the Tsitsikamma National Park's Otter Trail. Namibia's most famous trek is in the Fish River Canyon, the largest canyon in the southern hemisphere. There is also a 120km (74-mile) route in the Naukluft Mountains, which is considered to be the big daddy of Namibian treks.

# TICHKA TO TOUBKAL

*By Hamish Brown*

The South Pole was reached a dozen years before the highest summit of Morocco, Djebel Toubkal (4167m; 13,671ft), was first climbed by Europeans. The antagonism of Berber tribes kept the Atlas as *terra incognita* until France grabbed the country in 1912, making it the last country in Africa to be colonized. Toubkal was first climbed in 1923 by a French party. A Polish expedition explored the Western Atlas a decade later and a mere handful of surveyors would have seen the Tichka Plateau before World War II stopped mountain explorations. After the war, the struggle for independence kept Europeans away until 1956, and as a result it is only over the last 40 years that this mountain world, hardly changed in centuries, has

become more widely known. The first complete Tichka to Toubkal trek was undertaken in 1992, by me – and was nicknamed 'The Wonder Walk'.

The Atlas Mountains sweep across southern Morocco, dividing plains and cities from the deserts. Marrakech is the gateway to the Atlas and from its rooftops the horizon is seasonably rimmed with improbable snowy mountains. Berber clans – a tough, agricultural society, friendly and hospitable – have occupied the Atlas for millennia. On trek, their mules ensure unburdened freedom of movement, with enhanced camping and cooking facilities.

On this route trekkers will experience spectacular, varied scenery leading on, day

by day, from the remote Tichka Plateau, down the forests and gorges and villages of the Oued (river) Nfis, through a switchback of *tizis* (passes) to Imlil, and culminating on Toubkal, the highest peak in North Africa. The trek takes two weeks, plus a couple of days at the start and finish for travel.

Trekkers fly in to Marrakech, often changing at Casablanca. Several hotels offer a minibus service and will transport trekkers over the Atlas along the dramatic Tizi n' Test road to Taroudant,

ABOVE *The terrain here can be very rugged.*
OPPOSITE *Imaradene is the highest point on the north rim of the Tichka plateau, reached by an enjoyable scramble.*

briefly meeting the trek route by the Oued Nfis. From Taroudant, a *camionette* (pick-up truck) or Land Rover takes the party from the city through endemic argan forest, date palms, orange groves and walnut fields to the high, irrigated pastures of the Medlawa Valley, lodged in the heart of the mountains. The night is spent in the highest village, Awsagh-melt, in a friendly Berber house with traditional food and mint tea.

## TREK ROUTINE

The routine is an early start for trekkers, leaving the muleteers to strike communal tents, load the mules and follow; soon overtaking and speeding on to the next site to have welcome tea ready. Tents pitched, there is usually time to relax or explore the

flora and fauna, meet the local people and write notes, before supper at dusk in the big tent and then it's time to bed down.

From Awsaghmelt the Medlawa path ascends, twisting and turning for hours, to the Tizi n' Targa, a nick on the Tichka Plateau rim. At 3000m (10,000ft) some of the party may be puffing. The Tichka Plateau is a wedge-shaped hollow, the source of the Oued Nfis, rimmed with peaks, the outer sides falling precipitously for thousands of feet. Camp is a grass strip by the stream, dotted with mini daffodils early in season.

The 'lost world' feel to the plateau, enhanced the next day when ascending the highest rim peak, Imaradene (3351m; 10,994ft). The exposed crest calls for some scrambling. The Oued Nfis gives a succession

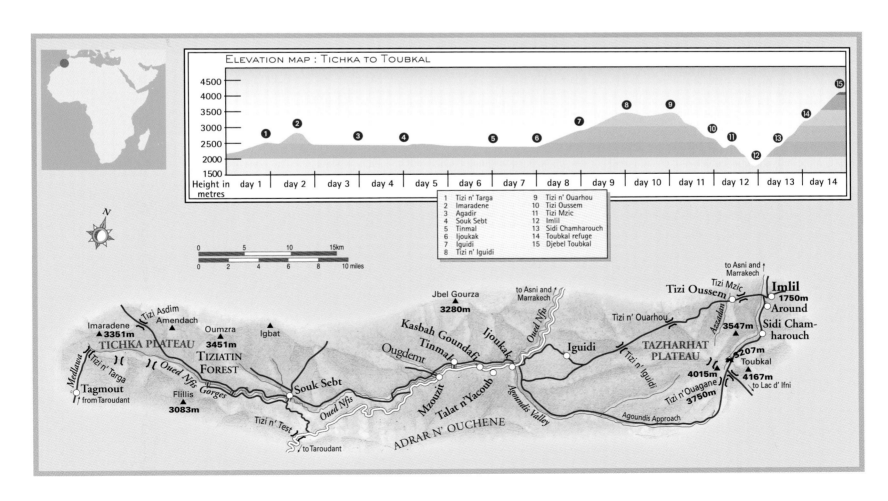

ELEVATION MAP : TICHKA TO TOUBKAL

| 1 | Tizi n' Targa | 9 | Tizi n' Ouarhou |
| 2 | Imaradene | 10 | Tizi Oussem |
| 3 | Agadir | 11 | Tizi Mzic |
| 4 | Souk Sebt | 12 | Imlil |
| 5 | Tinmal | 13 | Sidi Chamharouch |
| 6 | Ijoukak | 14 | Toubkal refuge |
| 7 | Iguidi | 15 | Djebel Toubkal |
| 8 | Tizi n' Iguidi | | |

LEFT *Crossing the Oued (river) Nfis. The river can be in spate after rain.*
BELOW LEFT *Local cooks preparing the group's food.*
OPPOSITE *Trekkers' camping and other equipment is carried by sure-footed mules.*

entirely on local stone and timber, with water channels, terraced fields, almond and walnut trees adding a touch of luxury.

## LORDS OF THE ATLAS

A few villages after Souk Sebt, the path enters forests of cool pine. Sleeping under the stars or swimming in river pools, each camp seems better than the last. The trail follows the river on the north bank while the tarred road on the south is rarely noticed. Tinmal, a fortified mosque restored in the 1990s, is starkly beautiful. From here, in the 12th century, the Almohads moved out to conquer Marrakech and create an empire reaching along North Africa and up through half of Spain.

The riverside Kasbah Goundafi is the derelict palace of one of the tribal chiefs, also known as 'Lords of the Atlas', who controlled the Nfis and the Tizi n' Test – proving a thorn in the side of British explorers Cunninghame Graham and Joseph Thomson. It was the driving of tarred roads over the Atlas that really brought about the end of tribal power.

Much of the road traffic takes a break at Ijoukak so it is full of foodstalls and cafés, and gives another temptation for a roof overnight and a tasty *tagine* (casserole) supper. Plenty of uphill walking lies ahead –

of oak forest, villages and pine forest before running parallel with the looping Tizi n' Test road, passing the historic sites of Tinmal and the Kasbah Goundafi to reach Ijoukak where the route forsakes the Nfis. After this the trail leaves the plateau.

The Tiziatin Forest of evergreen oak is overlooked by rocky peaks and the river cuts deep through a granite gorge for one stretch. The peaks become ever wilder; Oumzra's triple summits to the north are glimpsed up a side valley as the first village, Agadir, is reached. Villages perch along the north side every few miles, linked by mule tracks, and accommodation in houses is an option. The architecture in the area relies

and there are two options. One heads up the Agoundis side valley and over the Tizi n' Ouagane (3750m; 12,303ft) to the hut for Toubkal – but this is only possible late in the season when clear of snow. The other, standard route, climbs high to traverse the northern slopes of the 3980m (13,060ft) Tazharhat, the mountain between the Nfis and Agoundis valleys, crossing its northern spurs over some fine passes. There is a demanding pull up to gain height with the switchback track thereafter crossing the Tizi n' Iguidi and the Tizi n' Ouarhou before descending to the village of Tizi Oussem. From here, a last climb up to the 2489m (8166ft) Tizi Mzic leads over and down to the Imlil basin at 1750m (5740ft) and the busy world of the Toubkal trail. Imlil is humorously referred to as the Chamonix of Morocco, and a night in a *gîte* (small inn or hostel) here may be welcome.

An hour above Imlil lies Around, the last village on the trail towards Toubkal. The mountains close in and the path zigzags along to the sacred shrine of Sidi Chamharouch. The pass up to the east, the Tizi n' Tagharat (3442m; 11,293ft), was the height and distance reached by Hooker and Ball of the first real Atlas expedition in 1871. The Toubkal trail goes up like a coiled rope before a long rising traverse to Toubkal (ex-Neltner) refuge at 3207m (10,522ft).

From this well-appointed mountain hut the summit of Toubkal (4167m; 13,671ft) takes three to four hours. The trail cuts up a steep slope into the hanging valley of Ikhibi Sud, then follows a crest up to the summit wedge of mountain. Few treks can have such a grand ending – all but one of the country's 4000m (13,000ft) summits cluster round, and there are views of the Haouz Plain to the north and the tawny desert to the south.

Toubkal is not the end, of course. The toilsome boulders have to be descended – but how easy the path seems down to verdant Imlil! Even the drive out to Marrakech is fascinating and a couple of nights in this magical city will feel like a grande finale.

# CHOGORIA AND SUMMIT CIRCUIT ROUTES

*By Steve Razzetti*

Stretching in an enormous arc from the headwaters of the River Jordan in Palestine to the highlands of Mozambique, the Great Rift Valley is one of the most spectacular manifestations of plate tectonics on earth. Spanning a distance of over 5000km (3000 miles) and formed by the parting and sinking of the earth's crust along an ancient fault line, elevations on the valley floor range from 400m (1300ft) below sea level at the Dead Sea to over 1800m (5900ft) above sea level in Kenya. Most of the earth's volcanic and seismic activity occurs in the vicinity of such fault lines and, while there has been no volcanic eruption or major earthquake in Kenya for centuries, earth tremors can occasionally be felt in the highlands.

In eastern Africa, the Great Rift Valley divides into the Western Rift and the Eastern Rift, with the latter bisecting the Kenyan Highlands between the Aberdare Range and the Mau Escarpment. Scattered along the Great Rift Valley are numerous extinct rift volcanoes, the highest in Kenya being Mount Kenya (5199m; 17,058ft) and Mount Elgon (4321m; 14,177ft). Mount Kenya is the second highest peak in Africa, after Kilimanjaro (5895m; 19,341ft), and today consists of the eroded magma core of a volcano that once exceeded 6500m (21,300ft) in height.

Kenya takes its name from this mountain, and the word is a corruption of the Kikuyu name *Kere Nyaga* (meaning Mountain of Brightness). The Kikuyu believe the mountain to be the abode of their god Ngai, whom they refer to as Mwene Nyaga (Professor of Brightness). Located some 150km (90 miles) north of Nairobi and presenting an unforgettable spectacle as its rugged form soars above the fertile plains, Mount Kenya has blessed East Africa with a good deal more than its mere luminescence. In the immediate vicinity rise many rivers, fed by the melting snows above. These include the longest in the country, the Tana, which provides much of Kenya's electricity.

**ABOVE** *View from the top of Pt Lenana with morning light on Mt Kenya, and the mountain's shadow across the mists of the Rift Valley.*

Snow on the equator? Ludwig Krapf, travelling inland from Mombasa in 1849, apparently doubted his own eyes as he described how he 'could see the "Kegnia" more distinctly, and observed two large horns or pillars, rising over an enormous mountain to the northwest of Kilimanjaro, covered with a white substance.' His suggestions that there may be snow-capped peaks in equatorial Africa were ridiculed by geographical establishments back in Europe until, 33 years later, the affable Scot Joseph Thomson got closer. It certainly looked very much like snow.

The first European to make it through the surrounding jungle onto the mountain itself was an Austrian by the name of Count Samuel Teleki. He reached the snow line in 1887 and touched the stuff. White. Cold. Most definitely snow. Next came British geologist JW Gregory in 1893. He studied the physical structure of the mountain and gave European names to many of its prominent features, including the Teleki Valley on the Naro Moru side.

## FIRST ASCENT

Sir Halford Mackinder made the first ascent of the highest peak of Mount Kenya in 1899 accompanied by alpine guides Ollier and Brocherel. In those days, the railway had reached Nairobi, but there were no roads. Travel was not easy. In the bush there roamed elephant, lion, buffalo and rhinoceros, not to mention the local Kikuyu tribes, who were far from taken with the idea of European sportsmen trespassing on their sacred ground. To appease the locals, Mackinder named the highest summit (5199m; 17,058ft) after a Maasai *laibon* (witch doctor) named Mbatiang. The second highest (5198; 17,055ft) he named

after Mbatiang's brother, Neilieng, and the third (4985m; 16,356ft) and fourth (4704m; 15,434ft) after his sons, Olonana and Sendeyo. The first three have been anglicized to Batian, Nelion, and Lenana.

Thirty years later, on 6 January 1929, Englishmen Eric Shipton and Percy Wyn Harris established what is today known as the Normal Route up Nelion. Given the technical difficulty of the route, the fact that they had almost no idea where they were going and no crampons, this was certainly an audacious and pioneering ascent. Having waited by the road at Chogoria for two days for a lift, the climbers travelled back to Nairobi in a truck with a Dutch missionary. There they sold their incredible story to the *East African Standard* for the princely sum of £2 10s, and were somewhat taken aback when it appeared on the front page of the following day's paper under the

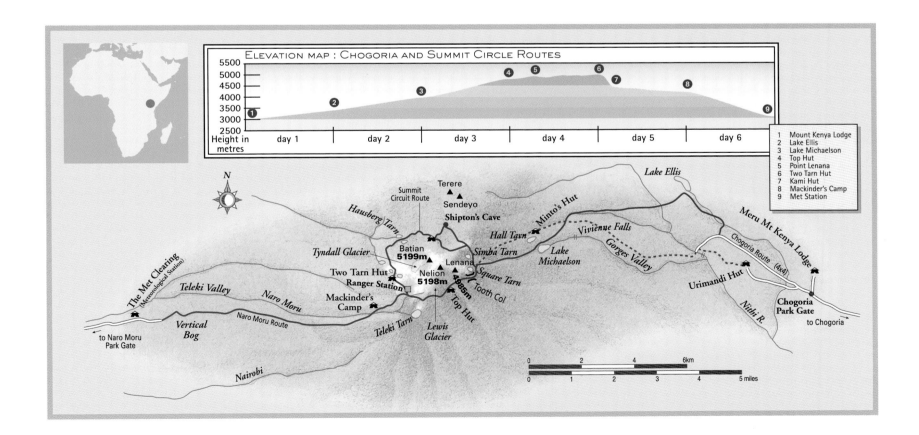

headline 'New Conquest of the Twin Peaks of Mount Kenya'. Shipton returned with Bill Tilman in August 1930 and completed both the first traverse of the mountain and the first circuit of the summits. After World War II, interest rapidly increased. In 1949, the ground above 3400m (11,100ft) was gazetted as a national park and the area mapped by the Colonial Surveys. That same year, the Mountain Club of Kenya was formed and soon huts were erected at various strategic locations.

Standing alone above the plains of the Rift Valley, Mount Kenya does not offer the opportunities for altitude acclimatization during the walk-in as do peaks of similar stature in the great ranges of the Himalaya and the Andes. Many trekkers underestimate both this fact and the seriousness of the terrain, and, for them, memories of aching limbs and pounding headaches obscure those of the magnificent views encountered. The Chogoria Route, pioneered in the 1920s by Earnest Carr, is the most beautiful approach and, at three days, by far the most gentle. Consider this especially if no prior acclimatization has been gained.

## OFF THE BEATEN TRACK

As with popular mountain journeys everywhere, there is much to recommend deviating from the main trails, and Mount Kenya is no exception. Instead of heading straight for Minto's Hut (4300m; 14,000ft) along the well-marked path from the Chogoria Park Gate and Mount Kenya Lodge, take your time and head off on the smaller track through rolling moorland to

LEFT *Approaching the screes and boulderfields of Hausberg Col from Hausberg Tarn on a clockwise circuit of Mt Kenya's Summit Circle.*
OPPOSITE *The Mountain Club of Kenya hut lies just below the ranger station at the head of the Teleki Valley on the Naro Moru route. In the foreground and to the right are giant groundsels (senecio species).*

Lake Ellis for your first night's camp. Spend the second by the idyllic shores of Lake Michaelson and make for the Top Hut (4790m; 15,715ft) via Square Tarn and Tooth Col from there. The pristine splendour of these lakes and the country surrounding them is far removed from the overcrowded squalor of a night at Minto's.

Point Lenana commands breathtaking views of the adjacent higher summits, and is reached after only 45 minutes of easy scrambling from Top Hut. Most people do this by the light of their head torches before dawn and stand at the top, in the bitter chill, waiting to watch the glorious spectacle of the African sun soaring into the sky. There then ensues a mad rush

back down to the hut where hearty breakfasts are scoffed and beelines made for the Teleki Valley and Met Station on the Naro Moru route far below. This is a shame, for an extra day or two spent completing the Summit Circuit Route really crowns what is the best high mountain walk in East Africa.

In either direction, this can be accomplished by fit and properly acclimatized walkers in less than eight hours. In order to properly savour all its aspects, however, an extra night at Two Tarn Hut (4990m; 16,370ft) or Kami Huts (4425m; 14,518ft) is highly recommended. The former commands stunning views of the Tyndall Glacier and the west face of Batian, while the latter looks out over the summits of

Sendeyo and Terere. Care is certainly necessary up here, as the trails are thin and traverse loose, exposed ground. Navigation may be problematic as thick mists envelop the peaks daily, obscuring landmarks, but the Summit Circuit Route certainly is a challenging and spectacular climax to a traverse of Mount Kenya. Whichever option you choose, do not hurry out down the Naro Moru route – the views back to the main summits from Mackinder's Camp are the best on the trip, and the vegetation on the final steep descent to the Met Station through the Vertical Bog surreal. Those craving a spot of unbridled luxury after all this exertion will not be disappointed at the Naro Moru River Lodge.

# MOUNT KILIMANJARO

*By Steve Razzetti*

Kilimanjaro, the highest peak in Africa, lies just 320km (200 miles) south of the equator in north-eastern Tanzania. From the Maasai steppe its snow-capped mass soars high above the grasslands, and, with grazing giraffe and elephant in the foreground, it presents a spectacle that is quintessentially African.

The very notion that there could be snow on the equator was ridiculed by the geographical establishment when missionaries Ludwig Krapf and Johann Rebmann, the first Europeans to set eyes on Kilimanjaro, returned from their travels there in 1848. 'A fortuitous combination of imagination and poor eyesight' quipped one pompous contemporary. On 5 October 1889 German geologist Hans Meyer, with alpine special-ist Ludwig Purtscheller and local guide Jonas Louwa, succeeded in reaching the summit. With typical colonial arrogance he named the peak Kaiser Wilhelmspitze after his emperor. When Tanzania gained inde-pendence in 1961 it was renamed Uhuru (Freedom) Peak.

Approaching Kilimanjaro across the plains of the Rift Valley, one is impressed by the sheer bulk of the mountain. Five vertical kilometres aloft, the dazzling whiteness tops a volcanic cone the ellipti-cal base of which measures some 80 x 40km (50 x 25 miles) – an area larger than that of Greater London. The mountain consists of the eroded remains of three huge volcanoes: Kibo (5895m; 19,340ft), Mawenzi (5149m; 16,893ft) and Shira (4006m; 13,140ft). All three were considered extinct until British mountaineer Bill Tilman discovered sulphur and fumaroles in the crater of Kibo in 1933, suggesting that it may just be dormant. The degree of erosion suggests that the most recent sig-nificant volcanic activity occurred millennia ago, and Shira may, originally, have exceeded 5000m (16,500ft) in height. Viewed from Stella Point (5700m; 18,701ft), Mawenzi, with its 600m (2000ft) of jagged needles and gullies topping the west face,

ABOVE *Kibo and Mawenzi, separated by The Saddle, seen from the Amboseli National Reserve near Kenya's border with Tanzania. If there is a quintessential image of Africa, this is surely it.*

is perhaps most impressive. However, the seldom-seen eastern aspect – comprising the Great and Lesser Barranco walls – is even more dramatic with 1200m (4000ft) of near vertical rock and ice.

Glacial retreat on Kilimanjaro has been dramatic. The ice dome in Kibo's crater, which was over 20m (65ft) high and covered an area in excess of 12km² (4 square miles) in 1912, has all but disappeared. At this rate the glaciers will be gone by the year 2020. It is now widely accepted that this accelerated depletion is largely due to pollution-induced global warming.

## ACCLIMATIZATION

The Kilimanjaro National Park headquarters are at Marangu Gate (1800m; 5905ft), southeast of Kibo, and it is from here that

the 64km (40-mile) Marangu Route (the 'tourist' route) commences. Sadly, the pristine and unique ecosystem on Kili is today straining under the weight of the unrestricted numbers climbing the mountain. Furthermore, lax enforcement of park regulations and woefully inadequate sanitation have made serious health hazards of all the major camps. Great care is needed with the hygienic preparation of food and the treatment of drinking water everywhere on the mountain.

The popular trekking routes on Kilimanjaro ascend much too fast to allow for proper altitude acclimatization and, consequently, the misery of a pounding headache mars the Kilimanjaro memories of many. A prior trip up either Mount Kenya or Kilimanjaro's lesser neighbour,

Mount Meru, will greatly enhance your enjoyment of the higher peak. Neither the effects of altitude nor the arctic conditions met on the summit of Kibo should be underestimated. It can be very, very cold up there! The most popular route is the Marangu, mostly done in five days (four nights). Parties usually make for the Mandara Huts (2700m; 8800ft) on the first day, followed by Horombo Huts (3720m; 12,200ft) on the second and Kibo Huts (4700m; 15,500ft) on the third day. Then it's up to the summit and back to Kibo, and finally all the way back to Marangu Gate on the fifth day. Thus the climb is three times faster than the recommended maximum rate of ascent.

While the Marangu route undoubtedly offers stunning vistas of both Kili and

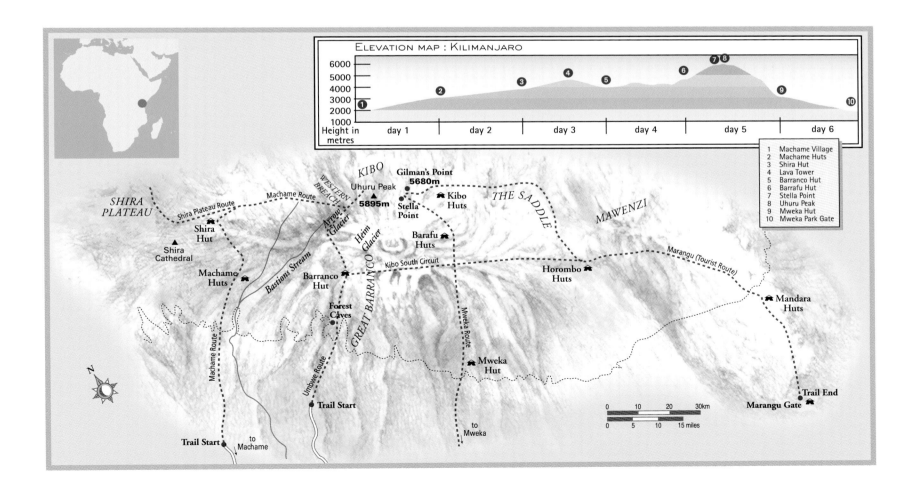

**ABOVE** *The constant interaction of cold, humid air and the power of the African sun creates many strange and beautiful ice formations on Kilimanjaro. Recent global warming is having a significant effect on the fabled snows and the summit ice cap, in fact, is diminishing.*

Mawenzi from The Saddle, the 'huts' are more like small villages and solitude will be hard to find. If you prefer a touch of tranquillity with your mountains, it's better to opt for a combination of the other routes.

## THE MACHAME-MWEKA ROUTE

The 69km (43-mile) Machame-Mweka route is the most diverse and requires a minimum of six days. From the end of the jeep track some 7km (4 miles) beyond Machame village (1920m; 6300ft), this relatively recent variation on the old Shira route starts with a steep five-hour slither up a muddy jungle trail to the Machame Huts (3000m; 10,000ft). A gentle pace will give legs and lungs a better chance to come to terms with the rigours of such rapid ascent, and allow an appreciation of the jungle's verdant and mysterious charms.

Montane forest forms a dense band between 1800 and 2700m (5900 and 8800ft) on Kilimanjaro. Under a humid, shady canopy of enormous yellowwood and pencil cedar trees, the broad mud highway weaves its way skywards. Look out for the surreal silhouetted forms of giant tree ferns in damp hollows and gullies. Bright balsam flowers and gladioli add vibrant splashes of colour to the impenetrable barrier of shrubbery that lines the trail. Common species include raspberries, elderberries and vernonia. Birdlife is abundant and vocal, but you will need a quick eye and patience to see the retiring turacos, hornbills and parrots making all the noise.

From the Machame Huts, the recommended stages are: Shira Hut (3840m; 12,600ft), Barranco Hut (3900m; 12,800ft), Barafu Huts (4600m; 15,090ft), Mweka Hut

(3100m; 10170ft) via Uhuru Peak, and down to Mweka village (1500m; 4920ft), ending with a drive to Moshi. This route affords wonderful panoramic views of the Western Breach and Kibo from the South Circuit Trail, covered between Wedge Shaped Buttress and Barafu. Though the stages between Shira and Barafu gain virtually no height, they are not easy and provide valuable time to acclimatize.

Those proficient with map and compass can add a day to their schedule from Shira Hut to make the seven-hour round-trip to the edge of the Shira plateau. Trails are very faint and few people venture here, but from Shira Cathedral (an exposed scramble along the summit ridge) the views are superb. Given clear skies, this three-day traverse of the southern flanks of Kibo is delightful. Jungle gives way to timber-line forest between 2500m (800ft) and 3000m (10,000ft), with stands of African rosewood and giant St John's Wort interspersed with giant heathers and heaths (ericas). These outrageous cousins of species familiar in many other parts of the world often attain heights in excess of 10m (33ft). Drier sites are home to African sage, sugarbush (a protea species) and aromatic evergreens (helichrysums).

## TROPICAL ALPINE CHAPARRAL

Above 3000m (10,000ft) the forest vanishes altogether and a sweeping band of open heath and moorland, properly called tropical alpine chaparral, extends to about 4000m (13,000ft). Liberally dotted across the tussocky grasslands here are magnificent otherworldly forms of giant groundsels (*Senecio* sp.), cabbage groundsels and lobelias, giving a bizarre character to these hillsides, especially when seen standing in silent ranks in the mist. Above the Barafu Hut, the climb to the crater rim at Stella Point is relentless and steep. Most trekkers set off before midnight, having struggled to eat their supper with an altitude-suppressed appetite and little or no sleep. Oxygen-starved brain cells rarely think with their normal clarity, so consider the contents of your backpack carefully. Though it may be cold (-10 to -15°C; 14 to 5°F) setting off, the exertion of the climb will soon have most people sweating. Immediately upon reaching the crater rim the exposure to the elements is extreme, and great care should be taken to avoid the sudden cooling of sweat-soaked bodies by the icy blast of the wind. The onset of hypothermia in such conditions can be rapid and debilitating, so pause to wrap up before you reach the rim and restrain your urge to stop for pictures at Stella Point.

Whatever the conditions, the hike along the crater rim to Uhuru Peak is a sensational and exhilarating skywalk. After dashing to have your photograph taken at the elaborate summit sign, take time to appreciate the wonders of Kilimanjaro. Few volcanoes can boast a crater as perfectly formed as the Reusch, and, as you head back from Uhuru Peak to begin the long descent, pause to admire the exquisitely delicate ice formations created by the ceaseless interaction of cold, humid air and the African sun, and look out for the white porphyritic crystals that weather out of the lava at the crater's rim.

## UMBWE ROUTE

Experienced and acclimatized trekkers seeking something more challenging should consider the Umbwe Route. Described by Iain Allan of the Mountain Club of Kenya as one of the 'finest non-technical mountaineering expeditions in Africa', this ascent is somewhat shorter (56km; 35 miles). It is also much more committing, and should only be undertaken by properly equipped parties with alpine experience. This route involves some fairly steep and exposed scrambling higher up and requires careful route-finding

**ABOVE** *Giant groundsels* (Senecio Kilimanjari) *are endemic to Kilimanjaro and are found throughout the moorland surrounding the peak. This view of Kibo shows the Western Breach from below the Barranco Wall.*

in poor weather, especially on the descent. The climb takes five days and makes its steep final ascent to Uhuru Peak via the Arrow Glacier and Western Breach.

Commencing at Umbwe Gate (1400m; 4590ft), the first two stages are to the Forest Caves (2850m; 9350ft) and Barranco Hut (3950m; 12,960ft), from where a day hike to the Great Barranco Breach Wall and Heim Glacier will further aid acclimatization. One could also opt to continue this way to Uhuru Peak (via Barafu Huts).

From Barranco Hut, which is more or less at the tree line, Umbwe Route heads north into the valley of the Bastions Stream before climbing very steeply up to the site of the Arrow Glacier Hut (4800m; 15,750ft), which has been destroyed by rockfall, necessitating a camp or chilly bivouac. From here the route ascends the Western Breach directly to the Great Western Notch on the crater rim. In good conditions and fine weather, this way offers an exciting scramble, with snowy sections offering those proficient with ice axe and crampons an opportunity to get off the loose and enervating screes. In less than perfect conditions, however, the route has major epic potential. Beyond the Notch lie the crater floor and the Furtwangler glacier, which must be crossed or circumvented before the final steep pull up to Uhuru Peak.

From Uhuru Peak one can descend any of the routes, though most will retreat the same way, having left their tent/equipment below on the way up. The descent of the western breach is especially difficult since it usually fills with cloud early in the day and route finding can be tricky.

# FISH RIVER CANYON

*By Mike Lundy*

The Fish River Canyon is one of the biggest river-gouged canyons in the world, second only to the Grand Canyon in Arizona, USA. In the same class as Victoria Falls and Kilimanjaro, it ranks as one of Africa's great natural wonders. The deafening silence, the unadulterated solitude and the billion stars every evening combine to provide a profoundly inspiring experience, and cleanse the soul.

The ancient sediments and lava forming the bottom of the canyon were originally deposited between 1800 and 1000 million years ago. Between 500 and 300 million years ago, during the Gondwana Ice Age, a series of north–south fractures were deepened by southward-moving glaciers.

Incision by the Fish River, in warmer times during the last 50 million years, has given the canyon its present shape.

Proclaimed a natural monument in 1962, six years later the Fish River Canyon was declared a game reserve by the South African government, which at that time was administering the mandated territory of South West Africa. The canyon is situated in the southwest corner of what, in March 1990, became Namibia, a country bigger than France and the United Kingdom combined, but with a population of only 1.5 million.

The canyon is over 600m (2000ft) deep in places and stretches for more than 160km (100 miles). The trek itself covers more than half that distance, and takes

five days to complete. Parts are so narrow that you feel you can almost reach out and touch both encroaching cliffs. As you progress downstream, the canyon widens until, at its broadest, it is a gaping 27km (17 miles) across.

The trail starts from the view site situated on the lip of the canyon about 12km (7 miles) from the Namibia Wildlife Resorts campsite at Hobas. Before you begin your descent, pause to look down on this awesome sight. Hell's Corner glowers back at you, but further downstream the vista is

ABOVE *Four Finger Rock is one of many fascinating geological features in the Fish River Canyon, sculpted by the sands of time.*

breathtaking, particularly in the early morning when the steep cliffs are awash with colour. The steep descent to the canyon floor is a journey through hundreds of millions of years of the earth's geological history. The river's shining ribbon gets closer and closer, until at last, an hour or so after beginning your descent with the aid of chains, you are able to plunge gratefully into the enormous pool waiting at the bottom, deep in the belly of the world's oldest canyon.

The first 16km (10 miles) to Palm Springs are notoriously rugged and slow, as the terrain is predominantly made up of large boulders interspersed with soft sand – not to mention the odd river crossing. For all the effort required, however, this is still the most rewarding and beautiful part of the

canyon. There is no marked trail but there is also no way you can get lost between the two enormous walls which dictate your route. There are also no set overnight stops. Simply call a halt for the day on any suitable terrain an hour before sunset. (After which it rapidly becomes dark and the temperature plummets.)

## STARTING STEEP AND DEEP

It's worth taking your time on the first two days when the canyon is at its steepest, deepest and most awe inspiring. Not long after starting down the canyon you will be surprised to come across the remains of a motor scooter. It is the result of a harebrained expedition against all the advice of the authorities by the Cape Town Vespa Club in 1968.

Even before you see the palm trees at Palm Springs, your nose will tell you that you are close. The 57°C (135°F) spring water is rich in fluorides, chlorides and sulphides, the latter being responsible for the unpleasant smell. This, despite the odour, is a great spot for a rest or even overnight, where weary limbs can be rejuvenated in the comfortably hot waters. The palm trees, while splendid specimens, are somewhat incongruous here. They are not indigenous and their presence has given rise to several stories. The most likely of these is that they grew from date stones discarded by two German prisoners of war, who had escaped from the POW camp at nearby Aus during World War I.

After Palm Springs, the going becomes easier and Table Mountain – not to be

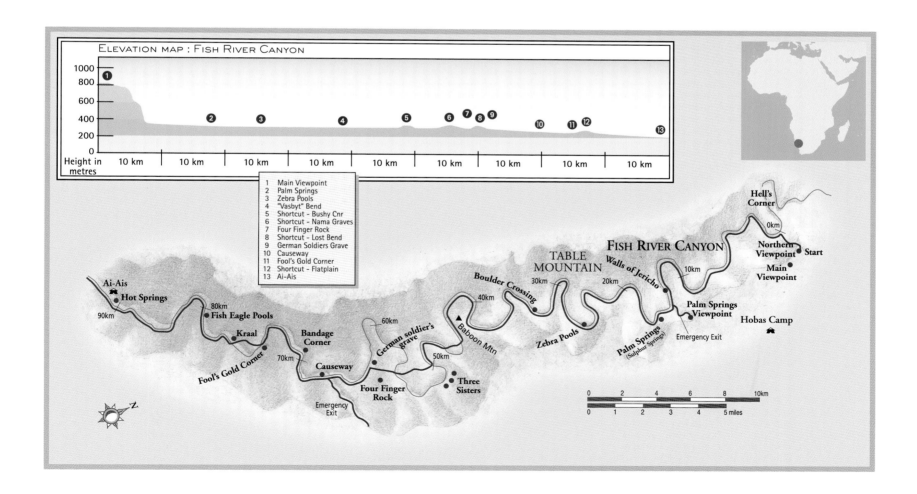

confused with the larger Table Mountain, symbol of Cape Town, some 900km (560 miles) to the south – comes into view, its flat top offering a landmark during the next few serpentine turns in the river.

The third day brings a series of interesting rock formations and pinnacles in such intriguing creations as the Three Sisters and Four Finger Rock. Once you leave the latter behind, the canyon begins to widen, the claustrophobic cliffs moving slowly further apart. It is in the region of these rock formations that you might find that the uneasy relationship between leopards and baboons can sometimes be too close for comfort. It is not uncommon for an

evening's silence to be shattered by the bloodcurdling screams of baboons under attack, as nature takes its course uncomfortably nearby.

Following a couple of shortcuts over ridges in the loop of hairpin bends, the canyon begins to widen, and you might see horse-like spoor, or dung. Unfortunately, this is probably all you will see of the shy Hartmann's mountain zebra, as they quench their thirst only under cover of darkness. There are two other species of zebra in southern Africa, but Hartmann's is endemic only to isolated mountainous areas of Namibia and southern Angola. More frequent sightings of the majestic kudu, a large

antelope with twisted horns, are likely. Wild horses are also often encountered.

On the fourth day, you might stumble across a German grave, its occupant enjoying for all eternity the rare solitude of this desert wilderness. Germany occupied Namibia as a colonial power for some 30 years before World War I, and fierce fighting with Nama tribesmen took place in this area. Lieutenant von Trotha was shot in the back during a skirmish in 1905 and buried where he fell.

This area has a history going back long long before the luckless lieutenant. There is evidence here of human settlements going back 125,000 years. There is almost a

spiritual presence you can feel. That's what happens in remote desert places.

On the final day, the canyon opens out into a wide open space and the trail continues mostly on soft sand. By now you have surely heard the call of Africa – the plaintive and haunting sound of the fish eagle, arguably the most regal and awe inspiring of all the raptors – and glimpsed some of its stars: the klipspringer ('rock jumper' buck) poised gracefully on the tips of its hooves like an agile ballet dancer. You would also have seen among the sparse vegetation the tree most associated with Namibia, the quiver tree, so named because the native Khoi people used the hollowed trunk to make quivers in which to carry their arrows. Confined mainly to the riverbanks, the camel thorn offers welcome shade and the ebony, with its drooping branches, gives the impression of wilting in the heat. Far from it. You have to be a survivor in this harsh wilderness.

The Fish River Canyon trek ends at Ai-Ais (pronounced 'eye-ice'), the Nama word for 'burning water', and the healing hot springs at this luxury oasis will soothe your aching joints. The resort, established in 1971, was almost entirely washed down the river one year later, during the biggest flood in recorded history.

RIGHT *The quiver tree acts as a water reservoir for animals in this arid region. It is indigenous to the hot and dry southern part of Namibia and can reach 300 years of age.*
OPPOSITE *An early morning start is the only way to beat the unforgiving midday sun.*

Namibia is a country that draws visitors back. It is hard to pinpoint why. There are miles of seemingly nothing, but there is an allure, a mystique about that nothing. The densely wooded lush green hills of the north, the arid desert plains of the south and the aptly named Skeleton Coast, constantly at war with the cold south Atlantic Ocean, show her in some of her moods.

# Northern Drakensberg

## By Tom Hutton

The Drakensberg, (the dragon mountain), form the spine of South Africa. Running north to south for over 200km (125 miles), they form a natural border between the province of KwaZulu-Natal and the tiny mountain kingdom of Lesotho, and offer endless opportunities for adventurous trekking.

The route discussed here, which will take a fit walker five days, winds its way along the escarpment edge at the northern end of the range. Starting at the mighty Sentinel, on the western boundary of the Royal Natal National Park, it passes some of the 'Berg's (as it is known for short) most famous landmarks: the Devil's Tooth, the Amphitheatre, Icidi Buttress, The Fangs, The Saddle, The Bell and, of course, the

magnificent Cathedral Peak. Along the way it traverses rugged, often trackless, terrain; slips back and forth across the Lesotho border; crosses the sources of some of the country's mightiest rivers; and then ends each day in the shelter of a hidden cave. The scenery throughout is awesome. Away from the escarpment edge, the landscape is barren and austere with only the occasional rocky peak or tumbling mountain stream to mark the way. But, after frequent forays across this impressive plateau, the trail repeatedly returns to the real spectacle – huge and broken basalt cliffs, adorned with needle-sharp pinnacles and knife-edge arêtes, that thrust up from the fertile hills of the Little Berg, at times over 1000m (3300ft) below.

The trek starts from the Sentinel Office, in the Free State Province, where permits can be obtained. A good track heads from here up towards the escarpment edge before tailing out into a narrow path that zigzags beneath the mighty Sentinel rock-tower. The views improve with every step and the climbing is made a lot easier by the distraction of the scenery to the north, towards the formidable walls of the Amphitheatre and the instantly recognizable spire of the Devil's Tooth. The track then traverses the flanks of the Sentinel

ABOVE *The trail to the amphitheatre climbs around the rock pillars, known as the Witches, and the rock castle of The Sentinel.*

before terminating in a dark and narrow cleft in the hillside. Here you take the much written-about, intimidating-looking chain ladders, up two levels, onto the plateau beneath Mont-aux-Sources. The path, slightly fainter at this stage, then heads southeast to the infant Tugela River. Follow its course down to the escarpment edge and stop to take in the full grandeur

of the Amphitheatre from the top of one of South Africa's most impressive waterfalls as it tumbles for 948m (3110ft). From this point onwards, the trek takes on a much wilder flavour as you leave the good paths behind and make your way across significantly more rugged terrain. Head south, to pick up a tributary of the Kubedu River, and follow this downstream to a major

confluence. Where the waters meet, you turn left and follow the second tributary uphill, pretty much due east, back onto the escarpment near the Ifidi Pass. Continue above the pass, where you'll see the dramatic Ifidi pinnacles, and then head due south to cross over the back of the Ifidi Buttress. This time you'll rejoin the escarpment close to the Icidi Pass where you'll spend the night. The Icidi Cave is little more than a shallow overhang on the southern side of the pass.

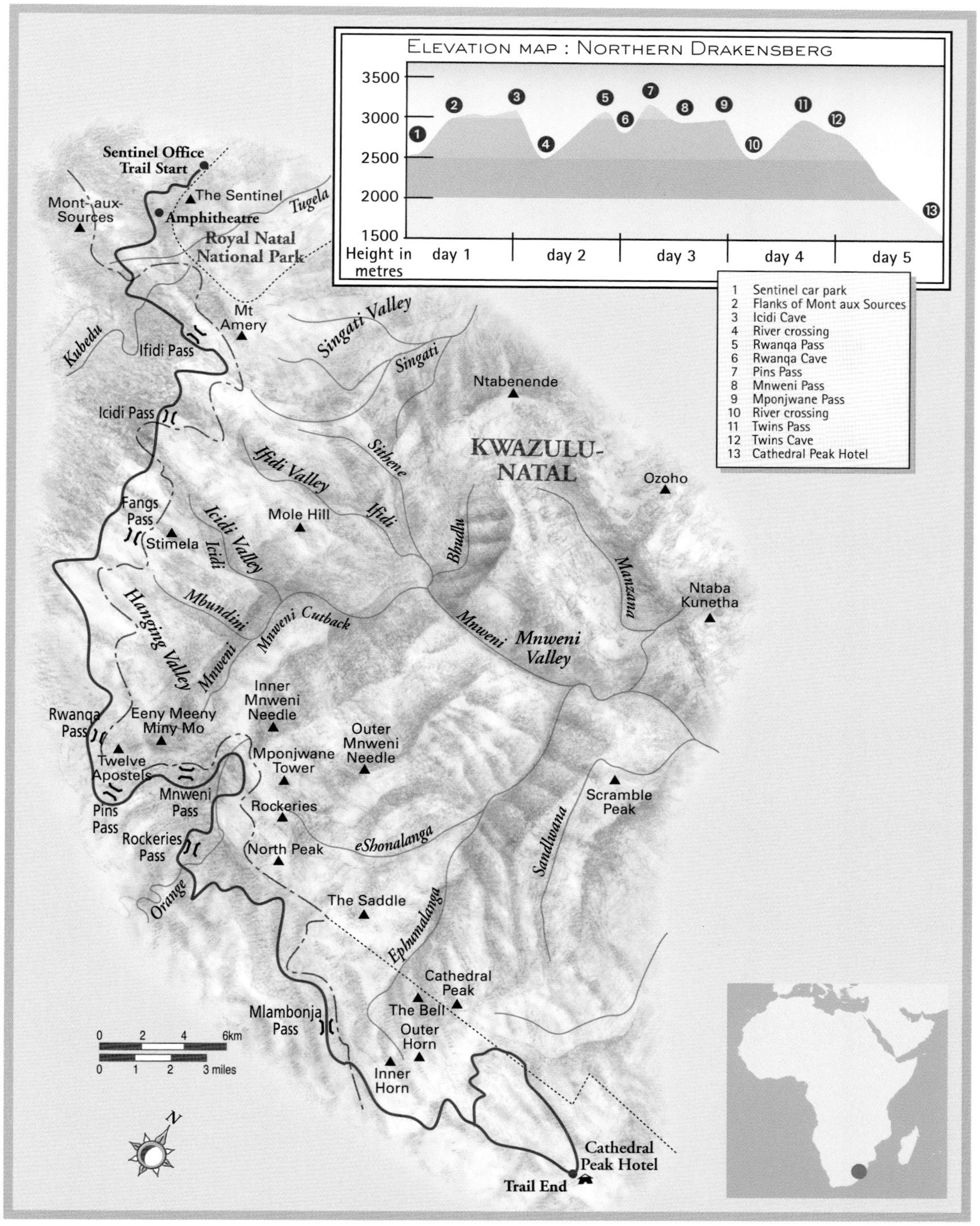

## MADONNA AND FOLLOWERS

From Icidi, the route continues south, behind the Icidi Buttress, before dropping to cross another of Kubedu's tributaries. Continue in the same direction; pass around the right of a small hill and then drop to another river. The best route heads east from here, back onto the ridge line, for a great view over the rock needles of Madonna and her worshippers. Stay on the escarpment edge, cross the top of Fangs Pass and veer southeast to pick up another river. Head upstream, still southeast and then, as the river meanders south, bear off to the left to locate the Rwanqa Pass. Drop down the pass for approximately 300m (985ft) and then scramble up to the cave in the cliffs on the right. The cave, considerably more comfortable than Icidi, is often frequented by baboons that, unlike their tamer cousins which frequent popular tourist spots, will make a hasty exit upon catching your scent. Other wildlife frequently seen along this section of the 'Berg includes rock hyrax (*Procavia capensis*), or *dassies*, as they are commonly

ELEVATION MAP : NORTHERN DRAKENSBERG

1 Sentinel car park
2 Flanks of Mont aux Sources
3 Icidi Cave
4 River crossing
5 Rwanqa Pass
6 Rwanqa Cave
7 Pins Pass
8 Mnweni Pass
9 Mponjwane Pass
10 River crossing
11 Twins Pass
12 Twins Cave
13 Cathedral Peak Hotel

views across the next section, above the Mnweni Cutback, are among the best of the whole trek. The Zulu people named the Drakensberg 'Quathlamba', meaning, literally, 'barrier of upright spears', and as you gaze along the escarpment from the top of Pins Pass, it's easy to see how formidable this barrier must have appeared. Continue south, following the line of the Lesotho border, over a rounded but distinct ridge and then contour around – first to the east and then to the northeast, to regain the clifftops near the wonderfully named pinnacles of Eeny, Meeny, Miny and Mo. The best line now heads due east into the Senqu Valley, where you'll cross the source of the Orange River before climbing back up above the Mponjwane Tower. This is the domain of cape vultures. Much maligned, these beautiful birds colonize the rocky towers along the escarpment and use the considerable updrafts created by the cliffs to glide effortlessly over the plateau edge searching for food. From close quarters it's possible to hear the wind in their wings and their calls echo eerily back from the surrounding rocks. They share the Drakensberg skies with black eagles, more solitary birds with deep and heavy wings, and with the much rarer lammergeier, or bearded vulture, a

known, and buck such as the largest of the antelopes – the eland – and also the smaller grey rhebuck.

The third day starts with a short climb back up the pass where a track leads west, down to the river again. Follow this southward and then, to avoid losing too much height, head southeast, back onto the cliff tops near Pins Pass. The escarpment swings around to the east here and the

stunning mountain dweller easily recognized by its diamond-shaped tail. Head south from the tower and track back onto the plateau slightly to round some rocky outcrops. Here, you'll locate a trail of cairns that will take you back onto the escarpment and down to the Mponjwane Cave, which, perched on a broad ledge, is probably the most spectacularly situated shelter of the whole tour. If water is proving difficult to find, Ledger's Cave, north of the Mnweni Pass, will be a better choice.

## TWINS CAVE

Sunrise from the cave should be enjoyed, but day four is a long one so break camp and head off as early as you can. A faint path heads south from the cave to the Rockeries Pass. The views across the jumble of rocky promontories and pinnacles are breathtaking and you should be able to make out the distinctive profile of The Bell, close to your finishing point yet still some way off in the distance. From the Rockeries, head southwest, away from the edge, where you'll pick up the Orange River once again. Follow this down to its confluence with the Koakoatsi and then backtrack to trace the meandering course of this river, almost due east, towards the Nquza Pass. Here, the river is channelled by a distinct valley that runs south to north and a pronounced ridge runs along its western side. Climb this, making your way through the occasional rock band and then descend by contouring around to the west, again avoiding rocky outcrops and small crags. The escarpment is regained above Ntonjelana Pass and from

**ABOVE** *Enjoying the early morning sun in the comfort of the Mponjwane Cave, while contemplating the start of day four.*

here, the trek follows the edge, as closely as possible, to Cathedral Peak. On the far side of the peak is the Mlambonja Pass, your final descent route. Follow this down into a saddle where you'll see another track leading down to the left. It ends in the relative luxury of Twins Cave, one of the largest and most popular of the 'Berg shelters. The views back along the escarpment to the north are really quite something and it's easy to make out the Devil's Tooth, so close to your starting point, four days earlier.

The final day is spent descending but there's no time to relax just yet. The path is tricky in places and there's an awful lot of altitude to lose before you finally reach civilization. The first task is to take the trail back up to the Mlambonja Pass. Once

reached, this is easily followed as it follows the course of the river down into a lush green valley where colourful ericas and proteas come in stark contrast to the barren mountain scenery you've grown accustomed to over the last few days. In places, the trail can be confusing, but the way is normally marked by a small cairn, perched precariously on a large boulder, somewhere close to hand. At the 2000m (6560ft) mark, the trail splits. The right-hand option is generally considered the better one. This contours for a while before climbing again and finally zigzagging steeply down to flatter ground. Soon after this, the trail leaves the Mlambonja Wilderness Area behind and picks up a waymarked track that leads down to the Cathedral Peak Hotel.

# WILD COAST TRAIL

## By Fiona McIntosh

South Africa's Wild Coast is remote and inaccessible, a land of deserted white beaches, dramatic cliffs, ruggedly beautiful green hills and friendly people. There are few roads, so the best way to explore is on foot, or on horseback, along the coastal paths.

A marked hiking trail once ran the length of the Xhosa republic of the Transkei, from the Umtamvuma River just south of Port Edward, 280km (174 miles) south to the Kei River near East London. The Transkei, which boasts Nelson Mandela as its most famous son, was a semi-autonomous 'homeland' until 1994 and it is still a very separate, distinct part of the country. Sadly, much of the trail has been neglected and is largely in disrepair with only hardy,

self-sufficient trekkers attempting the full whack. But the most popular and arguably the most spectacular section, the 100km (62 mile) section between Port St Johns and Coffee Bay, is one of the finest coastal walks in the world. And while the spectacular scenery cannot fail to impress, your memories will be as much about the fascinating people you meet along the way.

Named the Wild Coast after its treacherous waters, the area is certainly not a wilderness. Rather, it is heavily populated with villages – tiny clusters of thatched, circular *rondavels* (one-roomed huts) – dotting virtually every hillside. There are local shops at which to buy supplies, opportunist fishermen who offer crayfish (rock lobster) or their catch of the day and

enterprising women en route who produce crates of bottled beer – and other luxuries – from under their beds. You can still hike independently (for a paltry sum) or take a guided hike and stay with the communities enjoying AmaPondo hospitality at its best.

Most take five days on the trail and, make no mistake, it's a tough hike with steep hills, river crossings and long sections of beach. There are basic huts at roughly 12km (7½-mile) intervals, all in beautiful locations (and the odd hotel and

**ABOVE** *View across Second Beach, Port St Johns to Silaka Nature Reserve, the start of the Transkei Hiking Trail.*

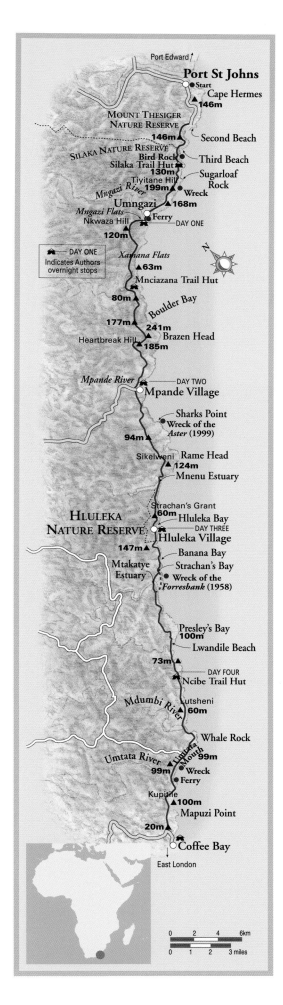

Port Edward
**Port St Johns**
Start
▲ Cape Hermes
146m
MOUNT THESIGER
NATURE RESERVE
146m
Second Beach
SILAKA NATURE RESERVE
Bird Rock
Silaka Trail Hut      Third Beach
130m
Tiyitane Hill      Sugarloaf
199m      Rock
*Mngazi River*      Wreck
**Umngazi** ▲ 168m
*Mngazi Flats*      Ferry
Nkwaza Hill      DAY ONE
▲
120m

🏠 DAY ONE
Indicates Authors
overnight stops

*Xauana Flats*
▲ 63m
Mnciazana Trail Hut
80m
*Boulder Bay*
177m
241m ▲
Heartbreak Hill      Brazen Head
185m

*Mpande River*      DAY TWO
●**Mpande Village**
Sharks Point
● Wreck of the
*Aster* (1999)
94m ▲
Sikelweni      Rame Head
124m ▲
Mnenu Estuary

Strachan's Grant
60m ▲
Hluleka Bay
**HLULEKA**      DAY THREE
**NATURE RESERVE** ●**Hluleka Village**
147m ▲
Mtakatye      Banana Bay
Estuary      Strachan's Bay
● Wreck of the
*Forresbank* (1958)

Presley's Bay
100m
Lwandile Beach
73m ▲
DAY FOUR
Ncibe Trail Hut
*Mdumbi River*      Lutsheni
60m
Whale Rock
*Umtata River*      99m
99m ●Wreck
● Ferry
Kupilile
▲ 100m
Mapuzi Point
20m ▲
🏠**Coffee Bay**
East London

0    2    4    6km
0    1    2    3 miles

backpackers' lodge) so, if you can, choose the independent, self-sufficient route. And although your pack will be crammed with essential gear, the presence of local trading stores means that you don't need to carry much food. The route is reasonably well marked, with the location of the next hut scrawled on rocks or signposts, but given the plethora of footpaths, you'll probably get lost on occasion. If in doubt, follow the coast – or ask the locals for directions to the next river crossing, village or store.

Deciding that this was as much a cultural experience as a trek, we opted for the chaperoned option, staying in communities. Our guide ensured that we were greeted as long-lost friends at every stop, shown to our clean overnight accommodation in a *rondavel*, and treated to local celebrations. Every evening we gathered to sample the local fare, samp and beans, or pap and sauce. The adventurous washed it down with the local brew, a milky white concoction, brewed from maize, but bottled beer is easily procured.

The high road, which begins along the dramatic cliffs to Port St Johns' Second Beach, is a fitting introduction to the Wild Coast. Although it boasts an asphalt surface and easy access from the main trunk road (the N2) Port St Johns is still a sleepy, relaxed seaside town. The views of the dramatic cliffs below the path are inspiring. We scrambled down a rickety ladder and over to The Gap, a popular, but exposed, angling spot where many a fisherman has come to grief, then down to the gorgeous coves of Second Beach where hawkers proffered huge crayfish.

## TRAILHEAD

From the trailhead at the Silaka Nature Reserve (at the end of Second Beach) the path climbs through coastal forest to cliff-top vantage-points from which you can survey the rounded promontories and sandy bays. The route then cuts briefly inland through grazing cattle to the pristine sands of Third Beach with its dramatic view of Bird Rock. Huge hardwood logs still litter the coastline, washed up a decade ago from a far-off shipwreck. Again you climb, to a high spot overlooking the wave-battered promontory of Sugar Loaf, following a track behind the coastal ridge until you descend towards Umngazi, where a holiday resort makes a pleasant stopping place while waiting for the ferry across the Mngazi River.

The pattern is pretty much set by now: a steep climb followed by a punishing descent and you're finally on the flat, walking on the beach to Mngazana and another ferry. The river, with its great sweeping bends, mudflats and vegetated banks is typical of the area but an unusual feature is the three types of mangrove that occur in this estuary – in most other estuaries along the coast only one variety is present.

Our first night's accommodation was in the village on the far side and after a shower we sat outside listening to the sounds of the crashing sea and trying to master a few words of Xhosa. Children poked their heads out from the kitchen while women with babies on their backs smiled as they cooked or passed by. Life is simple here, and tough, but looking at our happy, smiling hostess we felt the genuine welcome of these generous people.

Day two is a tough haul. You leave the coast behind and climb steep, steep hills, the exertion of climbing with packs, as well as the views, taking your breath away. The vegetation varies enormously, the scrubby, dry, north-facing slopes contrasting with the lush, greener southern slopes and clusters of forest along the streams and rivers. In places the heavily-grazed grasslands resemble mowed lawns, red pokers of aloes cling to the rocky cliffs and you'll spot colourful orchids, daisies, and everlastings among the tough grass. The flora of the Transkei coast is extraordinary, with the mix of three floral kingdoms, and close inspection reveals a profusion of tiny flowers. The climax of the day is to stand at Brazen Head, the highest point on the trail, and survey the green undulations of land from the vantage of the resistant dolerite intrusion. Heartbreak Hill, the next challenge, is appropriately named and then it's only a few more hills to the Mpande river, which is easily waded. Many of the rivers along the trail are relatively shallow, but you need to plan your approach carefully and aim to cross at low tide.

The *kraals* (enclosures) at Mpande, home for the second night, are visible from a long way off and after the toils of the day the sight is a welcome relief. All the villages are similarly structured, with small distinct clusters of huts, each with its own fenced-off cattle pen and vegetable garden. Visit the local backpackers' lodge and tourist drinking hole, The Kraal – a mini fortress with commanding views over the crashing ocean. The bar, decorated with washed-out, and washed-up driftwood, other

flotsam and shells, has the feel of a surfers' haunt. The food is excellent and a shuttle service from the N2 ensures that it's always full of travellers from all over the world.

## SLEIGH PATHS

On day three we followed sleigh paths behind oxen pulling basic sledges of wooden rails loaded with firewood and wide-eyed boys. The ubiquitous little black pigs snuffled around cleaning up all manner of waste, and sheep and goats grazed around the villages. We watched impromptu soccer games on sloping fields with rickety goalposts, passed the burnt-out skeletons

OPPOSITE *The trail takes you through dense coastal forest, past dramatic rock formations and empty golden beaches.*
BELOW *Xhosa woman smoking a pipe. Part of the attraction of the trail is staying with, and learning about, the local communities.*

of cars and boats and experienced one of the classic Wild Coast sights: cattle strolling along the beach, as if taking an evening promenade.

Local people also follow these trails and often a gaggle would fall in alongside us, trying to engage us with their few words of English. Horsemen slowed to ask where we were going and how we were enjoying their beautiful land and expressed their wish that we have the trek of our lives and take back happy memories of our stay.

After wading across the Mnenu estuary – you'll soon master the routine of tucking up your shorts and balancing your pack on your head – you enter the Hluleka Nature Reserve, a wonderful stretch of coastal forest. The wooden chalets, nestled behind the sheltered bay, are popular with fishermen and families, and the bay is perfect for a final swim or snorkel before you head inland to the Hluleka village. We celebrated our third night with beers at a pub in a *rondavel*. We sat long into the night until the empty beer crates that served as seats became too uncomfortable to endure.

Just beyond Hluleka lie the remains of the wreck of the *Forresbank*, a British freighter which caught fire and ran aground in 1958. Earlier on the trail we had passed one of the more recent wrecks – that of the *Aster* which went aground in 1999 at Sharks' Point near Mpande. Not much of either remains – the proximity to shore resulted in large-scale scavenging. However, the sight of the stem and broken wreckage in the spray and on the wave-cut platform is haunting. As you cross the Mtakatye estuary, look out for fish eagles

majestically soaring overhead. We were fortunate to spot the distinctive birds here and at Mngazana. We saw numerous other forest birds on the trail, but few coastal species. To our amazement, on the far side of the estuary we came across some cyclists valiantly pedalling along the narrow path. Competitors on the Imana Wild Ride, one of South Africa's most gruelling off-road events, these madmen and women were cycling over 200km (124 miles) from Kei Mouth to the Umngazi River. The thought of

navigating the steep paths, cliff-top trails and sandy beaches on bicycles made our efforts seem puny.

There is no village accommodation at the final overnight spot, Ncibe, so you sleep in the beautifully located hikers' huts – four *rondavels* facing out to sea. Our guide prepared an African dinner of samp and beans and we sat around regretting that the next day we would be back in 'civilization'.

The varied scenery on the last day was a fitting finale to this magnificent trek with stretches of dramatic cliffs, a long beach

walk and the final ferry crossing, at Umtata Mouth, achieved in a rather shaky craft skippered by a young boy. From there the trail heads inland again over the grasslands until Coffee Bay, a major town (by Wild Coast standards) and popular holiday resort with gorgeous beaches and rolling surf. A variety of accommodation to suit all tastes and budgets is available. Before you leave, be sure to visit one of the country's most dramatic coastal landforms, the Hole in the Wall, a wave-carved sea-arch a short hike further south.

# OTTER TRAIL

## By Mike Lundy

South Africa is a country with many different cultures, languages and creeds. It has an astonishing diversity of scenery, ranging from desert to subtropical jungle; and everything in between. This is the self-proclaimed Rainbow Nation, and the rainbow ends at the Otter Trail. Often referred to as 'the Prince of Trails', it is a 48km (30-mile) up-and-down roller coaster, with spectacular coastal scenery. Numerous river crossings add a little spice to the afromontane forest and *fynbos* that surround you. (Unique to this corner of Africa, *fynbos* is a group of flowering shrubs that make up a botanical treasure).

The plant world is divided into six distinctly separate botanical regions, called Floral Kingdoms. The largest – the Boreal Kingdom – covers most of the Northern Hemisphere and the smallest – the Cape Floral Kingdom – covers a tiny 0,04% of the world's land mass. But it is also the richest, with nearly 9000 different species of flowering plants concentrated in a minuscule corner of the southwestern tip of Africa.

**ABOVE** *View from the last hut of the daunting climb up to the escarpment and the final level stretch to the finish.*

**LEFT** *The Knysna Loerie is a relative of the European cuckoo. When in flight, contrasting colours of bright red wings and green body are most vivid.*

**OPPOSITE** *Time to chill out and cool off at one of the many deep dark pools.*

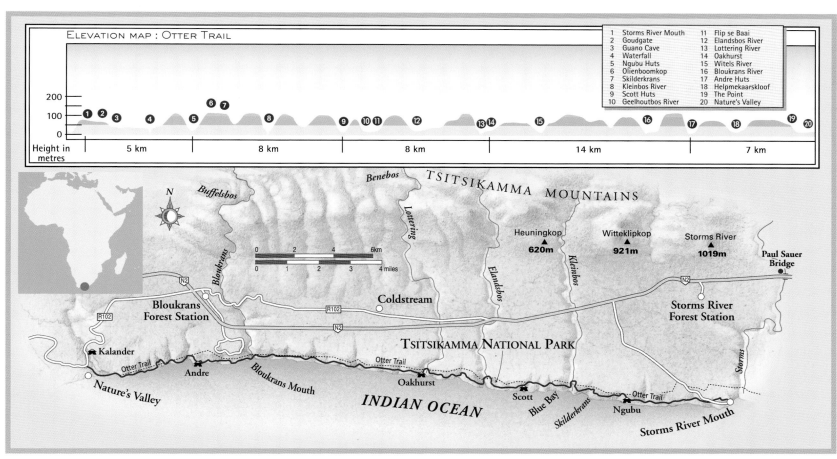

ELEVATION MAP : OTTER TRAIL

| | | | |
|---|---|---|---|
| 1 | Storms River Mouth | 11 | Flip se Baai |
| 2 | Goudgate | 12 | Elandsbos River |
| 3 | Guano Cave | 13 | Lottering River |
| 4 | Waterfall | 14 | Oakhurst |
| 5 | Ngubu Huts | 15 | Witels River |
| 6 | Olienboomkop | 16 | Bloukrans River |
| 7 | Skilderkrans | 17 | Andre Huts |
| 8 | Kleinbos River | 18 | Helpmekaarskloof |
| 9 | Scott Huts | 19 | The Point |
| 10 | Geelhoutbos River | 20 | Nature's Valley |

Height in metres

5 km   8 km   8 km   14 km   7 km

*Buffelsbos*

N

*Benebos*   TSITSIKAMMA MOUNTAINS

*Lottering*

Heuningkop ▲ 620m   Witteklipkop ▲ 921m   Storms River ▲ 1019m   Paul Sauer Bridge

*Bloukrans*   0 2 4 6km   0 1 2 3 4 miles

N2

Bloukrans Forest Station   R102   Coldstream   *Elandsbos*   *Kleinbos*   N2   Storms River Forest Station

R102   R102   N2

Kalander   TSITSIKAMMA NATIONAL PARK   *Storms*

Otter Trail   Otter Trail

Andre   Oakhurst

Nature's Valley   *Bloukrans Mouth*   INDIAN OCEAN   Scott   Blue Bay   Otter Trail   Ngubu

*Skilderkrans*   Storms River Mouth

The richness and abundance of the flora is well illustrated by heather of the genus Erica. The well-known heath flora of Europe has 21 species of Erica. In the Western Cape there are 657 Erica species.

The five-day Otter Trail starts at the picturesque Storms River Mouth rest camp. From here trekkers set out westward along the coastline, as they have done since the establishment of the trail in 1968. Moving through dense indigenous forest, you will emerge every so often at a secluded beach or a breathtaking viewpoint.

Huge jagged rocks stick straight out of the sea, guarding the coast like sentries. This is definitely not a place you would choose to be shipwrecked.

The path winds up and down steep wooded hillsides, occasionally interrupted by a river. You will walk an average of less than 9km (5½ miles) per day – which doesn't sound like much. But it is. Take your time and enjoy. Do not rush. For if you do, you will miss the magic.

The first part of the trek involves a fair bit of rock scrambling and boulder hopping, just on and above the high water mark. This short, 4.8km (3 mile) section to the first overnight hut is something of a baptism of fire for inexperienced trekkers, who can't quite seem to make the jump to

LEFT *The overnight huts (log cabins) are always in pairs, sleeping six each and at the water's edge.*
OPPOSITE *Hikers crossing the Bloukrans River at low tide. Crossing at high tide, not always avoidable, can be hazardous.*

the next rock, without climbing all the way down, and laboriously up again. Soon, however, all frustrations are washed away at a beautiful waterfall cascading into a deep, dark pool.

A mere three hours after starting you reach the first overnight huts. The Ngubu Huts were named after the park ranger who helped to develop the trail and later died in a fire. There are two spartan log cabins at each coastal overnight stop. They each sleep six people in bunks with foam mattresses, and have a table and two benches. Water and firewood are usually provided, but not guaranteed. *Lapas* (open cooking shelters) are planned for late 2006.

The second and third days, after more ups and downs, you might get the feeling that you are being watched. You are – by cheeky little vervet monkeys or brightly plumaged Knysna louries. At the end of this section you have to cross the mouth of the Lottering River to reach the Oakhurst Huts on the opposite bank. They could not be closer to the crashing waves where bottlenose dolphins frolic in the tumbling translucent breakers.

The fourth day brings with it the most feared obstacle on the trek: the Bloukrans (blue cliffs) River crossing. Its perceived dangers are almost without fail blown out of all proportion, and hikers often sleep fitfully

the night before in fearful anticipation. Strong currents and deep water at high tide are factors that warrant some consideration, but provided the crossing is undertaken at low tide, there is little to worry about.

The last day on the coast starts with a climb to a high plateau, before plummeting down to the seemingly endless beach at the aptly named Nature's Valley. The squabbling gulls; the rare African black oystercatchers trying to lure you away from their defenceless chick; the solitary cormorant drying himself out in the crucifix position – these coastal birds will bid you farewell.

# TSITSIKAMMA TRAIL

*By Mike Lundy*

The original inhabitants of this southern tip of Africa were the Khoisan or Bushman people. Light skinned and small in stature, they more than made up for their lack of size with superb hunting and survival skills. They called this place Tsitsikamma – where the clear waters begin – for these verdant mountains are the birthplace of many a river that gurgles its way down to the sea. Situated about three-quarters of the way between the coastal cities of Cape Town and Port Elizabeth, the mountainous six-day, 60km (37½-mile) Tsitsikamma Trail was South Africa's first officially accredited hiking trail, when it was established in 1968. In fact, the local authority claims it was the first accredited hiking trail in the

world. The South African Trail Owners Association (SATOA) describes it as having excellent trail facilities with standard to luxury accommodation in a pristine environment. They grade its level of exertion as moderate to difficult. But don't be put off by the 'difficult in parts' grading, for you will soon forget the occasional steep uphill gradient when surrounded by luxuriant woodland and the chattering of vervet monkeys. The trail meanders through the heart of the Tsitsikamma mountains, where extensive patches of indigenous afromontane forest and mountain fynbos still occur. (Fynbos is a vegetation type endemic to this part of South Africa, composed mainly of heather, proteas and reeds.)

Along the route, little contact is made with the outside world, except for the odd forestry activity here and there. These mountains jealously hide their forests, fynbos and sparkling swimming holes. Expect to encounter baboon and buck along the way. You might be lucky to run into a caracal (a lynx-like cat with tufted ears about the size of a medium dog), or have your food stolen by a large-spotted genet. The

**ABOVE** *The hike starts from Nature's Valley and follows the eastern bank of the Groot River lagoon and through the indigenous coastal forest.*
**OPPOSITE** *The mainly nocturnal caracal or African lynx grows up to 1m (40 inches) in body length and is extremely agile.*

spotted body and long striped tail makes the genet look like a cross between a mongoose and a cat. They are infamous for raiding camp kitchens. Even leopards occur in these mountains, but due to their nocturnal habit and skittish nature, they are seldom seen. But they might well be watching you.

Occasional tree ferns add a primeval air to the forest and the spectacularly coloured Knysna lourie will take your breath away, as it flies off, startled by your approach. Many streams and pools along the route provide ample opportunity for swimming and refilling of water bottles.

The first day's hike, from Nature's Valley to Kalender Hut, is only 3,6km (2,3 miles)

and will take about 1½ hours. The trail follows the eastern bank of the Groot River lagoon. Sounds of birdlife and the nearby Indian Ocean accompany you through the indigenous coastal forest to the overnight hut. The ocean and lagoon are a mere stroll away.

The second day's hike, from Kalender Hut to Bloukrans Hut is 13,5km (8,4 miles) and takes about six hours. The day begins with a climb up the escarpment. Most of the day will take you through indigenous afromontane forest as you progress inland towards the foothills of the Tsitsikamma Mountains. The Bloukrans Hut, perched precariously on a cliff edge, is a fitting end to the day. The views of the

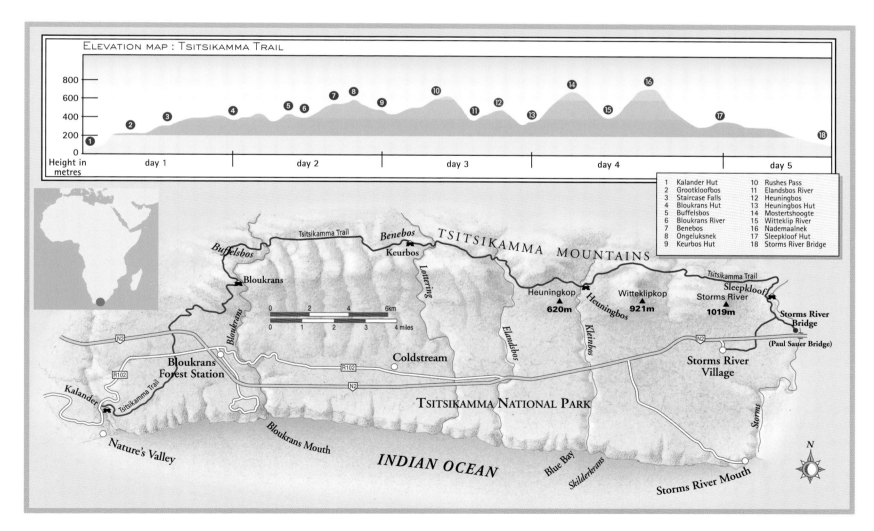

river gorges below and Formosa Peak in the distance will not easily be forgotten. Nor perhaps will the pair of large-spotted genets and a bush pig, who are regular visitors, ever hopeful that you've left some food unattended.

From Bloukrans Hut to Keurbos Hut the trail takes you deep into the Tsitsikamma Mountains and forest and even deeper into a remote world where you will experience a true sense of isolation. Not in any way an unpleasant feeling. This is a day of ups and downs, with Buffelsbos (buffalo forest) and Benebos (bones forest) adding a touch of

nostalgia. Elephant and African buffalo (two of the Big Five) once roamed these forests in great numbers. Alas, it took European settlers less than 100 years to wipe them out. The last buffalo (more feared and respected by hunters than even the lion or rhino) was shot in Buffelsbos in 1886.

## ENCHANTED PATCH

Still surviving, though, in great numbers, are tree ferns, giving the forest a feel of *Jurassic Park*. In this eerie and enchanted patch of forest, the trail begins its eastward course through the mountains and past

Formosa Peak, the highest peak in the Tsitsikamma range at 1675m (5496ft). This is a swimming day, with the crossing of the Bloukrans River a highlight. Towards the end of the day's walk there are rockpools resembling jacuzzis, offering a reward for all the effort.

The fourth day, from Keurbos Hut to Heuningbos Hut, is the same distance and also takes about six hours. This is a day of biodiversity, with some very different habitat types and a number of exciting river crossings, including the use of a newly constructed swing bridge. The Heuningbos (meaning 'honey forest') has many secrets, including a pleasant swimming hole close to the overnight hut.

The fifth day's hike is slightly longer and takes about seven hours. At 13,9km (8,7 miles) it is the longest day of the trail and possibly the most strenuous. On the way from Heuningbos Hut to Sleepkloof Hut you will reach the highest point of the trail, at 740m (2428ft) with two saddles to negotiate en route. Well worth the effort, though, is the pristine mountain fynbos through which it meanders. From a high point the view of the spectacular Storms River Gorge and the Sleepkloof Hut are just reward. At the Sleepkloof hut you will most certainly sleep, but the name actually means 'dragging ravine', and refers to the logs that were taken out through it.

The last day is only a two hour hike. Sleepkloof Hut to Storms River Village is about 5,5km (3,4 miles). The last lap takes the hiker through tall indigenous forest, joining up with various day walks in the area. If you'd planned well, there will be a car waiting at Storms River Village. If you're in a real hurry to get this wonderful hike over and done with – hard to imagine – then you can take a shorter route from Sleepkloof Hut to the Storms River Bridge.

On your way home from the finish of the trek, you cross the bridge over the Bloukrans River Gorge, which is a breathtaking 216m (709ft) high. Not surprisingly, operating here is the highest commercial bungi-jump in the world. You may want to finish your trek on a high note, with a major adrenaline rush!

ABOVE AND OPPOSITE *A pause to regroup, in the magnificent Tsitsikamma mountain range where the hiker will find a wide range of terrain from open savannah (opposite) to deep, dark ravines (above) in which a shower or dip in the cool, dark waters is often possible.*

# AUSTRALIA AND NEW ZEALAND

BY JACK JACKSON

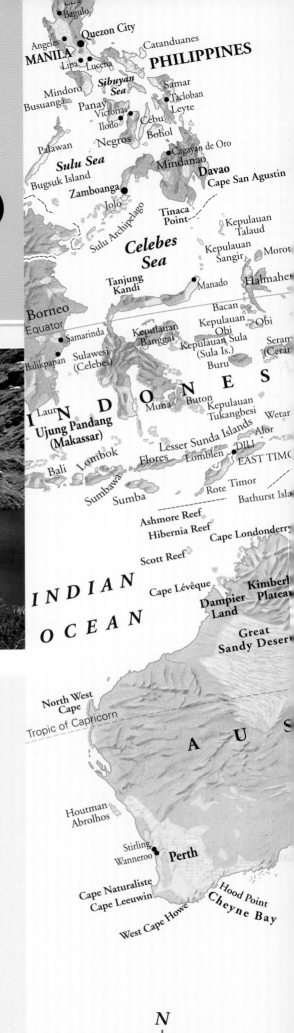

Australia and New Zealand are countries of diverse adventures. Australians and New Zealanders are known for their love of the outdoors so it is no surprise that bushwalking (Australia) and tramping (New Zealand) is popular. Some parts of Australia have dangerous animals, but New Zealand only has the poisonous Katipo spider, found on certain isolated beaches and it is so rare that it is classed as a protected species. However, you will need insect repellent.

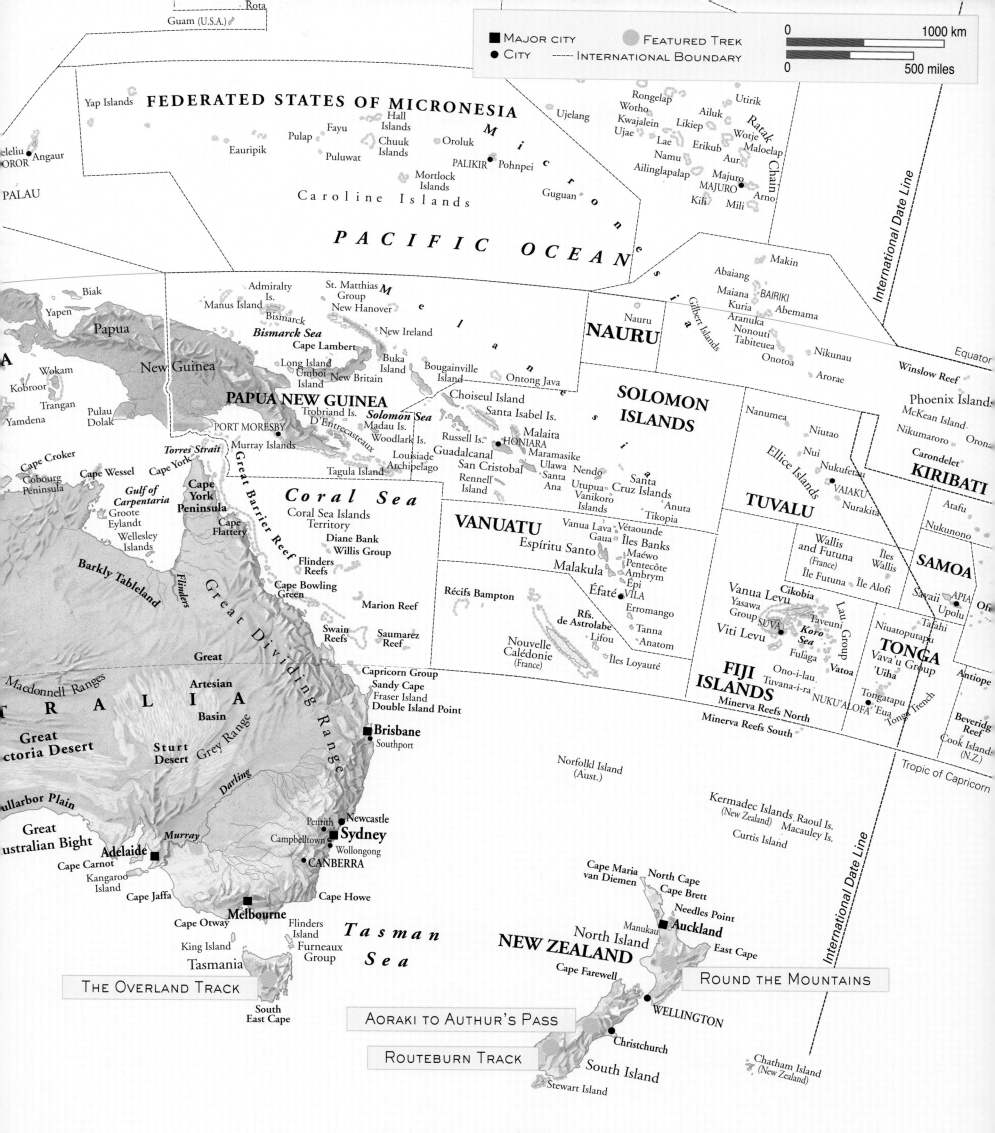

**Guam (U.S.A.)**
Rota

Yap Islands

# FEDERATED STATES OF MICRONESIA

Ujelang

Rongelap          Utirik
Wotho    Ailuk
Kwajalein  Likiep
Ujae    Lae  Erikub
Namu        Maloelap
Ailinglapalap  Majuro
MAJURO
Kili    Arno
Mili

*M*
*i*
*c*
*r*
*o*
*n*
*e*
*s*
*i*
*a*

Ratak
Chain

Hall
Islands
Fayu
Pulap
Puluwat
Chuuk
Islands
Oroluk
PALIKIR  Pohnpei

Eauripik

eleliu
OROR  Angaur

PALAU

Mortlock
Islands
Guguan

**Caroline Islands**

# PACIFIC OCEAN

International Date Line

Makin

Abaiang
Maiana  BAIRIKI
Kuria
Aranuka  Abemama
Nonouti
Tabiteuea
Onotoa

Nauru

# NAURU

Gilbert Islands

Nikunau
Arorae

Equator

Winslow Reef

Biak
Yapen

**Papua**

Wokam
Kobroor
Trangan
Yamdena
Pulau
Dolak

New Guinea

Admiralty
Is.
Manus Island
Bismarck
Cape Lambert
Long Island
Umboi
Island
New Britain

St. Matthias
Group
New Hanover

*M*
*e*
*l*
*a*
*n*

**Bismarck Sea**

New Ireland

Buka
Island

Bougainville
Island

Ontong Java

# SOLOMON
# ISLANDS

Nanumea

Niutao
Nui
Nukufetau

VAIAKU
Nurakita

Phoenix Islands

McKean Island
Nikumaroro  Orona

# KIRIBATI

Carondelet

# PAPUA NEW GUINEA

PORT MORESBY

Trobriand Is.
D'Entrecasteaux
Madau Is.
Woodlark Is.

**Solomon Sea**

Choiseul Island
Santa Isabel Is.

Russell Is.  Malaita
HONIARA
Maramasike

*s*
*i*
*a*

# TUVALU

Ellice Islands

Atafu

**Cape Croker**
Cape Wessel
Cobourg
Peninsula

Cape York

**Torres Strait**
Murray Islands

Guadalcanal
San Cristobal
Rennell
Island

Ulawa
Santa
Ana

Nendo
Utupua
Vanikoro
Islands

Santa
Cruz Islands

Anuta
Tikopia

Nukunono

Cape York
**Gulf of
Carpentaria**
Groote
Eylandt
Wellesley
Islands

Tagula Island
Louisiade
Archipelago

**Cape
York
Peninsula**
Cape
Flattery

**Coral Sea**

Coral Sea Islands
Territory

Diane Bank
Willis Group

# VANUATU

Vanua Lava
Vétaounde

Gaua  Îles Banks
Maéwo
Pentecôte
Ambrym
Épi

Wallis
and Futuna
(France)

Îles
Wallis

Île Futuna  Île Alofi

# SAMOA

Savaii  APIA
Upolu  Of

**Barkly Tableland**

Flinders

**Great Barrier Reef**

Flinders
Reefs

Cape Bowling
Green

Marion Reef

Espíritu Santo

Malakula

Récifs Bampton

Rfs.
de Astrolabe

Malakula

Éfaté
VILA
Erromango

Tanna

Cikobia
Vanua Levu
Yasawa
Group
Taveuni
Koro
Sea

Niuatoputapu

Tafahi

Savaii

**Great Dividing Range**

Swain
Reefs

Saumarez
Reef

Nouvelle
Calédonie
(France)

Lifou

Îles Loyauté

Anatom

Viti Levu
SUVA
Fulaga
Vatoa

# FIJI
# ISLANDS

Ono-i-lau
Tuvana-i-ra  NUKU'ALOFA

'Uiha

Vava'u Group

# TONGA

'Eua
Tongatapu

Antiope

Beverid
Reef

*Macdonnell Ranges*

**Great
ctoria Desert**

**Artesian
Basin**

Grey Range

**Sturt
Desert**

Capricorn Group
Sandy Cape
Fraser Island
Double Island Point

Minerva Reefs North

Minerva Reefs South

Norfolkl Island
(Aust.)

Tropic of Capricorn

International Date Line

Tonga Trench

**Great
ustralian Bight**

Adelaide
Cape Carnot
Kangaroo
Island
Cape Jaffa

ullarbor Plain

*Darling*

*Murray*

■ **Brisbane**
Southport

Penrith
Campbelltown
Newcastle
■ **Sydney**
Wollongong
● CANBERRA

Kermadec Islands
(New Zealand)  Raoul Is.
Macauley Is.

Curtis Island

**Melbourne**
Cape Otway

Cape Howe

Flinders
Island
Furneaux
Group

*Tasman*
*Sea*

Cape Maria
van Diemen

North Cape
Cape Brett

Needles Point

King Island
Tasmania

Manukau
North Island

Auckland

East Cape

South
East Cape

# NEW ZEALAND

Cape Farewell

WELLINGTON

Christchurch

Chatham Island
(New Zealand)

South Island

Stewart Island

Auckland Islands
(N.Z.)

## AUSTRALIA

Australia is the smallest continent (or the largest inhabited island) in the world, and is one of the driest lands on earth. The landscape consists mainly of a low plateau, skirted by coastal mountain ranges, the highest of which is the Great Dividing Range in the east. The country has two main climatic zones: the tropical one in the north has a wet summer and a dry winter, while the southern zone has a temperate climate with four seasons.

Call it trekking, hiking or bushwalking, it is popular all over Australia, but primarily in national parks, forests and reserves, encompassing many different environments including mountains, rainforests, desert areas, coastal trails, and aboriginal sites. Over 3000 of these parks are found in Australia and Tasmania, including the Blue Mountains, Kanangra-Boyd, Wollemi and the Hinchinbrook Island national parks. The Royal National Park was Australia's first and the world's second national park. The Snowy Mountains in the Kosciuszko National Park have the most extensive snowfields in Australia. The park contains Mounts Kosciuszko, Townsend, Twyam and Carruthers – the only peaks in Australia higher than 2134m (7000ft). The 2228m (7310ft) Mt Kosciuszko is Australia's highest mountain. The New South Wales government has changed the spelling from Kosciusko to what is now believed to be the correct spelling, Kosciuszko. Tasmania has scenic wilderness and the entire south-west region is protected by national parks.

As in the USA and Canada, there is a national trail. The Bicentennial National

**ABOVE** *Kea (Nestor notabilis) – the only mountain parrot in the world, is endemic to the South Island's high country, New Zealand.*
**PREVIOUS PAGE LEFT** *Old lava flows spill down the flanks of Mt Ngauruhoe, an active volcano in Tongariro National Park. The mountain continues to grow through further activity.*
**PREVIOUS PAGE RIGHT** *Lake Harris, near the Harris Saddle, the high point of the Routeburn Track at 1310m (4298ft), New Zealand's Southern Alps.*

Trail (BNT) is claimed to be the longest marked trekking route of its kind in the world, stretching 5330km (3305 miles) from Cooktown in tropical North Queensland, to Healesville in Victoria. The inspiration of the legendary bushman RM Williams, the trail follows historic coach and stock routes, old packhorse trails, and country roads, linking 18 national parks. The trail highlights historic sites and artefacts en route, and is waymarked (blazed) with red and yellow vertical striped triangles attached to trees

and posts along the way. There are 12 guidebooks, each covering a 400–500km (248–310-mile) section of the route. As with its North American counterparts, the development of the Bicentennial National Trail is coordinated by the BNT, a non-profit community organization, funded through membership subscriptions, donations and the sale of publications.

## NEW ZEALAND

1600km (1000-miles) southeast of Australia, New Zealand is tiny when compared with Australia. Roughly 1600km (1000 miles) long and 452km (280 miles) across at its widest point, it is stunningly beautiful, and remarkably empty with high mountains, active and extinct volcanoes, geysers and other thermal activity, lakes, fjords and rainforests. The North Island has seven small glaciers on the slopes of Mt Ruapehu and there are more than 360 glaciers in the Southern Alps.

The North Island, the smaller of the two main islands, is separated from South Island by the 26km (16-mile) wide Cook Strait and has the more benign climate. Rainfall is heaviest in the winter months and tends to be more evenly distributed than it is on the South Island. The North Island contains most of the population and the highest point is the 2797m (9176ft) Mt Ruapehu, one of three active volcanoes in the Tongariro National Park.

Almost three-quarters of South Island is mountainous. The central mountain chain of the Southern Alps runs northeast to southwest with 16 peaks above 3050m (10,000ft). The highest point is the 3764m

(12,349ft) Mt Cook. Flanked by the Hooker Glacier to the west and Tasman Glacier to the east, Mt Cook's Maori name 'Āoraki' means 'cloud piercer'. The range separates the narrow coastal strip of the Westland Plain (west) from the broad Canterbury Plain (east) and divides the island climatically, the forested western slopes and narrow coastal plain of Westland being much wetter than the eastern slopes and the wide Canterbury Plain. In the southwest, Fjordland, New Zealand's largest National Park, has magnificent scenery.

New Zealand tramping is a year-round activity, but November to April is most popular and some routes are only open at this time. The North Island's routes have more gentle terrain, while the South Island offers more isolated and more rugged routes. Some South Island routes can have four changes of weather in a few days. The most popular routes such as the Milford Track are collectively known as the Great Walks. However, most of these now have good overnight huts and have to be booked in advance. One of New Zealand's top routes, the Grand Traverse, crosses the Main Divide of the Southern Alps twice, combining the Routeburn Track and the Greenstone Valley Walk.

Ascending Mt Cook and Mt Tasman requires technical climbing but there are tramping routes lower down such as Āoraki to Arthur's Pass.

RIGHT *The 174m (571ft) Earland Falls, the outlet of Lake Roberts, are right beside the Routeburn Track, South Island, New Zealand.*

# OVERLAND TRACK, TASMANIA

## By Shaun Barnett

Tasmania's Overland Track has in recent years developed a reputation as Australia's finest multi-day trek. The 65km (40 mile) hike certainly has an abundance of attractions, including the spectacular Cradle Mountain, numerous alpine lakes, distinctive Australian wildlife and forests, and interesting Aboriginal and European history.

The Overland Track passes through rugged mountains, including Tasmania's highest peak, Mount Ossa. Although no glaciers exist today, the landscape bears the marks of heavy glaciation from the last ice age, which ended some 10,000–14,000 years ago. The trek traverses an impressive chunk of central Tasmania, a large wilderness area. In 1982, along with several other areas in Southwest Tasmania, Cradle Mountain–Lake St Clair National Park was granted World Heritage status, rightly recognizing its importance on a global scale.

### HUNTING GROUNDS

Aboriginal people have lived in Tasmania for over 30,000 years, and survived even the last ice age by retreating to coastal refuges. Although you always feel you are passing through pristine wilderness, many of the buttongrass plains that characterize the central part of the trek are actually the result of past Aboriginal fires. By lighting fires, Aboriginal hunters encouraged button grass to grow on the damp peaty soils, displacing eucalypt (gum) forest. The resulting plains made superb places for them to hunt wombats, wallabies and kangaroos. Europeans arriving in the late 1700s and early 1800s quickly recognized the hunting possibilities of the high plateau too, and trappers hunted possums, wallabies, wombats, and Tasmanian devils for their skins.

Not until the early 1900s did concerns for preserving the area overcome its more utilitarian past. Instrumental in getting protection for Cradle Mountain was an Austrian man, Gustav Weindorfer, who emigrated to Australia in 1900. With his

ABOVE *A hiker admires Cradle Mountain from Marion's Lookout. It is possible to climb the mountain on a side trail.*

wife Kate, Weindorfer made many visits to Cradle Mountain and was soon enraptured by the peak's beauty. The pair became convinced the area deserved national park status, but recognized more people needed to know the place before their dream could become a reality. To encourage visitors, Gustav built a chalet called Waldheim a short distance from the mountain, and opened it in 1912. There he served as guide and host, while continuing to campaign for the area's protection until his death in 1932. Although he lived long enough to see Cradle Mountain declared a scenic reserve in 1922, it was not until 1971 – some 39 years after Weindorfer's death – that the area finally gained national park status.

Trapper Bert Nicholls blazed the original Overland Track in 1930, and the first walk along the entire route was completed in January 1931. Since then the track has

**ABOVE** *A replica of Waldheim, the chalet Gustav Weindorfer built in 1912 to encourage visitors to the Cradle Mountain area.*

undergone many changes, and its popularity steadily grown. Although walking in either direction is allowed during the off-season (May to October), in the peak season (November to April) walkers are restricted to the north-south direction. This means starting at Cradle Mountain, the turreted peak that so captivated Gustav Weindorfer.

## IMPRESSIVE START

Officially this northern end of the Overland Track begins at Waldheim, but a much more impressive start to the tramp can be made on the shores of nearby Lake Dove, where Cradle Mountain dominates the views. Tracks from Lake Dove link with the main route at nearby Crater Lake.

On either route, trails pass through a mixture of eucalypt and beech forest, crossing burbling streams, and climbing steadily to Marion's Lookout at about 1200m (4000ft).

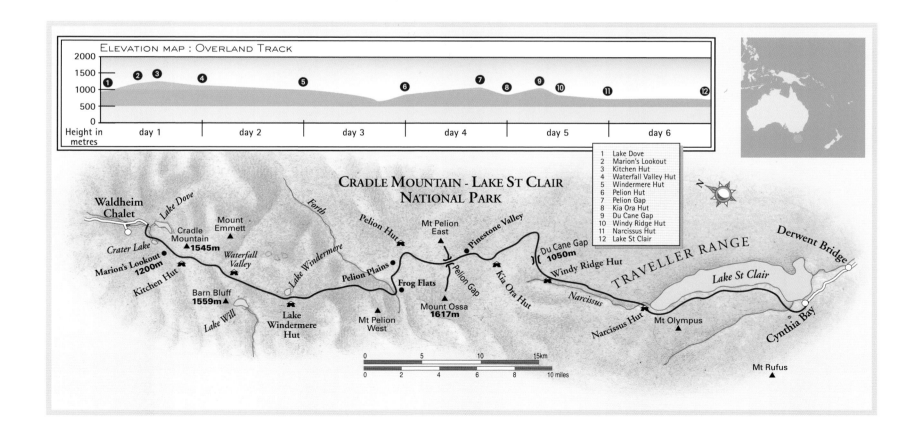

On a good day, you get uninterrupted views of the 1545m (5070ft) Cradle Mountain, now much more imposing, and the more distant monolith of the 1559m (5115ft) Barn Bluff. Although free of permanent snowfields, both bear the unmistakably chiselled imprint of the last ice age.

## ENDEMIC ALPINE SHRUBS

On many days, however, Marion's Lookout offers no views. Unimpeded by any landmass for over 14,000 km (8700 miles), westerly winds bring snow, hail and rain to Tasmania at any time of year, giving the island a reputation for unpredictable weather. This climate may sound bleak and uninviting, but rain forests as distinctive as Tasmania's inevitably require a lot of rain.

From Marion's Lookout, the trail begins a long sidle around the western flanks of Cradle Mountain, passing the rustic shelter of Kitchen Hut, before entering patches of endemic subalpine shrubs known as pandanni. Tasmania's plants share a common ancestry with those of New Zealand and South America when all were part of the supercontinent Gondwana. Since the super-continent fragmented some 80 million years ago, many Gondwanan plants have survived in comparatively cooler Tasmania, while their counterparts were replaced by more modern plants on the sun-baked Australian mainland.

Past a turn-off indicating a side-route to Barn Bluff, the main Overland Track begins a descent down to two huts at Waterfall Valley. One is a modern hut with accommodation for 20, while the other is an old cabin left over from the trapping days.

The next day sees a considerable stretch of travel across buttongrass plains, with the bulky Mt Pelion (1552m; 5092ft) visible for much of the day. Much of the route is now boardwalked, a necessary track development designed to cope with the notoriously peaty soils. Past use had turned much of the track into a quagmire, and the boardwalks, while jarring to walk on, are necessary both to prevent environmental damage, and to allow trekkers to walk at a reasonable pace.

Lake Windermere Hut appears set in a welcoming forest enclave, nestled near the attractive Lake Windermere. Hikers attempting the trail in five days will need to continue to Pelion Hut, while those with more time may wish to spend a night here.

## WALLABIES AND WOMBATS

Across the Pine Forest Moor the trail reaches the edge of Mt Pelion and sidles through eucalypt forest to the swampy Frog Flats and beyond to Pelion Hut. With 60 bunks it is the largest and newest of huts on the Overland Track.

From Pelion Hut the track climbs into the heart of Tasmania's highest peaks. A steady climb with many steps leads to the open expanse of Pelion Gap (1126m; 3694ft), an open pass with commanding views.

Taking ancient names from Greek mythology, Mounts Thetis, Achilles, and Ossa crowd the horizon, rising in long fluted columns at geometric angles. Mt Ossa is hardly a giant at 1617m (5305ft), but its buttresses and steep approaches demand respect. In summer the summit can be reached via a track from Pelion Gap,

ABOVE *Bennetts Wallaby, a large grazing marsupial commonly seen on the Overland Track.*

OPPOSITE *There are many cascades on the Overland Track, including Hartnett Falls, visible from a short side track near Du Cane Gap.*

but snow may deter an attempt. An easier scramble leads to the summit of the nearby Mount Pelion East.

From Pelion Gap, the track descends into the Pinestone valley and Kia Ora Hut. It is a good place to observe Bennetts wallabies, one of Tasmania's 31 marsupial species. More shy is the wombat, a short creature with a stout body and furry face. Although you may see wombats at dusk, you're more likely to find evidence in the form of their distinctive cube-like droppings.

Beyond Kia Ora Hut the trail soon crosses a low pass known as Du Cane Gap (1050m, 3445ft), then descends into the Narcissus Valley. The steep escarpments of the nearby Traveller Range are visible before the trail sinks into stately eucalypt forests. As the tallest flowering plants on earth, eucalypts can reach heights of 90m (300ft), with their trunks peeling bark in

great sagging strips. Quiet contemplation in these majestic forests, however, is often interrupted by loud screeches from flocks of sulphur-crested cockatoo. Another bird that often makes its presence felt is the crow-like black currawong. With beady yellow eyes and quick reflexes, they'll steal your lunch if you're not vigilant.

## AUSTRALIA'S DEEPEST LAKE

At the end of the valley, the darkly stained waters of the Narcissus River ebb into the head of Lake St Clair. Many of Tasmania's streams become coloured by tannins leached from button grass plains. While this lends it the appearance of strong tea, the water remains perfectly good for drinking. Narcissus Hut lies close by.

Despite having several tannin-stained streams feeding it, nearby Lake St Clair is a more traditional blue. After the last ice age gouged out its bed between Mt Olympus and the Traveller Range, Lake St Clair became Australia's deepest lake (167m; 548ft). Here, platypus – primitive egg-laying mammals – are quite common; best seen in the early morning or evening, quietly swimming across the lake.

Narcissus Hut is the last one on the Overland Track if you're heading north to south. Although a track skirts Lake St Clair past Echo Point on to Cynthia Bay, this last part of the trail has little merit. The better alternative is a leisurely cruise across Lake St Clair on the launch that operates regularly during summer. It's an enjoyable way to round off one of Australia's most satisfying outdoor experiences.

# ROUTEBURN TRACK

*By Kathy Ombler*

One of the most spectacular and popular of New Zealand's mountain hiking trails is the Routeburn Track. This historic, high quality trail explores remote mountain wilderness in two of the country's largest and adjoining national parks, Fiordland and Mt Aspiring, and traverses the heart of the World Heritage Area, Te Wahipounamu/ South West New Zealand.

Every day, sometimes every hour on the Routeburn, can reveal a changing landscape as the track winds its way through dense rainforests, tussock grasslands and summer-flowering alpine herb fields, past mountain streams, waterfalls and lakes, across glacier-gouged valleys, alpine passes and remnant glaciers – and all the way

hemmed on all sides by towering mountain peaks. Then there is the birdlife – over 30 species of New Zealand's native birds inhabit the forests, open river flats and alpine habitats along the trail.

The mountain weather can also have a huge impact, sometimes dramatically changing the Routeburn experience. Hot sun, moody mist, torrential rain, wind and perhaps snow can be delivered in unpredictable fashion. Even in summer it is possible to meet all these elements, each of which can suddenly change the landscape, during the course of a Routeburn trip. You can be be dealing with heat, sunburn and thirst one day, and the next be witness to a deluge, raging rivers and mountain walls draped with waterfalls.

Because of its beauty, and therefore popularity, the Routeburn walk is well served by park management and tourist operators. It is one of New Zealand's nine Great Walks, which are regarded as the premier hiking tracks in all New Zealand's national parks. The huts and tracks on the Great Walks are of a higher standard than other tracks, they have resident hut wardens during peak Great Walk season and many, including the Routeburn, are so popular they have booking systems during the season to manage visitor pressures.

**ABOVE** *Overlooking Hollyford Valley from the Routeburn Track, which traverses a spectacular range of alpine and forest environments.*

## TRACING HISTORIC FOOTSTEPS

No high-quality trail or hi tech boots graced the rock and tussock slopes of the Routeburn when people first crossed these mountains. Several hundred years ago New Zealand's first settlers, the Maori, were tenacious travellers, particularly when in pursuit of pounamu – a greenstone or nephrite jade highly valued for use in jewellery, tools and weaponry. Pounamu was found in the riverbeds of the South Island's west coast. In their pursuit of this valuable jade the early Maori forged a number of what became known as 'pounamu trails', from the more populated east coast to the west, and which necessitated travel over the great mountainous divide of the South Island.

Traces of the much-valued pounamu were also found in the Routeburn River, and the Routeburn became one such 'pounamu trail'. For centuries, flax-sandal-wearing Maori travellers negotiated the beech forests of the Routeburn valley, then climbed the steep mountains to the Harris Saddle (1277m; 4190ft), which they knew as Tarahaka Whakatipu and which marks the highest point of today's Routeburn Track. They continued across exposed mountain faces and descended into densely forested valleys to reach the west coast rivers and their pounamu treasure.

Later, British surveyors sought advice from Maori about routes through the mountains. In 1870, in a thoroughly optimistic manner, a new settlement was established at Martin's Bay, on the remote, southwestern coastline at the mouth of the Hollyford River – about as remote as one could get in New Zealand even by today's standards. Part of today's Routeburn Track negotiates the headwaters of the Hollyford valley.

## EPIC TREK

The provincial government of the time planned to build a bridle road to the west coast via the Harris Saddle, but realities of constructing this in the rugged, often snow-covered mountains, proved challenging and painfully slow. In the meantime, with alternative sea approaches to the new settlement thwarted by atrocious conditions, the Martin's Bay settlement was cut off and ran desperately short of provisions. One settler, William Homer, considered the settlement's most experienced bushman, set off overland with the aim of reaching Queenstown.

Travelling in September, in the New Zealand spring when snow and avalanche danger prevails in the mountains, Homer climbed for days to reach Harris Saddle. He struggled through deep snowdrifts, often sinking to his waist, until the ground gave way beneath him and he fell into a deep ice cave, well over his head. He managed to climb out, but retreated downhill and

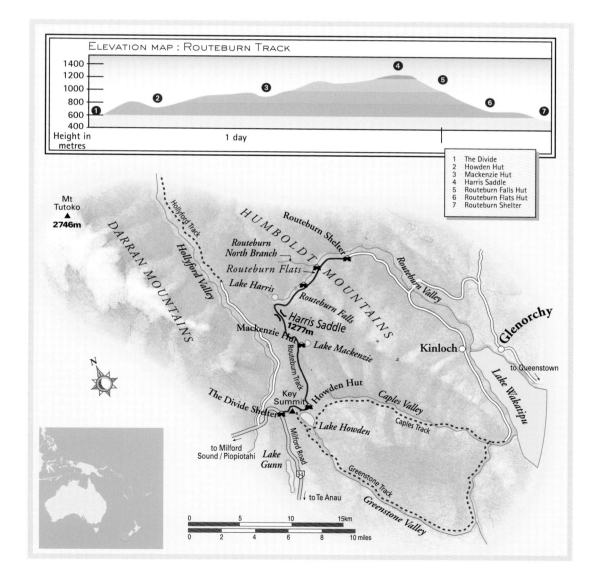

ELEVATION MAP: ROUTEBURN TRACK

Height in metres

1 day

1 The Divide
2 Howden Hut
3 Mackenzie Hut
4 Harris Saddle
5 Routeburn Falls Hut
6 Routeburn Flats Hut
7 Routeburn Shelter

Mt Tutoko
2746m

DARRAN MOUNTAINS

Hollyford Track
Hollyford Valley

Routeburn North Branch
Routeburn Flats
Lake Harris

HUMBOLDT MOUNTAINS

Routeburn Shelter

Routeburn Valley

Routeburn Falls

Harris Saddle
1277m

Mackenzie Hut

Routeburn Track

Lake Mackenzie

Kinloch

Glenorchy

to Queenstown

Lake Wakatipu

The Divide Shelter

Key Summit

Howden Hut

Caples Valley

Caples Track

to Milford Sound / Piopiotahi

Lake Gunn

Milford Road

Lake Howden

to Te Anau

Greenstone Track

Greenstone Valley

N

0   5   10   15km
0  2  4  6  8  10 miles

eventually found a way around the Hollyford headwaters, into the neighbouring Greenstone Valley, and thence to Queenstown. On arrival he was described as a 'moving bundle of rags, scratches and bruises'.

All attempts to establish roads and settlements were thereafter abandoned, thus the old Routeburn pounamu trail still traverses a remote mountain wilderness, one that is appreciated today by thousands of walkers from more modified environments. The names of landscape features here reflect the historic associations of both early Maori and British explorers. Ironically Homer Tunnel, a vehicle route that allows easy passage through a massive mountain wall on the Milford Highway, is William Homer's legacy.

### THE TRACK

From its eastern end there is a gentle start to the Routeburn Track. A well-formed, gently graded trail wends its way along the Routeburn valley floor, through beech forest where dappled light filters through the trees and friendly native birds, fantails and bush robins, will likely follow walkers' footsteps in search of insects. Footbridges cross side creeks that, in heavy rain, can be spectacular torrents. For a time the track sidles above the Routeburn Gorge, a spectacular jumble of giant boulders and deep, hidden chasms.

About one and a half hours from the start the track emerges from the bush onto the wide, open expanse of the Routeburn Flats. Towering mountain walls enclose the grassy flats, providing a hint of the alpine grandeur that lies ahead.

The Routeburn Flats hut and camp site nestle by the bush edge, where the peculiar 'honking' sound of paradise shelducks can be heard echoing across the flats. From the flats, the track starts climbing into true alpine terrain. The first hour is a steep pitch through beech forest, crossing a renovated section of the track that was obliterated by a massive slip in 1994. The higher portion of the track here is also within reach of avalanches, which is why this route should be avoided in winter and early spring.

Routeburn Falls Hut, at 1000m (3300ft) sits above the bush line on an imposing bluff overlooking Routeburn Flats, 500m (1600ft) below. Behind the hut, the Routeburn River itself cascades over a series of rock ledges before plunging to the valley floor. A little further uphill is the private, guided walkers' Routeburn Flats Lodge.

ABOVE Dracophyllum *sp, one of the profusion of shrubby plants that grow in subalpine areas, between the forest and mountain tops.*

Above the forest line now, the way ahead continues over rocky terrain, climbing among low-growing subalpine herbs and shrubs, snow tussocks and speargrass. Speargrass, with its stunning summertime flower, is yet the bane of hikers who absentmindedly touch its vicious, spear-like leaves. Above bush line there are different birds. Tiny rockwrens shelter among the rocks and tussocks, New Zealand falcon may soar above and kea, New Zealand's mountain parrot, is bound to make its cheeky presence known.

### SPECTACULAR BUT EXPOSED

The final climb to Harris Saddle at 1277m (4190ft) is spectacular but exposed. On a clear day the climb is straightforward, with mountain views expanding as altitude is gained. However, rain, cloud and wind can quickly combine to make this a dangerous adventure, requiring appropriate clothing and careful navigation.

At Harris Saddle, weather permitting, magnificent views of the sheer diorite (igneous rock similar to granite, but with less quartz) faces of the Darran Mountains are revealed across the forest-filled expanse of the Hollyford Valley. The 2746m (9009ft) Mount Tutoko is the highest mountain in the Fiordland's 1.2 million hectares (3 million acres), and the glacial-gouged Hollyford one of the longest rivers.

Closer at hand, in the swampy basin by the saddle, is a delightful profusion of plants, such as sundews, orchids, daisies, bog pines and bladderworts, which flourish in the boggy conditions. After the steady climb to the saddle, a small daytime shelter provides welcome respite for walkers, particularly in the event of inclement weather. On the other hand, if the weather is clear and the body willing, a magnificent, albeit steep, option for a side trip is the 250m (800ft) climb from the Saddle to Conical Hill. The views, even greater from this vantage point, extend all the way to the South Island's west coast.

## FLORAL DISPLAY

From here on, the Routeburn Track is just about all downhill. From the Saddle the trail descends steeply at first, then winds on a more gradual grade, still above bush line, along the exposed Hollyford Face. Again, great weather is synonymous with great views in this subalpine terrain. However, in summer, if mist and cloud conspire to hide the mountains there are other visual delights to enjoy beside the track itself, such as the flowering ourisias, gentians, daisies and the showy *Ranunculus lyalli*, commonly misnamed the Mount Cook lily.

The track descends a series of zigzags into the relative shelter of Mackenzie Basin, where in calm conditions the dark blue waters of Lake Mackenzie shimmer magnificent reflections of surrounding mountain peaks. Lake Mackenzie Hut, nestles at the forest edge beside the lake. The private Lake Mackenzie Lodge sits in a clearing just beyond the lake, while a park camp site is located in a clearing a few minutes further on.

From the stark and wild beauty of the uplands, the track continues now in a more sheltered environment, sidling along

**ABOVE** *Lake Mackenzie is one of two glacier-gouged lakes on the Routeburn Track. Lake Mackenzie Hut is splendidly appointed, right beside the lake edge, a refreshing spot for an end-of-day swim.*

the bush margin through a mix of mountain beech trees and snow tussock and passing small mountain tarns, or lakes. Soon after passing a small clearing dotted with distinctive-looking ribbonwood trees, the track cuts hard against near-vertical bluffs beneath the Earland Falls. These 80m (260ft) high falls are a highlight of the track, particularly after heavy rain.

## MUST-DO SIDE TRIP

As the track continues to descend it enters dense forest, silver beech trees dominate with a profusion of smaller trees and shrubs, ferns, lichens and mosses beneath. The mountain views are all but hidden until the track emerges in a clearing by Howden Hut, nestled beside the lake of the same name. A beautiful spot, but beware the hungry sandflies! From this point the final hour of walking offers yet more

scenic contrast. The well-graded track meanders through a great variety of forest. Growth is prolific in the heavy rainfall of 500mm per annum (20 in per annum).

A must-do side trip, just 15 minutes from Howden Hut, is the 30-minute climb to Key Summit. Once more (weather permitting), the mountains are revealed in all their splendour and, closer at hand, boardwalks lead walkers around delightful small tarns and over fragile, swampy areas matted with alpine herbs, mosses and bog plants.

The Routeburn Track ends beside the Milford Highway at The Divide, which is the lowest east-west crossing of the South Island's Southern Alps. From here transport connections can be made to Te Anau township, the Hollyford Valley (another major tramping route which starts just a few kilometres along the road) or to the scenic wonders of Milford Sound.

# ROUND THE MOUNTAINS

*By Kathy Ombler*

The volcanic landscape of New Zealand's Tongariro National Park, dominated by three magnificent volcanic mountains, is the fourth national park ever created and the first to be granted dual World Heritage Status for its outstanding natural and cultural values.

The Round the Mountains trek travels over and around these mountains, passing through stark and variable volcanic landscapes, deserts, beech forests, alpine herb fields, lakes and glacier-carved river valleys. The entire trek takes about seven to nine days, but there are several access points that allow for shorter trips.

Tongariro, Ngauruhoe and Ruapehu stand at the southern end of what is known as the Pacific Rim of Fire, a vast zone of volcanic and earthquake activity that results from tectonic movement of the great Pacific crustal plate. Mount Ruapehu, the highest of the three at 2797m (9177ft), dominates the surrounding countryside and is the only North Island mountain with glaciers. Indeed, glacial ice completely surrounds the mountain's volatile, steaming Crater Lake, one of the few such phenomena in the world.

## ACTIVE VOLCANO

Ruapehu is an extremely active volcano. As recently as 1996, massive showers of ash, rock and steam were blasted hundreds of metres from the Crater Lake and lahars (rivers of volcanic mud, water and debris) streamed down the mountain slopes. A modern, sophisticated monitoring system has been installed to provide early warning of an eruption, or lahar.

The 1968m (6459ft) Mount Tongariro may be lower than Ruapehu, but in both physical and spiritual terms it is the most significant mountain. In fact, its huge massif extends over 18km (11 miles) in length and encompasses numerous craters, steaming fumaroles, geothermal springs and volcanic vents, one of which is the higher, classical cone-shaped Ngauruhoe.

**ABOVE** *Mt Ngauruhoe, one of three mountain peaks gifted to the Crown by Ngati Tuwharetoa people that led to the creation of Tongariro National Park.*

The Tongariro mountains are of deep spiritual significance to Ngati Tuwharetoa, the Maori people who have lived in the region for around 1000 years. The mountains represent their ancestors and are sacred areas to be treated with respect.

Traditional stories describe the origins of volcanism in the park. When the ancestors of Ngati Tuwharetoa migrated to New Zealand in the canoe, *Te Arawa*, the navigator was the high priest Ngatoroitangi. After going ashore, he led his people inland, looking for a place to live. They settled by the great lake of Taupo, and Ngatoroitangi continued south to 'claim' the summit of Tongariro. As he crossed the barren desert, he spied a second priest travelling towards the mountain so he called for help from his gods, who sent a savage storm to vanquish his rival. Later, as Ngatoroitangi neared the icy summit, he became frozen in a snowstorm and prayed to his sisters in Hawaiiki, his traditional Polynesian homeland, for warmth. The name Tongariro, referring to the cold south wind, comes from this prayer. Ngatoroitangi's sisters blasted a fiery response, sending fire via an underground passage – the Pacific Rim of Fire – which erupted from a new crater we know today as Mt Ngauruhoe.

As the years passed, the spiritual significance of the volcanoes increased. To climb them was forbidden, travellers crossing the desert flanking Tongariro's eastern slopes used leaves as blinkers to prevent them from looking at the sacred summit. Early European explorers' attempts to climb the mountains were thwarted by local Maori, unless they made their journeys in secret.

In the 1880s, European immigration increased and the European system of land law was introduced throughout New Zealand, changing the very basis of traditional Maori tribal ownership.

In 1887, to prevent the sale of the sacred mountains, Ngatoroitangi's descendent Te Heuheu Tukino IV (Horonuku), made an historic decision and gave the three summits to the Crown, to preserve them forever as scared places. Thus they became the core of Tongariro National Park.

## THE TREK

From Whakapapa Village, the main entrance to the national park, the Tongariro Northern Circuit heads north, through a mix of open tussock fields and small stands of beech forest, across the lower, northern slopes of Mt Ruapehu. The classic cone of Mt Nguaruhoe looms ahead, alongside the lower, yet greater

ELEVATION MAP: TONGARIRO CROSSING

Height in metres

1 day (17 km)

| | |
|---|---|
| 1 | Mangatepopo Car Park |
| 2 | Mangatepopo Hut |
| 3 | Soda Springs |
| 4 | South Crater |
| 5 | Red Crater |
| 6 | Emerald Lakes |
| 7 | Central Crater |
| 8 | Blue Lake |
| 9 | Ketetahi Hut |
| 10 | Ketetahi Car Park |

mass of Tongariro. Heavily eroded in places, the track crosses many stream beds. The trail skirts around Pukekaikiore, one of the older vents of the Tongariro volcanic complex, and enters Mangatepopo Valley, close to Mangatepopo Hut.

From here the track turns into the valley, following the route of the popular, but challenging walk, the Tongariro Crossing, climbing gradually over a succession of lava flows that poured from Ngauruhoe during eruptions in 1949 and 1954.

A ten-minute detour at the head of the valley leads to the Soda Springs, which emerge from beneath an old lava flow and provide a fertile little oasis that fills with summer-flowering yellow buttercups and foxgloves, in this volcanic landscape.

The hardest climbing of the trek starts from here, as the rocky track zigzags its way high onto a saddle between Mounts Tongariro and Ngauruhoe.

A challenging side trip from the saddle, should one have energy to spare at this point, is to climb the cone-shaped summit of Ngauruhoe. This is not a poled route and is particularly steep and slippery underfoot. The route heads directly to the crater rim from the saddle, following a rocky ridge to the left of a scree slope. The summit area should be avoided if there are signs of increased volcanic activity (poisonous gases can be emitted) and do take care not to fall over the edge of the crater rim! Sliding down the loose scoria makes a quick descent but again, take care, it's very steep and a long way to a doctor.

Back on the saddle, the trek continues across the flat, dusty South Crater before

climbing again to the trek's highest point, the 1800m (5900ft) Red Crater. The going is steep, but the view more than compensates. Here is volcanic landscape at its finest: the stark blacks, reds and browns of lava rock contrasting strongly with the brilliant green and blue waters of Emerald and

A poled route is one above the forest line that's marked by poles placed in the ground at regular intervals. They are generally thin poles around 1.5m (5ft) high and mark the route so that people can find their way in bad visibility, for instance during whiteouts, snow and stormy weather. They are high enough to remain visible when snow covers the ground. There are also poles marking much of the Routeburn Track.

Blue Lakes, old explosion craters and, beside them, the massive trench in the earth that is Red Crater.

The brilliant colour of the lakes, named Ngarotopounamu (greenstone-hued lakes) by the Maori, are caused by minerals leaching from the adjoining thermal area. These lakes freeze in winter, thus hiding their brilliant hues.

If the weather is clear – and it needs to be to tackle this high, exposed section of the trek – the view extends eastwards, beyond volcanic landscape to the forest-covered Kaimanawa Ranges, part of the North Island's mountainous divide.

## SIDE TRIPS

Side trips from Red Crater include a walk to the summit of Tongariro (two hours return) or a walk down the northern side of Tongariro to Ketetahi Hut (two hours one way). From the hut you can see the steam coming off Ketetahi Springs a few ridges away. They are in a private enclave belonging to the Ngati Tuwharetoa people.

Back on the main trek, the trail to Oturere Hut branches southeast from beside Emerald Lakes, and descends through fields of jagged lava into Oturere Valley. Plant life here has been constantly repressed by volcanic eruptions, altitude and climate. Loose gravel also means that recolonization by plants is a slow process.

Some respite from open, rocky terrain comes as the trail descends to a lower level and enters the beech forests of Waihohonu Valley. Here there is a park hut, plus a restored historic hut that was built in 1903 for horse and coach passengers who once passed this way. At this point the park's 'Northern Circuit' trail turns west, to climb the low saddle between Mounts Ngauruhoe and Ruapehu.

The trek continues straight ahead across the Rangipo Desert, vast plains of wind-sculpted sands and volcanic rock flanking the eastern foothills of Ruapehu. Here, in the only true desert landscape of New Zealand, the altitude and harsh climate have combined to prevent the regrowth of forests devastated by volcanic eruption.

As it traverses the desert the trail passes Ohinepango Springs, which bubble up from beneath an old lava flow. The trail crosses the Tukino Mountain Road (a rarely used four wheel drive track) and the Whangaehu River to reach Rangipo Hut near the southern end of the desert.

From here the trek continues to Mangae-huehu Hut, traversing the southern slopes of Mt Ruapehu now, undulating through beech forest, tussock and steep river gorges. A feature of this section of the trek is the Waihianoa Gorge, which cuts a deep swathe right down the mountain side.

From Mangaehuehu Hut a gradual downhill traverse weaves through more open tussock country and beech forest. About three hours from Mangaehuehu, the track passes the highest falls in the park, Waitonga Falls, that tumble over the edge of an old lava flow. The trail then crosses Rotokawa, an alpine wetland where a boardwalk protects fragile wetland plants from hiker's boots. On a clear day, you can see Ruapehu's snowy peaks.

## LAVA AND LAHARS

The trail briefly joins the sealed Ohakune Mountain Road, which gives access to one of Tongariro's commercial ski fields. It then descends into a steep valley, crosses a lava ridge covered with alpine herbs and drops into the Mangaturuturu Valley beside the Cascades. This mountain stream tumbling over a spectacular rock fall has a creamy colour due to the silica deposits on the rocks. The trail follows this stream to Man-gaturuturu Hut nestling on the bush edge.

From Mangaturuturu Hut, the trail crosses the river of the same name, where the path of a lahar in 1975 is evident by the deeply scoured river bank and lack of veg-etation. A wooden staircase, built to protect fragile plants from hikers' boots, leads out of the valley and onto the final pitch of the Round the Mountain trek.

The final day's walk passes by an ensem-ble of lakes, steep gorges and waterfalls, beech forest, subalpine tussock and shrubs and wetlands, filled with summer flowering herbs. In good weather the views are expan-sive; Ruapehu's peaks loom above, while in the distant west the classic volcanic cone of Mt Taranaki (Egmont Volcano) stands above and beyond the forest-covered wilderness of Whanganui National Park.

From Whakapapaiti Hut there are two options to end the trek. The first is a higher level track that climbs above bushline to reach the Bruce Road (to the park's north-ern ski field) 4km (2.5 miles) above Whakapapa Village. The second is the lower forest track that heads directly to the village. The Whakapapa Village has a park, visitor centre, campsite, motel, cafés and the grand, historic hotel, Chateau Ton-gariro. There are also several short walks, with information signs that tell about the natural and historic features of the park.

RIGHT *Leaching minerals cause brilliant colourings in the Emerald Lakes, high up on Mt Tongariro.*

OPPOSITE *Celmisia incana, one of many hardy flowering plants and herbs that cover the subalpine regions of the park.*

# Āoraki to Arthur's Pass

*By Shaun Barnett*

A 600km (370-mile) long spine of glaciated mountains divides New Zealand's South Island down its entire length. Although not high by world standards, the peaks of the Southern Alps (or *Ka Tiritiri o te Moana* in Maori) nonetheless rise dramatically close to the ocean, reaching, at Āoraki/Mt Cook, a height of more than 3800m (12,500ft) within 30km (18 miles) of the coastline. Glaciers cover much of the region, including the famed Franz Josef and Fox Glaciers – both of which fall through temperate rainforest and nearly reach the sea.

To the west of the Alps lie gorged valleys and dense rainforests, as wet as anywhere on the planet. To the east are windswept dry grasslands and broad, braided rivers. In these varied habitats live many plants and animals unique to New Zealand, including the world's only alpine parrot, the inquisitive kea, and the showy Mount Cook lily – the world's largest buttercup.

Two national parks form the boundaries of the central Southern Alps: Āoraki/Mt Cook National Park in the south and Arthur's Pass National Park in the north. While both are popular and accessible locations for climbers and hikers, the country lying between remains remote, seldom visited, and with extensive opportunities for challenging transalpine hikes. Depending on the route taken and the weather encountered, trekkers will need to be prepared for glacier travel, river crossings, and bush navigation.

Travel on the western side of the Alps is slower, wetter and more difficult, but here lie some of the more spectacular landscapes, including the Bracken Snowfield, and the Garden of Eden and Allah ice plateaus. Hiking in the east often proves faster, but moraine and riverbed travel here can be monotonous, and several of the major rivers, the Rangitata, Godley and Rakaia in particular, may be difficult to cross. A fast party will need a minimum of ten days to tackle the eastern route, but two to three weeks is more likely, and if you intend to spend time on

ABOVE *The Godley Valley, one of several large braided rivers east of the Southern Alps.*

the western side of the alps, you should allow up to four weeks. All but the fastest trekkers will need to arrange a helicopter to fly in two or three strategically located food dumps.

## FIRST CLIMBERS

As early as the 1930s climbers began tackling long traverses in the central Southern Alps. Two of the first, GCT Burns and Max Townsend, crossed eight passes and ascended more than 7800m (25,590ft) between Arthur's Pass and Āoraki/Mt Cook in just 13 days during December 1934. More recently, in 1989 Michael Abbot completed an astonishing bold solo traverse of the entire 1600km (990-mile) South Island in 130 days, not only the Southern Alps.

## CHOICE OF ROUTE

These days an Āoraki to Arthur's Pass trek is attempted only once or twice a year. Most parties begin in the north at Arthur's Pass where the easier travel and fewer glaciers allows a gentler introduction to the trek. However, travelling in the opposite direction, beginning in the south at Āoraki/Mount Cook, has considerable merits. By tackling the bigger, more glaciated country earlier in the summer season, you are less likely to encounter problems with snowmelt swelling rivers and opening up crevasses.

The route described here begins in the south, and involves a mix of travel in both the west and east. The traverse begins at Mount Cook Village, where the immense pyramid of New Zealand's highest mountain, Mt Cook (Āoraki), the 3754m (12,317ft) 'sky piercer', dominates the view. From the village hikers face two options, both involving travel over glaciers. Most choose the Tasman Glacier, at 29km (18 miles) New Zealand's longest, while some opt for the Murchison Glacier, the second longest. While the Tasman offers more travel on white ice and less on gritty moraine, trekkers will eventually have to cross into the head of the Murchison regardless. Both routes start from the milky-white Tasman Glacier terminal lake, coloured by glacier-ground rock. Either way, both valleys are surrounded by some of New Zealand's highest mountains, and make a sublime – if daunting – introduction to the trip. From

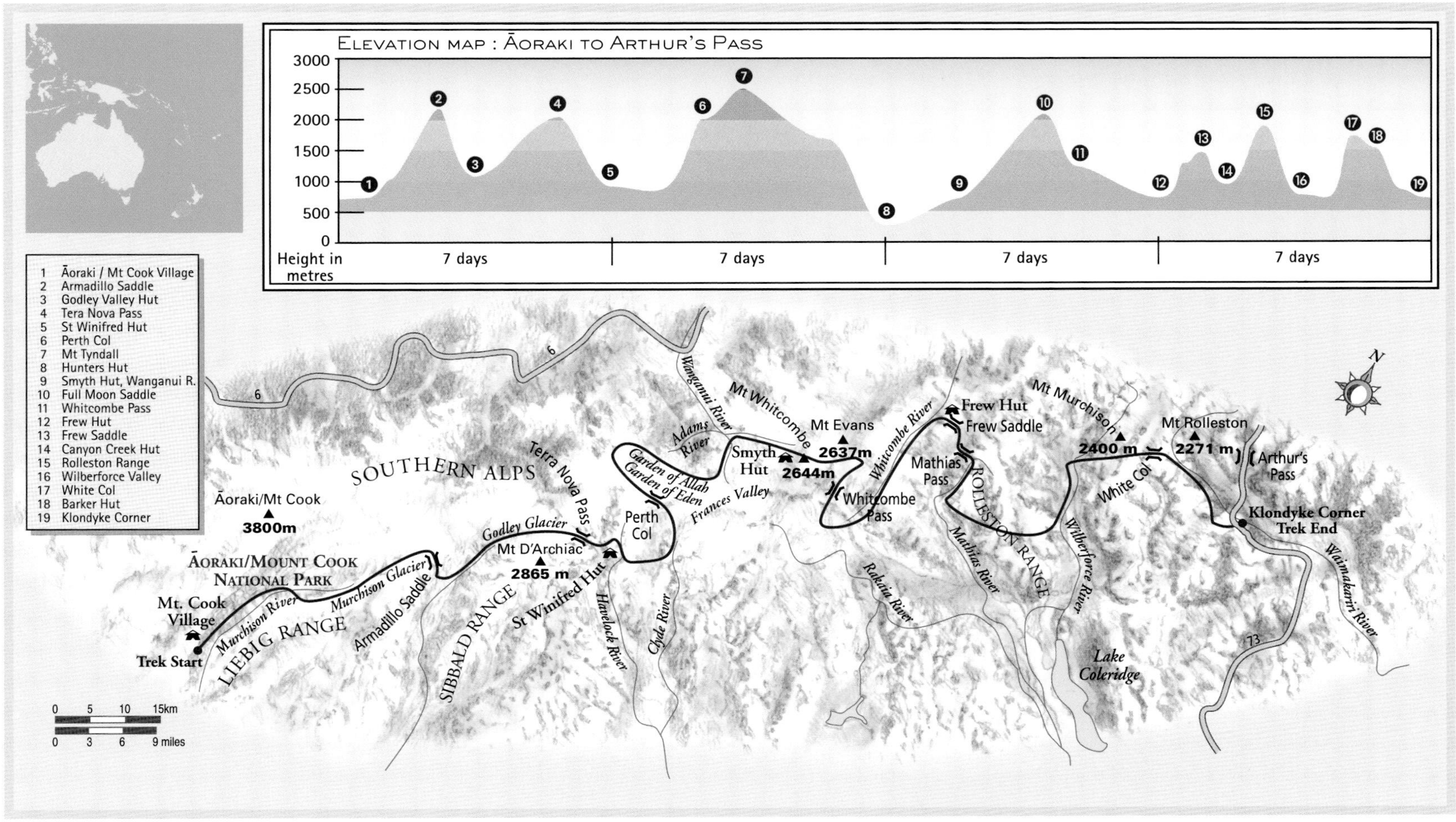

this angle Āoraki/Mt Cook appears like a giant parallelogram, with two prominent, massive glaciated faces.

While Āoraki impresses with sheer size, nearby Mount Tasman (New Zealand's second highest), exhibits more grace. Some have likened its two curved ice shoulders to a bird poised for flight.

Two or three days' trekking, some of it hard work under full packs while negotiating tottering piles of moraine, lead to the head of the Murchison Glacier. From the white ice of the upper Murchison, several routes lead into the Godley valley. While traditionally Classen Saddle has been the most popular, this route is now often cut off by bergschrunds. A better, though less direct, option is Armadillo Saddle. Both will require good climbing and navigation skills, and in the wrong conditions may prove impassable.

On a good day from Armadillo Saddle you'll have views of the attractive Godley

**ABOVE** *Sidling around obstacles, like this bank beside the flooded Murchison River, can be difficult with a heavy pack.*

### BRAIDED RIVERS

Braided rivers are peculiar to Alaska, Argentina and New Zealand. They occur where a river emerges from mountains to enter extensive flat plains, or a wide valley. Instead of flowing in one channel, the river splits and disperses into multiple channels (called braids) which rejoin, split then rejoin in succession. Almost all rivers on the eastern side of the central Southern Alps display this characteristic.

Valley, its silvery braids merging and splitting in endless variation to create striking patterns on the broad valley floor. Once across the river, progress is easy up-valley to the basic but comfortable Godley Hut.

The next stage of the trip involves crossing Terra Nova Pass, lying at the head of the Godley on the northern boundary of Āoraki/Mt Cook National Park. Getting there, however, may well be the hardest part of the trip, and parties are advised to wait for good weather in the shelter of Godley Hut.

The best option for negotiating the meltwater lake at the terminus of the Godley Glacier, a lake which has rapidly grown in recent years as the glacier recedes, is to

sidle around the true right (the left-hand side facing upstream), but this requires fording the Godley River. Rain or snowmelt quickly make the Godley River uncrossable, and beside Godley Hut its strength is concentrated into just one formidable flow rather than dispersed over several braids.

A second option involves sidling around the true left of the lake, but due to rock-fall and steep bluffs, this can prove very dangerous. Alternatively a high route over nearby tops is possible, but will require dexterous navigation and good visibility.

Terra Nova Pass leads from the head of the Godley Glacier, under the imposing helmet of Mt D'Archiac, eventually into the Havelock branch of the Rangitata River. Both the Havelock, and the other nearby branch of Rangitata River known as the Clyde, are liberally laced with small but welcoming huts. One of these, St Winifred, makes an excellent site for your first food dump. By now about a week of trekking will have elapsed.

The Havelock and especially the Clyde are very large rivers, and can only be crossed during periods of low-medium flow. Hikers should know river-crossing techniques, and never attempt fording alone or when the water level is high. During the early days of high country farming, drowning in such rivers was so common that for a while it was known as 'the New Zealand death.'

Loose rock is another danger. By now hikers will be well familiar with the easily shattered greywacke and schist that make up so much of the Southern Alps. Collision between the Pacific and Indo-Australian continental plates has uplifted New Zealand's relatively young mountains over the past five million years, raising them a total of 18,000m (59,000ft) – over twice the height of Everest. However, a wetter climate results in much greater rates of erosion than in the Himalaya, hence the more modest stature of the Southern Alps.

## GARDEN OF EDEN

From the headwaters of the Clyde, it is possible to traverse the Garden of Eden and Allah, large glistening ice plateaus straddling the western side of the Alps. They offer transalpine hiking par excellence, and are likely to be the highlight of your trip. Easiest access onto the Gardens is over a glaciated pass called Perth Col, lying at the head of the Frances valley, one of the Clyde's major tributaries. Travel is reasonably straightforward, although you'll need to rope up for glacier travel. It's a world of snow, ice and silence, with stupendous views back to Āoraki/Mt Cook and north to the lesser known, but equally inspiring, peaks of Whitcombe and Evans.

Difficulties multiply, however, when exiting the plateau into the Wanganui valley. The trail along the Adams River requires very tough bush bashing, while the adjacent Lambert Glacier and gorge are impassable. The best option is instead to take unmarked routes that sidle around Mount Lambert onto Lambert Spur between the two valleys. From Lambert Spur a sparsely marked trail leads down in the Wanganui Valley. Here a marked route of sorts exists upriver past Hunter Hut, but this is tough going, and parties choosing this route will be thankful to reach Smyth Hut (and its natural hot pools) near the valley head. By now another week will have passed, and Smyth is a good place for your second food dump.

From the headwaters of Wanganui you'll cross the Bracken Snowfield, a striking area of glaciers beneath the precipitous Mt Evans, then down to Whitcombe Pass. Like other passes in the Southern Alps, Maori once used Whitcombe Pass in search of pounamu, or greenstone – a type of jade used for weapons and ornaments. Nowadays, the tracks and huts of the Whitcombe Valley provide a useful way to

**ABOVE** *Climbers descend into Winifred's Stream across glaciated country near Terra Nova Pass.*

make progress directly northward. These huts, many of them built in the 1950s and 60s, provide shelter from the often unpredictable and stormy New Zealand weather. Rainfall on the West Coast is among the highest in the world, and one year a tributary of the Whitcombe recorded a staggering annual rainfall of 16.6m (54ft).

From the Whitcombe it takes two to three days to reach Frew Hut; with Arthur's Pass now just a week away. Valley hopping from Frew Hut over Frew Saddle leads to the Hokitika River. From here you cross Mathias Pass (the last of four routes by which you've crossed the main divide of the Southern Alps) to get to the Mathias River.

Crossing the Rolleston Range to the Wilberforce River, the not-so-distant mountains of Arthur's Pass draw ever closer. The upper reaches of the Wilberforce River offer several choices for reaching the boundary of Arthur's Pass National Park, among them Whitehorn Pass or White Col. Both lead into tributaries of the Waimakariri River, one of the major valleys of Arthur's Pass. Carrington Hut, at the junction of the White and Waimakariri Rivers is a large hut where you are likely to meet other hikers enjoying the national park. From there it is half a day out to the Arthur's Pass Highway and the trip's conclusion at Klondyke Corner.

Your legs will be weary. You'll have walked some 250km (155 miles) and crossed more than ten passes through demanding terrain. Yet you'll have had the satisfaction of woven a rarely used route through mountains that even few New Zealanders know exist.

# EUROPE

## UNITED KINGDOM

### PEMBROKESHIRE COAST WALK

**LOCATION** West Wales coast, UK

**START** St Dogmael's, Cardigan

**FINISH** Amroth Sands, near Saundersfoot.

**WHEN TO GO** Year round – the climate is mild, though often wet and windy in winter. Accommodation must be booked in busy holiday seasons

**DURATION** 10–14 days; ± 300km (186 miles)

**MAX. ALTITUDE** 175m (574ft)

**TECHNICAL CONSIDERATIONS** None

**TREKKING STYLE** The path is well way-marked, meaning that navigation is never really a problem. And plentiful accommodation allows for a flexible approach to daily distances

**MAPS** The whole route is covered by two 1:25 000 maps: Explorer OL 35 North Pembrokeshire; and Explorer OL 36 South Pembrokeshire, published by the Ordnance Survey. They are easily available from all local information centres and book shops or from www.ordnancesurvey.co.uk

**PERMITS/RESTRICTIONS** None

**DANGERS** Some sections pass close to cliff edges, so care should be taken, particularly on windy or stormy days

**INFORMATION** Pembrokeshire Coast National Park Visitor Centre, The Grove, St David's, Haverfordwest, Pembrokeshire, SA62 6NW Tel: (01437) 720392 http://stdavids.pembrokeshirecoast.org.uk

### SCOTLAND COAST TO COAST

**LOCATION** Central Highlands of Scotland

**WHEN TO GO** May or June. April and early May may have snow on ridges above 800m (2700ft). July and August are warmer but wetter and the biting midges can be troublesome. Deer stalking interrupts access from mid-August

**START** Acharacle 56° 44' N 5° 47' W: train from Glasgow to Fort William, then bus.

**FINISH** St Cyrus, near Montrose 56°46' N 2° 24' W: train and coach to Glasgow and Edinburgh

**DURATION** 11–14 days: 340km (211 miles); 15,500m (51,000ft) of ascent

**MAX ALTITUDE** Ben Nevis 1343m (4406ft); low-level routes remain below 750m (2461ft)

**TECHNICAL CONSIDERATIONS** Ability to select a route from the map and then follow it is essential. Ridges above 700m (2300ft) provide good going. At low levels paths or tracks should be followed. Very few paths are waymarked. Scrambling on Nevis, Alder, Lochnagar is not technical, but can be avoided in bad conditions

**TREKKING STYLE** Self-sufficient backpacking, with up to three days between resupply points at villages

**MAPS** Ordnance Survey 1:50 000 Landranger sheets 40, 41, 42, 43, 36, 44, 45

**PERMITS/RESTRICTIONS** Responsible access to all open country, including wild camping, is a legal right in Scotland

**INFORMATION** (www.access-scotland.com) www.visithighlands.com, +44 1506 83 2121 www.travelinescotland.com for transport www.yell.com, 'grocers' for food shops. Scottish Youth Hostels Association www.syha.org.uk; Central Bookings tel: ++44 1786 891400 and independent hostels (www.hostel-scotland.co.uk). Bothies

are basic unwardened huts with no facilities, see www.mountainbothies.org.uk Details of the Great Outdoor Challenge, and valuable accommodation listing, www.tgochallenge.co.uk

## FRANCE

### AIGUILLES ROUGES

**LOCATION** Near Chamonix, French Alps

**WHEN TO GO** Mid-July to mid-September

**START** Le Buet at 1350m (4429ft)

**FINISH** Le Buet at 1350m (4429ft)

**DURATION** 4–5days; 57km (35.5 miles)

**MAX ALTITUDE** Mont Buet 3096m (10,157ft)

**TECHNICAL CONSIDERATIONS** In good conditions none other than the short section of cables on the ascent of Mont Buet. However, fresh snowfall or *névé* remaining from the winter could make parts of this trek very difficult

**TREKKING STYLE** The Aiguilles Rouges is a natural reserve and thus protected. Camping is only tolerated from sunset until sunrise and far from the huts

**HEALTH AND SAFETY** Nothing unusual

**PERMITS AND RESTRICTIONS** None

**MAPS** IGN Top 25 GPS compatible series: 3630 OT Chamonix; 3530 ET Samoëns

**GUIDEBOOKS** *Trekking and Climbing in the Western Alps* by Hilary Sharp, pb New Holland

## FRANCE/ITALY/SWITZERLAND

### CHAMONIX–ZERMATT HAUTE ROUTE

**LOCATION** The trek is in the Pennine Alps, situated in the northern Alpine massif bordering France, Switzerland and Italy

**WHEN TO GO** July/August or early September. Before that time there is likely to be fresh, unconsolidated snow, which makes for difficult walking and can be dangerous. Later in September the weather is less likely to be stable. The huts close from about mid-September

**Start** Le Tour 1450m (4756ft)

**Finish** Zermatt 1600m (5248ft)

**Duration** 8 days;  80 km (50 miles) It has been assumed that any transport is taken as in the description and the length is measured excluding these sections. Purists need to add on another 28.5km (17.8 miles) to walk the whole distance

**Max Altitude** The Pigne d'Arolla – 3796m (12,451ft)

**Technical considerations** This trek takes place almost entirely on glaciers, so a good working knowledge of glacier travel is required, as is awareness of weather and snow conditions. It is essential to consult a detailed guide book as well as the map

**Trekking Style** There are plenty of huts along the route so it seems pointless to camp. Huts provide food and bedding and sell minimal hill food. Reservations are recommended

**Glaciers** The most visible effect of global warming from year to year is the recession of the end of the glaciers (the snout). Less apparent is the reduction in depth and volume. The hot summer of 2003 exposed labyrinths of enormous crevasses (the Plateau du Trient and the Col de Chermontane) in areas considered by many to be mostly benign. Routes over the glaciers are bound to change from year to year, even month to month. Early season will give better snow cover, mak-

ing quicker, more direct routes possible. Later in the more detours are necessary to circumnavigate areas of crevasses, making days longer

**Health and safety** Nothing unusual

**Permits and restrictions** None

**Maps** Carte Nationale de la Suisse 1:50 000 5003 Mont Blanc Grand Combin; 5006 Matterhorn Mischabel

**Guidebooks** *The Haute Route Chamonix Zermatt* by Peter Cliff pb Cordee

# France

## Provence: GR4 via Verdon Gorge

**Location** Provence, south of France

**When to go** Spring or autumn are best

**Start** Grasse 333m (1093ft)

**Finish** Moustiers Ste Marie 631m (2070ft)

**Duration** 9–10 days; 139km (86-miles)

**Max altitude** Col de Vauplane 1650m (5413ft)

**Technical considerations** None except that the Verdon Gorge should be avoided in unstable weather. Storms are especially dangerous in the gorge. For the rest of the route, the trail is waymarked with red and white paint flashes, but nevertheless some concentration and map reading is required, especially around villages and in forests where the route may have been changed slightly

**Trekking style** This trek is best done using accommodation rather than camping. Part of the joy of Provence is the food and culture and this is best experienced in the small village accommodation

**Health and safety** Nothing unusual

**Permits and restrictions** None

**Maps** IGN Top 25 GPS compatible series: 3643 ET Cannes Grasse; 3642 ET Vallée de l'Esteron and Loup; 3543 ET Haute Siagne; 3542 ET haute Esteron; 3542 OT Castellane; 3442 OT Gorges du Verdon

**Guidebooks** *Walking the French Gorges* by Alan Castle pb Cicerone Press; *Walks in Provence* by Robyn Marsack pb Robertson McCarta

# France

## Corsica GR20

**Location** Corsica is a French island off the French Mediterranean coast

**When to go** June to October are best, but early season there is the possibility of snow remaining in shady spots and later in the season storms, fires and a lack of water can be a problem

**Start** Calenzana 275m (902ft)

**Finish** Conca 252m (827ft)

**Duration** 12–20 days – 180km (112.5 miles) – for the complete trek. It can be divided at Vizzavona, the northern part taking 8–9 days and the southern 6–7. Extra days allow for the ascent of summits along the way, but time is easily lost due to bad weather or the need to leave the route to buy additional food

**Max Altitude** Brèche de Capitello 2225m (7298ft)

**Technical considerations** The terrain requires a good head for heights and there is some easy scrambling. The trail is waymarked throughout with red and white paint flashes

**Trekking Style** There is no guarantee of supplies of food, although the last few years more and more hut wardens have been setting up small shops. There is

always a water source at huts, although these can run low late in the season. All huts have toilet facilities and a cold shower. Basic food supplies can be bought at *bergeries*, and at several places en route, notably Haut Asco, Castel di Vergio, Vizzavona, Capanelle and Col de Verde

**HEALTH AND SAFETY** Nothing unusual

**PERMITS AND RESTRICTIONS** None

**MAPS** IGN Top 25 GPS compatible series: 4149 OT Calvi; 4250 OT Corte Monte Cinto; 4251 OT Monte d'Oro Monte Rotondo; 4252 OT Monte Renoso; 4253 OT Petreto-Bicchisano Zicavo; 4253 ET Aiguilles de Bavella Solenzara

**GUIDEBOOKS** *GR20 Corsica* by Paddy Dillon, pb Cicerone Press

## FRANCE AND SPAIN

### PYRENEAN HAUTE ROUTE

**LOCATION** The Pyrenees massif located in southwest France, forming the border with Spain

**WHEN TO GO** July, August and the first half of September are the best times

**START** Lac de Bious d'Artigues 1425m (4641ft)

**FINISH** Gavarnie 1525m (5002ft)

**DURATION** 10 days; 100km (62 miles). Those who walk from Torla to the Ordesa parking should add on another 7km (4.37 miles)

**MAX ALTITUDE** Petit Vignemale 3032m (9945ft); Monte Perdido 3355m (11,004ft) is an option

**TECHNICAL CONSIDERATIONS** This a non-glaciated trek but some sections of trail are exposed and care and judgement must be used in bad weather. Monte Perdido can only be climbed without crampons and ice axe when it's clear of snow late in the season. Snow or ice on

any of the summits or trails would make them very serious undertakings

**TREKKING STYLE** There are wardened refuges throughout, but camping is an option. If you do choose to wild-camp, outside official camp sites, discretion is essential, and no trace should be left of your visit. In the National Parks you are not allowed to camp within one hour of the roads or below 2000m (6560ft). Around the huts there are sometimes designated sites

**NOTE** Many of the Pyrenean huts are owned by the French Alpine Club (CAF) and are being systematically restored. During restoration the huts are closed for a couple of years, so check before setting out that the huts you plan to use are open

**HEALTH AND SAFETY** Nothing unusual

**PERMITS AND RESTRICTIONS** None

**MAPS** Institut Cartografic de Catalunya/ Rando Editions Carte de Randonées Pyrénées Gavarnie Ordesa 1:50 000

**GUIDEBOOKS** *Walks and Climbs in the Pyrenees* by Kev Reynolds pb Cicerone Press

## SPAIN

### PICOS DE EUROPA

**LOCATION** Parque Nacional Picos de Europa, Cordillera Cantabrica, northern Spain

**WHEN TO GO** June or September. July and August are hotter, more crowded, and afternoon thunderstorms are more frequent. Snow from October to May (can persist into June)

**START** Arenas de Cabrales 43° 18' N 4° 51' W; bus link to Llanes for trains and long-distance coaches from Santander, Bilbao

**FINISH** Covadonga 43° 17' N 5° 02' W; bus links to Arriondas for coach and train

**DURATION** 7 days (105km/65 miles; ascent 9800m/33,000ft)

**MAX ALTITUDE** Collada Bonita (2382m; 7815ft); Torre de Los Horcados Rojos (2506m; 8220ft)

**TECHNICAL CONSIDERATIONS** A tough trek involving scrambling, some difficult route-finding and continuous ascents/descents of 1200m (4000ft)

**TREKKING STYLE** Hut-to-hut walking and easy scrambling

**MAPS** 1:25 000 Picos de Europa sheets Central, and Occidental; 1:80 000 Picos de Europa for Day 1 and general orientation; all by Adrados Ediciones

**GUIDEBOOK** *Walks and Climbs in the Picos de Europa* by Robin Walker, pb Cicerone Press

**PERMITS/RESTRICTIONS** No permit required. Lightweight camping/bivvying is accepted around huts and above 1600m (5250ft); there are camp sites at Caín and Lagos de Enol. Otherwise no camping within the national park

**INFORMATION** www.picoseuropa.net (huts under 'refugios')
www.liebanaypicosdeeuropa.com
Tourist Information Potes ++34 942 730787 (for huts) Panes ++34 985 414008 http://turismo.cabrales.org
www.alsa.es (coastal coaches)

### THE WAY OF ST JAMES

**LOCATION** From the foot of the Pyrenees, in Navarra, to Santiago through northern Spain

**WHEN TO GO** Summer (July – August) is very crowded. The route is feasible from March to October, but the higher parts are covered in snow in winter and accommodation becomes scarce. The Camino is especially busy during a Holy Year, when the 25th July (St James' Day) falls on a Sunday

**Start** Roncesvalles, Spanish Pyrenées

**Finish** Santiago, capital of Galicia

**Duration** A month on foot or horseback, or two weeks by bicycle; 750km (465 miles)

**Max altitude** Cruz de Hierro, Galicia, 1504m (4934ft)

**Technical considerations** The route is generally easy, provided sensible distances are covered each day. The area is hot and dry in high summer so carry plenty of water and try to find shade to rest in. Set out early to reach the day's destination before it gets too hot. After a siesta, enjoy a bit of culture and a meal before nightfall

**Trekking style** Backpacking, but with ready access to pilgrim refuges and other accommodation. Camping is possible. Most pilgrims walk, but a large number cycle, at variance to the walking route, and a few ride on horseback

**Permit/restrictions** No permit is required, but walkers wishing to use the pilgrim refuges should obtain a *credencial* at Roncesvalles and ensure it is stamped daily to prove you are genuinely covering the distance. A fully stamped *credencial* is needed at Santiago to claim the *compostela* certificate

**Information** Websites: www.csj.org.uk (Confraternity of St. James) www.xacobeo.es (official Camino website).

**Guidebooks** *The Way of St James* by Alison Raju pb Cicerone Press. *A Practical Guide for Pilgrims – The Road to Santiago* by Millán Bravo Lozano, Editorial Everest. The world's oldest guidebook, the 12th century *Codex Calixtinus*, described the Way of St James in thirteen unequal stages

## SWITZERLAND

### TOUR OF THE MATTERHORN

**Location** Circumnavigates the Matterhorn summit, which straddles the Swiss-Italian frontier towards its western end

**When to go** Mid-July to mid-September. Late snow can remain on shady slopes until well into the summer season. This can be difficult to negotiate, especially early in the morning when it's frozen

**Start** Zermatt 1620m (5315ft)

**Finish** Zermatt 1620m (5315ft)

**Duration** 8–12 days; 123km (76 miles) if all transport options described are taken. Purists can add 30km (19miles)

**Max altitude** Testa Grigia at 3479m (11,414ft) or Théodule Pass at 3301m (10,830ft), or the Breithorn at 4164m (13,661ft) if included

**Technical considerations** The trek crosses two glaciers; it is essential to be equipped for, and to know the techniques of, glacier travel. The trails are generally waymarked, but in bad weather map reading would be required

**Trekking Style** This is a hut-to-hut trek, so minimum gear is carried. Camping is permitted near the huts, but you must request permission from the hut guardian. In the villages there are plenty of hotels

**Health and safety** Nothing unusual

**Permits and restrictions** None

**Maps** Landeskarte der Schweiz 1:50 000 No. 5006 Matterhorn Mischabel, and the Istituto Géografico Centrale 1:50 000 No. 5 Cervino – Matterhorn e Monte Rosa

**Guidebook** *Tour of the Matterhorn* by Hilary Sharp pb Cicerone Press

## ITALY

### THE DOLOMITES – ALTA VIA 2

**Location** The Dolomites, at the eastern end of the Alps, just south of the Austro-Italian border

**When to go** July to early September. Any earlier and there is likely to be considerable snow remaining on the high passes, any later the refuges may be closed and fresh snow may fall at low altitudes

**Start** Bressanone (Brixen) 550m (1804ft)

**Finish** Passo di San Pellegrino 1919m (6294ft)

**Duration** 6–8 days; 67km (42 miles), plus 6km (3.75 miles) if you walk instead of taking the Plose cable car

**Max altitude** Forcella della Marmolada 2910m (9545ft), Sass de Putia 2875m (9430ft), Piz Boé 3152m (10 339ft) or Forcella Pordoi 2829m (9279ft), depending on whether any summits are included and which route is taken past the Marmolada

**Technical Considerations** Care should be taken on the via ferrata – this is not a walk for those who don't like exposure. The terrain is non-glaciated, except for the optional Marmolada crossing, and scrambling is moderate in difficulty. There are some long, steep ascents and descents. The crossing of the Marmolada (optional) usually requires ice axe, crampons and a rope, and knowledge of glacier travel

**Trekking style** This is a hut-to-hut trek, so minimum gear is carried. Basic picnic supplies are available at the huts and at the road passes

**Health and safety** Nothing unusual

**Permits and restrictions** None

**Maps** Tabacco 1:50 000 sheet 9 Bressanone/

Brixen Val di Fundres/Pfunders Val di Funes/Villnöss; sheet 2 Val di Fassa – Alta Badia Val Gardena/Gröden

**GUIDEBOOKS** *Treks in the Dolomites Alta Via 1 and 2* by Martin Collins and Gill Price, pb Cicerone Press

## SLOVENIA

### THE JULIAN ALPS – TRIGLAV

**LOCATION** Julian Alps, Slovenia

**WHEN TO GO** June–September; snow may be a problem higher up in June and (less so) in September. The main huts are open throughout July–September, and tend to be crowded mid-July to mid-September

**START** Bohinjska Bistrica 46° 16′ N 13° 57′ E; train from Klagenfurt in Austria, or direct coach from Ljubljana

**FINISH** Rateče 46° 30′ N 13° 40′ E; bus to Jesenice, from where you can take a train

**DURATION** 10 days; approx 140km (87 miles); 12,000m (39,000ft) of ascent

**MAX ALTITUDE** Triglav 2864m (9396ft)

**TECHNICAL CONSIDERATIONS** One exposed, chain-assisted scramble to Triglav (could be omitted), undemanding scrambling at many points, and more serious scrambling options to harder peaks alongside

**TREKKING STYLE** Hut-to-hut on well-maintained, waymarked paths; scrambling trips from huts

**MAPS** Geoclub 1:50 000 Triglavský Národní Park for overview; Planinska zveza Slovenije 1:25 000 for Triglav. Most easily obtained locally – these distinguish normal/moderate/difficult paths.

**GUIDEBOOKS** *Mountaineering in Slovenia* by Tine Mihelič pb Sidarta; *The Julian Alps of Slovenia* by Justi Carey and Roy Clark pb Cicerone

**PERMITS/RESTRICTIONS** No permits needed. Camping at designated sites only. National Park rules include staying on the waymarked trails

**INFORMATION** Rail www.oebb.at
Slovenian Tourist Board ++386 1 306 4575
www.slovenia.info
www.bohinj.si ++386 4 574 7590
www.kranjska-gora.si ++386 4 588 17 68
Huts: www.pzs.si
Triglav National Park www.gov.si/tnp

## POLAND/SLOVAKIA

### THE HIGH TATRAS

**LOCATION** White Tatras (Belianske Tatry) and High Tatras, in Poland and Slovakia

**WHEN TO GO** Mid-June to early October. Paths in Slovakia are closed until 15 June. Huts are crowded in July and August

**START** Zdiar, Slovakia 49° 16′ N 20° 16′ E; bus from Zakopane (Poland) or Poprad (Slovakia), each reachable by inexpensive sleeper train from Prague

**FINISH** Kuźnice near Zakopane, Poland 49° 16′ N 19° 58′ E; bus to Zakopane and then Krakow for trains, airport

**DURATION** 6 days 80km (50 miles); 7200m (23,622ft) of ascent. Alternatively omit Orla Perć, but continue to Polana Chochołowska: 7 days 110km (68 miles); 9000m (29,528ft) of ascent

**MAX ALTITUDE** Rysy 2502m (8209ft)

**TECHNICAL CONSIDERATIONS** The route described includes exposed scrambling protected by fixed chains; the alternative route is on good paths

**TREKKING STYLE** Hut-to-hut, on well-maintained, waymarked paths with side trips to peaks from huts, other peaks crossed on the route

**MAPS** Vojenský Kartografický ústav (Slovak) 1:25 000 sheet 2 (Vysoké Tatry) for the main range, plus sheet 3 if including the Western Tatras; with 1:50 000 sheet 113 (also Vysoké Tatry) for approaches

**GUIDEBOOK** *The High Tatras* by Colin Saunders and Renáta Nárožná pb Cicerone Press

**PERMITS/RESTRICTIONS** No permits required. No camping in the national park, whose rules (either side of the border) include staying on the marked trails. Only members of recognized climbing clubs may leave the waymarked path network. With both countries now in the EU, border crossings, now Rysy summit only, should eventually be unrestricted

**INFORMATION** trains www.polrail.com
www.tanap.sk (Slovak side)
www.zakopane.pl ++48 18 20122-11 (Polish side, including hut phone numbers listed as 'hostels')
Polish mountain guide centre Zakopane ++48 18 20637-99

## SWEDEN

### KUNGSLEDEN

**LOCATION** The Kungsleden runs through the mountains of Lapland in northern Sweden, straddling the Arctic Circle

**WHEN TO GO** The lodges are open and the ferries operate from around 20 June to 20 September, after which the ferries and rowing boats are removed from the lakes before they freeze. The lodges are also open from early March to early May when you can ski along the route

**START/FINISH** The Kungsleden starts at Hemavan in the south and finishes at

Abisko in the north. Hemavan can be reached by bus from Umeå, itself accessible by train or plane from Stockholm. Abisko is on the railway from Stockholm

**DURATION** 2–4 weeks; 450km (279 miles)

**MAX ALTITUDE** 1150m (3773 ft), Tjäktja Pass

**TECHNICAL CONSIDERATIONS** The path is way-marked and clear with no technical difficulties. However, it is long and in remote country and good fitness is required

**TREKKING STYLE** Hut-to-hut walking between Hemavan and Ammarnäs and Kvikkjokk and Abisko. Backpacking for the 180km (112 miles) between Ammarnas and Kvikkjokk

**STF ACCOMMODATION** Along the route there are 16 self-service STF lodges. These are wardened and provide bedding, heating and cooking equipment. Ten of them sell food supplies. The STF also has hostels in Hemavan and Ammarnäs and large, luxurious fjällstations at Kvikkjokk, Saltoluokta, Kebnekaise and Abisko

**PERMITS/RESTRICTIONS** None

**MAPS** Fjällkarten 1:100 000 BD6, BD8, BD10, BD14, BD16, AC2

**INFORMATION** Svenska Turistföreningen, www.stfturist.se

Swedish Tourism, www.visit-sweden.com

**GUIDEBOOKS** *The Laponian Area: A Swedish World Heritage Site* by Claes Grundsten pb Swedish Environmental Protection Agency

# GREECE

## NORTH PINDOS

**LOCATION** The northwest corner of mainland Greece, near the border with Albania. Access International flights to Preveza airport (about 2.5 hours' drive from Vitsa

village); or fly to Corfu and transfer to Igoumenitsa by ferry. Buses connect Preveza and Igoumenitsa with Ioannina, the area capital, which also has a local airport. There are regular bus services from here to Zagoria villages

**WHEN TO GO** May-October. (May and June are best for wildflowers). The alpine areas are snowbound in winter

**START** Vitsa or Monodendri (adjacent villages), North Pindos mountains

**FINISH** Tsepelovo, North Pindos

**DURATION** 5-6 days; 60km (37 miles)

**MAX ALTITUDE** Gamila 1, one of Greece's highest peaks (2497m; 8192ft); or Astraka Col/Refuge (1950m; 6397ft), if the ascent of Gamila is not included in the route

**TECHNICAL CONSIDERATIONS** Some difficulties may be encountered on the alpine section, around Gamila, early in the season (May and early June); this would be impassable without skis or snowshoes in winter. Although the Pindos mountains are close to the Albanian border, this does not affect visitors in any way except that accurate (military) maps are not available

**TREKKING STYLE** Backpacking on a way-marked trail, with the option of ascending two peaks. Paths are marked with red paint flashes indicating the O3 national trail for most of the route, with blue and yellow markings in the final stages. You need to be fairly fit, and enjoy walking in wild surroundings. Route-finding is usually straightforward. There are plenty of climbs and descents, but paths follow the most sensible lines so even gaining height is fun. Guesthouses in isolated villages and the mountain hut on Astraka col

provide comfortable accommodation and excellent food. Guided and self-guided walks with luggage transfer also available

**MAPS** Maps from the Hellenic Alpine Club (from Korfes mountaineering journal), with contour intervals at 200m (655ft), have been adapted from the 1:50 000 military series, sheets 55-60

**PERMITS/RESTRICTIONS** None

**INFORMATION** Ioannina EOT (tourist office), Napoleonda; Zerva 2, Ioannina; National Tourist Office of Greece, 4 Conduit St., London W1R ODJ; Adventure Center, 1311 63rd St, Suite 200, Emeryville, CA 94608; tel: +1-510-6541879, fax: 6544200 Websites: www.sherpaexpeditions.com www.adventure-center.com/Explore

# NORTH AMERICA

## CANADA/USA

### THE CONTINENTAL DIVIDE TRAIL

**LOCATION** The length of the Continental Divide from Canada to Mexico through the states of Montana, Idaho, Wyoming, Colorado and New Mexico

**WHEN TO GO** North-south: late June to November. South-north: late April to October. Hiking the CDT over two or more seasons is easier than a through-hike: mid-July to mid-September is the best time for the mountains, spring or autumn for the low, hotter areas (Great Divide Basin and most of New Mexico)

**START/FINISH** South: Antelope Wells or Columbus on the USA/Mexico border in New Mexico. North: Glacier National Park (Montana)/Waterton Lakes National Park (Alberta) border

**Duration** 4–6 months

**Max Altitude** 4081m (13,391ft). Parry Peak, Front Range, Colorado

**Technical considerations** This is a trail for experienced backpackers with good navigation skills as there are many sections where the route isn't waymarked. Some very steep and rough sections. Some dry sections where water must be carried. Resupply points are far apart; food for a week or more will often have to be carried. The weather is hot and dry in the deserts; warm in the mountains with afternoon thunderstorms common. There is snow in autumn, winter and spring

**Trekking Style** Backpacking. Camping essential

**Permits/Restrictions** Permits are needed for Glacier, Yellowstone and Rocky Mountain national parks. Contact the CDTS or CDTA (see below) for up-to-date information

**Dangers** Bears occur all along the Divide. They are not usually a problem. Black bears are found in most places, the larger grizzlies in Glacier and Yellowstone national parks and adjacent wilderness areas. Up-to-date information on any potential bear problems should be obtained from rangers. Knowledge of bears and the precautions to take are needed. A good book on this is Dave Smith's *Backcountry Bear Basics* pb The Mountaineers, 1997. Encounters with bears are unlikely, however. You'll be lucky to even see one. Much bigger threats are the usual rugged wilderness hazards of hypothermia, lightning, falling off a cliff, stream fords, getting lost and injury in a remote area

**Information** Continental Divide Trail Society, 3704 N. Charles St. (#601), Baltimore MD 21218, USA. www.cdtsociety.org, email: mail@cdtsociety.org

Continental Divide Trail Alliance, PO Box 628, Pine, CO 80470, USA. www.cdtrail.org; email: info@cdtrail.org

**Guidebooks** *Guide to the Continental Divide Trail* (Volumes 1-7) by Jim Wolf pb CDTS; *CDT Long Distance Planning Guide* pb CDTA

## USA

### The Highline Trail

**Location** Wind River Range (Rockies), northwest Wyoming, USA

**When to go** End-July to mid-September. Expect snow in early season

**Start** Big Sandy trailhead, lodge and campground (2775m; 9100ft), reached by dirt road from US191 near Pinedale

**Finish** Green River Lakes trailhead and campground in the north (2430m; 7970ft), reached by dirt road from US 191 near Pinedale. Hitchhiking to and from trailheads is normally easy, and a bus runs daily through Pinedale along US191

**Duration** Min 8–10 days. 108km (67 miles)

**Max Altitude** Texas Pass (3475m; 11,400ft)

**Technical considerations** Trails are mostly good, but occasionally rough. Only experienced backpackers should attempt a trek of this length, remoteness and altitude. Snow may be encountered on the high passes at any time and may prove problematic in places until mid-August. Several fords are required

**Trekking style** Backpacking, mostly above timber line, in spectacular high-altitude alpine country. Camping is required

throughout. Backpacking at over 3050m (10,000ft) requires fitness and determination; the Winds are remote mountains with no short escape routes. You will acclimatize as you go, but plan for short days and allow time for rest days and side trips

**Permits/Restrictions** Apart from the Shoshone and Arapaho Wind River Indian Reservation on the east side of the Winds, the entire range has wilderness designation. Access to the trek described here is unrestricted. No permits are required. In areas designated Special Management Units (e.g. Big Sandy Lake, Titcomb Basin), camp sites must be 60m (200ft) from lakes and designated trails, and open fires are prohibited. Inquire at the address below

**Dangers** Black bears can be a problem at trailhead camp sites and precautions should be taken everywhere, especially in forest; cook and store food away from the tent. Streams may contain *giardia*. All drinking water should be boiled, filtered or treated with iodine

**Maps** Northern Wind River Range, Southern Wind River Range, 1:48 000 pb Earthwalk Press

**Information** District Ranger, Pinedale Ranger District, PO Box 220, Pinedale, Wyoming 82941; tel +1-307-367-4326).

**Websites** www.pinedaleonline.com www.fs.fed.us/btnf

### Sawtooth

**Location** The Rocky Mountains, south-central Idaho, USA.

**When to go** End July to mid-September, although snow may be encountered on the north side of passes until mid-August.

**Start** Tin Cup Hiker trailhead (2135m; 7000ft) on Pettit Lake, 29km (18 miles) south of Stanley

**Finish** Iron Creek trailhead and campground (2040m; 6700ft), 9km (5.5 miles) west of Stanley. For a small fee, commercial whitewater rafting companies in Stanley will drive your car from starting trailhead to finishing trailhead

**Duration** 8–10 days (82km; 51 miles)

**Max altitude** The Cramer Divide (2900m; 9514ft)

**Technical considerations** Excellent trail throughout, but a trek of this length and wildness should be attempted only by experienced backpackers. Snow obliterates high elevations of the trail in early season. The fording of several rivers is necessary

**Trekking style** Backpacking, often above timber line, with views unhampered by forest cover. Well-maintained trails and signposts. Camping necessary throughout. If there is a need to curtail the trek for any reason, many side trails provide easy escape routes

**Permits/Restrictions** None. Do make use of voluntary self-registration facilities at trailheads, as hiker counts influence trail budgets. Inquire at SNRA Visitor Center (address below) about restrictions on camp sites and open fires (e.g. at Sawtooth Lake)

**Dangers** There are small numbers of black bears, which have been known to annoy campers at trailhead campgrounds, but seldom venture into the high country. Nevertheless, it is wise to cook and store food away from the tent. Streams may contain *giardia*. All drinking water should be boiled, filtered or treated with iodine

**Maps** Sawtooth Wilderness, Idaho, 1:48 000 pb Earthwalk Press

**Information** Stanley Ranger Station, Star Route, (5km/3 miles south of) Stanley, Idaho 83278; tel: +1-208-774-3681. SNRA Visitor Center, Star Route, (13km/8 miles north of) Ketchum, Idaho 83340; tel: +1-208-726-7672)

Stanley Chamber of Commerce, Box 59, Stanley, Idaho 83278; tel: +1-208-774-3411)

**Websites** www.stanleycc.org www.fs.fed.us/r4/sawtooth

## Grand Canyon

**Location** Northwest Arizona, 126km (78 miles) north of Flagstaff

**When to go** April to May (June is usually too hot for safe hiking); and October to November. South Rim trailheads and Grand Canyon Village open all year; North Rim trailheads from mid-May to mid-October. The road to the North Rim, Highway 67, remains open until closed by snowfall in November or early December. Facilities close in mid-October

**Start/Finish** The route can be walked in either direction. Start at South Rim, Grand Canyon Village, with shuttle bus to South Kaibab trailhead. Finish at trailhead for North Kaibab Trail, North Rim, then shuttle to Grand Canyon Lodge or exit transportation

**Duration** 3–4 days; 35km (22 miles)

**Max altitude:** 2400m (8000ft) at North Rim

**Technical considerations** Both winter and summer weather can make trekking in the Grand Canyon impossible or dangerous. Snow and ice at the highest points on the 'rims' is common well into spring.

Blistering heat from late spring onwards in the canyon makes sunburn and dehydration likely. Drink plenty of water even if you are not thirsty and replenish your electrolytes, especially salt. Footpaths are generally wide and flat, but often with precipitous drop-offs. All refuse must be carried out

**Trekking style** Backpacking

**Permits/Restrictions:** The National Park Service regulates access to the canyon's trails to prevent crowding, but this makes reservations difficult. Backcountry permits ($10, plus $5/person/night) are required for all overnight treks into the canyon. Permits can be reserved up to four months in advance by contacting: Backcountry Information Center, PO Box 129, Grand Canyon, AZ 86023, tel 928-638-7875, www.nps.gov/grca

## Appalachian trail

**Location** USA; eleven east coast states (Georgia, North Carolina, Tennessee, Virginia, West Virginia, Maryland, Pennsylvania, New Jersey, New York, Connecticut, Massachusetts, Vermont, New Hampshire, Maine)

**When to go** Spring through autumn: southern states March through November; northern states April through mid-October. Nearly year-round trekking is common in southern lowlands. Best hiking is August through colourful autumn, especially in New York and New England

**Start/Finish** Through-hikers generally start in Georgia and walk north to Maine. Many people make the trek in sections over a number of years

**Duration** 4–6 months for a continuous through-hike. Discrete sections (one of the national parks, for example) make a fine two- to three-week expedition

**Max altitude** Clingman's Dome, North Carolina (2024m; 6642ft)

**Technical considerations** Winter conditions can close sections of the trail in early spring or mid-autumn. The entire AT is blazed white, with a simple vertical bar painted on trees and rocks. Side trails are blazed blue, orange, red, etc. Lean-tos generally provide outhouses and spring water (purification is still strongly advised), but backcountry AT hikers should come prepared to camp well off the trail and without amenities

**Trekking style** Backpacking

**Permits/Restrictions** No permits are required for the trail. Within Great Smoky Mountains National Park, lean-tos are reserved for through-hikers. Trekkers on shorter trips should carry a tent

**Information:** www.internationalat.org/SIAIAT/ The organization is called Sentier International des Appalaches in French. For further information contact Jean-François Boily, in Montreal, 514-873-9899, www.sepaq.com email: boily.jeanfrancois@sepaq.com

## Evolution Loop

**Location** High Sierra Nevada Mountains, central California, USA

**When to go** July to October, with snow on high passes until early August, and sometimes all summer at Muir Pass

**Start** South Lake trailhead (2975m; 9755ft), 34km (21 miles) southwest along

Highway 168 from Bishop, on US395

**Finish** North Lake trailhead (2870m; 9415ft), 32km (20 miles) southwest along Highway 168 from Bishop. Inquire locally about shuttle services between trailheads

**Duration** Min 8–10 days (85km; 53 miles)

**Max Altitude** Muir Pass (3660m; 11,995ft)

**Technical considerations** A trek of this length, remoteness and altitude should be attempted only by experienced backpackers. Several river fords are required. Camping necessary throughout

**Trekking style** Backpacking, often above timber line in high-altitude alpine country. Once onto the west side of the Sierra crest the country is remote, with no short escape routes. Owing to the altitudes reached, and the height differential between high and low points, the trek requires fitness and determination. You will acclimatize as you go, but plan for short days and allow time for rest days. In an emergency there are backcountry ranger stations, manned in summer, in Le Conte Canyon and Evolution Valley

**Permits/Restrictions** Permits are required for overnight backcountry travel and should be booked well in advance from the Backcountry Office (address below). In some locations there are restrictions on open fires and camping near water sources (e.g. Dusy Basin, Evolution Basin). Inquire at the Backcountry Office before setting out

**Dangers** Black bears are numerous in the High Sierra, especially in popular areas where they are used to humans. At forest camp sites especially, cook and store food away from the tent. Streams may contain

*giardia.* All drinking water should be boiled, filtered or treated with iodine

**Maps** USGS (United States Geological Survey) 1:63 360, John Muir Wilderness – National Parks Backcountry. One map covers the central section of the JMT, one covers north and south sections. Both are required

**Information** Backcountry Office, White Mountain Ranger District, 798 N. Main St, Bishop, CA 93514; tel: +1-619-873-4207)

**Websites** www.bishopvisitor.com www.r5.fs.fed.us/inyo

## John Muir Trail

**Location** Sierra Nevada, California USA

**When to go** Much of this trek takes place above 2700m (8858ft) and the winters are very snowy. This snow can linger until well into the summer so mid-summer is the best time – mid-July to the end of August. The resupply lodges close in mid to late September

**Start** Yosemite Valley Happy Isles 1230m (4035ft)

**Finish** Whitney Portal, near Lone Pine 2548m (8360ft)

**Duration** 3 weeks; 345km (214 miles)

**Max Altitude** Mount Whitney 4418m (14,496ft)

**Technical considerations** None in normal summer conditions

**Trekking style** Backpacking with a few lodges and camp sites with wardens in the first part

**Permits/Restrictions** Permits are required for the whole trek. If starting in Yosemite these are available from Yosemite National Park, must be reserved well in advance, and cost US$5 in 2004

**Dangers** Bears are present throughout the region of the JMT. Food must be stored in bear-proof canisters, available for hire from Yosemite National Park, or hung from a tree at least 4m (12ft) above the ground and 3m (10ft) out from the trunk. *Giardia lamblia*, which causes Giardiasis (Beaver Fever), and *Cryptosporidia* are present in water sources in the region so all drinking water must be boiled or filtered and sterilized with iodine. In certain areas forest fires are not permitted above a certain altitude. A stove is necessary for cooking

**Maps** The best available are the 13 maps contained within the John Muir Trail Map Pack: Tom Harrison's Maps

**Guidebooks** *Guide to the John Muir Trail* by Thomas Winnett and Kathy Morey pb Wilderness Press; *The John Muir Trail* by Alan Castle pb Cicerone Press

### Alaska on foot

**Location** Kenai Peninsula, Chugach National Forest in southern Alaska

**When to go** May through to October. The best time to complete this trek is during the last week in August and the first week in September. At this time, there will be few mosquitoes and the first autumn colours will touch the forest

**Start** Resurrection Pass northern trailhead, near the town of Hope, Kenai Peninsula. There is no public transport to Hope

**Finish** Exit Glacier, near Seward, southern Kenai Peninsula. Daily bus and train services from Anchorage to Seward during the summer season

**Duration** 5 to 7 days, 72 miles (115km)

**Max Altitude** Resurrection Pass 792m (2600ft)

**Technical Considerations** Moderate grade; moderate fitness required. No climbing or scrambling

**Trekking style** Backpacking. Good unmarked trail, except for the Resurrection River Trail (final 16 miles of the trek) that is often overgrown with possible difficult river crossings. Several huts en route run by the US Forest Service. Camping is possible at numerous maintained wild sites near the huts and at points between

**Dangers** Backpacking in Alaska is no different to backpacking in other areas of the world, except for the greater isolation of most of the treks, mosquitoes (very bad between June and August), and some large wildlife unused to humans, i.e. bears and moose

**Permits/Restrictions** No permits needed for the area. No restrictions on wild camping in the Chugach National Forest

**Maps** U.S.G.S maps 1:63 360 series, two sheets cover the northern half of the trek, SEWARD (D-8) QUAD & SEWARD (C-8) QUAD. The southern half of the trek is covered by Trails Illustrated Topo map, Sheet 231; Kenai Fjords National Park, approx 1:100 000 scale;
The whole area and surroundings can be seen in The Alaskan Atlas and Gazetter. 1:300 000 by Delorne Mapping

**Guide books** *Hiking in Alaska* pb Lonely Planet; *Alaska's Parklands* by Nancy Simmerman

**Information** Website for all things Alaskan: www.alaskan.com
Alaska Division of Tourism,

PO Box 110801, Juneau, AK 99811 Mountaineering Club of Alaska, PO Box 102037, Anchorage, AK 99510. Email: mca@alaska.net Alaska Public Lands Information Centre, 605 West 4th Avenue, Anchorage, Alaska 99501. This office handles all the information for Alaska's network of national parks

# South America

## Peru

### Inca Trail

**Location** Machu Picchu Historical Sanctuary, Cuzco, Peru

**When to go** May to September is the dry season. Closed February. UNESCO applying pressure for closure from January through March

**Start/Finish** The Classic Trail has 3 starting points: Km77, Km82 and Km88. Km77 and Km82 can be reached by road or train from Cuzco, Km88 only by train. (Only the 'Backpacker' train stops at these places).
• Nearly all Inca Trail groups drive to trailhead at Km77 or 82. Finish trek at Machu Picchu. 6km (4-mile) bus ride to Aguas Calientes for 4-hour train ride to Cuzco.
• The Salkantay Inca Trail starts at Cruzpata, near Mollepata (4hr drive from Cuzco towards Abancay), finishing at Machu Picchu.
• The Km104 Trail starts at the Km104 railway stop 8km (5 miles) before Aguas Calientes (only 'Backpacker' train stops at Km104), finishing at Machu Picchu

**Duration** • The Classic Inca Trail takes 3–4 days: 45km (28 miles) from Km77 and 40km (25 miles) from Km82 or 36km (22 miles) from Km88. • Salkantay Inca Trail

takes 6 days. • The Urubamba Valley Trail via Km104 takes 2 days. • The Km104 Trail takes 6–7 hours

MAX ALTITUDE Abra Warmiwañusca (4200m; 13,780ft)

TECHNICAL CONSIDERATIONS A few days' acclimatization around Cuzco (3360m; 11,000ft) is essential. Limit of 500 people/ day on trail. Must book through approved agency. For high season, book at least a month in advance! Many agencies organize fixed departure groups (cheaper), or you may prefer private group (more expensive). Whichever, you must be accompanied by official guide. • Weighing station at Km82 checks porters are not exceeding 20kg load. • Leave litter in pits provided at designated camp sites. • Use latrines provided at all designated camp sites, or bury ablutory waste well away from trail or water

TREKKING STYLE Backpacking along a well-defined trail with designated camp sites. May no longer trek independently

PERMITS/RESTRICTIONS May only hike in one direction. Park fees: Classic Inca Trail, Salkantay Trail or Urubamba Valley Trail, $55. Km104 Trail, $25. Second-day re-entry to Machu Picchu, $20. Access to all trails, except Machu Picchu, limited to organized groups

MAPS Editorial Lima produce a 1:50 000 map of the trail available from map websites or in Peru

INFORMATION South American Explorers Club, Avenida Republica de Portugal (off Alfonso Ugarte, 2 blocks from Plaza Bolognesi), Breña, Lima (Casilla 3714, Lima 100); or US office: 126 Indian Creek Road, Ithaca, NY 14850

## HUAYHUASH CIRCUIT

LOCATION The Andes of northern Peru. Nearest towns are Chiquián and Cajatambo

WHEN TO GO May–September, dry season

START/FINISH Llamac; several daily buses from Lima to Chiquián (8hrs) and Huaraz to Chiquián (3hrs). From Chiquián, daily morning and afternoon minibus to Llamac. Note that transport for Llamac can be hired in Huaraz or Chiquián. An alternative starting point is Pocpa

DURATION 11–13 days; 190km (118 miles). Longer if side valleys are explored. Alternative half-circuit (7–9 days) from Llamac to Cajatambo or vice versa

MAX ALTITUDE Punta Cuyoc (4950m; 16,240ft). Average altitude is well above 4000m (13,124ft)

TECHNICAL CONSIDERATIONS Steady acclimatization before starting trek is essential. For security and health reasons, the trek should not be attempted alone

TREKKING STYLE Backpacking or expedition. Recommended to hire donkeys at Llamac to transport gear. (It is the trekker's responsibility to feed the donkey driver during trek). No designated camp sites but good wild camping spots abound. No huts

PERMITS/RESTRICTIONS The Huayhuash has no protected status and no permit is required, but 4 communities – Llamac, Queropalca (Mitucocha/Carhuacocha), Tupac Amaru (Huayhuash/Viconga) and Huayllapa (Guanacpatay/ Sarapococha/ Punta Tapush) – each levy a per-person access fee totalling approximately $15 for the whole circuit. The Huayhuash may soon gain national reserve status

## ALPAMAYO

LOCATION North end of Cordillera Blanca. Nearest town Caraz, nearest city Huaraz

WHEN TO GO June to September is the dry season; sunny days and cold nights

START/FINISH Huaraz (3090m; 10,138ft) is start and acclimatization point for treks into the Cordillera Blanca. Has dozens of hotels and agencies and several equipment-hire shops. Daily buses from Lima (7½hrs). • Starting point at northwestern end of trail is Hualcayán (4hrs from Huaraz). Hire transport or take public transport, changing at Caraz (2200m; 7218ft). • Starting point at southern end of trail is Vaqueria (4hrs from Huaraz). Hire transport or take public transport, changing at Yungay (2500m; 8202ft)

DURATION About 10 days; 140km (90 miles). Recommended 2-day trek extension from Vaqueria via Portachuelo de Llanganuco to Quebrada Llanganuco. Transport to Huaraz available above Cebollapampa camp

MAX ALTITUDE Paso de los Cedros (4850m; 15,913ft).

TECHNICAL CONSIDERATIONS Can be trekked in either direction. Scenically preferable to start at northwest and trek east and south, but trekkers need very good acclimatization due to rapid altitude gain and the need to camp very high on the first two nights. Also, no escape route between passes 1 and 2. For acclimatization, trekking in the other direction is better. Possible escape route from Quebrada Jancapampa: 4hr walk east along valley to road head at Pomabamba town. Daily buses to Huaraz (about 9hrs). Weather conditions in the mountains can change rapidly so carry suitable clothing to cover all eventualities. Weather usually wetter to east of watershed. Plenty of stream water, but sterilize with iodine

**TREKKING STYLE** Backpacking or expedition. No huts or designated camp sites except in Huaripampa valley. Mainly wild camping in remote and beautiful valleys

**PERMITS/RESTRICTIONS** Trek (most of) is in Huascarán National Park. Buy trekking permit (US$20) at the Llanganuco park gate, either at start or end of trek. Must register with passport

## CHILE

### TORRES DEL PAINE

**LOCATION** Southern Chile, 12th Region. 110km (68 miles) north of Puerto Natales, 400km (250 miles) north of Punta Arenas

**WHEN TO GO** October – April; long daylight hours

**START/FINISH** Several daily bus trips to the park from Puerto Natales. Stops include Laguna Amarga gate, Pudeto (3 daily lake crossings) and park HQ. Exit from same points. The park can now also be accessed by vehicle from the southwest, entering via the Rio Serrano

**DURATION** About 10 days; 135km (84 miles) including side trips and rest day(s). Alternative 5-day W trek: Grey – Pehoe – Valle Francés – Torres, exiting via Laguna Amarga (buses to and from Puerto Natales stop here)

**MAX ALTITUDE** Paso John Gardner pass, also known as Paso Paine (1250m; 4100ft)

**TECHNICAL CONSIDERATIONS** Trails, marked with orange paint, are not immaculate. There are occasional bogs to cross,

streams to ford and gullies to negotiate. Anti-clockwise is recommended as it avoids the toughest ascent early on. Winds around 160kph (100mph) can hinder progress and require caution on exposed ground. Snow often lies deep near the pass and can obscure the trail, especially early in the season

**TREKKING STYLE** Backpacking. Most camp sites are private and charge a fee; a few are public and free. The refugios (private) offer bunks and meals, but in high season beds and food should be booked in advance. Most refugios also have a small shop selling basic supplies

**PERMITS/RESTRICTIONS** Park fee (US$13) payable in Chilean pesos on entering park (must register with passport and sign out on leaving). Park is well managed by CONAF and wardens are helpful

## BOLIVIA

### ILLAMPU CIRCUIT

**LOCATION** Cordillera Real, western Bolivia. About 150km (90 miles) from La Paz

**WHEN TO GO** May to September (dry season) is best. Sunny days and cold nights

**START/FINISH** Trek starts and finishes at subtropical Sorata (2695m; 8842ft) at the foot of the Illampu and Ancohuma mountains. Bus service from La Paz (4hrs)

**DURATION** 6–7 days; 62km (39 miles)

**MAX ALTITUDE** Abra Calzada (5045m; 16,553ft). Total ascent and descent during the trek is 4300m (14,100ft)

**TECHNICAL CONSIDERATIONS** Trek goes into remote highland areas. Spend several days at altitude before setting off to ensure adequate acclimatization. Strong

sun and high altitude combine to increase the risk of dehydration; drink plenty of water. Stream water is readily available, but should be filtered and sterilized with iodine. Rubbish should be carried out, and human waste disposed of responsibly

**TREKKING STYLE** Backpacking and expedition. Wild camping; no designated sites. It is best not to camp near villages

**PERMITS/RESTRICTIONS** There are no restrictions on trekking or climbing in the area and no permits are required for the trek. It is advisable to hire a local guide

**TECHNICAL CONSIDERATIONSS** Guides and donkeys are available from the guides cooperative association in Sorata; the Asociación Guías Turísticas Sorata (tel: 813 5044; fax: 813 5218) located on Plaza Peñaranda facing Residencial Sorata. The guides will know the way, but will probably only speak Spanish and may be poorly equipped. Check that any local people you contract have suitable equipment for spending nights out in the mountains

**MAPS** There are many: • Club Andino Aleman Cordillera Real Nord (Illampu), and Instituto Geográfico Militar (IGM) maps Sorata 58461 and Warizata 5846 11. There are two IGM sales offices in La Paz, the most accessible is in Edificio Murillo. Take your passport with you. For maps go to the back of the building. Open Monday to Friday 09:00–12:00 and 15:00–19:00. The second office is at the Estado Mayor. Open Monday to Friday, 08:30–16:30. • The New Map of the Cordillera Real by Liam O'Brien is also useful, as it shows the whole Cordillera Real range. This, and the Club Andino Aleman map are

normally available at Los Amigos del Libro (Av 16 de Julio at Edificio Alameda) and other good bookshops in La Paz. You can also find them internationally at good bookshops, some tour companies and at offices of South American Explorers

# ASIA

## TURKEY

### THE LYCIAN WAY

**LOCATION** Fethiye to Antalya on the central southern coast of Turkey

**WHEN TO GO** All year round, but the parts of the route over 1500m; 5000ft (Myra – Finike and Çıralı – Antalya) may be covered by snow from December to April. Alternative, low-level sections allow trekking from February – June and September – November. Water may be scarce in September-November, but is always available at mosques. Not recommended in July and August, when it is too hot

**START/FINISH** Start at Ovacık, 10km (6 miles) south of Fethiye, and finish at Hisarçandır, 20km (12 miles) SW of Antalya. Nearest airports are at Dalaman, 20 minutes from Fethiye, and Antalya. Transport to the start by regular buses and minibuses from Dalaman, change at Fethiye bus station. Transport from finish by taxi to Antalya

**DURATION** 21–28 days; 509km (220m)

**MAX ALTITUDE** 1811m (5942ft) – İncegeriş hill, Finike. Optional climb of Mount Olympos (2366m, 7763ft)

**TECHNICAL CONSIDERATIONS** The path is way-marked and has no technical difficulties, although it gets progressively more

difficult and remote. An 'update' page on the website www.trekkinginturkey.com gives latest information on bad waymark-ing, re-routing and snow conditions, and should be studied before starting

**TREKKING STYLE** Choice of accommodation in village houses and pensions on most of route. Accommodation is listed on the website www.trekkinginturkey.com; e-mail the site for Internet bookings. No accommodation on the two high sections. Plenty of wild camping places near natural water supplies

**PERMITS/RESTRICTIONS** Camping is forbid-den in Culture Ministry historic sites

**MAPS** Sabri Aydal's map of Lycia at 1:250 000 is available at local museums and bookshops. There are some downloadable GPS waypoints on website

**INFORMATION** www.trekkinginturkey.com

**GUIDEBOOKS** *The Lycian Way; Turkey's First Long-Distance Walk* by Kate Clow, (English or German) pb Upcountry

### THE KAÇKAR MOUNTAINS

**LOCATION** The Kaçkar Mountains are the highest part of the Pontic Alps. The Pon-tics stretch from the Caucasus and the Georgian border for about ⅔ of the length of the Turkish Black Sea coast

**WHEN TO GO** The trekking season is very short – either July to September for sum-mer treks, or mid-February to mid-March for snowshoe trekking. Commercial treks only operate in summer, generally with mule support

**START/FINISH** The trailhead on the southern side is at Yusufeli, about 4hrs by bus from Erzurum (airport; scheduled flights from

Istanbul). There is a northern trailhead at Ayder, accessed via two buses from Trab-zon (airport; scheduled flights from Istanbul). This trek starts at Yaylalar, about 2hrs/52km (32 miles) along a dirt road (local buses) from Yusufeli, and finishes at Barhal, which is between Yusufeli and Yaylalar

**DURATION** 10–14 days (depending on optional climbs of Mt Kaçkar and Altıpar-mak ridge), but is broken into two sections of 7 and 6 days

**MAX ALTITUDE** Highest pass (unnamed) (3305m, 10,843ft); Mount Kaçkar (3922m, 12,867ft)

**TECHNICAL CONSIDERATIONS** The path is not waymarked, but is clear on the ground or marked with cairns. The majority of the route is above the tree line so visibility is good except in locally dense mists

**TREKKING STYLE** No permanent accommo-dation or food above the start and finish points; most treks are supported by muleteer(s). Supplies are available in Yaylalar, Yukarı Kavron and Barhal. Guides and muleteers can be hired at Yaylalar or Yukarı Kavron, or booked though one of the sources on www.kackarmountains.com There are a few level camp sites, often alongside lakes

**PERMITS/RESTRICTIONS** None

**MAPS** Only sketch maps available on vari-ous websites. Turkish large-scale military maps are not available

**INFORMATION** www.kackarmountains.com

**GUIDEBOOKS** *The Mountains of Turkey* by Karl Smith pb Cicerone; *Kackar Dağları* (Kaçkar Mountains) by Tunç Fındık, pb Homer Kıtabevi is being translated into English

## PAKISTAN

### GONDOKORO LA – HUSHE TO CONCORDIA

**LOCATION** Karakoram Range, Baltistan province, northern area, Pakistan

**WHEN TO GO** Early June to early September

**START** Hushe village; international flights to Karachi or Islamabad (recommended), then by air (1hr) or road (Karakoram Highway, 18–30hrs) to Skardu. Overnight there, then to Hushe by jeep (10hrs)

**FINISH** Askole village; There is now a jeep road through the Braldu Gorge. Jeep to Skardu (6–10hrs, depending on road conditions), then by air or road to Islamabad/Rawalpindi

**DURATION** Min 22 days; 130km (80 miles)

**MAX ALTITUDE** Gondokoro La (5585m; 18,324ft)

**TECHNICAL CONSIDERATIONS** Party must consist of proficient glacier travellers and be equipped for roped glacier travel and crevasse rescue. Some fixed ropes may be required on the upper sections of the Gondokoro La. Some stone-fall danger here also – helmets recommended

**TREKKING STYLE** Expedition. Must be completely self-sufficient

**PERMITS/RESTRICTIONS** Trekking permit and a liaison officer now required for this route (it's close to the disputed border with India). Permit only available through trekking agent in Pakistan. Licensed Pakistani mountain guides may double as liaison officers

### BIAFO–HISPAR TRAVERSE

**LOCATION** Central Karakoram, Pakistan

**WHEN TO GO** June to September

**START** Askole village. International flights to Islamabad, then by air (1hr) or road (KKH, 18–30hrs) to Skardu. Overnight there, then to Askole by jeep (6–10hrs)

**FINISH** Nagar village. Jeep to Karimabad (on the KKH in the Hunza Valley, 1½hrs), then by bus or jeep to Gilgit (3–4hrs). Gilgit–Islamabad by bus (14–18hrs) or air (45mins, weather permitting)

**DURATION** 14–20 days, depending on side trips, pace and weather

**MAX ALTITUDE** Hispar Pass (5151m; 16,900ft)

**TECHNICAL CONSIDERATIONS** Party must consist of proficient glacier travellers and be equipped for roped glacier travel and crevasse rescue

**TREKKING STYLE** Expedition. Self-sufficient all the way

**PERMITS/RESTRICTIONS** The trek is in a restricted area requiring prior permit (US $50 per person per month); plus services of a licensed guide; and insurance for porters and any other staff (cook etc.). For more info see www.nazirsabir.com
The permit is issued by the Ministry of Tourism through a local agent, you can't apply yourself. It takes only one day on receipt of photocopies of the info and visa pages of your passport

### LUKPE LA

**LOCATION** Northern and central Karakoram ranges, Pakistan

**WHEN TO GO** July–early September offer the best chance of stable, fine weather. Crevasses open up as summer progresses

**START** Shimshal village, Hunza. International flight to Islamabad, then flight (1hr) or KKH (14–20hrs) to Gilgit. Jeep or bus to Passu on the KKH (5hrs), jeep to Shimshal (5hrs)

**FINISH** Askole village in Baltistan. Jeep to Skardu (6–10hrs), flight (1hr) or drive (18–30hrs) to Islamabad

**DURATION** Approximately 21 days (200km; 125 miles)

**MAX ALTITUDE** Lukpe La (5700m; 18,700ft)

**TECHNICAL CONSIDERATIONS** Expertise in prolonged glacier travel is essential

**TREKKING STYLE** Backpacking with porters

**PERMITS/RESTRICTIONS** Advance permit necessary; US$50 is charged per person for one month

**MAPS** From US Army Map Service, 1:250 000, series U-502, sheet No. NJ 43–15 (Shimshal)

**DANGERS** Avalanches are a real threat on Lukpe La. Trekkers need to be able to recognize signs of crevasses under fresh snow, judge deteriorating snow conditions and avalanche potential, and understand oncoming bad weather and fronts. Also, come prepared for potential hypothermia with suitably warm wet- and windproof clothing, and learn how to recognize the early signs of this condition

**INFORMATION** Nazir Sabir Expeditions (outfitter for Karakoram range, Pakistan): e-mail: info@nazirsabir.com Website: www.nazirsabir.com

## INDIA

### LADAKH AND ZANSKAR

**LOCATION** Ladakh Himalaya, Jammu and Kashmir and Himachal Pradesh, India

**WHEN TO GO** June to November. Like the Karakoram in Pakistan, the Ladakh and Zanskar ranges are mountain deserts that lie in the 'rain shadow' of the main

Himalayan Range, and are barely affected by the summer monsoon

**Start** Lamayuru Gompah; international flights to New Delhi, then by air (1hr) or road (3 days) to Leh. Local transport (jeep or bus) to Lamayuru takes half a day

**Finish** Darcha; local bus to Manali (8hrs). Then either by road to Delhi (12hrs) or to Kulu by road (3hrs) and by air to Delhi (1hr – unreliable due to weather). Alternatively, travel to Chandigar by road (8hrs) and on to Delhi by air (35mins) or train (Shatabdi Express, 3½hrs). Note: the road conditions from Chandigar to Delhi (4hrs) are extremely dangerous

**Duration** 23 days minimum

**Max Altitude** Shin-Kun La (5096m; 16,720ft) or Phirtse La (5250m; 17,225ft)

**Technical considerations** None

**Trekking style** Backpacking or expedition. Very basic local accommodation is possible, but food cannot be guaranteed

**Permits/Restrictions** No permits required

## Singalila to Kangchenjunga

**Location** Sikkim Himalaya, India

**When to go** March to May or September to December

**Start** Dhodray; international flight to Delhi, Bombay or Calcutta, then by train, bus or plane to Bagdogra (West Bengal) and up to Darjeeling by toy train (8hrs), bus or jeep (3–4hrs). Overnight in Darjeeling, then by road (2hrs) to Dhodray

**Finish** Yuksom; jeep to Kalimpong or Darjeeling, then on to Bagdogra for rail, road and air links to Delhi, Bombay or Calcutta. Land crossing into Western Nepal is also possible from Karkabitta (near Siliguri)

**Duration** About 21 days

**Max Altitude** Goecha La (4800m; 15,700ft)

**Technical considerations** After snowfall, the Goecha La may not be reachable without an ice axe at least

**Trekking style** Backpacking or expedition. Some lodges on the Singalila Ridge between Dhodray and Phalut. Basic food only

**Permits/Restrictions** Trip may not be done independently; must hire local guide or agent. Permit for Phalut Dzong Ri section only available at tourist office in Gangtok. No fee for permits, but fees for yaks, porters, cameras and tents on a per day basis for trekking

**Maps** Sikkim Himalaya – SSAF 1:150 000

**Information** Rimo Expeditions rimo@vsnl.com; info@rimoexpeditions.com http://www.rimoexpeditions.com

## Zanskar River Trek

**Location** Zanskar River, Ladakh, northern India

**When to go** The most reliable period for river-ice formation is mid-January to mid-February, although conditions vary from year to year

**Start/Finish** A round trip via Padum, starting and finishing at the current road-head at Chilling (about 3 hours from Leh by bus); trekkers usually walk in and out of Zanskar on the Zanskar River route

**Duration** about 14 days; 250km (155 miles). Poor river ice conditions may increase the duration. Shorter variations of the trek are possible by simply retracing the route before reaching Padum. The trek to Lingshed is a popular 4-day (8-day round trip) option

**Max Altitude** depending on destination: Padum 3590m (11,775ft); Lingshed 3700m (12,136ft): deviations to avoid poor river ice conditions may exceed these altitudes

**Technical considerations** Serious expedition. Trekkers must be fit and well versed in living in extreme cold. They must also be prepared to wade through open water and undertake exposed rock climbing and scrambling, all in subzero temperatures. Usual daytime temperatures in the shade range from -5° to -25°C (23° to -13°F)

**Trekking style** Ice trekking with a local guide, cook and porters. Trekkers overnight in caves and Zanskari houses. Itinerary and day-length are subject to local river-ice conditions. It is not advisable to undertake the trek without an experienced guide

**Permits/Restrictions** Currently none, but it is advisable to check the political situation in Zanskar and neighbouring areas

**Maps** A 1:350 000 map of the area is published by Éditions Olizane, Genève

**Information** www.snowleopardtrails.com www.ibexexpeditions.com www.jktourism.org For Padum – Manali (Himachal Pradesh) helicopter see www.himachal.com

## Kangchenjunga

**Location** Kangchenjunga Himal, eastern Nepal

**When to go** April–June or October–December

**Start and Finish** International flights to Kathmandu, then by air (55mins) or road and foot – night bus to Biratnagar (14hrs), local bus to Hille (5hrs), then 3 days' walk – to Tumlingtar. Alternatively, night bus to

Biratnagar, overnight there, then early morning flight to Taplejung (±40mins). Return by the same route. Flight from Taplejung to Biratnagar, bus or flight back to Kathmandu

**Duration** Min 28 days

**Max Altitude** Pang Pema (5100m; 16,700ft)

**Technical considerations** If there is snow, parties opting to cross the Lapsang La (high route from Tseram to Ghunsa) should take ice axes for cutting steps, especially for porters

**Trekking style** Backpacking or expedition

**Permits/Restrictions** Trekking permit required. Must be obtained through accredited agency

## Nepal

### Dhaulagiri Circuit

**Location** Dhaulagiri Himal, Nepal

**When to go** April to May and September to December

**Start** Beni; international flight to Kathmandu, then by road or air to Pokhara and on to Beni by bus or jeep (poor road)

**Finish** Jomsom; flight to Pokhara (20mins) and on to Kathmandu either by air (25mins) or by road (8hrs). Or walk out from Tukuche down the Kali Gandaki to Poon Hill/Ghorepani/Birethanti (4 days walk to the road, 2–3hrs bus to Pokhara)

**Duration** Min 21 to 23 days

**Max Altitude** French Pass (5300m; 17,389ft)

**Technical considerations** French Pass in bad weather needs skilful navigation. Though ostensibly close to some of the busiest trails and airstrips in Nepal, much of this route is extremely remote, and organizing a retreat/evacuation in an

emergency could be time consuming at best. Parties travelling here should prepare, equip and conduct themselves with this in mind

**Trekking style** Backpacking or expedition

**Permits/Restrictions** Trekking permit required. Must be obtained through accredited agency

**Maps** For latest availability and supply of all maps of Nepal, visit www.omnimap.com/catalog/int/nepal.htm *Dhaulagiri: The High Route Around Dhaulagiri Across High Passes*, 1:87 500, Nepal, Kathmandu. The map covers Thapa Pass, Hidden Valley, French Pass, Dhaulagiri Base Camp, West Dhaulagiri Glacier. One of Nepal's earlier maps, the topographic base map is not as detailed as the later maps although the hiking information is still there and the map is quite useful. With latitude and longitude markings and 500 metre contours. Not indexed. US$12.95 Note that Himalayan Map House/Nepal Maps has several outlets in Kathmandu and Pokhara

### Manaslu and Annapurna Circuit

**Location** Larkya Himal, Nepal

**When to go** March to May or September to December

**Start** International flight to Kathmandu, then by road to Gorkha via the Prithvi Highway (7hrs)

**Finish** Jomsom; flight to Pokhara (20mins) and on to Kathmandu either by air (25mins) or by road (8hrs)

**Duration** 22 days

**Max Altitude** Thorung La (5400m; 17,700ft).

**Technical considerations** None

**Trekking style** Gorkha–Thonje, backpacking. Thonje–Jomsom, tea-houses and lodges available all the way. Most people doing the Manaslu & Annapurna circuit camp all the way

**Permits/Restrictions** Gorkha–Thonje stretch is a notified area – a permit and a liaison officer are required. Thonje–Jomsom is an open area, and no permit is necessary

## Nepal and Tibet

### Jumla to Mount Kailas

**Location** Ngari province, southwest Tibet. Approach through Humla, northwest Nepal

**When to go** May to June; late September to December

**Start** International flight to Kathmandu, then to Nepalganj by air (50mins) or road (bus 14hrs). Overnight there and early morning flight to Jumla (25mins) or Simikot (50mins)

**Finish** Simikot; flight to Nepalganj (50mins) and on to Kathmandu by air or road (night bus 12–14hrs)

**Duration** 28 to 30 days

**Max Altitude** Dolma La (5600m; 18,400ft)

**Technical considerations** In view of the remoteness of Kailas and the extreme altitude attained on this trek, a close watch should be kept for the onset of altitude sickness. Getting below 4000m (13,000ft), once in this part of Tibet, will be difficult and helicopter evacuation impossible

**Trekking style** Backpacking or expedition

**Permits/Restrictions** Standard Nepali trekking permit required for Jumla-Simikot section. Must be obtained through accredited agent. Section from

Simikot to border requires a special permit. Limi requires notified area permission. Arrangements for visas and the Kailas sector must be made in advance through an accredited agency in Nepal or Tibet. Expensive

**Information** Gyurme Dorje / Trans Himalaya info@trans-himalaya.com

**Guidebooks** *Kailash Mandala* by Tsewang Lama pb HCDA, Nepal, 2002; *The Sacred Mountain* by John Snelling pb East-West Publications, London, 1990

## Bhutan

### Tiger's Lair and Sacred Peak

**Location** Along the eastern Himalaya, between Nepal, India, Bangladesh and China

**When to go** Spring (April to June) and Autumn (October and November)

**Start** Drukgyel Dzong, near Paro, west Bhutan. International flights to Paro, Bhutan's only airport (sit on the left of the aeroplane when flying to Bhutan for an incredible view of Mt Everest); or travel by road via Phuentsholing

**Finish** Drukgyel Dzong

**Duration** 6-7 days (116km; 72 miles)

**Max Altitude** Jangothang (4090m; 13,420ft).

**Technical considerations** Paths are easy to follow and the ascent is gradual, but you will start to notice the effects of altitude as you gain height up the Paro Chhu valley. Arriving at Jangothang base camp you may feel short of breath and a little light-headed. Here, at 4000m (13,000ft), altitude sickness is a possibility. Be aware of the symptoms and ensure that your guide has experience of this too

**Trekking style** Pleasant hiking on good trails through wild and beautiful terrain. You must trek with a guide and a trek support team of horseman, cook and at least one helper; make the most of it by interacting with them and the local people you meet along the way. Camping equipment supplied may be basic – take your own sleeping bag and mat

**Permits/Restrictions** Tourists need a visa to enter Bhutan, and must pre-arrange their itineraries through recognized tour operators. An all-inclusive daily rate is charged; this covers transport within the country, food, accommodation, guide, trek support team, and so on. The rate, quoted in US dollars, may seem high but it offers good value for money, providing access to a unique country and culture

**Information** www.himalayankingdoms.com www.bhutan-info.org

### Snowman Trek

**Location** Bhutan, eastern Himalaya

**When to go** May to June or October. Bhutan gets a much heavier monsoon than Nepal. The weather is generally less settled, windier and colder

**Start** Drukyul Dzong. International flight to Paro. (The only airline serving Bhutan is Druk Air, with a fleet of 2 BAe146/Avro RJ aircraft, and services from Bombay, Delhi, Bangkok and Kathmandu.) Overnight in a lodge and then by road to the trailhead

**Finish** Dhur village, Bumthang. By road to Thimpu (4hrs), overnight in hotel, international flight from Paro

**Duration** Minimum of 25 days, Drukyel Dzong–Dhur. Add 5 days for rests, contingency and/or side trips

**Max Altitude** Gophu La (5230m; 17,160ft)

**Technical considerations** None

**Trekking style** Backpacking or expedition

**Permits/Restrictions** No permits for independent travel are issued for anywhere in the country. All treks must be booked through an accredited agency. Must travel on fixed itineraries approved by the Tourist Authority of Bhutan

**Maps** Maps of Bhutan are notoriously difficult to acquire

**Guidebooks** *Bhutan – A Trekkers Guide* by Bart Jordans pb Cicerone, UK, 2005. Jordans lived in Bhutan for four years

# Africa

## Morocco

### Tichka to Toubkal

**Location** High Atlas Mountains of Morocco, North Africa

**When to go** May to October

**Start/Finish** Tichka Plateau, north of Taroudant; descending to Marrakech from Djebel Toubkal. Flights to/from Marrakech and hotel minibus for start/finish

**Duration** 14–18 days; 140km (87 miles), including days at start/finish for access. The major peaks of Imaradene (start) and Toubkal (end) can be omitted if required, though they are not technical ascents

**Max altitude** Djebel Toubkal (4167m; 13,672ft)

**Technical considerations** This is essentially a summer trek, the earliest dates being dependent on mule access to the Tichka Plateau, while Djebel Toubkal can bear summit snow into June. Take local advice. The trekking is mostly on good paths/tracks suitable for any fit person but there are some long ascents to tizis. Nights can feel cool, days can be hot and, while generally sunny, storms can occur during any season

**Trekking style** Backpacking or expedition

**Permits/Restrictions** None, and trekking costs are modest

## KENYA

### CHOGORIA AND SUMMIT CIRCUIT ROUTES

**Location** East of the Rift Valley, Kenyan Highlands

**When to go** January to February, August to September

**Start** Mount Kenya Lodge (3000m; 10,000ft). International flights to Nairobi, then by road (3hrs) to the old Scottish mission station at Chogoria. There is a transit hotel here, and porters may be arranged. The *bandas* (huts) of Mount Kenya Lodge are 3½hrs further by 4x4 – if the road is dry

**Finish** Naro Moru Meteorological Station. The Naro Moru River Lodge operates a basic lodge and camp site here. The River Lodge is 1hr away by jeep, and from Naro Moru the journey to Nairobi takes 3hrs

**Duration** Min 6 days

**Max Altitude** Point Lenana (4985m; 16,356ft)

**Technical considerations** Acclimatization to altitude is a must

**Trekking style** Backpacking or expedition

**Permits/Restrictions** None, but park and hut/camping fees must be paid on entry (in US Dollars)

## TANZANIA

### MOUNT KILIMANJARO

**Location** North-eastern Tanzania, around 500km (300 miles) from Dar es Salaam; nearest town is Moshi

**When to go** January – February and August – September

**Start** Machame – Mweka route: 7km (4 miles) from Machame village (southeast of Kili); Umbwe route: Umbwe gate

**Finish** Machame-Mweka routes: Marangu Gate

**Duration** Machame-Mweka route: min. 6 days; Umbwe route: 5 days

**Max Altitude** Uhuru Peak (5865m; 19,243ft)

**Technical considerations** Altitude and weather

**Trekking style** Backpacking with porter support. Most trails are waymarked and cairned. Huts other than those on the Marangu Route may be unfit for use, so camping or bivouac equipment will be needed. Generally food is supplied by outfitters who arrange for porters to carry and cook

**Permits/Restrictions** Ascents of Kilimanjaro must be organized through a tour company. The use of guides and porters in the national park is mandatory. Many are superb, but some are scoundrels. Modest fees are payable for time spent within park boundaries

**Dangers** All trekkers must be familiar with the symptoms of, and necessary action for, Acute Mountain Sickness (AMS). Its dangers should not be underestimated. Rules of thumb are: do not ascend once symptoms manifest, and descend if symptoms worsen at any given altitude

**Maps** *Map and Guide to Kilimanjaro*, 1:75 000 by Andrew Wielochowski. *Kilimanjaro Map and Guide*, 1:50 000 by Mark Savage

**Information** www.intotanzania.com/safari/ tanzania/north/peaks/kilimanjaro/ kilimanjaro-01-intro.htm
www.gorp.com/gorp/location/africa/ tanzania/home_kil.htm
www.tanzaniaparks.com/
www.tanzania-online.gov.uk/tourism/ kilimanj.html

**Guidebooks** *The Mountain Club of Kenya Guide to Mount Kenya and Kilimanjaro* Ed Iain Allan, 1998 *Kilimanjaro – To the Roof of Africa* by Audrey Salkeld pb National Geographic 2002

## NAMIBIA

### FISH RIVER CANYON

**Location** Namibia; near the border with South Africa

**When to go** Mid-April to mid-September. June and July are the best months. Due to extreme weather conditions, the canyon is closed during the remainder of the year. In April or May some years, you might find so much water in the canyon that you need to cross the river dozens of times a day. On the other hand, in September and October you could be fighting your best friend to drink from a puddle of stagnant water. Conditions can vary considerably, depending on rainfall that particular year. In 2003 the canyon had no water at all, and all hikes were cancelled

**Start** Hobas, 10km (6 miles) from the canyon, 650km (404 miles) from Windhoek, 900km (560 miles) from Cape Town or 1200km (750 miles) from Johannesburg

**Finish** Ai-Ais; hot-spring oasis in the

semi-desert. Range of accommodation from luxury apartments to basic huts and permanently erected tents with camp beds. Spa complex has a restaurant, filling station and swimming pool

**Duration** 5 days. 100km (62 miles) along the river course, or around 86km (53 miles) using short cuts

**Max Altitude** 820m (2700ft)

**Technical considerations** Take a book to read between 11h00 and 15h00, when it is too hot to walk

**Trekking style** Backpacking

**Permits/Restrictions** Groups can consist of 3 (min) to 40 (max) people. A medical certificate of physical fitness, issued within 40 days of the trek, must be submitted to the ranger at Hobas before starting. For permits apply to the central reservations office of Namibia Wildlife Resorts Ltd in Windhoek

**Information** www.nwr.com.na; email reservations@nwr.com.na

## South Africa

### Northern Drakensberg

**Location** Northern Drakensberg mountains, forming the border between Lesotho and KwaZulu-Natal, South Africa

**When to go** April and May (autumn/fall), June (winter), September and October (spring) or November (early summer) are generally considered the best months. Winter is drier but any precipitation at that time can fall as snow

**Start** The Sentinel carpark, Free State Province; or from the Royal Natal National Park (add around 5 hours to walk up to the Sentinel Office)

**Finish** The Cathedral Peak Hotel

**Duration** 5 days; about 65km (40 miles)

**Max Altitude** 3400m (11,155ft)

**Technical considerations** No climbing involved but proficiency in navigation and a good understanding of general mountain knowledge are required.

**Trekking style** Backpacking across an exposed and mainly untracked high mountain plateau, following the edge of a rugged and rocky escarpment. Apart from water, which is available from the rivers, all food and supplies must be carried

**Permits/Restrictions** A permit can be purchased at the office in the Sentinel Car Park (Witsieshoek). Fees for hiking in the wilderness area are currently about R15 pp admission, plus R20 pppn

**Dangers** Weather is extremely fickle: a hot summer's day can produce a midday thunderstorm with lightning, dense fog can roll in, a crisp frosty winter morning can turn into a blinding snowstorm. Come well prepared. Also, be aware that the rural people of Lesotho are very poor and that any items left lying around camp sites are likely to become part of the redistribution of wealth programme. There have been several incidents of this sort recently and it is not recommended to trek in small groups

**Maps** 1:50 000 maps available from the KwaZulu-Natal Nature Conservation office

**Information** KwaZulu-Natal Nature Conservation Services, PO Box 13053, Cascades 3202, KwaZulu-Natal tel: +27-33-8451000/2. (www.rhino.org.za/) For guides or guided treks try www.ctsm.co.za

### Wild Coast

**Location** Eastern Cape

**When to go** The trail can be walked year round but winters are cool and pleasant for hiking. The Wild Coast has a mild, humid climate with most rain falling during summer. The temperature range is quite small with average monthly air temperatures of 17–23°C (63–73°F)

**Start/Finish** Port St Johns/Coffee Bay

**Duration** 5 days over 100km (62 miles). Full trail is 25 days over 280km (174 miles)

**Max Altitude** Brazen Head 239m (784ft)

**Technical considerations** Although steep at times this is a straight-forward trail with no scrambling or exposed sections

**Trekking style** Guided hike staying in communities, or independent trek

**Permits/Restrictions** Maximum of 12 hikers on each day of the trail. Permits available through the Department of Economic Affairs, Umtata. Contact Port St Johns Tourism for guides

### Otter Trail

**Location** Eastern Cape

**When to go** Although this is a year-round rainfall area, avoid August to November when it is above average. Warmest months are December to March with an average temperature of around 20°C (68°F)

**Start** Storms River Mouth; 500km (310 miles) east of Cape Town; 250km (150 miles) west of Port Elizabeth

**Finish** Nature's Valley

**Duration** 5 days; 43km (26 miles)

**Max Altitude** About 200m (656ft), between Scott and Oakhurst huts

**Technical considerations** None

**Trekking style** Backpacking, although trail has huts for overnight stays. Otter Trail huts have 6 bunks each (2 huts at each stop)

**Permits/Restrictions** Permits are required and can be obtained from the SA National Parks. Tel +27 12 428-911 or e-mail reservations@sanparks.org Website: www.sanparks.org

## Tsitsikamma Trail

**Location** Eastern Cape

**When to go** Although this is a year-round rainfall area, avoid August to November when it is above average. Autumn and winter (April to July) have the lowest rainfall, but always be prepared for rain. Warmest months are December to March with an average temperature around 20°C (68°F)

**Start** Nature's Valley, about 600km (375 miles) from Cape Town and 200km (125 miles) from Port Elizabeth)

**Finish** After hiking 60km (37 miles) in an easterly direction, the trail ends at the Storms River Bridge

**Duration** 6 days/5 nights 60km (37 miles)

**Max Altitude** 740m (2400ft)

**Technical considerations** None

**Trekking style** Backpacking. Huts can accommodate 30 people, but the maximum has been set at 24 per day to reduce pressure on the facilities. Each hut has an adjacent *lapa* (cooking shelter), equipped with barbeque grids, kettles, cast iron pots and pans. There are 24 bunks and mattresses, 2 flush toilets 2 showers with a hotwater shower-bucket. Firewood is supplied. Equipment and backpack porterage is possible at a cost approximately

equivalent to the basic charge for the trail. Guides with knowledge of the fauna and flora, forest ecology, geology and history of the area can accompany your group on any section of the route at an additional cost. Non-hiking family or friends can be transported to certain overnight huts to overnight with the hikers

**Information** MTO Ecotourism, tel +27.44.874-4363. Fax +27 44 874-6397. E-mail ivy@cyberperk.co.za www.mtoecotourism.co.za

# Australia

## Tasmania Overland

**Location** Cradle Mountain-Lake St Clair National Park in central Tasmania

**When to go** Summer (December to February) usually offers the best weather but this is when the trail is most crowded. Autumn (March to May) is pleasant, when the colours of the deciduous beech are changing. During winter and spring snow may cover large parts of the trail

**Start** Cradle Mountain, near Devonport in northern Tasmania

**Finish** Lake St Clair in the centre of the island some 100km (62 miles) northwest of Hobart, the state capital. Daily buses service both ends during summer

**Duration** 5–7 days, 65km (40 miles)

**Max Altitude** Marion's Lookout 1200m (4000ft)

**Technical considerations** Moderate grade, suitable for people of moderate fitness. No climbing or scrambling necessary

**Trekking style** Backpacking. Well-formed and waymarked track with several huts en

route. Huts have no mattresses or cooking facilities. Camping is possible near most huts, and in a few other locations, but walkers are requested to use only the tent platforms provided. Guided walks using private huts, with meals supplied, are also available

**Permits/Restrictions** Because of the track's increasing popularity a booking system has been introduced for independent walkers during the peak season of November to April. In these months hikers must walk in the north – south direction, starting at Cradle Mountain. However, in the off-season (May to October) the trail can walked in either direction All Tasmania's national parks charge entry fees. Trekkers intending to visit more than one park should consider the 8-week holiday pass. During peak season, additional fees for walking the Overland Track apply

**Maps** Tasmap produces a 1:100 000-scale park map which is suitable for trekking

**Information** Tasmanian Parks and Wildlife Service: Cradle Mountain, PO Box 20, Sheffield, TAS 7306 tel: +61-3-64921133; Lake St Clair, Derwent Bridge TAS 7140, tel: +61-3-62891172; www.parks.gov.au; www.overlandtrack.com.au Lake St Clair ferry service: tel: +61-3-62891137

**Guidebooks** *The Overland Track, A Walker's Notebook* pb Parks and Wildlife Service Tasmania, 1996

# New Zealand

## Routeburn

**Location** Southwest corner of the South Island

When to go Summer and autumn (October to May/June). During the 'Great Walk' season (October to April) bookings are essential to guarantee your hut or camp site accommodation. At other times hut tickets can be purchased from most Department of Conservation offices. During winter much of the country above bush line is likely to be covered by snow, which can make the track impassable as a through route. Snow and ice on the Hollyford Face can be extremely hazardous. During late winter and spring, depending on snow and weather conditions, there can be serious avalanche risk, in particular near the Earland Falls, above Lake Mackenzie, on the Hollyford Face and above Lake Harris. Huts remain open during winter but are not staffed. A winter crossing should only be attempted by experienced and well-equipped parties

Start/Finish The track can be walked in either direction, from Routeburn Shelter, one hour's drive from Queenstown or The Divide, on the Milford Highway, 1½hrs drive from Te Anau. Several companies operate shuttle services for trampers to and from each end of the Routeburn Track, which are separated by over 350km (217 mile) of road

Duration 3–5 days, 33km (20 miles), with options of continuing onto the adjacent Greenstone and/or Caples Tracks for extended trekking. Be aware that bad weather may cause delays over open, exposed track sections

Max Altitude Harris Saddle (1280m; 4200ft)

Technical considerations On this alpine trail storms can occur at any time of the

year. Walkers should be cautious and carry suitable clothing for cold, wet and windy conditions

Trekking style Backpacking. There are four park huts on the track, Howden, Lake Mackenzie, Routeburn Falls and Routeburn Flats. These huts are supplied with gas cookers, lighting and heating, cold water, toilets and communal bunkrooms with mattresses. Camping is only permitted at two designated camp sites, at Routeburn Flats and Lake Mackenzie. These have toilets, water supply and a shelter for cooking. During the Great Walk season park staff are stationed at each hut and camp site. They are equipped with radios for use in emergencies and for weather forecasts, and they provide an evening talk discussing the track conditions, weather forecast and what features walkers might expect to see the following day. One company is licensed to operate a guided walk over the Routeburn Track

Permits/Restrictions No permits are required for hiking in any New Zealand national park, but passes are required for staying in huts or camp sites. During the Great Walk season these must be pre-purchased. Outside of the Great Walk season backcountry hut tickets or annual passes can be purchased in advance from any park visitor centre or Department of Conservation office. The cost varies from season to season. Camping is permitted at the two designated camp sites, anywhere else tents must be pitched more than 500m (1600ft) off the track

Information email: greatwalksbookings@doc.govt.nz

### Round the Mountains

Location Central North Island

When to go Summer (November to March) is the safest and most popular time. During winter snow, ice and avalanche danger are likely

Start/Finish Whakapapa Village, 40 minutes' drive from Turangi. Regular public transport and hiker shuttle services are available from Turangi and Whakapapa. Hikers should complete a 'trip intentions' form at the park visitor centre before they leave, and sign out when they have completed their trek

Duration 7–9 days; 85km (55 miles)

Max Altitude Red Crater, Mount Tongariro (1800m; 5900ft)

Technical considerations The standard of the trail varies. Part of it is unformed and marked only by poles, in other places it follows a well-formed, benched trail or boardwalk. There are clear signs at all trail junctions. Much of the route is exposed to changeable mountain weather, at any time of the year. During winter snow and ice cover much of the route, necessitating climbing equipment and expertise. Some river crossings might not be feasible during or after heavy rain. In the event of sudden volcanic activity, trekkers should move out of valleys and onto high ridges to avoid danger from lahars (volcanic mud flows). Follow the advice of park staff, should any be in the vicinity. Eruptions can be spectacular, viewed from a safe distance, and extremely dangerous for those who venture too close

Trekking style Backpacking. There are nine park huts with facilities that include toilets, bunks and mattresses, water supply and benches for cooking. During summer, four huts on Mount Tongariro (Mangatepopo, Ketetahi, Oturere and Waihohonu) also have gas cookers and heaters, and resident hut wardens. Camping is permitted

**PERMITS/RESTRICTIONS** No permits are required for hiking in any New Zealand national park. Backcountry hut tickets or annual hut passes are required to stay in huts. These should be purchased in advance from any park visitor centre or Department of Conservation office, the cost varies from season to season and depending on the standard of hut. Children under 11 are free. Bunk space in park huts is available on a first-come, first-served basis. During the season Great Walk passes are required for the Mangatepopo, Ketetahi, Oturere and Waihohonu huts and for camp sites near the huts (passes should be pre-purchased, there is a surcharge if purchased from a hut warden) and camping is prohibited within 500m (1600ft) of the trail

## ĀORAKI TO ARTHUR'S PASS, SOUTHERN ALPS

**LOCATION** Central Southern Alps

**WHEN TO GO** The summer months of December to January are probably best, although winter (July-September) ski-touring trips are possible

**START** Āoraki/Mount Cook Village

**FINISH** Klondyke Corner, Arthur's Pass

**DURATION** West and east mixed route: 3–4 weeks. Eastern route: 2-3 weeks

**MAX ALTITUDE** 2460m (8071ft) on the crossing of the Garden of Eden, beside Mt Tyndall

**TECHNICAL CONSIDERATIONS** A traverse of the central Southern Alps is a major undertaking. Expect to encounter flooded rivers, glaciers, high alpine passes and lots of moraine; only people with considerable transalpine hiking experience should attempt this. Any trip into the area will require meticulous planning, map consultation and serious study of the guidebook. Depending on your route, you'll also need to pre-arrange a helicopter to fly in at least one food dump – probably two or three. Although guided trips are theoretically possible, the length of the trip will mean it is both costly and difficult to find a willing guide

**TREKKING STYLE** Full self-reliance is required; there are some tracks and huts in most of the major valleys but rarely any on alpine ground. Huts are basic – with bunks, mattresses and wood burner, but you must carry your own stove and fuel. A modest charge is payable to the Dept of Conservation

**PERMITS/RESTRICTIONS** No restrictions, fees or permits in any NZ national park. The only fees are for staying in huts overnight

**DANGERS** Rock fall, flooded rivers, avalanches and crevasses. The weather is notoriously unpredictable, and fast-approaching storms with rapidly falling temperatures and winds gusting up to 150kph (90mph) are not uncommon – even in summer

**MAPS** A series 1:50 000 scale detailed topographical maps by Terralink NZ are ideal for the entire trip

Two Suggested Routes:
- West and East mixed Route (allow 3-4 weeks) Āoraki/Mt Cook Village, Murchison Glacier, Armadillo Saddle, Godley Valley, Terra Nova Pass, Havelock River, Clyde River, Frances Valley, Perth Col, Garden of Eden, Garden of Allah, Lambert Spur, Wanganui River, Bracken Snowfield, Whitcombe Pass, Whitcombe River, Frew Saddle, Mathias Pass, Rolleston Range, Wilberforce River, White Col, Waimakariri River, Klondyke Corner, Arthur's Pass.
- Eastern Route (allow 2-3 weeks) Āoraki/Mt Cook Village, Murchison Glacier, Armadillo Saddle, Godley Valley, Terra Nova Pass, Havelock River, Clyde River, McCoy Stream, McCoy Col, Rakaia River, Ragged Range, Mathias River, Rolleston Range, Wilberforce River, White Col, Waimakariri River, Klondyke Corner, Arthur's Pass.

**INFORMATION** Mount Cook National Park Visitor Centre, PO Box 5, Mount Cook, tel: +64-3-4351819, website: www.doc.govt.nz Alpine Guides (Mount Cook) Ltd, PO Box 20, Mount Cook 8770, tel: +64-3-4351834, e-mail: mtcook@alpineguides.co.nz, website: www.alpineguides.co.nz Adventure Consultants/Guy Cotter, PO Box 97, Wanaka, tel: +64-3-443-8711, e-mail: info@adventure.co.nz, website: www.adventure.co.nz

**GUIDEBOOKS** *Tramping in the South Island: Arthur's Pass to Mt Cook* by Elise Bryant and Sven Brabyn pb Brabyn Publishing, Christchurch (updated edition 2004); *The Mountains of Erewhon* by T.N. Beckett pb Reed, Wellington, 1978

JACK JACKSON – well-known author, photographer and lecturer – has carved an impressive reputation for himself as a mountaineer and diver through his exploration of rugged landscapes and the charting of unknown destinations in sea, mountain and desert terrain. Originally an industrial chemist working in the oil and photographic film industries, Jack found a stronger calling in his love for mountains and adventure. He gave it all up for expeditionary travel in the Himalaya, making a living from lecturing and photography, and has explored the remoter areas of Asia, Africa, Europe and the Far East, both on his own account and as leader of scientific, cultural and tourist expeditions. Some of the more challenging countries he has trekked in include Morocco, Afghanistan, Iran, Oman, Nepal, northern India, Borneo, Iceland and Greenland

Jack is a member of the Alpine Club, the Climbers' Club, the Scientific Exploration Society and the Outdoor Writers' Guild, a Fellow of the Royal Geographical Society and a consultant to the Expedition Advisory Centre at the Royal Geographical Society.

SHAUN BARNETT is a Wellington-based writer and photographer with a passion for tramping and wild places. He's tramped extensively in New Zealand and Tasmania, as well as in Nepal, Canada, Alaska and South America. With co-author Rob Brown he won the 2000 Montana Book Award in the Environment category for their book *Classic Tramping in New Zealand*. In January 2001 he completed a 28-day, 248km (154 mile) tramp through the central Southern Alps, and two years later tackled a two-week section from Āoraki/Mt Cook south to Makarora. Now he has just three short sections to complete a traverse of the Southern Alps.

PADDY DILLON, born and reared among the Pennines of Northern England, is a prolific outdoor writer with over thirty guidebooks to his name. He has walked dozens of long-distance trails and climbed hundreds of mountains, but is equally happy exploring moorlands, woodlands, coastlines and islands. He writes regularly for a number of leading outdoor magazines and other publications, as well as producing literature for tourism organizations. He currently lives on the fringe of the English Lake District and regularly walks among the high fells. He has walked in most parts of Britain, even to the extent of walking in, and writing about, every single county. His exploits in Ireland have earned him the title of Mr Walking in Ireland. Paddy has enjoyed walking in many parts of Europe, as well as in places as diverse as Nepal, Tibet and the Canadian Rockies. He has led many guided walking holidays and travels extensively. As a committed user of public transport, Paddy links rail and bus services to reach nearly all his walking destinations. Once he hits the trail, he walks for a month or more through all kinds of terrain and weather. When engaged in guidebook research, Paddy works directly onto a palmtop computer, so that his words are generated at the very point that his readers will make use of them. He is a keen photographer and often draws his own maps to accompany the route descriptions in his guidebooks.

DEAN JAMES is a mountaineering guide who specializes in trips to the quiet offbeat areas of the world. He has climbed and trekked extensively throughout six continents, with many first ascents and

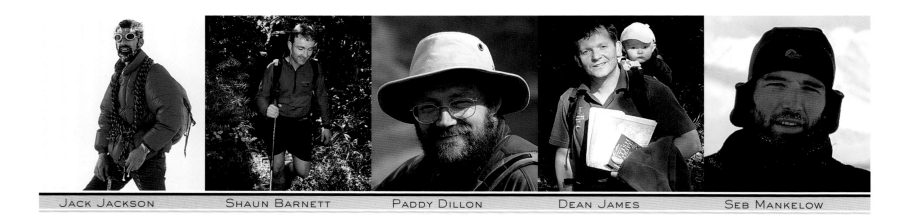

JACK JACKSON     SHAUN BARNETT     PADDY DILLON     DEAN JAMES     SEB MANKELOW

first British ascents of peaks in the Himalaya, Karakorum, Pamirs, Antarctica and North America. His favourite area is the little publicized Alaska and the Canadian Yukon to which he had led 25 expeditions. Here he has made many first ascents and first British ascents of the huge snow and ice peaks, traversed numerous vast, untrodden glaciers and backpacked across its pristine wilderness. In his time off he writes for various British outdoor magazines about his experiences and takes every possible opportunity to amble over his beloved hills of Wales.

SEB MANKELOW is a keen trekker, free-heel skier, occasional climber and amateur naturalist, Seb has expeditioned and travelled in the mountains of North America, East Africa and South Asia. He has visited the Zanskar region of Ladakh almost annually since 1994, where he has trekked extensively (including four winter *chaddar* trips) and undertaken both agricultural and anthropological research. Pursuing his passion for this corner of the world, Seb also has a Masters Degree in South Asian Area Studies from the School of Oriental and African Studies, London.

RALPH STORER was born in England, but has lived in Scotland since his days at university there. After a career as an IT training consultant in industrial and educational computing, and as a lecturer at the Napier University of Edinburgh, he is today a full-time writer. Ralph is the author of a number of outdoor books, including a best-selling series of guides to the mountains of Scotland. Although he feels particularly at home in the Scottish highlands, his passion for the outdoors has expanded recently to the mountains of the American West.

RONALD TURNBULL is an all-weather walker, writer and photographer based in southern Scotland. His special interest is in multi-day backpack trips over rough country, and he has completed 19 different coast-to-coast journeys across various parts of the UK. He has achieved comfortable nights without tent on over 50 UK hilltops. He also enjoys hut-to-hut across hot, rocky and preferably Spanish-speaking bits of Europe.

HILARY SHARP is a qualified Trekking Guide and runs her own business,

Trekking in the Alps. Although British, she lives permanently in the French Alps. She is the author of *Trekking and Climbing in the Western Alps*, published by New Holland; *Snowshoeing: Mont Blanc and the Western Alps*; *Mont Blanc Walks*; and the *Tour of the Matterhorn* published by Cicerone Press UK. She regularly contributes to the mountaineering press in the UK.

JUDY ARMSTRONG is a New Zealander, with bases in England and the French Alps. As a photojournalist, she has travelled extensively by foot, kayak, horse, bike and skis throughout Europe, Africa, South and Central America, and Asia. Judy works regularly for magazines and newspapers specializing in adventure travel and outdoor pursuits. Recent assignments include ski joering (being towed behind a horse on skis), alpine trekking and paragliding.

MIKE LUNDY has spent a lifetime trekking through many parts of southern Africa. He has written five books and numerous magazine features on the subject. He has been a columnist for two South African newspapers, producing over 200 hiking features, as well as a weekly

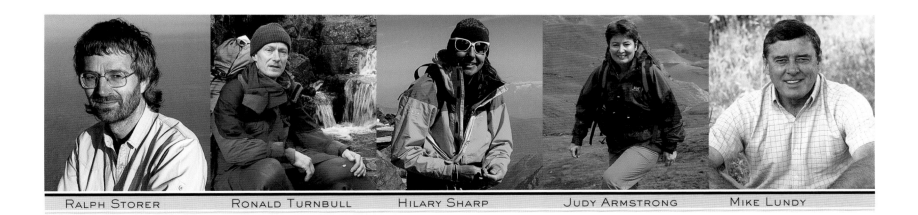

RALPH STORER    RONALD TURNBULL    HILARY SHARP    JUDY ARMSTRONG    MIKE LUNDY

hiking report on radio. In 1996 Mike received the Merit Award from the Hiking Federation of Southern Africa for what they described as his 'exceptional service to the hiking community of southern Africa.' Mike lives in Cape Town, which he describes as the 'scenic hiking capital of the world.' Having travelled extensively to over 50 countries worldwide, he feels both qualified and, he hopes forgiven for such home-town chauvinism. He and his wife, Barbara, work from home as trader and travel agent respectively.

**STEVE RAZZETTI** has been a compulsive Himalayan wanderer ever since his first season in Nepal and India in 1984. He has spent 20 springs, summers and autumns leading commercial treks and making his own exploratory expeditions, from the Pamirs and Central Asia to the Eastern Himalaya and Bhutan. Author of New Holland's *Trekking and Climbing in Nepal* and editor of *Top Treks of the World*, his most recent project has been travelling the world with BBC presenter Michael Wood taking the photographs for his book *In Search of Myths and Heroes*. Visit his web site at www.razzetti.com.

**DAVID EMBLIDGE** edited *The Appalachian Trail Reader* (Oxford) and the series *Exploring the Appalachian Trail* (Stackpole). He has trekked extensively in the US and in Europe and has made two forays to Asia, one a trek on the Annapurna Circuit in Nepal and the other to the Great Wall of China. Formerly Editor-in-Chief at The Mountaineers Books (Seattle), he now teaches at Emerson College (Boston) in the graduate programme in publishing.

**KATHY OMBLER** is a freelance writer whose interests lie in conservation, nature tourism and the travel and tourism industries. In the past 25 years Kathy has either lived in, or visited, all of New Zealand's national parks. Kathy has written several books and magazine articles on conservation and tourism, including two comprehensive books on New Zealand's National Parks.

**HAMISH BROWN** is a professional author, mountaineer, photographer, educationist and lecturer who has become the English-speaking authority on the Atlas Mountains of Morocco. Born in Colombo to Scottish parents, he discovered the great

outdoors early in life and has wandered the world ever since. His climbs and expeditions have ranged from the Arctic to the Andes, from the Alps to the Himalaya – but it is the Atlas Mountains which have 'stolen his heart away'. Having spent winters there in 1965 and 1966, he now leads small exploratory treks into the Atlas for up to five months each year. Along with local guide Ali, from Taroudant, Hamish was the first to realize the potential of the Western Atlas and, again with Ali, has made complete traverses afoot of the Anti- and the High Atlas, the latter a 96-day, 900km (560-mile), 30-peak venture.

Hamish starred in a television feature on the Western Atlas and, in 2000, was made an honorary Fellow of the Royal Geographic Society. He is currently working on a book about the early exploration of the Atlas Mountains.

**KATE CLOW** was born and educated in the UK, and pursued a career in the computer business while indulging a hobby of off-road motorcycling. On annual motorcycle journeys through France and Spain she followed the Roman road network, and visited many

STEVE RAZZETTI     DAVID EMBLIDGE     KATHY OMBLER     HAMISH BROWN     KATE CLOW

historic sites in the mountains. Taking a job in Istanbul, Kate learned Turkish while selling computers to the Turkish government and studying at Istanbul University. Eight years ago she moved to Antalya at the foot of the fabulous Taurus range. Immediately, she started collecting maps and researching the ancient road system on foot and motorbike. Turkey's first long distance walk, the Lycian Way, is a result of this research. Today, Kate earns a living from writing and photography, and leading groups of trekkers on the old paths.

**CHRIS HOOKER**'s love of the great outdoors and his work as a guide have taken him to many remote corners of the globe. But Chris's great love remains Latin America, where he was born, grew up and has spent much of his adult life. Years of guiding, trekking, climbing and cycling, from the Amazon to the Andes and from Peru to Patagonia, have given him an intimate knowledge of the continent. He is usually to be found (or not) somewhere remote, either leading treks or planning new routes. Chris is co-owner of Andean Trails, a travel company based in the UK, specializing in wilderness expeditions to South America.

**KATHY JARVIS** grew up in Scotland, where she was introduced to the joys of hill walking at an early age. Her career in South America began when she went to work as a tour guide in Chile and Peru in the early 90s, and she has been going back regularly ever since. For a few years all of her free time between tours was spent exploring the Andes, but now she spends more time in her office as a partner in the trekking and mountain biking company, Andean Trails, organizing tours to Peru, Bolivia and Patagonia. This provides a great excuse for leading groups on her favourite treks and spending a few months each year exploring new routes throughout the Andes. Kathy has no particular favourite among the Andean countries, anywhere with dramatic scenery, empty spaces, local people or wildlife and the freedom to walk, is just fine.

**TOM HUTTON** is a freelance writer and photographer with a passion for nature and the outdoors. He seeks out particularly remote or dramatic landscapes, where he indulges his love for walking, climbing, skiing and cycling. He was a contributing author to *Classic Treks* (David & Charles).

**FIONA MCINTOSH** is a passionate outdoor enthusiast who has trekked on every continent including Antarctica. A photo journalist, she is the editor of *Out There Adventure* and *Out There Travel* and the author of various books on hiking and other adventures. She considers herself extremely privileged to live on the slopes of Table Mountain in Cape Town, one of the world's premier hiking destinations.

**CHRIS TOWNSEND** is the author of 15 books on hiking and ski touring; his latest book, *Crossing Arizona*, is the story of his 1290km (800-mile) trek along the Arizona Trail. He also writes every month for *TGO* (*The Great Outdoors*) magazine. Chris has hiked the Continental Divide and Pacific Crest trails, through the mountains of Norway and Sweden, through Canada's Yukon Territory, the length of the Canadian Rockies (the first time this walk was attempted), and over all of Scotland's highest mountains. Chris lives in the Scottish Highlands.

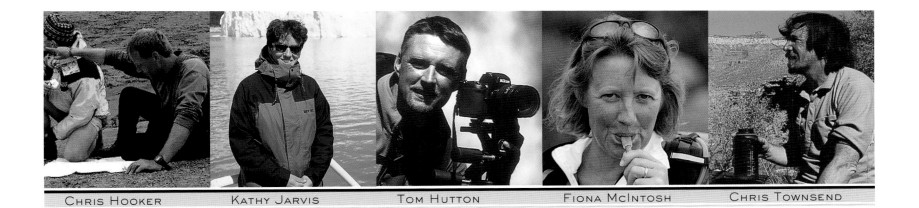

CHRIS HOOKER    KATHY JARVIS    TOM HUTTON    FIONA MCINTOSH    CHRIS TOWNSEND

# PHOTOGRAPHIC CREDITS

Copyright © in photographs rests with the following photographers and/or their agents as listed below.

BR/SB=Black Robin/Shaun Barnett; CE/DJ=Cloudwalker Expedition/Dean James; CT=Chris Townsend, DH=Dave Hansford; DR=David Rogers; GI=Gallo Images/Gettyimages.com; HB=Hamish Brown; HS=Hilary Sharp; IOA=Images of Africa; JA=Judy Armstrong; JdM=Jon de Montjoye; JJ=Jack Jackson; KC=Kate Clow; KJ=Kathy Jarvis; KO=Kathy Ombler; NG=National Geographic; PD=Paddy Dillon; PH=Photo Access; PA/FO/S=Photo Access/Fantuz Olimpio/Sime; PA/G/CL=Photo Access/Getaway/C.Lanz; PA/NG=Photo Access/N.Greaves; PA/PS=Photo Access/P. Steyn; PA/KY=Photo Access/K. Young; RS=Ralph Storer; RT=Ronald Turnbull; SA=Shaen Adey; SM=Seb Mankelow; SR=Steve Razetti; TH=Tom Hutton

| | | | | | | | | | |
|---|---|---|---|---|---|---|---|---|---|
| 1 | | KJ | | 88 | | GI | | 199-203 | SR |
| 2-3 | | SR | | 89-90 | | RS | | 204-207 | JA |
| 4-5 | | SR | | 91-92 | | GI | | 208-211 | SR |
| 6-7 | | GI | | 93 | | CT | | 212 | left | SA |
| 10 | | RT | | 94-104 | | RS | | 212 | right | SR |
| 12 | | BR/SB | | 105 | | GI | | 214 | | SR |
| 13 | | JJ | | 106 | | NG | | 215 | | GI |
| 14-15 | | SR | | 108 | | GI | | 216-219 | | HB |
| 16 | | KJ | | 109 | | RS | | 220 | | SR |
| 18 | | BR/SB | | 110 | | GI | | 222-223 | | JJ |
| 19-21 | | SR | | 111-116 | | RS | | 224-226 | | GI |
| 22 | left | JA | | 118 | | HS | | 227 | | IOA |
| 22 | right | RS | | 119 | | RS | | 228 | | PA/G/CL |
| 24 | | JA | | 120-124 | | CE/DJ | | 230 | | GI |
| 25 | | HS | | 125 | top | CE/DJ | | 231 | | PA/FO/S |
| 26-29 | | TH | | 125 | bottom | GI | | 232 | | RS |
| 30-33 | | RT | | 126-129 | | KJ | | 234 | top | RS |
| 34-38 | | HS | | 130 | | BR/SB | | 234 | bottom | TH |
| 39 | | JA | | 132 | | KJ | | 235 | | TH |
| 40 | top | JA | | 133 | | BR/SB | | 236-239 | | SA |
| 40 | bottom | HS | | 134-141 | | KJ | | 240 | top | DR |
| 41-51 | | HS | | 142 | | SR | | 240 | bottom | PA/NG |
| 52 | | JA | | 144-145 | | BR/SB | | 241-243 | | DR |
| 53 | | HS | | 146-149 | | KJ | | 244 | | PA/PS |
| 54-57 | | RT | | 150-152 | | SR | | 245-246 | | IOA |
| 58-61 | | PD | | 153 | | JJ | | 247 | | PA/KY |
| 62-69 | | HS | | 154-161 | | KC | | 248 | left | DH |
| 70-76 | | RT | | 162-177 | | SR | | 248 | right | KO |
| 77 | | RS | | 178 | | JJ | | 250-259 | | BR/SB |
| 78-81 | | CT | | 179-183 | | SR | | 260 | | JA |
| 82-85 | | JA | | 184-187 | | SM | | 262-267 | | BR/SB |
| 86 | left | CT | | 188-196 | | SR | | 295 | centre | JdM |
| 86 | right | GI | | 198 | | BR/SB | | | |